Law and Visual Jurisprudence
Volume 16

The Series Law and Visual Jurisprudence seeks to harness the diverse and innovative work within and across the boundaries of law, jurisprudence, and the visual in various contexts and manifestations. It seeks to bring together a range of diverse and at the same time cumulative research traditions related to these fields to identify fertile avenues for interdisciplinary research.

In our everyday lives, we experience law as a system of signs. Representations of legality are visually manifested in the materiality of things we see and spatially experience. Methodologically, aesthetic texts of legality semiotically emerge as examples of visual jurisprudence and illustrate the constitutive waltz between social governance, formal law, and materiality.

***

In its tangled relationship to regulation, the visual complexity of law is semiotically articulated as an ongoing process of meaning imbued with symbolism, memory, and cultural markers. Through a legal semiotics framework of symbolic articulation and analysis, the examination of law that happens in conjunction with the visual expands understandings of how law is crafted and takes root. Additionally, such an inquiry challenges the positivist view of law based within the courtroom as disciplinary spatial practices, the observation of everyday phenomenon, and the visible tethering of regulation to cultural understandings of legality generate a framework of visual jurisprudence. The Series seeks to enliven such frameworks as those in which law happens precisely without formal institutions of law and through which a visual-based methodology of law is crafted through everyday instances of ordinariness that contextualize the relationship between law, culture, and banality.

The Series welcomes proposals–be they edited collections or single-authored monographs–emphasizing the contingency and fluidity of legal concepts, stressing the existence of overlapping, competing and coexisting legal discourses, proposing critical approaches to law and the visual, identifying and discussing issues, proposing solutions to problems, offering analyses in areas such as legal semiotics, jurisprudence, and visual approaches to law.

Keywords: Legal Visual Studies, Popular Culture, Everyday Law, Spatiality, Legal Semiotics, Legal Geography, Legal Materiality, Legal Transplant, Bioethics, Cyber Law, Communication, Heritage and Territory, Design, Marketing, Packaging, Digitalization, Arts.

Alexandra Juster

Law, Literature and Legal Counterfactuals

A Method of Contrastive Discourse Analysis Using the Example of Contemporary Literature

Springer

Alexandra Juster
Comparative Literature
University of Innsbruck
Innsbruck, Austria

ISSN 2662-4532 ISSN 2662-4540 (electronic)
Law and Visual Jurisprudence
ISBN 978-3-032-03791-6 ISBN 978-3-032-03792-3 (eBook)
https://doi.org/10.1007/978-3-032-03792-3

Translation from the German language edition: "Juristische Kontrafaktik. Eine Methode der kontrastiven Diskursanalyse von Recht und Literatur am Beispiel von Gegenwartsliteratur " by Alexandra Juster, © Velbrück Wissenschaft 2025. Published by Velbrück Wissenschaft. All Rights Reserved.

This Springer imprint is published by the registered company Springer Nature Switzerland AG
The registered company address is: Gewerbestrasse 11, 6330 Cham, Switzerland

Contents

Chapter 1
Introduction

> *"The fact that law and poetry*
> *had risen from a bed,*
> *is not hard to believe"*
>
> *Jacob Grimm: On poetry in law (1815)*

Based on the long-established American *law and literature* movement, the interdisciplinary research field of 'law and literature' is also beginning to hesitantly establish itself in Europe, whereby the Münster Collaborative Research Centre (SFB) 1385 *Law and Literature* has provided an important impetus for this development. The present work builds on the latter and aims to develop a contrastive interdisciplinary research method ('legal counterfactual') that claims to offer a methodological basis for the further development of the young research field of 'law and literature'. The particular focus herein is on law *in* literature, neglecting 'law as literature' and the 'law of literature'. Taking the American *law and literature movement* as a starting point, an overview of the heterogeneous research approaches in Italy, France, Belgium, and Germany is first provided. Thereafter, the focus shifts to a theoretical examination of the methodological concepts of interdisciplinarity and counterfactuality on the one hand, and the specific approaches to the text—namely discourse and hermeneutics—on the other. Based on these theoretical 'building blocks', the dividing lines between legal and literary studies are drawn in the first step, to identify the resulting intersections in the second step: the written text as a common working basis and the inseparable link with human society on the one hand, and hermeneutics and discourse as a means of analysing texts on the other. This realisation makes it possible to access literary texts from which the fictional legal discourse is methodically extracted and contrasted with the real-world text in a juxtaposing manner. The aim of this counterfactual contrast is to determine the degree of correspondence between diegetic and real law. Such an approach enhances the quality of the interdisciplinary understanding between literary and legal scholars and leads to an improved understanding of both, the literary text and the legal discourse it addresses. To consolidate this method of legal counterfactuals, five works of contemporary literature are tested and demonstrated in practice: *La décision*

A. Juster, *Law, Literature and Legal Counterfactuals*, Law and Visual Jurisprudence 16, https://doi.org/10.1007/978-3-032-03792-3_1

(2022) by Karine Tuil, *Sworn Virgin* (2014) by Elvira Dones, *Unorthodox* (2012) by Deborah Feldman, *Repenti* (2017) by Claude Chossat, and *A Slap in the Face* (2018) by Abbas Khider. The selection of these works is motivated by an interest in touching on different areas of law that have received little attention in interdisciplinary law and literature research to date, such as French anti-terror legislation, Albanian customary law of the *Kanun*, Talmudic law, Corsican feudal law of *vendetta*, and German asylum law. The analysis of these works, using the counterfactual method of investigation, reveals the numerous points of intersection between law and literature and opens positive perspectives for further interdisciplinary research approaches in the field of 'law and literature'.

The research project itself was made possible by an ESPRIT research grant from the Austrian Science Fund FWF (*Fonds zur Förderung der wissenschaftlichen Forschung*) and draws on my dual career as a lawyer and attorney, as well as my experience as a researcher in German and comparative literature. The first impulse came from my dissertation on Juli Zeh's *Corpus Delicti. Ein Prozess* (2009) (engl. *The Method,* 2014) which, among other interdisciplinary and intertextual references, deals with the legal discourse in the fictional diegesis of the novel. The second impulse came from the realisation that in Austria—in contrast to the Collaborative Research Centre (SFB) 1385 *Law and Literature* at the University of Münster (2019–2024)—no structured, interdisciplinary research in the field of *law and literature* has taken root to date. A third impulse is the realisation that there is sometimes little (or, in some cases, no) interdisciplinary understanding between legal and literary scholars and that a stronger methodological link between the disciplines is needed to facilitate their development. A current example from practice illustrates the persistent barriers to understanding: In one of my abstracts for an academic article, I referred to a 'split between legal entity and law'. These are two basic concepts of law, i.e. legal entities are persons or companies that are in a position to possess and exercise rights and obligations. The extent of the lack of understanding is shown by the comment of peer reviewers when they comment, with a remarkable and at the same time disturbing self-confidence, albeit in ignorance: "Term unclear. In general, the holder of rights. In the new federal states, 'Rechtsträger' also refers to the body that was previously authorised to dispose of public property. The term 'legal entity' still has meaning in connection with the regulation of unresolved property issues (Property Act)[1] because the regulations on the allocation of property or an authorisation to dispose of property are often linked to the registration (land register)."[2] This example clearly highlights the urgency of improving interdisciplinary understanding.[3] It is therefore my endeavour, on the one hand, to address the aforementioned research deficit in the EUROPEAN research landscape—and

[1] Beyond the obvious lack of understanding that emerges from the comment, the peer reviewer refers to websites that have nothing to do with my use of the term 'legal entity': https://wirtschaftslexikon.gabler.de/definition/vermoegensgesetz-50761

[2] https://wirtschaftslexikon.gabler.de/definition/grundbuch-33315

[3] Cf. Homann and Suchanek (1989), p. 84.

not the well-established American movement, which I will nevertheless mention briefly in the beginning of this work—and, on the other hand, to identify interfaces between law and literature that can form the basis of an interdisciplinary working method. Gil Charbonnier and Franck Petit, whose work I encountered during the course of my research, agree with this analysis: they understand the connection between the strengthening of the interdisciplinary development between law and literature in the comparison between legal and literary–theoretical methods on the one hand and the investigation of the representation of legal relationships and debates in literature on the other: "3. Law compared with literature: a comparison of literary and legal methods. 4. Law in literature: the way in which literature represents the law, justice and the major problems of the law [...]."[4] At this point, reference should also be made to the comment by Angela Condello and Tiziano Toracca that research has so far paid too little attention to the development of theoretical foundations for an interdisciplinary examination of law and literature: "The attempts to engage with theories of law and literature, are still not copious."[5]

Based on these premises, the present research work, following on from the investigations by Eric Achermann and Klaus Stierstorfer as part of the SFB 1385, focuses on law *in* literature to "(re)open a highly innovative and relevant research area in the field of law and literature research, which has the aforementioned history, but opens up new territory in the direction envisaged here."[6] I especially see this 'new territory', which I would like to enter, in the fact that, as far as I have been able to ascertain in the course of my research, the approaches of legal and literary research in most cases only deal with analysing, explaining, and commenting on legal relationships in literature, but rarely convey a clear understanding of the real-world aspects of these legal relationships negotiated in fiction. Walter Müller-Seidel has already recognised this, insisting that the reader must not only be presented with the literary side but also the legal side, because this juxtaposition "cannot simply be left to the reader. The linking and integration of the other [Müller-Seidel refers here to the law, author's note] remains to be done on a case-by-case basis, actually from sentence to sentence."[7] For, as Christoph Rodiek clearly indicates, and as will be discussed in more detail in the chapter on counterfactuals, readers can only become aware of the interplay between real-world legal relationships and real and/or fictitious legal assertions in the diegesis if they have any knowledge of real-world law. In contrast, if they are not informed about this, they are fundamentally unable to recognise counterfactual conditions, as they are not in a position to make a contrastive comparison between the real and the fictitious.[8] This is where the ambition of my attempt to uncover the legal discourse in literary fiction and simultaneously explicate the

[4] Charbonnier and Petit (2023), p. 26.

[5] Condello and Toracca (2020), p. 19.

[6] Achermann and Stierstorfer (2022), p. 6.

[7] Müller-Seidel (1986), p. 90.

[8] Cf. Rodiek (1993), p. 273; cf. also Wittmann (2018), p. 11.

corresponding real-world law becomes relevant, as well as innovative. The approach to these matters should furthermore be explicable and applicable methodologically to the study of law in literature at will.

It appears that the development of such a counterfactual methodology of legal analysis in literature, with simultaneous juxtaposition to real law, could also pave the way for a systematic and structured approach to not only shed light on obvious but also inconspicuously slipped-in legal information and allusions with legal sensitivity. At the same time, such an endeavour could serve to address the call of Eric Achermann and Klaus Stierstorfer for a stronger, more detailed interlocking of law and literature—similarly formulated in France by Christian Biet[9]—and will be tested based on selected works of contemporary German, German-American, French, and Italian-Albanian literature. This comparative, cross-border, and interdisciplinary approach is preceded by an introduction to the emergence of the *Law and Literature* movement in the United States and its reception in France, Germany, and Italy. As the works used to test the counterfactual research method originate from these three cultural areas, the geographical overview will certainly provide a useful introduction to the actual research project, which is divided into a conceptual-methodological and a practical phase: Here, the concepts of interdisciplinarity, discourse, and counterfactuality are explained as methodological auxiliary concepts (step 1, Chap. 3) for the development of the actual method of legal counterfactuality (step 2, Chap. 4). The method of legal counterfactuality itself is tested and illustrated using the novels *La décision* (2022) by Karine Tuil, *Sworn Virgin* (2014) by Elvira Dones, *Unorthodox* (2012) by Deborah Feldman, *Repenti* (2017) by Claude Chossat, and *A Slap in the Face* (2018) by Abbas Khider (step 3, Chap. 5).

References

Achermann, Eric, and Klaus Stierstorfer. 2022. Squaring Law and Literature: Materiality – Comparativity – Constitutivity. *Law & Literature* 35 (3): 457–489.

Biet, Christian. 2000. Introduction. Droit et littérature, un lien nécessaire. *Littératures classiques. Droit et literature* 2000 (40): 5–22.

Charbonnier, Gil, and Franck Petit. 2023. *Quand la littérature moderne (ré) invente le droit. Œuvres choisies du XXe siècle à aujourd'hui*. Paris: LexisNexis.

Chossat, Claude. 2017. *Repenti*. Paris: Fayard.

Condello, Angela, and Tiziano Toracca. 2020. *A Theory of Law and Literature. Across Two Arts of Compromising*. Leiden/Boston: Brill.

Dones, Elvira. 2014. *Sworn Virgin*. London/New York: And Other Stories.

Feldman, Deborah. 2012. *Unorthodox*. New York: Simon & Schuster.

Homann, Karl, and Andreas Suchanek. 1989. Methodologische Überlegungen zum ökonomischen Imperialismus. *Analyse & Kritik* 11:70–93.

Khider, Abbas. 2018. *A Slap in the Face*. Calcutta: Seagull Books.

[9] Biet (2000), pp. 17–18.

Müller-Seidel, Walter. 1986. *Die Deportation des Menschen. Kafkas Erzählung 'In der Strafkolonie' im europäischen Kontext*. Stuttgart: J. B. Metzler.
Rodiek, Christoph. 1993. Prolegomena zu einer Poetik des Kontrafaktischen. *Poetica* 1993 (25): 262–281.
Tuil, Karine. 2022. *La décision*. Paris: Gallimard.
Wittmann, Jan. 2018. *Recht sprechen: Richterfiguren bei Kleist, Kafka und Zeh*. Berlin/Heidelberg: J. B. Metzler.
Zeh, Juli. 2014. *The Method*. New York: Vintage.

Chapter 2
Law and Literature, with a Special Focus on Law *in* Literature

The word is not only the supporting pillar of literature but also of law: without words, law could not be objectified, understood, interpreted, applied, and 'spoken'. As Jacob Grimm noted, the word makes law and literature possible in the first place: "It is not hard to believe that law and poetry rose from the same bed together."[1] Both are rooted in human life and coexistence, to which they relate by narrating and observing (literature) or 'narrating' and standardising (law). Every legal case is based on a 'story' to which legal texts are applied, the wording of which must be interpreted to lead to a judicial decision, which in turn—how could it be otherwise—is formulated in words. Every literary text must be understood and interpreted in words. Kieran Dolin therefore justifies the close link between law and literature with the fact that law is expressed through words, albeit more stringently than in literature: "The law can only be articulated in words. While the order of a court will be imposed [...], it will originally have been spoken as a sentence. This is the fundamental connection between law and literature."[2] According to Dolin, the narrative of law and jurisprudence involves not only language but also cultural references that are conveyed through literature and language.[3] References to literature in legal judgements therefore seem to clarify the understanding of legal texts: "Literature and law, it seems, can work together in the production of cultural ideals and values" because "no set of legal institutions or prescriptions exists apart from the narratives that locate it and give it meaning."[4] Claudio Magris, on the other hand, weakens Dolin's strongly affirmative position to the extent that he recognises not

---

[1] Grimm (1816), p. 30.

[2] Dolin (2007), p. 2.

[3] Cf. ibid., p. 2: Dolin refers to the example of the case *Plaut v. Spendthrift Farm Inc.* In its ruling, the American Supreme Court implicitly referred to Robert Frost's poem *Mending Wall* with the sentence "good fences make good neighbours" on the assumption that the semantics of this statement were generally known in American culture.

[4] Cf. ibid.

A. Juster, *Law, Literature and Legal Counterfactuals*, Law and Visual Jurisprudence 16, https://doi.org/10.1007/978-3-032-03792-3_2

only relationships between law and literature that promote understanding but also possible barriers between the disciplines.[5] However, it cannot be overlooked that law and literature make use of the word, with law exercising a stringent function of 'prescribing', 'threatening', and 'sanctioning', while literature entertains, explains, describes, fantasises, or imaginaries. Law appears in literature through the discourse that results from the combination and recurrence of certain words,[6] whether explicitly or implicitly. Thanks to narrative techniques, literature can convey knowledge about law as a factor in certain cultural, historical, social, societal, or political circumstances, it can raise philosophical and ethical questions, or it can become a source of legal history, e.g. if the law has not been documented in writing in history.[7] According to Thomas Weitin, further similarities between law and literature arise not only from the word as a unifying 'raw material', but also from methodological overlaps in the field of hermeneutics.[8]

A glance at the history of literature indicates that law and literature meet in an interdisciplinary way beyond these methodological points of reference; this aspect will be discussed in more detail under Chap. 3. As Bernhard Greiner indicates, the treatment of legal issues in literature as a medium of social reflection is as old as literature itself and can be traced back to the Greek tragedy *Oresteia* by Aeschylus in antiquity.[9] Stephanie Blum refers to Johann Fischart's sonnet cycle *Etlich Sonnet* as an example of early modern German literature of the sixteenth century that takes a legal stance against the rule of Catherine de Medici.[10] Heiko Ulrich highlights the legal confrontation with the office of a judge in antiquity in Georg Rudolf Weckherlin's short epic *Urtheil des Paris* in the seventeenth century.[11] Guglielmo Gabbiadini traces the human rights discourse in Friedrich Maximilian Klinger's fragment *Das zu frühe Erwachen des Genius der Menschheit* against the backdrop of the violent upheavals of the French Revolution.[12] In 1892, Ernest Huffcut convincingly formulated the thesis of the close interdisciplinary interlocking of law and

---

5 Magris (1994), p. 9.

6 Frank L. Schäfer and Monika Fludernik provide a broad concept of law as a text corpus of narratology to which they include "all legal norms and the associated legal literature." "Legal norms include not only parliamentary laws, executive ordinances, statutes of public corporations, customary law and internal administrative instructions, but also administrative acts and court decisions as well as individual contracts and general terms and conditions, i.e. all stages of the application of the law from the abstract legal basis to the concrete individual case or to private agreements." (Schäfer and Fludernik 2022, p. 7).

7 An example of literature as a source of legal history in German-speaking countries is Hartmann von Aue's Middle High German legend Gregorius, which provides information about the legal consequences of incest in the twelfth century. Cormeau and Stömer (2007), pp. 120–121.

8 Weitin (2010), p. 44ff.

9 Greiner (2010), p. 7.

10 Blum (2014), pp. 13–29.

11 Ulrich (2014), pp. 31–48.

12 Gabbiadini (2014), pp. 49–66. Cf. also Mölk (1996a).

literature: "historically it is probably true that no branches are more closely united and interwoven."[13]

Although law has been a possible literary subject since antiquity, it is only since the first half of the nineteenth century, when the first works by John Wigmore and Benjamin Cardozo appeared in the United States, that we can speak of an actual structured, cultural-scientific field of research into *law and literature*, to which the current of law *in* literature owes its origin. John H. Wigmore published a catalogue of *legal novels* as early as 1908,[14] with the conviction that the reading of literary fiction should be an integral part of any legal education. In this context, Richard Weisberg emphasises Wigmore's visionary anticipation of the *Law in* Literature *movement*:

> Wigmore had no interest in directing them towards literature as a mere hobby. Fiction-reading instead was to be a lifelong professional duty. If Continuing Legal Education existed in his day, most of the credits required of lawyers and judges would have involved instruction in literary criticism. Balzac, Dickens, Jane Austen, George Eliot, Katherine Anne Porter—these and scores of others were to be lifelong companions to the practicing lawyer or sitting judge.[15]

Wigmore views literature as a pedagogical tool to explain the complex human relationships that are essential for a good application of the law to lawyers, legal scholars, judges, and attorneys:

> The novel—the real work of fiction—is a catalogue of characters taken from nature. And a lawyer must understand human nature. He must work comprehensively with its variations and its motivations. He will not be able to find all of this in his own immediate circle; life is not long enough nor [are] his contacts diverse enough to teach him personally what he will need to know in some unforeseeable new case. To acquire this knowledge, he must have recourse to fiction, which is a portrait gallery taken from nature.[16]

In 1925, Benjamin Cardozo wrote: "I am told at times by friends that a judicial opinion has no business to be literature. The idol must be ugly, or he may be taken for a common man."[17] With this appeal to also pay attention to literary writing in legal practice, Cardozo, as does Richard H. Weisberg emphasises, the relevance of writing style for the meaning of legal texts: "In fact […] attention to the literary is *mandatory* [italics in original] in all acts of legal communication, because style controls meaning; it is not added for fun."[18] According to this view, form, structure and content comprise a necessary unit to ensure 'good' legal communication in all its forms, both written and oral. The view that high-quality legal texts should be written according to literary criteria has led to the trend of law *as* literature, which,

[13] Huffcut (1892), p. 52. See also: Frank (2010), p. 70.

[14] See Cf. Wigmore (1908), pp. 574–593.

[15] Weisberg (2009), p. 130.

[16] Wigmore (1908), p. 579.

[17] Cardozo (1947), p. 339.

[18] Weisberg (2018).

however, can only be touched on in passing here in favour of the focus on law *in* literature.

After Cardozo's legal-literary prelude, the publication of James Boyd White's work *The Legal Imagination* (1973)[19] provided a further decisive impetus, which again placed lawyers at the centre of the text. This profession-specific reference is already emphasised in the introduction: "I want to begin calling this an advanced course in reading and writing, a study of what lawyers and judges do with words."[20] Boyd's work marked the beginning of the division of the *literature and law* movement into 'law *in* literature' and 'law *as* literature'. Law *as* literature regards linguistic analysis as an aid to finding the law and attempts to apply literary theories of text interpretation and understanding (hermeneutics, deconstructivism, structuralism, post-structuralism, linguistics) to legal texts,[21] to give lawyers more profound access to them.[22] Law *in* literature, which is the primary focus here, *is concerned with the explicit and implicit treatment of legal phenomena and appearances in literature.* A third area of interdisciplinary interdependence, which is not examined in this work, concerns the copyright protection of literary works. Stephan Kirste also includes 'poetic justice', i.e. the justice "that the law cannot provide", in the research area of *law and literature.*[23] However, this seems to be more of a thematic approach to law *in* literature than an independent perspective.[24] Since, as already indicated, the focus of this work is on the research field of 'law *in* literature', the other subdisciplines will not be discussed in the following. *The focus here is exclusively on the examination of law, legal systems, legal figures and legal cases that are explicitly or implicitly dealt with in literary diegesis.*

Richard Posner, known for his critical stance on the *law and literature movement*, goes beyond identifying commonalities between the disciplines to examine the mutual implications of literature in law and law in literature. According to Posner, the difficulty of dealing with law in literature lies in the fact that law, as a complex system of norms and institutions, cannot be portrayed and is therefore not easy for laypeople to grasp: "Law is a complex of rules and institutions from which a writer can borrow but which does not lend itself to being imitated."[25] In this context, Posner undertakes a critical analysis of the legal interpretations in selected literary works from the perspective of American and foreign law to highlight what he considers lay deviations and inconsistencies from a legal perspective.[26] According

[19] White (1973).

[20] Cf. ibid. p. xxi.

[21] Cf. Baron and Epstein (1997), pp. 141–187.

[22] Cf. Schramm (2007), pp. 581–585.

[23] Kirste (2021), p. 351.

[24] Cf. the very detailed work by Christine Baron on the divergence of the perception of justice between law and literature: Baron (2023).

[25] Posner (1988), p. 23.

[26] Cf. Schramm (2007), p. 582. See also Gaakeer (2012), pp. 44–72. Julie Stone Peters makes the same criticism of 'amateurishness' of lawyers who, when they deal with literature, do not have a solid knowledge of literary theory: Stone Peters (2005), pp. 442–453.

to Posner, literary figures are not qualified to plausibly present legal relationships. Nevertheless, Posner indicated that law in literature can contribute to the study of comparative law."[27] Posner's disdain for the legal expertise of writers is hardly concealed here. Along the same lines as Posner, Robert Weisberg also denies literature any legal added value, but at least concedes it an educational value in terms of 'humanity': "Even though these texts [literary texts, author's note] can tell us little or nothing about the legal situation, they can still educate lawyers about the human condition."[28] In this sense, Robert Weisberg ascribes contextualising qualities to literature, which are not sufficient to reliably and competently depict legal relationships, but which at least contribute to outlining the wider socio-historical-cultural framework. This is precisely what my work aims to contribute to by showing that the law can also be accessible to writers through a methodically structured approach, thus effectively countering the accusation of incompetence. In this way, by reducing or at least alleviating prejudices on the part of lawyers and inferiority complexes on the part of writers, an improvement in interdisciplinary cooperation can be hoped for.

After these hesitant approaches, interdisciplinary research on law and literature received an important impetus in the 1980s from Richard Weisberg (not to be confused with Robert Weisberg) and Jean-Pierre Barricelli, who recognise a connecting element between law and literature in the fact that both disciplines are concerned with representing reality through language: "Law is associated with literature from its inception as a formalized attempt to structure reality through language."[29] Neglecting the literature *in* law trend, reference is only made here to Richard Weisberg's advocacy of the pedagogical approach of law *in* literature in line with Robert Weisberg, to whom Ian Ward also refers: "Whereas for White the value of such texts lies chiefly in the style and rhetoric which they deploy, Weisberg suggests that such texts are justified in legal studies simply "for the situation which they seek to describe and for the social and political contexts which they imply."[30] In his studies on the Holocaust in France, Richard Weisberg focused, in particular, on the literary and legal portrayal of the Vichy regime, bitterly stating that the "source of Holocaust predictions and reappraisals is lost in the meaningless verbiage of legal protagonists."[31] Albert Camus' novels *The Stranger* (1942) and *The Fall* (1956) helped Richard Weisberg in his investigations into how non-lawyers shape legal contexts in literature.[32] In the course of his study of law in the works of Dostoyevsky, Melville, and Flaubert, Weisberg realised that writers had replaced heroism and religiosity with the principle of legality as the controlling authority of

[27] Gaakeer (2012), p. 43.

[28] Ward (1995), p. 14.

[29] Weisberg and Barricelli (1982), p. 150.

[30] Ward (1995), pp. 7–8; quite differently James B. White, who argues for the priority of the text over the literature, insofar as it is primarily the style and rhetoric of a text that determine the relationship between text and reader and thus its effectiveness (White 1973). Stanley Fish takes the same stance in (1989).

[31] Weisberg (2013), p. 13.

[32] Weisberg (1999), pp. 81–91.

modern society: "But law, nothing more than a relativistic method for ordering reality through language, took the same position toward spontaneous life as the philosophical or priestly forms of earlier texts."[33] C.R.B. Dunlop confirms Richard Weisberg's thesis of the educational function of law in literature, as it is essential for future lawyers to connect law with politics, morals, ethics, and culture: "Literature provides legal scholars with an ideal vehicle to see law as a part of the surrounding culture."[34] Marta Nussbaum, another supporter of Weisberg's approach, insists on literature as a means of perfecting the 'good' lawyer and judge, who, in addition to professional expertise, must not only have knowledge of social contexts but must also possess human qualities and empathy without immediately falling into emotional arbitrariness.[35] According to Nussbaum, literature is important because

> the novel is a living form and in fact still the central morally serious yet popularly engaging fictional form of our culture. [...] the novel constructs a paradigm of style of ethical reasoning that is context specific without being relativistic, in which we get potentially universalisable concrete prescriptions by bringing a general idea of human flourishing to bear on a concrete situation, which we are invited to enter through the imagination.[36]

In addition to the cultural-humanistic value of literature advocated by Nussbaum, there is another argument in favour of including law in literature, which is emphasised above all by Hans Müller-Dietz, Donato Carusi,[37] and Peter Häberle. They convincingly argue that literature portrays societal and social developments, shortcomings and needs, which law receives with a time lag, even if, as Müller-Dietz ironically notes, it is often too late:

> Apart from times of drastic epochal change or even revolutionary upheaval, law usually lags behind social developments due to its traditionally conservative character, working through their late changes (often too late). This 'cultural lag', the cultural tardiness of law [...] is contrasted with the more seismographic character of literature, which picks up on social change processes earlier and more quickly, if not even assuming a pioneering function.[38]

Peter Häberle ascribes the same pioneering role to literature in recognising society's legal needs, because literature provides the "'stuff' from which the law and the lawyers of an open society can draw a great deal of inspiration and 'material' as well as (orienting) 'values' in the short, medium and long term."[39] According to Häberle, the "'lay' pre-formulation of reform wishes and necessities, of people's

---

[33] Weisberg (2013), p. 12.

[34] Dunlop (1991), p. 69. Other supporters of the humanistic-educational function of law in literature are Cook (1991), 387–411; Getman (1988), 577–588.

[35] Cf. Nussbaum (1995), pp. 118–121.

[36] Ibid. p. 6.

[37] Carusi (2022), p. 6.

[38] All translations from non-English original texts into English are done by myself. Müller-Dietz (1990), p. 21. Cf. also: Schwarz (2009), pp. 213–238.

[39] Häberle (1983), p. 98.

new needs and hardships, of hopes and wishes" is[40] reason enough to "approach literature and writers […]."[41]

Despite the divergent positions on literature and law, and the debates concerning the advantages and disadvantages of confronting lawyers with literature and writers with law, the growing interest in the subject of 'law and literature' at most renowned law faculties in the United States, and gradually, albeit less consistently and more fragmentedly, also in Europe, testifies to the success of the *law and literature* movement.[42] In Germany, the first explorations of law in literature began as early as the nineteenth century, while France only followed at the beginning of the twenty-first century. In Italy, which has always sought proximity to the United States, the interest in law and literature was evoked at the same time as it started becoming a topic for its American counterparts. European *law and literature* research is now attempting to emancipate itself from the American *law and literature* movement through independence[43] and is fertilising the field through its own debates and expansions. As Greta Olson emphasises, there will continue to be a plurality of currents within the movement in the future, taking country-specific characteristics into account, whereby one of the main tasks of the *Law in* Literature *movement* will be to highlight normative gaps and grievances in line with the social 'Zeitgeist': "The traditional Law and Literature movement would be to state that through the emotionally evocative means of narrative literature, the failings of law to ensure social justice are uncovered, and that the literary presents a necessary supplement to law."[44] With Olson's findings in mind, we will now turn to the state of the law and literature movement in France, Italy, and Germany.

2.1 Law and Literature in the French-Speaking World

The Belgian lawyer, university professor, playwright, and author François Ost notes a belated development of the law and literature movement in the French-speaking world,[45] whereby Ost himself can be seen as a pioneer of the movement in Belgium. It was not until the beginning of the second decade of our century that Christian Biet[46] became a pioneer of law and literature in France. Since his untimely death,

[40] Ibid. p. 100.

[41] Ibid.

[42] See Witteveen (1998), p. 155.

[43] See Olson (2010), pp. 338–364.

[44] See Olson (2015), p. 60.

[45] Ost et al. (2001), pp. 7–10. See also Malaurie (1997); Teissier-Ensminger (1999); Ost (2004); Ost (2021).

[46] Biet (2004).

Christine Baron,[47] together with Denis Salas[48] and Sandra Travers de Faultrier,[49] has been leading the French law and literature movement since the 2010s. Other contributors such as Claire Bouglé-Le Roux,[50] Marion Mas,[51] Jean-Pol Masson,[52] and Jean-Marc Sorel,[53] have also helped to revitalise and strengthen the French current in recent years. The foundation of the journal *Revue Droit & Littérature* in 2017, which is now published annually by Lextenso in Paris, also testifies to the gradual growth of interest in this field of research.[54] A 3-year Law and Literature (*Droit-Lettres*) degree programme has even been set up at the University of Aix-en-Provence.[55]

The representatives of the young French school agree, without any notable differences, that literature, as a fictional and free medium, can soften the rigidity and sometimes situational non-conformity of law and see a fruitful interdisciplinary approach precisely in the dialectic between the 'you-may-not' of law and the 'you-can-anything' of literature. In this context, Antoine Garapon and Denis Salas contrast the conservative rigidity of the actual state of law with the imaginary openness of literature and ask how law and literature can be thought of together, despite their disciplinary peculiarities:

> 'Law and literature', a strange association. Everything seems to separate the two universes: law fences the real, literature opens the doors to fiction. On the one hand, the formalism of the law and on the other, the fantasy of the imagination. How can the literary character's 'anything is possible' be reconciled with the legal subject's 'you must not'? How can the abstraction of the rule be reconciled with the embodiment of the story? The generality of principle and the singularity of destiny? The rigidity of the prescriptive and the fluidity of the descriptive?[56]

Biet emphasises that literature always inevitably revolves around questions of law and attempts to fill institutional, normative, political or moral gaps: "Literature never ceases to revisit the law, to invest it, to cast doubt on it, and to enter into the institutional, normative, political and moral gaps that it has left open."[57] According to Biet, narrative fiction has the advantage of the freedom to 'play' with the law and thus yields new insights and perspectives.[58] Even if the staging of trials, judges,

---

47 See Baron (2021); Baron (2020); Baron (2016), pp. 371–382.

48 Garapon and Salas (2008); Salas (2013).

49 Travers de Faultrier (2021); Travers de Faultrier (2012), pp. 25–41.

50 Bouglé-Le Roux (2021).

51 Mas and Roman (2023), pp. 5–15.

52 Masson (2022).

53 Sorel (2023).

54 The journal *Revue Droit & Littérature* is accessible at https://www.cairn.info/revue-droit-et-litterature.htm and deals with law in literature (e.g. in the novels of Victor Hugo, Marcel Proust), with questions concerning the writer's responsibility, and with rebellion and Europe in literature.

55 Cf. https://formations.univ-amu.fr/fr/licence/3HLF/PRHLF3AE

56 Garapon and Salas (2008), p. 7.

57 Biet (2000), p. 5; see also Roman (2023), pp. 16–18.

58 Cf. ibid., pp. 5–9.

prosecutors, legal debates, or pleadings in literary texts is evident in many cases, as Biet further emphasises, legal discourses in texts can also be implicit, which must be recognised to enhance the understanding of the text: "But if the law exists in literature in an explicit way through the appearance of precise legal notions, it also appears in an implicit way, and it is then necessary to determine, what in the texts which do not speak explicitly about justice, calls upon legal knowledge that can change the deep understanding that we have of a literary work."[59] Biet refers here to an important point to which particular attention should be paid in this study, namely that in addition to the explicit legal discourses in literature, it is also a matter of tracking down implicit legal relationships. Only by uncovering the non-obvious in fiction, according to Biet, can the interdisciplinary connection between law and literature be fully realised, as not only legal but also ideological or cultural insights can be derived from it. In this sense, the legal voids and gaps, the aporias and paradoxes in literary fiction point to fundamental social, legal, and cultural issues that need to be recognised.[60] Through the fictional 'game', literature positions itself as a covert, critical, ironic, or aesthetic observer of society, capable of visualising the imperfection, incoherence, or inadequacy of legal systems.

Christine Baron draws attention to the ability of literature to imagine the law where it is lacking or fails in reality on the one hand and to denounce normative overproductions that restrict freedom and stand in contradiction to democracy on the other.[61] Literary narratives open up the possibility of building bridges between legal jargon and the emotionally charged vernacular, between the legal and human-cultural understanding of concepts (justice,[62] freedom, dignity, etc.) and between the legal and pragmatic interpretation and application of norms. According to Baron, they fill the legal vacuums, they allow the 'law to speak' where it has fallen silent, and they point the finger at miscarriages of justice or incongruent interpretations of the law. By describing concrete cases, literature opens up novel perspectives on the law that were previously inaccessible to the jurist: "Literature and sometimes cinema offer original perspectives on norms by narrating them, by exposing them, by putting them to the test in concrete cases, by posing alternatives that lawyers are sometimes unable to face."[63] Marc Verdussen similarly emphasises the function of literature as a means of illustrating interpersonal relationships in the social fabric that is decisive for the production of law:

> More generally, they [the literary works, author's note] provide a better understanding of the social framework of the production of law and, more specifically, of the representations of human nature and the configurations of human relations, an understanding of which is indispensable for legal thought and the production of law.[64]

[59] Cf. ibid., pp. 17–18.

[60] Cf. ibid., p. 18.

[61] See Baron (2023), pp. 16–25.

[62] Christine Baron analyses the relationship between law and literature with reference to the understanding of the principle of 'justice'.

[63] Cf. ibid., p. 17.

[64] Verdussen (2007), p. 60.

François Ost emphasises the creative and heuristic potential of literature in relation to the rigidities of law. Literature slips into the interstices of positivist law to emphasise its fallibility all the better and to generate new insights. It exchanges stereotypical legal subjects and abstract legal situations for concrete cases centred on changeable and evolving human beings.[65] According to Ost, the potential of the dialogue between law and literature lies between the commanding or sanctioning rationality of law and the boundless freedom of fiction, between the legal 'you-may-not' and the literary 'everything-is-possible': "Rather than a dialogue of the deaf between a codified, instituted law, entrenched in its rationality and effectiveness, and a literature that rebels against all conventions, jealous of its fictionality and its freedom, it is a question of mutual borrowings and implicit exchanges."[66]

Gil Charbonnier's reference to the complementary function of literature in relation to the restrictive normativity of law also fits into the same logic of mutual dialogue between the disciplines, whereby he insists that, for example, family law cannot be fully grasped without the writings of André Gide. A marriage without the emotional dimension, which is limited only to the law, would be a "pretty poor marriage."[67] As an example of the concrete influence of literature on the development of family law, Charbonnier and Petit cite Jean Cocteau's novel *Les parents terribles*, which led to the abolition of the prerogatives of the *pater familias* in Article 213 of the French Civil Code of 1938, which obliged women to obey their husbands.[68] True to its tradition of strong ties to social 'being', contemporary French literature remains committed to those legal issues that are currently highly topical, such as incest, the failure of French justice, or the fight against terrorism.[69]

In contrast to the more recent developments in the French-speaking world, the law and literature movement in Italy was already taking hold at the beginning of the twentieth century, as the Sect. 2.2 indicates. While the role of literature as an observer of legal shortcomings or deficiencies was emphasised in France, in Italy the theses on the pedagogical value of literature for lawyers and its predictive function for future legal developments coexisted.

---

[65] Cf. Ost (2004), pp. 10–15.

[66] Ibid., p. 19.

[67] Carbonnier (2014), p. 28. Carbonnier refers here to André Gide's work *Fruits of Earth* (1897). In France, the family as a legal and social institution is the focus of several novels that deal with the taboo subject of incest. Cf. Angot (2022); Kouchner (2022); Springora (2020); Enthoven (2020); Moix (2019).

[68] Charbonnier and Petit (2023), p. 16.

[69] On the subject of incest, see footnote no. 67. On false testimony and document forgery, see Robert-Diard (2022); Jaenada (2023). On the terror trial, see Tuil (2022); Carrère (2022); Trévidic (2011).

2.2 Law and Literature in Italy

In Italy, the first contributions and reflections on law and literature emerged as early as 1923, synchronised with the development of American *law and literature* studies, which followed the American theses on the educational potential of literature for lawyers. In this sense, Roberto Vacca points out that literature offers a better insight into human nature than any dusty work of legal philosophy or psychology.[70] Piero Calamandrei, on the other hand, recognises the pedagogical value of literature in making law understandable in a more profane way.[71] Antonio d'Amato, whose publication *La letteratura e la vita del diritto* (1936) is regarded as the actual starting point of interdisciplinary research in the field of law and literature in Italy, defines both disciplines as part of spiritual activity ("*branche dell'attività dello spirito*"[72]), whereby literature, like a seismograph, provides information about the legal sensibility of a population ("*termometro della sensibilità di un popolo*"[73]).[74] Donato Carusi comments on d'Amato's realisation of the anticipatory and preparatory function of literature in relation to the subsequent development of law: "It states that literature 'follows the law in its stages' and that when the latter hesitates and 'stalls' the former prepares its evolution."[75] Ferruccio Pergolesi's work *Diritto e giustizia nella letteratura moderna narrativa e teatrale* (1956), in which the many facets of law, justice, and morality are analysed in a selection of nineteenth and twentieth-century European literature, was another interdisciplinary advance that would subsequently prove to be very significant.[76] Since the 1980s, the Italian current of law and literature has been analysed by Mario A. Cattaneo,[77] Giorgio Rebuffa,[78] Antonio Bevere,[79] Remo Danovi, Fabrizio Cosentino, and Adelmo Cavalaglio.[80]

Contemporary Italy is characterised by a lively interest in the research field of *law and literature* on the part of lawyers, legal historians, legal philosophers, judges, and lawyers, whereby the dominance of lawyers over writers can be attributed to the historically deeply rooted doctrine of legal philosophy in Italian culture. In addition to today's leading legal scholars Felice Casucci,[81] Giovanni Rossi[82] and Donato

---

[70] Cf. Vacca (1923).

[71] Cf. Calamandrei (1924), p. 204.

[72] D'Amato (1936), p. 14.

[73] Ibid.

[74] Cf. Condello and Toracca (2015), pp. 1–2; see also Barenghi (2023), p. 772.

[75] Carusi (2022), p. 6, where Donato Carusi agrees with Heinz Müller-Dietz that literature anticipates the law (cf. Müller-Dietz 1990, p. 21).

[76] Sansone and Mittica (2008), p. 4.

[77] Cattaneo (1985, 1991).

[78] Rebuffa (1992), pp. 65–88.

[79] Bevere (1996).

[80] Cf. ibid., pp. 4–5.

[81] Casucci (2015, 2019).

[82] Cf. Rossi et al. (2023).

Carusi,[83] who have provided—and continue to provide—an important impetus for the development of the regional university research groups[84] and publication series,[85] the abundance of contemporary contributors to the research field of *law and literature* should be mentioned, albeit without any claim to completeness: Gabrio Forti,[86] Fabrizio Cosentino,[87] Michele Navarra, Guido Alpa,[88] Giuseppe Mastrominico,[89] Aldo Mazzacane, Giuseppe Guizzi,[90] Torre.

Torre,[91] Cristina Vano, Jerome Bruner,[92] Domenico Marafioti,[93] Remo Danovi,[94] Daniela Carpi,[95] Andrea Errera,[96] Daniele Cananzi,[97] Massimo Meccarelli,[98] Francesca Scamardella,[99] Arianna Sansone,[100] Anna Sansa,[101] Gustavo Zagrebelsky, Giovanni Tuzet,[102] Federico Spantigati,[103] Maria Paola Mittica,[104] Giulio Itzcovich,[105] Maurizio Cau, Giulio Marchetto,[106] Anna Jellamo[107] and Carla Faralli, to name but a few. Since 2008, the *Italian Society for Law & Literature* (ISLL) has also been the

[83] See Carusi's most recent publication on a European history of the links between law and literature: Carusi (2022).

[84] *Ius in Fabula* at the University of Verona (since 2016), *Diritto e letteratura* at the University of Naples (since 2008/2009), DiGiES at the Mediterranean University of Reggio Calabria (Daniele Cananzi, since 2019), courses in '*Diritto e Letteratura*' at the Universities of Genoa (Donato Carusi), Bologna (Carla Faralli), Urbino (Maria Paola Mittica), Sassari (Michele Navarra), Naples (Fulvia Abbondante), Macerata (Massimo Meccarelli), Roma Tre (Emanuele Conte), and Teramo (Emilia Musumeci).

[85] *Ius in Fabula, Collana di studi sul Diritto e Arti* (since 2017), *Diritto e Letteratura* (since 2010), *Quaderni di Diritto e Letteratura* (since 2015), *LawArt - Rivista di Diritto, Arte, Storia / Journal of Law, Art and History* (since 2020).

[86] Forti (2024); Forti et al. (2022, 2023).

[87] Cf. Condello and Toracca (2015), p. 3.

[88] Alpa (2017).

[89] Mastrominico (2017).

[90] Guizzi (2020).

[91] Torre (2017).

[92] Bruner (2002).

[93] Marafioti (2002).

[94] Danovi (2004).

[95] Carpi (2005).

[96] Errera (2023), pp. 371–399.

[97] Cananzi (2020).

[98] Meccarelli (2020), pp. 207–234.

[99] Prisco (2017), pp. 5–8.

[100] Sansone (2001).

[101] Sansa (2023).

[102] Tuzet (2005), pp. 179–204.

[103] Spantigati (2006).

[104] Mittica (2006).

[105] Itzcovich (2007), pp. 239–268.

[106] Cau and Marchetto (2004).

[107] Jellamo (2005).

central body for research communication and dissemination. However, despite the extensive interest in the discipline, the positions on the intensity and form of the interdisciplinary proximity of *law and literature* are inconsistent, ranging from the denial of the connection between the two disciplines to the postulation of a purely ethical or pedagogical function of literature for the lawyer, without any claim to legal expertise.

In more recent research, Paolo Cherchi cites the ancient *Controversiae*[108] as an early example of the close link between law and literature,[109] a proximity that, according to Cherchi, was called into question by the redefinition of the disciplines and the rise of theories of interpretation of literary texts.[110] This has led to a separation between the disciplines, since legal norms are abstract, while literature creates conceivable figures.[111] Bernardo Picichè agrees with Cherchi's denial of the close link between law and literature, albeit for different reasons since, according to Picichè, it is the respective objectives of law and literature that cannot possibly be made to coincide. Thus, law must not claim to be literature, and literature must not take the place of law. From a teleological point of view, the law enables social coexistence in real space, while literature is located in the sphere of making the impossible possible, filling legal vacuums or making the unthinkable conceivable: "While it is true that art often offers an exhaustive key to understanding reality, it must not usurp the place of disciplines that exist because, by basic axiom, they are rooted in reality, such as legal, historiographic, sociological or economic investigation."[112] Although people are at the centre of both, law and literature, they are viewed from different perspectives. Law is concerned with man as a 'social animal' ("animale sociale"), while literature illuminates him from as many different angles as there are writers,[113] which is why, according to Picichè, it is challenging to understand literature as a source of law.[114] At best, it could help the lawyer to make himself better understood through literary language.[115] In contrast to Cherchi and Picichè, Vincenzo Vitale, on the other hand, takes an affirmative position concerning the synergy between law and literature, as literature is a medium for the formation of conscience and the jurist's understanding of justice ("*la letteratura rappresenta una dimensione*

[108] *Controversiae*: didactic practice speeches on legal cases (*genus iudiciale)*, which primarily served as preparation for the court speeches (Zinsmaier 2006). The aim was for learners to apply fictional law to a dilemmatic legal case and to present (impossible) solutions that could only arise from the imagination: "Questi sono gli episodi in cui la letteratura prende in consegna 'casi controversi' e li trasforma in novelle o aneddoti. Sono gli episodi in cui legge e letteratura sono coinvolte in ugual misura, e in una coesistenza che non le mantiene autonome, bensı` in una relazione dialettica in cui una 'partorisce' l'altra" (Cherchi (2019), pp. 252–253).

[109] Cf. Cherchi's more detailed remarks: Cherchi (2019).

[110] Cf. ibid., p. 251.

[111] Cf. ibid., p. 211.

[112] Picichè (2019), p. 205.

[113] Ibid.

[114] Cf. ibid., p. 206.

[115] Cf. ibid., p. 207.

costitutiva della coscienza giuridica"),[116] by revealing the diversity of facets of the human being, right down to the most intimate and hidden.[117] For Massimo Meccarelli, literature places the law in the social environment of the narrative, thereby directing the perspective towards the contextualised legal norm and allowing the jurist to gain the necessary distance for understanding.[118] Finally, Donato Carusi favours the introduction of the teaching of *law and literature* at law faculties and argues that the study of literature can provide lawyers with knowledge about the law in societies other than their own. A literary perspective can also support the development of imagination and sensitivity to justice.[119]

Even if the approach to law and literature in Italy can be described as 'dynamic' in comparison to France, it remains just as fragmented and unstructured, as is the case in France. This may also have something to do with the nature of Italians, who have always been very individualistic and have little regard for restrictive imperatives. From France's relatively uniform understanding of literature as a stopgap for law (perhaps as an expression of historical centralism?) to Italy's broad cacophony with regard to law and literature as a pedagogical instrument, as a seismograph for legal developments, as separate or, on the contrary, connected disciplines, we will now move on to the situation in Germany, where lawyers and writers share the field and, with Josef Kohler, provided the first approaches to the scientific study of law *in* literature as early as the nineteenth century.

2.3 Law and Literature in German-Speaking Countries

As early as the eighteenth century, criminal phenomena in the German-speaking cultural area were narrated in the form of case histories[120] and court reports[121] in which the guilt and atonement of the criminal took centre stage. In the Weimar period, the view of the justice system and its misdemeanours expanded.[122] While both high and popular literature was already familiar with questions of criminal law, the academic debate primarily began, as Ekkehard Gerstenberg points out, with Josef Kohler, whose volume *Shakespeare vor dem Forum der Jurisprudenz* (1883) was the first to address the law (law of guilt, revenge, mercy) in literature

[116] Vitale (2019), p. 240.

[117] Cf. ibid., p. 239.Vitale refers here to the second chapter "Salvation Through Literature" in Bauman and Mazzeo (2016).

[118] Cf. Meccarelli (2020), p. 209.

[119] Cf. Carusi (2022), p. 8.

[120] The case history became known through the collection of interesting criminal cases by the French jurist de Pitaval (2019). On the case history, see also Juster (2022), pp. 167–172. See also Lüdemann (2014), pp. 115–127.

[121] See also Holiczi (1972).

[122] Cf. Müller-Dietz (1990), pp. 25–33.

(Shakespeare's *Merchant of Venice* and *Hamlet)* in a groundbreaking way.[123] As Klaus Lüderssen comments, Kohler seems to have anticipated the *Law and* Literature *movement* when he sensed in Shakespeare's "ongoing legal and aesthetic studies [...] a new endeavour" that "shone into the world of poetry."[124] According to Kohler, the literature that followed him proves that his intuition was correct:

> Following on from my approach, which has immersed itself in the most diverse poetic works; now one has dealt with a jurisprudence in Goethe, in Richard Wagner, in Ibsen and others; one has finally understood that no world development is possible without law and that every world poet must also see the legal problems in his world. A piece of world history is what the poet offers, and woe betide the jurist who is unable to recognise the progress of law in world history![125]

Although Klaus Lüderssen ironizes Kohler's enthusiasm as exaggerated, he acknowledges his serious merits in the field of criminological studies based on Shakespeare's work[126] and in establishing a "relationship between law and literature [...]."[127] Since little research has been conducted on law in older literature in the German-speaking world,[128] the studies on law *in* literature from the works of Goethe to the present day are just as rich.[129] Indeed, since the end of the nineteenth century, there has been an increase in the number of writings about Goethe as a man of letters[130] and a lawyer.[131] Georg Müller undertakes 'legal forays' in his work *Das Recht in Goethes Faust* (1912).[132] Eight years later, Gustav Radbruch published a remarkable study on the philosophy of law in Goethe's *Wilhelm Meisters Wanderjahre* (1821/1829),[133] followed by Hans Fehr's cultural studies publications *Das Recht in der Dichtung* (1931) and *Die Dichtung im Recht* (1936). Works such as Thomas Würtenberger's *Die deutsche Kriminalerzählung* (1941),[134] Erik Wolf's *Vom Wesen des Rechts in deutscher Dichtung* (1946),[135] and, 20 years later, Paul Bockelmann's *Das Problem der Kriminalstrafe in Deutscher Dichtung* (1967)[136] continue this interdisciplinary research. Works on legal history can be found in Albert von

[123] Gerstenberg (1954), p. 98. Cf. in more detail on Shakespeare in German philology: Lieb (2022), pp. 273–279.

[124] Kohler (1883), foreword.

[125] Ibid.

[126] Cf. Lüderssen (1997), pp. 1108–1109.

[127] Ibid., p. 1109.

[128] Cf. Mölk (1996a), pp. 186–228.

[129] Wolf (1941); Fechner (1952); Schneider (1987); Roxin (1997); Diederichsen (1996), pp. 186–228; Schmidhäuser (1996); Großfeld (2005); Müller-Dietz (2009), pp. 360–364; Müller-Dietz (2016), pp. 37–59.

[130] Lüderssen (1996), pp. 328 ff.

[131] Cf. Lieb (2022), pp. 268–273.

[132] Ibid., p. 99. Cf. Müller (1912).

[133] Cf. Schramm (2007), p. 583; Radbruch (1920), pp. 152–162.

[134] Würtenberger (1941).

[135] Wolf (1946).

[136] Bockelmann (1967).

Schirnding,[137] Klaus Lüderssen,[138] Rolf Meier,[139] Michael Kilian,[140] Hans-Albrecht Koch,[141] Peter Ensberg,[142] and Hermann Weber.[143] In addition to academic essays, there are also the literary figures themselves, such as Heinrich von Kleist, Gotthold Ephraim Lessing, Johann Gottfried Herder, Johann Wolfgang von Goethe, Johann Ludwig Tieck, E.T.A. Hoffmann, Franz Grillparzer, Johann Nestroy, Theodor Storm, Heinrich Heine, Ludwig Thoma, Georg Heym, Franz Kafka, Werner Krauss, Friedrich Georg Jünger, Martin Beradt, Kurt Tucholsky,[144] and, in the immediate contemporary literature, Alexander Kluge, Herbert Rosendorfer, Rolf Henrich, Fred Breinersdorfer, Manfred Zach, Martin Mosebach, Bernhard Schlink, Georg M. Oswald, Juli Zeh, Ferdinand von Schirach, etc., who combine law and literature in their works.[145] In Thomas Bernhard's story "Ist es eine Komödie? Ist es eine Tragödie?" (*"Is it a comedy? Is it a tragedy?")* the 'fool' states: "'The world is an entirely and thoroughly legal one, as you may not know. The world is one monstrous jurisprudence'."[146]

In this context, Hans Müller-Dietz points to the dominance of the thematization of the breach of norms, insofar as the depiction of crime serves the reader's expectations of right and wrong, justice and injustice, and can also be vividly depicted in literature.[147] Jan Wittmann also confirms this when he states that criminal law is given a strong preponderance over civil law in literature, which can probably be explained by the fact that

> The figure of the criminal exposes an anthropological category, evil, that has always affected people. Far from motivational psychological explanations on the part of the recipients, which refer to the fascination of evil and the monstrous, it is on the other hand the connection of literature to the dispositive of life, which 'in the second half of the 18th century [...] became a central, discourse-bearing concept' and with the telling of life stories and case histories in criminal law practice refers to a counterpart in the field of law. In civil law, on the other hand, especially in property law, the offence is not linked to life, but to property.[148]

According to Wittmann, it is not only the disciplinary one-sidedness of legal references in literature that is to be criticised *but also the focus on legal figures without*

[137] von Schirnding (1990).

[138] Lüderssen (1991).

[139] Meier (1994).

[140] Kilian (1987).

[141] Koch (1998).

[142] Ensberg and Marquardt (2002).

[143] Cf. Zeuch (2006), pp. 78–79.

[144] Cf. Wambach (2000). Jünger's prediction of the "erosion" of the law in the "machine society" and Krauss' outline of caricatural legal systems in National Socialism are noteworthy here (p. 7).

[145] Nilges (2014a). See also Weber (2005); Nilges (2014b); Schramm (2007), p. 584.

[146] Bernhard (1988), p. 85.

[147] Cf. Müller-Dietz (1990), pp. 18–19.

[148] Wittmann (2018), p. 10. Cf. also: Bergengruen (2011), pp. 133–165.

at the same time conveying legal knowledge.[149] It is precisely this observation that forms the basis of my work; proposing a common working method that is suitable for both writers and lawyers and that simultaneously conveys concrete legal knowledge through the contrastive comparison of fictional legal discourse and real law.

Contrary to the usual top-heavy treatment of criminal law topoi in literature, the German scholar Walter Müller-Seidel also devoted himself to the literary criticism of legal institutions and the contradictory legal practice of various legal subjects in Goethe's ballad *Vor Gericht*, in Schiller's dramas, and in the works of Kleist, Heinrich Mann, and Kafka.[150]

Bernhard Schlink points out that literary treatises on law often focus on individual writers in order to 'paint a picture of their lives and work' and to show "where the writer's interest in law comes from, how it develops and how it is expressed."[151] The most recent example of this is the volume published in 2024, *Der Jurist Johann Wolfgang von Goethe. Eine Spurensuche in Werk und Wirken* (2024) by Hans Hugo Klein.[152]

Among the academic publications, the *Neue Juristische Wochenschrift* has been publishing individual articles on the subject of law and literature every year since 1982,[153] since 2013 the series *Recht und Literatur* has been publishing by Nomos-Verlag with four volumes to date,[154] on the occasion of the SFB[155] 1385 *Recht und Literatur* of the University of Münster the specialist book series *Literatur und Recht* has been issued by the publisher J.B. Metzler from 2022.

In contrast to the American *law and literature* movement, no structured development of this field of research can be observed in Germany, France, or Italy. As Stephan Kirste emphasises, "the coherent treatment of the topic [...] is still largely lacking in German-speaking countries, despite the lengthy discussion of 'law in literature'."[156]

The 5-year research project of the Collaborative Research Centre (SFB) 1385 *Law and Literature* at the University of Münster, which was launched on 1 July

[149] Wittmann (2018), p. 11.

[150] Müller-Seidel (2017), pp. IX-XIX; Müller-Seidel (1983b), pp. 436–450; Müller-Seidel (1985), pp. 7–38; Müller-Seidel (1983a), pp. 103–127. Müller-Seidel (1996), pp. 356–369.

[151] Schlink (2013), p. 278.

[152] Klein (2024).

[153] Cf. *Neue Juristische Wochenschrift* (1982/12), pp. 601–673.

[154] Publication series, edited by Arnd Koch, Helmut Koopmann, Edward Schramm, Thomas Weitin, Fabian Wittreck. "The series provides a forum for academic papers that link law and literature thematically and theoretically, analysing interconnections and differences, similarities and commonalities. Studies are presented that deal with law as a literary subject and, conversely, those that look at the literary work of lawyers as writers." https://www.dike.ch/wissenschaftliche-schriftenreihen/schriftenreihen-kooperationspartner/recht-und-literatur-rul

[155] Collaborative Research Centre.

[156] Kirste (2021), p. 351. Cf. on the Swiss attempt at implementing a more standardised approach: Kilcher et al. (2013).

2019 and had to be discontinued on 30 June 2024 because the DFG[157] did not agree to its extension, provided an initial promising approach for structured research. However, it remains to be seen whether this will develop into a continuous line of academic research.[158] Until the most recent developments, Christine Künzel laments, in agreement with Stephan Kirste, that the two fields of law and literature have tended to move dispassionately side by side,[159] rather than seeking interdisciplinarity. Ulrich Mölk regrets that the dialogue between philologists and legal scholars is not conducted jointly, but predominantly by legal scholars.[160] Even more than legal and literary scholars, numerous poet-jurists deal with law in literature and populate the literary scene.[161]

Contemporary research on law and literature in Germany has been enlivened and fertilised by the legal scholars Bodo Pieroth, Heinz-Müller Dietz († October 2022), Tonio Walter, Edward Schramm, Klaus Lüderssen, Fabian Wittreck, Hermann Weber, as well as the literary scholars Klaus Stierstorfer, Eric Achermann, Thomas Weitin, Gideon Stiening, Ino Augsberg, and Jan Wittmann.[162] Their works deal with the literary contributions of 'poet-judges' and with the term 'poet-judge' itself,[163] whereby the figure of the judge[164] or the lawyer[165] is also thematised. Outside the topoi of procedural law, the discussions refer conceptually to certain literary works, such as questions of democracy, justice, morality, violence, war, causality, sanity, truth, citizenship, etc. Thematically more open are the research projects that look for points of contact between the two disciplines of law and literature.[166] Heinz Müller-Dietz offers an in-depth approach to various areas of law, including customary law, on the Albanian *Kanun* under the title "*Blutrache in literarischer Sicht - am Beispiel des Romans 'Der zerrissene April' von Ismail Kadare*"[167] and Andreas Bloch on matrimonial law in his contribution "*Sophie von La Roche's 'Geschichte*

---

[157] German Research Foundation.

[158] See also: https://www.uni-muenster.de/SFB1385/. It says here: "Literary studies and jurisprudence are working together here as equal partners more intensively than has been the case in Germany to date. The aim of the interdisciplinary dialogue is to open up and map a field of research in order to systematically investigate areas of relationship between the two disciplines and document them using relevant examples."

[159] Cf. Künzel (2007), pp. 115–132. Künzel deals here with the question of the proximity or distance of law and literature from the perspective of *gender studies* and uses the metaphor of the marriage crisis to describe the state of the law-literature relationship (pp. 129–132).

[160] Mölk (1996b), p. 7.

[161] Cf. Albrecht et al. (2021), p. 122.

[162] Achermann and Stiening (2022); Achermann and Stierstorfer (2022), pp. 457–489; Müller-Dietz (2010); Müller-Dietz (2011), pp. 34–54; Müller-Dietz (2009, 2016); Pieroth (2015, 2018, 2019, 2021); Weber (2003, 2010, 2014, 2017); Walter and Schramm (2021); Lüderssen (1991, 1999, 2007a, 2007b, 2014).

[163] Nilges (2014a). Cf. also Weber (2005, 2009); Wambach (2000, 2002); Vormbaum (2005, 2016).

[164] Wittmann (2018); von Schirnding (1990).

[165] Quabeck (2021).

[166] Koegler et al. (2021); Greiner et al. (2010); Becker (2016).

[167] Müller-Dietz (2011), pp. 34–54.

des Fräuleins von Sternheim' (von 1771) - Ehe und Eherecht im Werk und in der Wirklichkeit des 18. Jahrhunderts."[168]

Other approaches attempt to work out close links between law and literature; they see literature as a medium of the possible, in which law is distanced in perspective and scrutinised in terms of what is or could have been, as Katrin Trüstedt explains:

> Literature forms its own sphere – that of the possible – and thus provides law with a margin of contingency in relation to the modalities of what *is* and what *should be*; of what *could also have been*. The sphere of narration and imagination gives law a distance from itself [...].[169]

Trüstedt extends her approach to literature as a mirror of the legal realm of possibilities by the assumption that literature, beyond the level of representation, could even be the impetus for legal changes and thus become a normative source of law.[170] However, the assertion that literature can become a *normative* source of law in the legal sense must be doubted insofar as the normative character of law can only be constituted by legally legitimate reasons:

> Texts have a normative effect as soon as [...] authority is ascribed to them. [...] Normativity thus refers to the legitimisation or justifying quality of norms, i.e. the quality that gives them the character of ought in the eyes of their subjects. Normative orders are thus understood as orders of justification, as the totality of more or less institutionalised norms, rules, values, etc., which are based on [...] justifications and need such justifying reasons in order to maintain themselves.[171]

In this sense, literature would have to be *instituted* as a normative source of law through legislative bodies, legal acts, *usus*, etc., whereby if this were the case, it would no longer be possible to speak of literature, but only of normative legal texts. However, literature can function as a documentary *historical* source of law if it shows legal relationships in the social context of different epochs. Trüstedt, on the other hand, citing Pierre Legendre,[172] refers to a cultural normativity that cannot be used analogously to the legal concept of normativity. She sees cultural-critical literature as having the potential to create new legal references by utilising the triangle of text—cultural reference—text recipient to bring about a change in the reader's cultural-normative referentiality.[173] Ascribing *normative* character to literature, in whatever form, inevitably leads to misleading references to legal normativity in the sense of legal production by legitimised legal authorities and should therefore be avoided. Rather, one could speak of cultural references in the sense of seismographic effects, as Heinz Müller-Dietz and Albert von Schirnding cite, ascribing to

---

[168] Bloch (1995), pp. 835–840.

[169] Trüstedt (2012), p. 61.

[170] Cf. ibid., p. 61.

[171] Duss Jacobi (2013), pp. 364–365.

[172] Becker refers to Legendre's view that art has normative power (see Becker 2016, p. 128, cf. footnote 174). See also: Legendre (2012), p. 128.

[173] Cf. on this Becker (2016), pp. 109–146.

literature the sensitivity to recognise or anticipate social changes, which in turn entail legal changes.[174] This characteristic of literature will be revisited later in greater detail.

A proposal for dealing with law in literature that is relevant to the present work comes from Peter Schneck, who, in agreement with the French researcher Christian Biet,[175] refers to the inner, implicit, or invisible legal discourse in literary texts, to paraphrase Michael Foucault:

> The representation of law in literature inevitably involves an interpretation of the law's founding authority, which in turn serves as a basis for literature's own performative authorisation. Consequently, the presence of the law in literature can (and must) be felt even where its forms, processes, and practices are not the immediate object of representation at certain points in a specific literary text.[176]

As has been stated previously regarding Christian Biet, not only the obvious legal or procedural subject matter in the literature but also implicit discourses in the literature that are not immediately obvious can, out of their context, result in a legal discourse. It is precisely the disclosure of these 'inconspicuous features' through the legally sensitive reading of a text that can reveal new legal contexts and discourses that remain hidden to the legal layperson. The success of such fine-meshed examinations of the law in literature naturally requires a strongly interdisciplinary approach that recognises the possibility of the closest methodological and substantive links between law and literature.

In this context, a very recent study by Eric Achermann and Klaus Stierstorfer should be mentioned, which attempts to show the thematic connections and the mutual influence of literature and law.[177] According to the two authors, the basis of this hyphen is the triangle of "materiality - comparativity - constitutivity",[178] which is intended to encourage a new reflection on the comparison of the two disciplines as part of a common socio-cultural context: "It is not so much on the relations that connect two things in genealogies or systems, but on the analysis of the two things thus combined with regard to a third, a tertium, that is a property, structure or function which sets up a paradigm on the basis of which conformity or difference can be defined."[179] This new perspective could forge a closer link between literature and law through structural, functional, or disciplinary methods. According to Achermann and Stierstorfer, such an interweaving of disciplines would also promote access to research into the potential for mutual influence as well as the development of "constitutive normative concepts within law and literature research."[180] The two authors believe that there is potential for future research here by replacing generalised

174 Cf. Müller-Dietz (1990), p. 21; cf. von Schirnding (1990), p. 27.

175 Cf. Biet (2000), pp. 17–18.

176 Schneck (2011), p. 18.

177 Achermann and Stierstorfer (2022).

178 Achermann and Stierstorfer (2023), p. 3.

179 Ibid., p. 466.

180 Achermann and Stierstorfer (2022), p. 471.

conceptualisations with precise analyses at the interface between the two disciplines and possibly laying the foundations for a third cultural studies discipline.

Bernhard Schlink already surmised that this interdisciplinary potential is far from being exhausted in his epilogue to Richard Weisberg's *Legal Histories* in 2013:

> Despite the long tradition of lawyers writing about literature, the study of law and literature is still in its infancy in Germany. Its greatest significance, its greatest impact, is as a gateway to the history of law, culture and mentality and to legal philosophy. In Germany, the door has only just been opened; it will be pushed wide open in the coming years. The potential of dealing with law and literature in teaching is too great to remain unutilised.[181]

Since Schlink's statement, legal and literary research has taken a step forward, especially through the work of the Collaborative Research Centre 1385 'Law and Literature' at the University of Münster,[182] but the research potential, especially in methodological and interdisciplinary terms, has not been exhausted. Consequently, the present work aims to build on this research to refine and supplement it methodologically.

Moreover, it is simultaneously based on the observation that previous studies on law *in* literature rarely offer a precise step-by-step analysis of the legal discourse in the narrative in comparison to the real legal discourse. Unless they are larger-scale studies of interdisciplinary intersections, they usually analyse a thematic focus or concept in detail and relate it to the literary text without developing an interdisciplinary methodology. The design of the *counterfactual method* also implies the provision of the prerequisites for recognising legal-counterfactual connections in literature, and this requires the recipient to have knowledge of real-world law in comparison to the fictional, semi-real, or factual law in the diegesis. If this knowledge is not imparted to the reader, they cannot arrive at a counterfactual reading due to a lack of possibilities for critical contrast.

As indicated earlier, this study is limited to the field of law *in* literary texts, which thus not only excludes analyses of legal texts from a literary and linguistic perspective but also literary creations by so-called poet-lawyers,[183] insofar as their stories do not directly or indirectly refer to legal issues or topics.

---

181 Schlink (2013), p. 289.

182 On 1 July 2019, the German Research Foundation (DFG) established the Collaborative Research Centre 1385 "Law and Literature" at Münster University (until 30 June 2024) with the aim of researching fundamental questions about law and literature, the disciplines involved, their basic concepts and methods as well as their social and cultural significance. The specialist book series 'Literature and Law', which has been published by J.B. Metzler since 2022, documents these latest research findings and, at the same time, testifies to the revitalisation of interest in interdisciplinary work between literature and law.

183 Yvonne Nilges' broad concept of the 'poet-lawyer' includes writers who have worked or are working as lawyers as well as those who have started or completed a legal education (Nilges 2014c, p. 10). The term 'poet-jurist' itself was introduced by Eugen Wohlhaupter. See Wohlhaupter (1957). Among the jurists who also used their legal knowledge in literature are Jacob Grimm, Josef Kohler, Gustav Radbruch, Jutta Limbach, Michael Stolleis, Wolfgang Graf Vitzthum (Greiner 2010, p. 8).

After this brief comparative overview of the state of research on *law and literature*, the following section will attempt to define the concept of 'interdisciplinarity' for the purposes of the study and to explore the spectrum of interdisciplinary points of contact between law and literature. Methodologically, the more recent drafts by Eric Achermann and Klaus Stierstorfer on the triangle of "materiality - comparativity - constitutivity" as well as the theories of discourse, interdiscourse, and hermeneutics are used as possible 'cement' between the disciplines. The establishment of a common interdisciplinary, methodological basis is intended to facilitate the development and presentation of methodological and counterfactual work between intradiegetic and real-world, extradiegetic law.

The aim of this research will be to use this approach to show how law and literature can be methodically linked, on the one hand, and to attempt to bring the counterfactual perspective to full fruition by contrasting diegetic law with real-world law, on the other. The following five selected contemporary novels will be used to test and illustrate the legal-counterfactual method conceived in this way: *La décision* (2022) by Karine Tuil, *Unorthodox* (2012) by Deborah Feldman, *Sworn Virgin* (2014) by Elvira Dones, *Repenti* (2017) by Claude Chossat, and *A Slap in the Face* (2018)[184] by Abbas Khider. In these studies, the conversation will turn to terror legislation (*La décision*), unwritten law (*Repenti*, *Sworn Virgin*), administrative law (*A Slap in the Face*), and Talmudic law (*Unorthodox*).

References

Achermann, Eric, and Gideon Stiening. 2022. *Vom "Theater des Schreckens" zum "peinlichen Rechte nach der Vernuft"*. Berlin/Heidelberg: J. B. Metzler.

Achermann, Eric, and Klaus Stierstorfer. 2022. Squaring Law and Literature: Materiality – Comparativity – Constitutivity. *Law & Literature* 35 (3): 457–489.

Achermann, Eric, and Klaus Stierstorfer. 2023. Einleitung: Materialität – Komparativität – Konstitutivität. In *Literatur und Recht: Materialität. Formen und Prozesse gegenseitiger Vergegenständlichung*, ed. Eric Achermann, Andreas Blödorn, Corinna Norrick-Rühl, and Petra Pohlmann, 3–43. Berlin/Heidelberg: J. B. Metzler.

Albrecht, Timo M., Svenja Brand, Leonore Merth, et al. 2021. 'Recht und Literatur'. Ein interdisziplinärer Forschungsüberblick mit Werkstattbericht. *Göttinger Rechtszeitschrift* 2021 (2): 120–130.

Alpa, Guido. 2017. *Giuristi e interpretazioni. Il ruolo del diritto nella società postmoderna.* Genoa: Marietti.

Angot, Christine. 2022. *Le voyage dans l'Est*. Paris: J'ai lu.

Barenghi, Andrea. 2023. L'umanesimo giuridico in un libro di Donato Carusi. *Intersezioni* (2): 771–775.

Baron, Christine. 2016. La littérature auxiliaire de l'acte de juger?. *Les Cahiers de la justice* (2): 371–382.

Baron, Christine. 2020. *Contextes littéraires, émotions judiciaires*. Paris: Classiques Garnier.

Baron, Christine. 2021. *La littérature à la barre*. Paris: CNRS éditions.

[184] Engl. translation: *The Slap in the Face* (2018).

Baron, Christine. 2023. *Le tribunal du récit: Désir de justice et littérature*. Le Kremlin-Bicêtre: mare & martin.

Baron, Jane, and Julia Epstein. 1997. Is law narrative? *Buffalo Law Review* 45 (1): 141–187.

Bauman, Zygmunt, and Riccardo Mazzeo. 2016. *In Praise of Literature*. Cambridge/Malden: Polity.

Becker, Katrin. 2016. *Zwischen Norm und Chaos: Literatur als Stimme des Rechts. Legendre, Kafka, Hoffmann*. Paderborn: W. Fink.

Bergengruen, Maximilian. 2011. Betrügliche Schlüsse, natürliche Regeln. Zur Beweiskraft von forensischen und literarischen Indizien in Kleists 'Der Zweikampf'. In *Ausnahmezustand der Literatur. Neue Lektüren zu Heinrich von Kleist*, ed. Nicolas Pethes, 133–165. Göttingen: Wallstein.

Bernhard, Thomas. 1988. Ist es eine Komödie? Ist es eine Tragödie? In *Erzählungen*, ed. Thomas Bernhard, 35–42. Suhrkamp: Frankfurt am Main.

Bevere, Antonio. 1996. *La giustizia in prosa e versi*. Ancona: Nuove Ricerche.

Biet, Christian. 2000. Introduction. Droit et littérature, un lien nécessaire. *Littératures classiques. Droit et literature* 2000 (40): 5–22.

Biet, Christian. 2004. *Droit et littérature sous l'ancien régime. Le jeu de la valeur et de la loi*. Paris: Honoré Champion.

Bloch, Andreas. 1995. Sophie von La Roches Geschichte des Fräuleins von Sternheim (von 1771) – Ehe und Eherecht im Werk und in der Wirklichkeit des 18. Jahrhunderts. *NJW* 1995 (13): 835–840.

Blum, Stephanie. 2014. 'Darum Gott alles recht erschuf': Recht und Geschlecht in Johann Fischarts Sonettzyklus 'Etlich Sonnet'. In *Dichterjuristen. Studien zur Poesie des Rechts vom 16. bis 21. Jahrhundert*, ed. Yvonne Nilges, 13–29. Würzburg: Königshausen & Neumann.

Bockelmann, Paul. 1967. *Das Problem der Kriminalstrafe in Deutscher Dichtung. Vortrag gehalten vor der juristischen Studiengesellschaft in Karlsruhe am 14. März 1967*. Karlsruhe: C. F. Müller.

Bouglé-Le Roux, Claire. 2021. *La littérature française et le droit, du Roman de Renart à Michel Houellebecq. Anthologie illustrée*. Paris: LexisNexis.

Bruner, Jerome. 2002. *La fabbrica delle storie. Diritto, letteratura, vita*. Rom/Bari: Laterza.

Calamandrei, Piero. 1924. Le lettere e il processo civile. *Rivista di diritto processuale civile* I:202–204.

Cananzi, Daniele, ed. 2020. *La città dell'imperfezione. Follia e gioco tra diritto e letteratura*. Torino: Giappichelli editore.

Carbonnier, Jean. 2014. *Flexible droit. Pour une sociologie du droit sans rigueur*. Paris: LGDJ.

Cardozo, Benjamin. 1947. Law and Literature. In *Selected Writings of Benjamin Nathan Cardozo*, ed. Margaret E. Hall, 339–356. New York: Fallon.

Carpi, Daniela, ed. 2005. *Property Law in Renaissance Literature*. Frankfurt am Main: Peter Lang.

Carrère, Emmanuel. 2022. *V13. Chroniques juidiciaires*. Paris: P.O.L.

Carusi, Donato. 2022. *Sua maestà la legge? Tre secoli di potere, diritto e letteratura*. Florence: Olschki.

Casucci, Felice. 2015. *L'ingiuria tra diritto e letteratura*. Naples: Edizioni Scientifiche Italiane.

Casucci, Felice. 2019. *La rosa del diritto. Per un libro dei giorni tra vita, letteratura e diritto*. Naples: Edizioni Scientifiche Italiane.

Cattaneo, Mario. 1985. *L'illuminismo giuridico di Alessandro Manzoni*. Sassari: Edizione presso la facoltà di Sassari.

Cattaneo, Mario. 1991. *Carlo Goldoni e Alessandro Manzoni. Illuminismo e diritto penale*. Milan: Giuffré.

Cau, Maurizio, and Giuliano Marchetto, eds. 2004. *Droit et littérature (Serie Laboratoire italien. Politique et société)*. Vol. 5. Paris: ENS éditions.

Charbonnier, Gil, and Franck Petit. 2023. *Quand la littérature moderne (ré) invente le droit. Œuvres choisies du XXᵉ siècle à aujourd'hui*. Paris: LexisNexis.

Cherchi, Paolo. 2019. Il genere delle controversie fra diritto e letteratura. *Forum Italicum* 53 (2): 250–263.

Chossat, Claude. 2017. *Repenti*. Paris: Fayard.

Condello, Angela, and Tiziano Toracca. 2015. *Letteratura e Diritto*: breve tracciato di una disciplina. Il caso italiano: qualche riflessione, https://www.academia.edu/en/21498058/Letteratura_e_Diritto_breve_tracciato_di_una_disciplina.

Cook, Nancy. 1991. Shakespeare Comes to the Law School Classroom. *Denver Law Review* 1991 (68): 387–411.

Cormeau, Christoph, and Wilhelm Störmer. 2007. *Hartmann von Aue*. Munich: C. H. Beck.

D'Amato, Antonio. 1936. *La letteratura e la vita del diritto*. Milan: Ubezzi & Dones.

Danovi, Remo. 2004. *Tra fantasia e diritto. List of novels*. Milan: Giuffrè.

de Pitaval, François Gayot. 2019. *Causes celèbres et intéressantes, avec les jugements qui les ont décidées*. Paris: Hachette.

Diederichsen, Uwe. 1996. Shakespeares *Kaufmann von Venedig*: Jurisprudenz auf dem Forum der Bühne. In *Literatur und Recht: Literarische Rechtsfälle von der Antike bis zur Gegenwart*, ed. Ulrich Mölk, 186–228. Göttingen: Wallstein.

Dolin, Kieran. 2007. *A Critical Introduction to Law and Literature*. Cambridge: Cambridge University Press.

Dones, Elvira. 2014. *Sworn Virgin*. London/New York: And Other Stories.

Dunlop, C. R. B. 1991. Literature Studies in Law Schools. *Cardozo Studies in Law and Literature* 3 (1): 63–110.

Duss Jacobi, Vanessa. 2013. Die Korrelation von Text und Normativität im Recht. In *Beiträge zur Rechtsgeschichte Österreichs (BRGÖ)*, ed. Kamila Staudigl-Ciechowicz, Philipp Klausberger, Ramon Pils, et al., vol. 2, 363–373. Vienna: Verlag der Österreichischen Akademie der Wissenschaften.

Ensberg, Peter, and Hans-Jochen Marquardt, eds. 2002. *Recht und Gerechtigkeit bei Heinrich von Kleist*. Stuttgart: Heinz.

Enthoven, Raphaël. 2020. *Le Temps gagné*. Paris: Flammarion.

Errera, Andrea. 2023. Il diritto nella produzione letteraria di Claudio Magris: uno scrittore al cospetto delle norme, *LawArt. Rivista di Diritto, Arte, Storia – Journal of Law, Art and History* 2023 (4): 371–399.

Fechner, Erich. 1952. *Recht und Politik in Adalbert Stifters 'Witiko': Stifters Beitrag zur Wesensbetrachtung des Rechts und zur Charakterologie und Ethik des politischen Menschen*. Tübingen: H. Laupp.

Fehr, Hans. 1931. *Das Recht in der Dichtung*. Bern: Francke.

Fehr, Hans. 1936. *Die Dichtung im Recht*. Bern: Francke.

Feldman, Deborah. 2012. *Unorthodox*. New York: Simon & Schuster.

Fish, Stanley. 1989. *Doing What Comes Naturally, Change, Rhetoric, and the Practice of Theory in Literary and Legal Studies*. Durham: Duke University Press.

Forti, Gabrio. 2024. *Il tempo della parola giusta. Scritti di diritto penale, criminologia e letteratura*. Milan: Vita e Pensiero.

Forti, Gabrio, et al., eds. 2022. *L'ombra delle 'colonne infami'. La letteratura e l'ingiustizia del capro espiatorio*. Milan: Vita e Pensiero.

Forti, Gabrio, Giuseppe Rotolo, and Arianna Visconti, eds. 2023. *Tra giustizia e letteratura. Un'avventura del Pensiero*. Milan: Vita e Pensiero.

Frank, Catherine O. 2010. *Law, Literature, and the Culture in England, 1837–1925*. Farnham/Burlington: Ashgate.

Gaakeer, Jeanne. 2012. European *Law and Literature*: Forever Young – The Nomad Concurs. In *Dialogues on Justice: European Perspectives on Law and Humanities*, ed. Helle Porsdam and Thomas Elholm, 44–72. Berlin/New York: De Gruyter.

Gabbiadini, Guglielmo. 2014. Welttheater, Revolution und usurpierte Menschenrechte: Über Friedrich Maximilian von Klingers Fragment *Das zu frühe Erwachen des Genius der Menschheit*. In *Dichterjuristen. Studien zur Poesie des Rechts vom 16. bis 21. Jahrhundert*, ed. Yvonne Nilges, 49–66. Würzburg: Königshausen & Neumann.

Garapon, Antoine, and Denis Salas, eds. 2008. *Le droit dans la littérature*. Paris: Michalon.

Gerstenberg, Ekkehard. 1954. Das Recht in der Dichtung. Einführung in die Literatur und Bibliografie. *Archiv für Rechts- und Sozialphilosophie* 41 (1): 98–109.
Getman, Jules. 1988. Voices. *Texas Law Review* 1988 (66): 577–588.
Greiner, Bernhard. 2010. Das Forschungsfeld 'Recht und Literatur'. In *Recht und Literatur. Interdisziplinäre Bezüge*, ed. Bernhard Greiner, Barbara Thums, and Wolfgang Graf Vitzthum, 7–26. Heidelberg: Winter.
Greiner, Bernhard, Barbara Thums, and Wolfgang Graf Vitzthum, eds. 2010. *Recht und Literatur. Interdisziplinäre Bezüge*. Heidelberg: Winter.
Grimm, Jacob. 1816. Von der Poesie im Recht. *Zeitschrift für geschichtliche Rechtswissenschaft* 1816 (2): 25–99.
Großfeld, Bernhard. 2005. *Poesie und Recht – Rechtsvergleichende Zeichenkunde*. Paderborn/Munich: F. Schöningh.
Guizzi, Giuseppe. 2020. *Il "caso Balzac". Storie di diritto e di letteratura*. Bologna: Il Mulino.
Häberle, Peter. 1983. *Das Grundgesetz der Literaten. Der Verfassungsstaat im (Zerr?) Spiegel der Schönen Literatur*. Baden-Baden: Nomos.
Holiczi, Walter. 1972. *Die Entwicklung der Gerichtsberichterstattung in der Wiener Tagespresse von 1848 bis zur Jahrhundertwende*. Vienna: Notring.
Huffcut, Ernest W. 1892. The Literature of Law. *The Green Bag* 4 (2): 52–54. https://www.repository.law.indiana.edu/cgi/viewcontent.cgi?article=2982&context=facpub.
Itzcovich, Giulio. 2007. Pinocchio e il diritto. *Materiali per una storia della cultura giuridica* 37 (1): 239–268.
Jaenada, Philippe. 2023. *Sans preuve & sans aveu*. Paris: Éditions Points.
Jellamo, Anna. 2005. *Il cammino di Dike. L'idea di giustizia da Omero a Eschilo*. Rome: Donzelli.
Juster, Alexandra. 2022. *Juli Zehs "Corpus Delicti: Ein Prozess". Intertextuelle Perspektiven*. Münster: LIT.
Khider, Abbas. 2018. *A Slap in the Face*. Calcutta: Seagull Books.
Kilcher, Andreas, Matthias Mahlmann, and Daniel Müller Nielaba, eds. 2013. *"Fechtschulen und phantastische Gärten": Recht und Literatur*. Zürich: vdf Hochschulverlag.
Kilian, Michael, ed. 1987. *Jurisprudenz zwischen Techne und Kunst – von Hippokrates bis Heine: Philosophisches und Literarisches zum Verhältnis Kunst und Recht*. Tübingen: Attempto.
Kirste, Stephan. 2021. Literatur und Recht. In *Handbuch Rechtsphilosophie*, ed. Eric Hilgendorf and Jan C. Joerden, 351–362. Berlin/Heidelberg: J. B. Metzler.
Klein, Hans H. 2024. *Der Jurist Johann Wolfgang von Goethe*. In *Eine Spurensuche in Werk und Wirken*. München: C. H. Beck.
Koch, Hans-Albrecht, ed. 1998. *Grenzfrevel. Rechtskultur und literarische Kultur*. Bonn: Bouvier.
Koegler, Caroline, Jesper Reddig, and Klaus Stierstorfer. 2021. *Citizenship, Law, and Literature*. Berlin/Boston: De Gruyter.
Kohler, Josef. 1883. *Shakespeare vor dem Forum der Jurisprudenz*. Würzburg: Stahel.
Kouchner, Camille. 2022. *The Familia Grande: A Family's Silence Weighs on Everyone*. London: Brazen.
Künzel, Christine. 2007. 'Aus einem Bette aufgestanden'. Anmerkungen zum 'Verhältnis' zwischen Recht und Literatur. In *Figures of Law. Studies in the Interference of Law and Literature*, ed. Gert Hofmann, 115–132. Basel: Francke.
Legendre, Pierre. 2012. *Über die Gesellschaft als Text. Grundzüge einer dogmatischen Anthropologie*. Vienna/Berlin: Turia + Kant.
Lieb, Claudia. 2022. *Germanistiken: Zur Praxis von Literatur- und Rechtswissenschaft 1630-1900*, 273–279. Berlin: Metzler Verlag.
Lüdemann, Susanne. 2014. As the Case May Be. Über Fallgeschichten in Literatur und Psychoanalyse. In *Was der Fall ist. Casus und Lapsus*, ed. Inka Mülder-Bach and Michael Ott, 115–127. Stuttgart: W. Fink.
Lüderssen, Klaus. 1991. *Produktive Spiegelungen. Recht und Kriminalität in der Literatur*. Frankfurt am Main: Suhrkamp.
Lüderssen, Klaus. 1996. *Genesis und Geltung in der Jurisprudenz*. Frankfurt am Main: Suhrkamp.

Lüderssen, Klaus. 1997. Die Juristen und die schöne Literatur – Stufen der Rezeption. *Neue Juristische Wochenschrift* 1997 (50): 1106–1113.

Lüderssen, Klaus, ed. 1999. *Die wahre Liberalität ist Anerkennung. Goethe und die Jurisprudenz.* Baden-Baden: Nomos.

Lüderssen, Klaus. 2007a. *Eichendorff und das Recht*. Frankfurt am Main: Insel.

Lüderssen, Klaus. 2007b. *Produktive Spiegelungen II. Recht im künstlerischen Kontext*. Berlin: Berliner Wissenschaftsverlag.

Lüderssen, Klaus. 2014. *Produktive Spiegelungen III. Recht im künstlerischen Kontext*. Berlin/Boston: De Gruyter.

Magris, Claudio. 1994. Who is on the Other Side? Considerations about Frontiers. In *Frontiers*, ed. Christopher Mac Lehose, 8–25. London: Harper Collins.

Malaurie, Philippe. 1997. *Droit et littérature: une anthologie*. Paris: Cujas.

Marafioti, Domenico. 2002. *Giustizia e letteratura*. Milan: Spirali.

Mas, Marion, and Myriam Roman. 2023. Écrire le droit: un enjeu pour les études dix-neuvièmistes. *Romantisme* 199 (1): 5–15.

Masson, Jean-Pol. 2022. *Le droit dans la littérature française*. Brussels: Larcier.

Mastrominico, Giuseppe. 2017. *Diritto e letteratura. Dissapori medievali e moderni*. Neaples: Editoriale Scientifica.

Meccarelli, Massimo. 2020. Diritto e letteratura tra storia e memoria. Prime riflessioni a partire da due romanzi sulla transizione. *LawArt. Rivista di Diritto, Arte, Storia – Journal of Law, Art and History* 2020 (1): 207–234.

Meier, Rolf. 1994. *Dialog zwischen Jurisprudenz und Literatur. Richterliche Unabhängigkeit und Rechtsabbildung in E.T.A. Hoffmanns 'Das Fräulein von Scuderi'*. Baden-Baden: Nomos.

Mittica, Maria P. 2006. *Raccontando il possibile. Eschilo e le narrazioni giuridiche*. Milan: Giuffrè.

Moix, Yann. 2019. *Orléans*. Paris: Grasset.

Mölk, Ulrich, ed. 1996a. *Literatur und Recht. Literarische Rechtsfälle von der Antike bis in die Gegenwart*. Göttingen: Wallstein.

Mölk, Ulrich. 1996b. Vorwort. In *Literatur und Recht. Literarische Rechtsfälle von der Antike bis in die Gegenwart*, ed. Ulrich Mölk. Göttingen: Wallstein.

Müller, Georg. 1912. *Das Recht in Goethes Faust, juristische Streifzüge durch das Land der Dichtung*. Berlin: Heymann.

Müller-Dietz, Heinz. 1990. *Grenzüberschreitungen. Beiträge zur Beziehung zwischen Literatur und Recht*. Baden-Baden: Nomos.

Müller-Dietz, Heinz. 2009. Jenseits von Bologna – Jurisprudentia literarisch – von Woyzeck bis Weimar, von Hoffmann bis Luhmann. *Zeitschrift der Savigny-Stiftung für Rechtsgeschichte: Germanistische Abteilung* 126 (1): 360–364.

Müller-Dietz, Heinz. 2010. *Recht und Kriminalität in literarischen Spiegelungen*. Berlin: BWV.

Müller-Dietz, Heinz. 2011. Blutrache in literarischer Sicht – am Beispiel des Romans 'Der zerrissene April' von Ismail Kadare. *Goltdammer's Archiv für Strafrecht* 158 (1): 34–54.

Müller-Dietz, Heinz. 2016. Literarische Verarbeitung von Recht in Gegenwartsromanen. In *Recht Populär. Populärkulturelle Rechtsdarstellungen in aktuellen Texten und Medien*, ed. Patrick Meier and Franziska Stürmer, 37–59. Baden-Baden: Nomos.

Müller-Seidel, Walter. 1983a. Justizkritik im Werk Heinrich Manns. Zu einem Thema der Weimarer Republik. In *Heinrich Mann. Sein Werk in der Weimarer Republik. Zweites internationales Symposion Lübeck 1981*, ed. Helmut Koopmann and Peter-Paul Schneider, 103–127. Frankfurt am Main: Vittorio Klostermann.

Müller-Seidel, Walter. 1983b. *Vor Gericht*. Balladendichtung und Justizkritik. Zu einem wenig bekannten Gedicht Goethes. In *Gedichte und Interpretationen, vol. 2: Aufklärung und Sturm und Drang*, ed. Karl Richter, 436–450. Stuttgart: Reclam.

Müller-Seidel, Walter. 1985. Todesarten und Todesstrafen. Eine Betrachtung über Heinrich von Kleist. In *Kleist Jahrbuch 1985*, ed. Hans-Joachim Kreutzer, 7–38. Berlin: Erich Schmidt.

Müller-Seidel, Walter. 1996. Alfred Döblin. *Die beiden Freundinnen und ihr Giftmord*. Psychiatrie, Strafrecht und moderne Literatur. In *Literatur und Recht. Literarische Rechtsfälle von der Antike bis in die Gegenwart*, ed. Ulrich Mölk, 356–369. Göttingen: Wallenstein.

Müller-Seidel, Walter. 2017. *Rechtsdenken im literarischen Text. Deutsche Literatur von der Weimarer Klassik zur Weimarer Republik*. Berlin/Boston: De Gruyter.

Nilges, Yvonne, ed. 2014a. *Dichterjuristen. Studien zur Poesie des Rechts vom 16. bis 21. Jahrhundert*. Würzburg: Königshausen & Neumann.

Nilges, Yvonne, ed. 2014b. *Recht und Juristen im Spiegel von Literatur und Kunst. Tagung im Nordkolleg Rendsburg vom 6. bis 8. September*. Münster: LIT.

Nilges, Yvonne. 2014c. Einleitung. In *Dichterjuristen. Studien zur Poesie des Rechts vom 16. bis 21. Jahrhundert*, ed. Yvonne Nilges, 9–11. Würzburg: Königshausen & Neumann.

Nussbaum, Martha C. 1995. *Poetic Justice. The Literary Imagination and Public Life*. Boston: Beacon Press.

Olson, Greta. 2010. De-Americanizing Law and Literature Narratives: Opening Up the Story. *Law & Literature* 22 (2): 338–364.

Olson, Greta. 2015. Futures of Law and Literature: A Preliminary Overview from a Culturalist Perspective. In *Recht und Literatur im Zwischenraum / Law and Literature In-Between. Aktuelle inter- und transdisziplinäre Zugänge / Contemporary Inter- and Transdisciplinary Approaches*, ed. Christian Hiebaum, Susanne Knaller, and Doris Pichler, 37–69. Bielefeld: transcript.

Ost, François. 2004. *Raconter la loi. Aux sources de l'imaginaire juridique*. Paris: Odile Jacob.

Ost, François. 2021. *Nouveaux contes juridiques*. Paris: Dalloz.

Ost, François, and Laurent Van Eynde. 2001. Le droit au miroir de la literature. In *Lettres et lois. Le droit au miroir de la littérature*, ed. François Ost, Laurent Van Eynde, Philippe Gérard, et al., 7–10. Brussels: Presses universitaires Saint-Louis Bruxelles.

Pergolesi, Ferruccio. 1956. *Diritto e giustizia nella letteratura moderna narrativa e teatrale*. Milan: Zuffi.

Piciché, Bernardo. 2019. Diritto e letteratura a dialogo nella tradizione italiana: Introduzione al volume. *Forum Italicum* 53 (2): 201–231.

Pieroth, Bodo. 2015. *Recht und Literatur. Von Friedrich Schiller bis Martin Walser*. München: C. H. Beck.

Pieroth, Bodo. 2018. *Deutsche Schriftsteller als angehende Juristen*. Berlin: De Gruyter.

Pieroth, Bodo. 2019. *Recht und britische Literatur. Von William Shakespeare bis George Orwell*. Munich: C. H. Beck.

Pieroth, Bodo. 2021. *Recht und französische Literatur. Von Jean de la Fontaine bis Albert Camus*. Munich: C. H. Beck.

Posner, Richard. 1988. *Law and Literature*. Cambridge Massachusetts/London: Harvard University Press.

Prisco, Salvatore. 2017. Diritto, letteratura, discipline umanistiche. Teorie, metodi, casi. Un programma culturale e un progetto di ricerca per il Dipartimento di Giurisprudenza. In *Il diritto incontra la letteratura*, ed. Stefania Torre, 5–8. Naples: Edizioni Scientifiche Italiane.

Quabeck, Franziska. 2021. *The Lawyer in Dickens*. Berlin/Boston: De Gruyter.

Radbruch, Gustav. 1920. Wilhelm Meisters sozialpolitische Sendung. Eine rechtsphilosophische Studie, *Logos. Internationale Zeitschrift für Philosophie und Kultur* 1920 (8): 152–162.

Rebuffa, Giorgio. 1992. Il trionfo del codice civile nella testimonianza di Honoré de Balzac. *Materiali per una storia della cultura giuridica* XXII (1): 65–88.

Robert-Diard, Pascale. 2022. *La petite menteuse*. Paris: Éditions L'Iconoclaste.

Roman, Myriam. 2023. *Le droit du poète: la justice dans l'œuvre de Victor Hugo*. Saint-Étienne: Presses Universitaires de Saint-Étienne.

Rossi, Giovanni, Daniele Velo Dalbrenta, and Cecilia Pedrazza Gorlero, eds. 2023. *L'arte di giudicare. Percorsi ed esperienze tra letteratura, arti e diritto*. Naples: Edizioni Scientifiche Italiane.

Roxin, Claus. 1997. *Karl May, das Strafrecht und die Literatur*. Tübingen: Klöpfer & Meyer.

Salas, Denis. 2013. *Kafka: Le combat avec la Loi*. Paris: Michalon.

Sansa, Anna. 2023. *Carlo Goldoni 'Avocat vénitien'. Droit et théatre à Venise au XVIIIe siècle*. Paris: Presse Universitaire Paris-Sorbonne.

Sansone, Arianna. 2001. *Diritto e letteratura. Un'introduzione generale*. Milan: Giuffré.

Sansone, Arianna, and Paola Mittica. 2008. Diritto e letteratura. Storia di una tradizione e stato dell'arte. *Italian Society for Law and Literature* 2008 (1): 1–9. https://amsacta.unibo.it/id/eprint/5552/1/ISLL_Papers_Vol_1_2008.pdf.

Schäfer, Frank L., and Monika Fludernik, eds. 2022. *Erzählen und Recht. Narrative and Law.* Baden-Baden: Ergon.

Schlink, Bernhard. 2013. Das Bilderbuch des Rechts. In *Rechtsgeschichten. Über Gerechtigkeit in der Literatur*, ed. Richard Weisberg, 275–289. Berlin: Suhrkamp.

Schmidhäuser, Eberhard. 1996. *Verbrechen und Strafe: Ein Streifzug durch die Weltliteratur von Sophokles bis Dürrenmatt.* Munich: C.H. Beck Verlag.

Schneck, Peter. 2011. *Rhetoric and Evidence: Legal Conflict and Literary Representation in U.S. American Culture.* Berlin/Boston: De Gruyter.

Schneider, Peter. 1987. *... ein einzig Volk von Brüdern.* In *Recht und Staat in der Literatur.* Frankfurt am Main: Athenäum.

Schramm, Edward. 2007. Law and Literature. *Juristische Arbeitsblätter*: 581–585.

Schwarz, Claudia. 2009. Sentenced to 'Storification'. A Trial on Legal Narratives. In *Legal Narratives. European Perspectives on U.S. Law in Cultural Contact*, ed. Gudrun M. Grabher and Anna Gamper, 213–238. Vienna/New York: Springer.

Sorel, Jean-Marc. 2023. *Les lectures du monde: La sphère juridique internationale dans la littérature.* Le Kremlin-Bicêtre: mare & martin.

Spantigati, Federico, ed. 2006. *Ritorno al diritto: I valori della convivenza.* Milan: Franco Angeli.

Springora, Vanessa. 2020. *Consent. A Memoir.* New York/London: HarperVia.

Stone Peters, Julie. 2005. Law, Literature, and the Vanishing Real: On the Future of an Interdisciplinary Illusion. *Publications of the Modern Language Association* 120 (2): 442–453.

Teissier-Ensminger, Anne. 1999. *La beauté du droit.* Paris: Descartes et Cie.

Torre, Stefania, ed. 2017. *Il diritto incontra la letteratura.* Naples: Edizioni Scientifiche Italiane.

Travers de Faultrier, Sandra. 2012. Les mots du droit sur et dans l'œuvre. *Les Cahiers de la justice* 4:25–41.

Travers de Faultrier, Sandra. 2021. *Afin que du réel advienne... Quand droit et littérature dialoguent.* Le Kremlin-Bicêtre: mare & martin.

Trévidic, Marc. 2011. *Au cœur de l'antiterrorisme.* Paris: JC Lattès.

Trüstedt, Katrin. 2012. Nomos und Narrative. Zu den Verfahren der Orestie. In *Die Innenwelt der Außenwelt der Innenwelt des Rechts. Annäherungen zwischen Rechts- und Literaturwissenschaft*, ed. Ino Augsberg and Sophie Charlotte Lenski, 59–77. Munich: W. Fink.

Tuil, Karine. 2022. *La décision.* Paris: Gallimard.

Tuzet, Giovanni. 2005. Diritto e letteratura: finzioni a confront", In *Annali dell'Università di Ferrara* (Sezione 5: Sc. Giuridiche Nuova Serie), 179–204.

Ulrich, Heiko. 2014. Der 'augenschein / Der nackenden wahrheit': Juristische Rhetorik und poetische Ästhetik in Weckherlins 'Urtheil des Paris'. In *Dichterjuristen. Studien zur Poesie des Rechts vom 16. bis 21. Jahrhundert*, ed. Yvonne Nilges, 31–48. Würzburg: Königshausen & Neumann.

Vacca, Roberto. 1923. *Il Diritto Sperimentale.* Turin: Fratelli Bocca.

Verdussen, Marc. 2007. L'étranger. Sur les révoltes fondatrices d'Albert Camus contre le Mensonge, l'Injustice et la Violence. In *Droit et littérature*, ed. François Jongen and Koen Lemmens, 45–61. Wavre: Anthemis.

Vitale, Vincenzo. 2019. Cosa cercano i giuristi nella letteratura? *Forum Italicum* 53 (2): 232–249.

von Schirnding, Albert. 1990. *Recht und Richter im Spiegel der Literatur.* München: Boorberg.

Vormbaum, Thomas, ed. 2005. *Anton Matthias Sprickmann – Dichter und Jurist.* Berlin: Berliner Wissenschaftsverlag.

Vormbaum, Thomas. 2016. *"Als Doktor beider Rechte". Heinrich Heine, das Recht und die Jurisprudenz.* Münster/Berlin: LIT.

Walter, Tonio, and Edward Schramm. 2021. *Dichtung und Wahrheit – und Recht.* Baden-Baden: Nomos.

Wambach, Lovis Maxim. 2000. *Grenzgänger zwischen Jurisprudenz und Literatur. Werner Krauss, Kurt Tucholsky, Friedrich Georg Jünger und Martin Beradt*. Baden-Baden: Nomos.

Wambach, Lovis Maxim. 2002. *Die Dichterjuristen des Expressionismus*. Baden-Baden: Nomos.

Ward, Ian. 1995. *Law and Literature. Possibilities and Perspectives*. Cambridge: Cambridge University Press.

Weber, Hermann, ed. 2003. *Reale und fiktive Kriminalfälle als Gegenstand der Literatur*. Berlin: Berliner Wissenschaftsverlag.

Weber, Hermann. 2005. *Recht und Juristen im Bild der Literatur*. Berlin: Berliner Wissenschaftsverlag.

Weber, Hermann. 2009. *Juristensöhne als Dichter: Hans Fallada*. In *Der Konflikt mit der Welt ihrer Väter in ihrem Leben und ihrem Werk*, ed. R. Johannes and Becher und Georg Heym. Berlin: Berliner Wissenschaftsverlag.

Weber, Hermann. 2010. Strafrecht und Religion in Dantes 'Göttlicher Komödie'. In *Literatur, Recht und Religion. Tagung im Nordkolleg Rendsburg vom 18. bis 20. September 2009*, ed. Hermann Weber, 57–90. Münster: LIT.

Weber, Hermann, ed. 2014. *Recht und Juristen im Spiegel von Literatur und Kunst. Tagung im Nordkolleg Rendsburg vom 6. bis 8. September 2013*. Münster: LIT.

Weber, Hermann, ed. 2017. *Das Recht als Rahmen für Literatur und Kunst. Tagung im Nordkolleg Rendsburg vom 4. bis 6. September 2015*. Berlin/Boston: De Gruyter.

Weisberg, Richard H. 1999. Vichy Law and the Holocaust in France: Précis of a Talk to the Hofstra Conference. In *Law and the Arts*, ed. Susan Tiefenbrun, 81–91. Westport/London: Greenwood Press.

Weisberg, Richard H. 2009. Wigmore and the Law and Literature Movement. *Law & Literature* 21 (1): 129–145.

Weisberg, Richard H. 2013. *Rechtsgeschichten. Über die Gerechtigkeit in der Literatur*. Berlin: Suhrkamp.

Weisberg, Richard H. 2018. Cardozo's 'Law and Literature': A Guide to his Judicial Writing Style. *Touro Law Review* 349: Cardozo Legal Studies Research Paper Nr. 551, Cardozo School of Law, https://papers.ssrn.com/sol3/papers.cfm?abstract_id=3216255.

Weisberg, Richard H., and Jean-Pierre Barricelli. 1982. Literature and the Law. In *Interrelations of Literature*, ed. Joseph Gibaldi and Jean-Pierre Barricelli, 150–175. New York: MLA.

Weitin, Thomas. 2010. *Recht und Literatur*. Münster: Aschendorff.

White, James B. 1973. *The Legal Imagination*. Chicago/London: University of Chicago Press.

Wigmore, John H. 1908. A List of Legal Novels. *Illinois Law Review* 08 (/2): 574–593.

Witteveen, Willem J. 1998. Law and Literature: Expanding Contracting Emerging. *Law & Literature* 10 (2): 155–160.

Wittmann, Jan. 2018. *Recht sprechen: Richterfiguren bei Kleist, Kafka und Zeh*. Berlin/Heidelberg: J. B. Metzler.

Wohlhaupter, Eugen. 1957. *Dichterjuristen*. Vol. 3. Tübingen: Mohr Siebeck.

Wolf, Erik. 1941. *Der Rechtsgedanke Adalbert Stifters*. Frankfurt am Main: Vittorio Klostermann.

Wolf, Erik. 1946. *Vom Wesen des Rechts in deutscher Dichtung. Hölderlin, Stifter, Hebel, Droste*. Frankfurt am Main: Vittorio Klostermann.

Würtenberger, Thomas. 1941. *Die deutsche Kriminalerzählung. Vortrag*, Erlanger Universitätsreden Nr. 27.

Zeuch, Ulrike. 2006. Recht und Literatur um 1800 im Kontext des *law and literature movement*. *Internationales Archiv für Sozialgeschichte der deutschen Literatur* 31 (1): 77–84.

Zinsmaier, Thomas. 2006. Controversiae. In *Der neue Pauly*, ed. Hubert Cancik, Helmuth Schneider, and Manfred Landfester. Tübingen: Brill. https://doi.org/10.1163/1574-9347_dnp_e304890.

Chapter 3
Auxiliary Methodological Concepts: Interdisciplinarity, Discourse, Hermeneutics, Counterfactuals

The historical references to the research field of law and literature, focusing on law *in* literature, have outlined the field geographically, provided national tendencies and outlined the state of research as a starting point for the present investigation. If the attempt to develop a 'legal method of counterfactuality' is to succeed against this background, the relationship between law and literature must first be defined more precisely: How exactly are the two disciplines related to each other? Where do they intersect, where do they touch, where do they separate? Are there previously undiscovered points of contact that could be utilised for the development of a methodological link? Answers to these questions are herein sought on four methodological levels, the combined interface of which is intended to determine the correlation between law and literature for the purposes of the present work: interdisciplinarity means cooperation on the basis of shared paradigms, discourse provides points of reference for a common 'speech', hermeneutics as a method of textual analysis is familiar to both disciplines and counter factuality links fiction and non-fiction as a product of mutual reflection. Each of these four concepts is explained below, first in general terms and then specifically for the field of law *in* literature.

3.1 Interdisciplinarity[1]

3.1.1 Theoretical Preliminary Remarks

Eric Hilgendorf recalls that Francis Bacon already advocated interdisciplinary research to promote the cross-fertilisation and correction of disciplines:

[1] Frank Fürbeth provides a rich bibliography on interdisciplinarity in his article "Was heißt, wozu dient und wohin führt uns Interdisziplinarität", in: *Zeitschrift des Mediävistenverbandes* (1999), pp. 7–16, here: pp. 7–8.

A. Juster, *Law, Literature and Legal Counterfactuals*, Law and Visual Jurisprudence 16, https://doi.org/10.1007/978-3-032-03792-3_3

> The rule [should be] that all divisions of knowledge be understood and used as lines to mark and distinguish rather than as cuts to sever; so that this interruption of continuity in the sciences is always avoided. For the opposite has caused individual sciences to become unfruitful, shallow and erroneous, since they are not fed and maintained and corrected by the general source and nourishment.[2]

In the 1960s, Helmut Schelsky founded the Bielefeld Centre for Interdisciplinary Research (Zentrum für Interdisziplinäre Forschung ZiF) in Germany, which is still active today, with the aim of "integrating the specialising sciences into a cooperation between the various disciplines" to promote the "mutual conceptual and methodological understanding of the disciplines" and to contribute to the "development of overarching theoretical concepts."[3]

Interdisciplinarity is a common term today, which is often used synonymously with transdisciplinarity, without yet having an established, standardised definition. As Doris Pichler states, this term is "much in need of specification and clarification."[4]

The term 'interdisciplinarity' is often used to refer to collaboration between two or more disciplines, but without specifying exactly what this collaboration should look like. 'Interdisciplinary' degree programmes and competencies seem to be in vogue, and it is not uncommon for them to be attributed an academic added value as compared to 'monodisciplinary' degree programmes. Nevertheless, on the one hand, there is great resistance to genuinely interdisciplinary research, and on the other hand, the term is used in an inflationary and incorrect manner. The inclusion of other fields of knowledge or the associative work of several disciplines in one project is often wrongly treated as 'interdisciplinary'. However, even if the definitions of interdisciplinarity diverge, they nevertheless coincide in the point that an understanding between the disciplines must take place via a common 'language', which renders a common research result reachable, through the application of shared concepts and methods. Merely 'pooling' knowledge is certainly not enough. Markus Käbisch emphasises the vagueness of the term by questioning its contours:

> Is 'interdisciplinarity' extra research with its own terms and rules or does it mean the intermediate position of a research subject when it is not possible to decide which discipline it belongs to? Or does interdisciplinarity mean [...] curiously looking around at other disciplines [...]? Likewise, 'interdisciplinarity' could also mean that the science that has fallen apart is amid a science that is actually unified and only needs to be grasped metatheoretically.[5]

The uncertainties here range, to paraphrase Jürgen Mittelstraß, from the mere restoration, via neologisms, of the internal scientific structure of an unjustly fragmented discipline,[6] to the creation of an entirely new discipline. In this context, Rainer Greshoff attempts to comprehensively tame the concept of interdisciplinarity:

---

[2] Hilgendorf (2021), here: p. 493; Bacon (2006), p. 216.

[3] Hilgendorf (2021), p. 493.
See today's ZiF: https://www.uni-bielefeld.de/einrichtungen/zif/.

[4] Pichler (2015), here: p. 15. See also Weingart and Stehr (2000), pp. 1–2. Balsiger (2005).

[5] Käbisch (2001), pp. 13–31.

[6] Mittelstraß (1989), p. 73.

> I use the term 'interdisciplinary' to refer [...] to those endeavours that are supported by the intention of correcting assumed or presumed limitations, one-sidedness and 'blind spots' of concepts, hypotheses or premises of respective disciplines, in which research is carried out on the same topics or at least somehow overlapping topics, through interdisciplinary work.[7]

Regardless of the definition used, interdisciplinary work needs to ensure common objects of study, terminology, concepts, methods and theories, without which fruitful integrative research is difficult to achieve in order to, as Jürgen Mittelstraß argues, "eliminate subject-specific and disciplinary narrow-mindedness where this stands in the way of problem development and appropriate research action."[8] Frank Fürbeth points out that actual interdisciplinarity requires a clear statement of common interest in knowledge—and the resulting development of common methods and objects—even before the disciplines themselves do so, whereby the disciplines "have to give up their own and dissolve into something common."[9] Greshoff does not go as far as the aporia of cancelling out the disciplines by merging them into the 'common ground', but he emphasises that it is essential to at least create a "conceptual basis for mediation" between the disciplines by coordinating the terms used in each case and relating them to each other.[10] To put it more simply: it must be verified that both disciplines are talking about the same 'thing', because "one of the biggest obstacles to interdisciplinary work is the problem that often 'wrong' elements from different scientific theories are related to each other."[11] Helmut Reinalter refers, in particular, to the problem of the commonality of linguistic concepts, which is sometimes exacerbated by adherence to one's own discipline and blindness to different questions.[12] Eric Hilgendorf emphasises the frequently encountered difficulty of the disciplines in working through "legal formula stuff", whereby the desire for linguistic clarity and unambiguity can break down interdisciplinary barriers.[13] Ultimately, however, as Reinalter and Greshoff note, it is precisely this integrative, albeit not unproblematic, terminology that gives rise to "transdisciplinarity."[14] The conceptual distinction between the terms interdisciplinarity and transdisciplinarity also proves to be blurred, which is why the question arises as to whether or not they should be used synonymously. Mittelstraß argues that transdisciplinarity is a synonym for interdisciplinarity in the sense of an integrative research principle because it "cancels out subject-specific and disciplinary constrictions where these stand in the way of problem development and appropriate

---

[7] Greshoff (2000), here: p. 29.

[8] Mittelstraß (2005), here: p. 19. See also Mittelstraß (1989), pp. 60–88. Cf. also Jahraus (2013), pp. 373–378.

[9] Fürbeth (1999), p. 11.

[10] Greshoff (2000), pp. 30–31.

[11] Homann and Suchanek, "Methodologische Überlegungen", p. 84.

[12] Reinalter (1993), here: pp. 9–13.

[13] Hilgendorf (2021), pp. 494–495.

[14] Mittelstraß (2005), p. 19; Greshoff (2000), pp. 30–31.

research action; it is in fact transdisciplinarity."[15] Mittelstraß does not want 'transdisciplinarity' to be understood as an independent theory or method, but rather as an "*internal scientific* principle relating to the organisation of scientific knowledge and scientific research itself […], but also as a form of scientific research and work when it comes to solving concrete problems in the world rather than scientific problems posed by science itself."[16] The concept of time allows a fine distinction to be made between the two terms if one assumes that interdisciplinary research refers to temporary projects, while transdisciplinary cooperation is aimed at long-term, usually institutionally anchored, collaboration. However, if one follows Mittelstrass, a synonymous use of the terms appears to be unproblematic, despite this slight temporary difference:

> While scientific cooperation generally means the willingness to cooperate in science and interdisciplinarity generally means a concrete temporary cooperation in this sense, transdisciplinarity means that cooperation leads to an ongoing scientific systemic order that changes the subject and disciplinary orientations themselves.[17]

In this respect, for the purposes of the present study, it does not appear to be inappropriate to simply speak of 'interdisciplinarity' instead of differentiating between interdisciplinarity and transdisciplinarity. It should also be emphasised in this context that interdisciplinarity/transdisciplinarity does not lead to a new subject or disciplinary context, i.e. no new discipline is created.[18]

The concept of interdisciplinarity today therefore stands for a means that is often only half-heartedly used to correct the progressive atomisation of scientific disciplines[19] and to start where a single discipline[20] alone is not able to develop the "methodological and theoretical ideas"[21] necessary to solve certain problems. According to Mittelstraß, interdisciplinary work requires a "reorganisation of scientific practice and scientific awareness",[22] whereby the boundaries between the

[15] Mittelstraß (2005), p. 19.

[16] Mittelstraß (2018), here: p. 202.

[17] Mittelstraß (2005), p. 20.

[18] Mittelstraß (2012), here: p. 13.

[19] See Mittelstraß (1989), pp. 67–69.

[20] Interdisciplinarity initially presupposes disciplinarity. In this regard, Mittelstraß complains about the lack of clarity in today's definition of what constitutes a discipline and how it is contoured (Mittelstraß 1989, p. 71). In terms of scientific theory, a discipline is determined by the object of knowledge, the method of knowledge, and the interest in knowledge (Gräfrath 2005, here p. 237). From an empirical perspective, disciplines emerge historically, in practice, and are determined by their methods, theories and research purposes (Lorenz Krüger 1987, pp. 106–128). Michel Foucault defines the term 'discipline' in particular as "a domain of objects, a set of methods, a corpus of propositions considered to be true, a play of rules and definitions, of techniques and instruments: all this constitutes a sort of anonymous system at the disposal of anyone who wants to or is able to use of it, without their meaning or validity being linked to the one who happened to be their inventor" (Foucault 1970, p. 9).

[21] Mittelstraß (1989), p. 74.

[22] Ibid.

concepts of interdisciplinarity and transdisciplinarity are, as we have seen, blurred, and it is fundamentally about nothing other than the restoration of "the old disciplinarity."[23]

In this context, Julie Thompson scales different levels of intensity of interdisciplinary cooperation, ranging between: The transfer of knowledge between disciplines, joint problem solving, building bridges between disciplines that are separated, the development of synthetic theories across scientific boundaries and the establishment of new joint fields of research based on overlapping research topics from several disciplines.[24]

Like Mittelstraß, Thompson does not see the emergence of a new discipline but rather seems to think of a relatively loose, topic-specific cooperation. If one follows Jürgen Mittelstraß and Julie Thompson, then neither interdisciplinary nor transdisciplinary forms of academic practice can lead to a new discipline, as Eric Achermann and Klaus Stierstorfer seem to be striving for when they speak of a modification of the basic understanding of law and literature: "Work on constitutivity addresses those encounters which rupture disciplinary boundaries and affect the core understandings constitutive of the respective literary and legal fields."[25] Although it is clear from this statement that the interdisciplinary work between law and literature has an impact on the basic understanding of both disciplines, it is not clear to what extent a third discipline could be formed that methodologically synthesises law and literature. Here the question arises of whether Achermann and Stierstorfer are essentially concerned with restoring the original disciplinary proximity between law and literature, as seemed to be a matter of course at the founding meeting of German Studies in 1846, if one recalls the text of the invitation to the latter: "Fostering German law, German history and the German language" in order to "promote academic stimulation, personal acquaintance and the balancing of opposites."[26] Could there be a new fusion of law and literature in the sense of the original German studies if, as Stephan Kirsten suggests, "academics working on a permanent interdisciplinary basis who are familiar with the sciences involved, i.e. who understand their language (concepts, methods) and can provide translation services" endeavour to do so?[27]

Before an answer to these questions can be sought, with reference to law *in* literature, it is first necessary to work out the conceptual, methodological, and linguistic similarities between law and literary studies, insofar as they can be found. Against this background, the following Sect. 3.1.2 examines the pragmatic applications of the concept of interdisciplinarity with a focus on the research field of law and literature.

---

[23] Ibid.

[24] Kirste (2016b), here: p. 56.

[25] Achermann and Stierstorfer (2022), p. 479.

[26] Lämmert (1999), pp. 7–22.

[27] Cf. Kirste (2016b), p. 76.

3.1.2 The Interdisciplinarity of Law and Literature

According to Kirste, the writer "artistically transforms legal problems into literature; the lawyer, who deals with the law in this foreign form, asks himself whether he cannot learn from this transformation for his work."[28] While, according to Gideon Stiening, to understand this correlation between writers and lawyers, it must be considered that although literature has the unlimited field of legal "standardisation of human behaviour" at its disposal,[29] it is limited by the difficulty of its sensually representable dimensions.[30] In other words, literary studies finds it challenging to present the abstract concept of normativity in writing. Despite possible interdisciplinary hurdles, according to Walter Müller-Seidel, the opening of literary studies to other academic disciplines is essential for its continued existence:

> But it will only be able to survive as a humanities discipline […] if it wants to be more than itself; if it does not remain in its shell but opens the windows and looks outwards. The modern industrial society in which we find ourselves can hardly be explained without the developments in the areas of social life, technology and natural science, and literary studies have every reason to concern themselves with these areas without disappearing into them, if only because literature itself concerns itself with them.[31]

As a mirror and seismograph of society, literature cannot—and must not—close itself off to an interdisciplinary approach. This applies today more than ever, in a world in which complex challenges, such as the Anthropocene, to name just one striking example, can hardly be mastered in a monodisciplinary way. Literary texts are not created in a vacuum—they are characterised by 'intertextuality' and 'multi-referentiality'—, different spheres of knowledge influence them and are reflected by them in a protean way. Walter Müller-Seidel's understanding of textual indexing is to be understood in this sense and in that of Hans Gadamer's hermeneutic circle, which will be discussed in more detail later. In order to be able to fully decipher a text, the necessary interdisciplinary prior and background knowledge is required, as Müller-Seidel shows using the example of Kafka's writing *In der Strafkolonie* (1919).[32] Its correct interpretation requires not only an examination of the literary text itself but also psychological and sociological insights, as well as knowledge of German criminal law and the discussions surrounding the deportation penalty at the turn of the eighteenth and nineteenth centuries, both of which flow into Kafka's

[28] Kirste (2021), p. 357.

[29] Hans Kelsen testifies to an infinite 'playing field' for the legal norm: "A legal norm is not valid because it has a certain content, that is, because its content can be derived from that of a presupposed basic norm by way of a logical conclusion, but because it is created in a certain way, and in the last instance in a way determined by a presupposed basic norm. […] *Therefore, any content can be law. There is no human behaviour which, by virtue of its content, would be excluded from being the content of a legal norm* [emphasis added by the author]" (Kelsen 2017, p. 354).

[30] Stiening (2022), here: p. 59.

[31] Müller-Seidel (1986), pp. 88–89.

[32] Kafka (1995). In German: *In der Strafkolonie.*

text.[33] According to Müller-Seidel, the reader is not only entitled to literary-historical knowledge but must also be 'supplied' with other information, i.e. "it must be made clear to him what the one has to do with the other. This cannot simply be left to the reader. The linking and integration of the other must be done on a case-by-case basis, actually from sentence to sentence."[34] If the reader is not provided with this 'marginal knowledge', the hermeneutic work of the literary scholar remains unsatisfactory, where the literary potential cannot be optimally developed. It is therefore fair to say that legal relationships in a literary work that is not grasped by the recipient neither allows adequate access to the text nor does justice to its potential for development. Michel Foucault, who is known to have dealt with the development of criminal law, also advocates the interdisciplinary connection between law and the human sciences:

> Instead of treating the history of penal law and the history of human sciences as two separate series whose overlapping appears to have had on one or the other, or perhaps on both, a disturbing or useful effect, according to one's point of view, see whether there is not some common matrix or whether they do not both derive from a single process of 'epistemologico-juridical' formation.[35]

Ian Ward believes that this common 'matrix' underlying law and literature has 'enormous potential' and sees the work between the two disciplines as one of the most exciting interdisciplinary tasks in better understanding law.[36] As indicated, Christophe Biet agrees with this line when he calls for not only explicit, but also implicit law to be uncovered in literature to promote sensitivity to legal relationships. Hans Müller-Dietz also sees the crossing of boundaries between disciplines as an attractive source of knowledge.[37] However, Ward criticises the fact that it is primarily lawyers who are interested in literature, while writers deal with legal material far less frequently.[38] Lorenz Kähler also regrets the asymmetry between literature and law, insofar as it is primarily lawyers who seek an interdisciplinary connection to literature.[39] The difficulty of reception in the humanities lies in the special nature of the legal discipline, which is, if we follow Luhmann, characterised by contingency and normative over-complexity: The validity of norms is thus ultimately based on the complexity and contingency of the field of expectation, in which they have their function as reductions".[40] According to Kähler, however, its reception can be "promoted by working out general principles, by developing

[33] Müller-Seidel (1986), pp. 46–60.

[34] Ibid., p. 90.

[35] Foucault (1977), p. 23.

[36] Ward (1995), p. IX.

[37] See Müller-Dietz (1990).

[38] Mölk (1996a, b), p. 7.

[39] Kähler (2018), here: pp. 109–110.

[40] Cf. Luhmann (1985), p. 31. Elena Esposito explains Luhmann's approach to 'contingency' as a reference to the "realm of the possible, which cannot be determined without checking what is the case in each case [...]. Contingency forces us to refer to the real and to project the possibilities from it, instead of starting from a possible that includes reality as an abstract instance" (Esposito

abstract concepts and by analysing recurring patterns."[41] According to Doris Pichler, a balancing of this imbalance in favour of literary scholars does indeed seem to be underway.[42] This is evidenced by the high proportion of literary scholars in the aforementioned SFB 1385 'Law and Literature' at the University of Münster. Depending on their specialist expertise, the motivation and research focus shifted within this framework, even if access to law still seems to be more difficult for literary scholars than for lawyers. One of the challenges is therefore to "find a common language that can be understood by literary scholars and lawyers."[43] In this context, Stephan Kirste argues for a softening of the positivist-abstract closedness of law in favour of an opening to other disciplines, which in turn should enable and establish a connection to the law. What is needed, according to Kirste, is to

> exchange with other sciences that use their methods to observe those areas of society that are not accessible to jurisprudence as such. This exchange is the actual task of interdisciplinarity. Interdisciplinarity specifically includes those aspects that had to be excluded in the technicality of legal-dogmatic disciplining.[44]

The difficulty of the interdisciplinary approach of law, in comparison to other disciplines therefore primarily lies in conceptual, terminological, and linguistic problems when it comes to developing common terms, methods, and concepts, understanding the same terms in the same way, and making legal terminology more accessible to other disciplines. To counter these difficulties, Ian Ward argues in favour of an expansion and simplification of legal and literary research and does not shy away from advocating a separate identity for 'law and literature':

> Intellectual pretentiousness is the pervasive evil in so much contemporary legal scholarship, and law and literature must seek to avoid falling into this trap. What law and literature scholarship must do is to remember that its purpose is to broaden, not merely to deepen. At the same time, importantly, it must strike out and establish its own identity [...].[45]

However, what exactly is meant by 'own identity' is difficult to determine. Does Ward mean a separate branch of research, common methods, or even a new discipline that unites law and literature? Regardless of the perspective taken, opinions on whether, to what extent, and in what way interdisciplinary research should be conducted between law and literature are not uniform, as has already become evident in the previous chapter and sections. In fact, the spectrum ranges from the denial of an interdisciplinary connection to all possible gradations of linkage to the affirmation of a possible fusion into a new discipline.[46]

2012, here p. 40). Contingency for jurisprudence refers to the necessity of applying the abstract norm to the concrete case, which can be one way or another, depending on the concrete situation.

[41] Kähler (2018), p. 139.

[42] Pichler (2015), p. 17.

[43] Ibid., p. 19.

[44] Kirste (2016a), here: p. 148.

[45] Ward (1995), p. X.

[46] Cf. Achermann and Stierstorfer (2023), pp. 4–5.

Despite these divergent findings, the primary concern here will and must be to assert the close connection between law and literature—if one wants to plausibly analyse law *in* literature—which is why my research intention is to identify the connecting elements. The focus will lie on the authentication of the transfer of law into literature. To this end, it will be necessary to investigate whether the two disciplines can be related to each other through a third, "namely a characteristic, structure or function", from which agreement or divergence arises,[47] or whether literature can function as a source of law, whether it can abolish or modify law, and how it represents legal relationships in general.[48] The series of tasks and questions seems long and confusing, but can be reduced to a simpler denominator, which will serve as a guideline in the following: What commonalities between the two disciplines can promote interdisciplinary work between law and literature and make it possible in the first place? The search for an answer to this question will, as we shall see, lead from the realm of interdisciplinarity to that of discourse, interdiscourse, and hermeneutics.

At first glance, the relative thematic dissolution of boundaries that is characteristic of both law and literature is striking. Hans Kelsen formulates it as follows: "Therefore, any content can be law. There is no human behaviour which as such, by virtue of its content, would be excluded from being the content of a legal norm."[49] In contrast to the literature, the thematic dissolution of boundaries for the law is to be regarded as relative, i.e. object-related, insofar as limiting factors such as practicability, taboos, judgements, and legal classifications each play a role.[50] The fundamental dissolution of thematic boundaries—possibly limited by censorship, unconstitutionality, formal aesthetic demands or reader expectations[51]—applies to literature to an even greater extent: while literature can refer to "everything that is"[52] and "everything that is not", law can only refer to "external human actions."[53] These far-reaching possibilities of literature are materially limited by only one condition, namely, its sensual representability. Literature cannot, as Gideon Stiening points out, "depict rational validity and binding force in itself",[54] for it lacks the normative functional immanence of law. It follows that literature is dependent on making legal processes 'visible', for which criminal trials are particularly suitable. Juli Zeh's

47 Cf. ibid., p. 16. The authors refer to the designation of the comparative function by name in the two sub-disciplines of 'general and comparative literature' and 'comparative law' as well as to the long-standing demarcation as a unit of comparison.

48 On the genesis of the concept of constitutivity in literature and law, see ibid., pp. 22–35.

49 Kelsen (2017), p. 354.

50 Achermann and Stierstorfer illustrate this relative openness using the example of the questionable nature of making the exchange of flower gifts the subject of a legal norm (Achermann and Stierstorfer 2023, p. 8).

51 Ibid., pp. 10–13. Cf. also Stiening (2022), pp. 51–52.

52 Here reference is made to Spinoza's first axiom: "That which is in itself, and that which is in something else ("*Omnia, quae sunt, vel in se vel in alio sunt*"): de Spinoza (1901), p. 14.

53 Stiening (2022), p. 57.

54 Ibid., p. 58.

novel *The Method* (2014)[55] or, if one revisits the nineteenth century, the collection of criminal histories of the *Pitaval*[56] are examples of this. As a result of the lack of normativity *in itself*, literature cannot become a normative source of law, but it can represent, depict, criticise, model, modify, explain or even invent the law.

In this context, Hans Müller-Dietz refers to the commonality of language as an organ of communication in law and literature, whereby literature admittedly has a much larger (playing) field[57] than that of law, whose linguistic expression is canonised and purpose-bound. Nevertheless, both disciplines are committed to *object adequacy*, i.e. "both are united by the telos of the greatest possible appropriateness with regard to object and statement. […] Object adequacy rather aims to make the – respective – object speak in the form appropriate to it."[58] Certainly, the subject of a novel, or the case to be legally regulated, determines how language is used, with the difference that literature can go to the limits of linguistic possibilities, while legal language always remains anchored in its target immanence and its formal and formulaic nature.[59] The essential medium of language for both disciplines is the text, which, as Jean-Philippe Agresti emphasises in the foreword to the recently published volume *Quand la littérature moderne (ré)invente le droit* (2023),[60] connects them: "The text. Always the text as a source of reflection […]. The authors emphasise the constant movement of texts between the legal discipline, which is rooted in reality, and the literary discipline, which appeals to the imaginary […]."[61] According to Jean-François Lyotard, literature takes on the role of a balancing 'guardian' where the law does not fulfil its function of enabling an appropriate decision. In this sense, Lyotard's literary 'guardian function' refers to the assumption that literary texts imagine solutions to conflicts that the law has not (or has not yet) found, as Lyotard puts it: "What is at stake in a literature, in a philosophy, in a politics perhaps, is to bear witness to différends by finding idioms for them."[62] Angela Condello and Tiziano Toracca take Lyotard's analysis further when they advocate the idea that literature, in its function of finding compromises, can overcome legal normativity by giving different, because unconscious, rules and regulatory strategies a right to exist. In this sense, literature can endure contradictions and allow them to exist, whereas the law must make a clear decision. For example, the refusal to repay a loan is not legally tenable, while the contradiction between the legal obligation to repay the loan and the desire to keep the money for living expenses is seen as compromising in literature: "Literature can claim that one thing is at the same time just and

55 Zeh (2014). Orig. *Corpus Delicti. Ein Prozess*, 2009.

56 Hitzig and Alexis (1842), pp. 1842–1890. Cf. Löhr (2022), pp. 249–256.

57 Müller-Dietz alludes here to Wittgenstein's 'language game'. See also: Schulte (2022), pp. 387–392 (cf. here especially section 78.3 on the diversity of language).

58 Müller-Dietz (1990), p. 49.

59 Cf. ibid., pp. 46–48.

60 Charbonnier and Petit (2023).

61 Agresti (2023).

62 Lyotard (1988), p. 13.

unjust: law, instead, must take responsibility and decide which reason should prevail."[63]

However, literature not only can resolve conflicts, but it can also address where the law is still lacking, and where there are gaps in the law. This realisation leads Hans Müller-Dietz to the observation that both literature and law reflect the 'Zeitgeist', although it is usually literature that grasps social development trends faster than the law, which often 'lags behind' literary allusions and insights.[64] Albert von Schirnding also shares this anticipatory relationship between literature and legal developments when he ascribes to literature the power of imagination to anticipate "developments that do not have to occur with compulsive necessity."[65] By reacting sensitively to social influences, literature influences, according to Klaus Kastner, "the whole of public life and consciousness."[66] The literary seismograph observes, anticipates, and points out, while the law follows and searches for answers to new social questions. The correlation between the two disciplines functions, according to the scheme of 'cause' and 'effect', through the temporal discrepancy between the discovery of the cause and the adequacy of the reaction or response. Stephan Kirste describes this correlation as a "circular structure" in which empiricism precedes the object of research: "Although in both the humanities and the natural sciences the discipline is identified by the method and the interest in knowledge, knowledge is not only the result of the scientific process, but also the beginning of the further development of the object of knowledge."[67] Cognition in legal research, as in literary research, is 'nourished', albeit in a temporally differentiated way, by practical experience, from which the object of investigation in turn emerges. As Erich Nossack indicates, this happens when literature anticipates the criminal law qualification for future circumstances:

> The legally ascertainable and standardisable crime is of little interest to the writer, but what goes on under the covers as a prerequisite for both the crime and the law has always been the field of literature. Literature observes and reflects with realistic vigilance on events that are only called crimes after the fact and when it is too late.[68]

As Müller-Dietz points out, the temporary relationship between law and literature is determined by the influence of the 'Zeitgeist', which is why the correlation between law and literature does not necessarily arise *a priori*, but only because of certain cultural-historical circumstances that have a 'legitimising' effect. In other words, this means that external societal, political, and social circumstances favour the interaction between law and literature, such as when Juli Zeh in her novel *The Method* incorporates the law of the medieval Inquisition with the specific intention of

[63] Condello and Toracca (2020), p. 7.
[64] Cf. Müller-Dietz (1990), p. 21.
[65] von Schirnding (1990), p. 27.
[66] Kastner (2004), here: p. 1.
[67] Kirste (2016b), p. 40.
[68] Nossack (1968), p. 26.

denouncing the feared loss of democracy and freedom against the backdrop of the Middle Ages as a thematic template.[69]

To summarise the topic of 'interdisciplinarity', it can be said that law and literature already come close to each other through at least three important points of connection: language and text as 'raw material', the wide-ranging material of variation possibilities, and the interaction with the social Zeitgeist'. Both disciplines are near social events, needs, and demands; they are inconceivable without reference to the real environment. While the law may initially appear to be closer to reality, a closer examination reveals that literature also cannot do without the template of reality, even when it moves in purely fictional spheres, insofar as people cannot think about non-existent or invented things without reference to their world.

As indicated, the search for unifying elements between law and literature will now turn to the area of discourse, and later, hermeneutics. While the examination of interdisciplinarity has led to the realisation of enumerative 'character commonalities', it is ideally assumed that methodological points of contact between law and literature could arise from a closer examination of discourse and, later, hermeneutics. In the following two sections, the specific treatment of law and literature is preceded by a general theoretical section.

3.2 Discourse

3.2.1 Theoretical Preliminary Remarks

The preoccupation with discourse as an object of knowledge can be traced back to Aristotle's *Peri Hermeneias* or Descartes' *Discours de la méthode* (1637) as 'speech', and as 'mental running back and forth'. If we skip back several centuries to the twentieth century, we cannot help but recognise Michel Foucault and Jürgen Habermas as the fundamental theorists of discourse,[70] whereby Foucault's approach to implicit discourse in texts is of particular interest in this context. If one tries to escape the incredible complexity and, admittedly, also the confusion of discourse studies, one could perhaps initially venture an extreme simplification of the concept of discourse as an "ensemble of meaning-creating practices"[71] and statements without a specific speaker. Foucault speaks of a "group of rules that are immanent in a practice and define it in its specificity."[72] Foucault is concerned here with an object- and knowledge-constitutive, authorless and diffuse 'speaking' in texts, books, and other written media, the rules and particularities of which need to be analysed:

[69] See Juster (2022), pp. 66–67.

[70] Cf. Angermüller (2014), here: p. 18.

[71] Van Dyk et al. (2014), here: p. 350.

[72] Foucault (1972), p. 46.

> These schemata make it possible to describe – not the laws of internal construction of concepts, not their progressive and individual genesis in the mind of man – but their anonymous dispersion through texts, books, and oeuvres. A dispersion that characterizes a type of discourse, and which defines, between concepts, forms of deduction, derivation, and coherence, but also of incompatibility, intersection, substitution, exclusion, mutual alteration, displacement, etc.[73]

Foucault explains the interest in investigating this diffuse, object-constitutive character of discourse with the challenge of finding the rules that underlie the emergence of these objects of discourse: "To define these objects without reference to the *ground*, the *foundation of things*, but by relating them to the body of rules that enable them to form as objects of a discourse and thus constitute the conditions of their historical appearance."[74] Rolf Parr summarises Foucault's concept as "a practice of thinking, writing, speaking and also acting, which at the same time systematically produces the objects it deals with."[75] To illustrate the elusive concept of discourse, Jürgen Fohrmann and Harro Müller use the comparison with the unknown game: "It looks as if the rules of an unknown game can be found by observing the course of the game."[76] While Johannes Angermüller suggests distinguishing between discourse theory as a triangle between "language, communication and meaning",[77] and discourse analysis as a methodological "interplay of 'language', 'practice' and 'context'",[78] Alexander Preisinger, Pascale Delormas, and Jan Standke understand literary discourse analysis less as a method and more as a specific "approach or research perspective"[79] with "different research styles."[80] This view probably arose from the fact that, due to the fluid boundaries between the social sciences and humanities, no standardised discourse method has yet been able to emerge for literary studies. It is precisely in this context that the achievements of intercultural literary studies for discourse analysis should not go unmentioned, as they have led to a "departure from the hermeneutic understanding of texts" on the one hand and to the transdisciplinary "connectivity of literary studies" on the other.[81] In other words, cultural studies offer literary studies an alternative to the complicated and often diffuse rules of hermeneutics—which will be discussed in more detail later—and a method of interdisciplinary connection through 'interdiscourse', which enables literature to think together different disciplines through the medium of the text. The figurative idea of a road junction where different types of vehicles (cars, motorbikes, lorries, buses, etc.) meet can perhaps better illustrate this idea.

---

[73] Ibid., p. 60.

[74] Ibid., pp. 47–48.

[75] Parr (2020a), here: pp. 274–275.

[76] Fohrmann and Müller (1988), here: p. 16.

[77] Angermüller (2014), p. 23.

[78] Ibid., p. 25.

[79] Preisinger et al. (2014), here: p. 139.

[80] Wedl et al. (2014), here: p. 540.

[81] Preisinger et al. (2014), p. 139.

As indicated, Michel Foucault's discourse theories are of particular importance for the development of discourse research in literary studies, which are presented above all in his essay *What is an author?* (1969), in *The Order of Discourse* (1972), and in *The Archeology of Knowledge* (1981). Foucault's discourse and interdiscourse theory can also be found scattered and varied in other writings, so that for Achim Geisenhanslüke no "concise theory of discourse analysis"[82] can be derived from Foucault's work. Moreover, Foucault can also not be clearly assigned to either post-structuralist or critical realist discourse theory, as his works deal with both the social function of language "for the production of order, reality and structure in social space" (post-structuralism) and with discourse as a power structure (critical realism).[83] Dietrich Busse dares to attempt to grasp Foucault's discourse theory in its diffuse plurality: "What we have become accustomed to calling 'discourse analysis' following Foucault [is] actually the analysis of the social in the borderline or overlapping area of thought, language and social knowledge. But if one analyses the social in terms of 'power' and 'critique of power', then it can initially only be an analysis of the power of the structures themselves."[84] Foucault's diffuse pluralism results from the numerous and highly diverse discourse topics in connection with the corresponding social dimensions (prohibitions, human madness, will to truth, sexuality),[85] which are determined and contoured by various institutions[86] (prisons, psychiatric institutions, scientific institutions, etc.). Alongside these externalised and institutionalised discourses of power circulates the subliminal 'inner' discourse that pervades society, which arises from a series of random events,[87] and is of relevance to the study of legal discourse in literature insofar as it describes how disciplines 'express themselves'. Rainer Diaz-Bone builds on this idea of the discursive constitution of knowledge and objects when he outlines his understanding of discourse analysis as the investigation of "statements in this world […] not as statements *about* the world, but as performative elements of the systematic *production of* this world." This breaks with referential thinking and the claim that statements have the capability to objectively depict this world. At the same time, this break enables a special discourse-analytical approach to interpretation that examines a system of statements concerning the rules of production that exist within them.[88] This gives the statement a constitutive character because it is only through the latter that reality is created.[89] It is, therefore, a question of how statements are created, under what

[82] Geisenhanslüke (2008), p. 7.

[83] Angermüller (2014), pp. 22–23.

[84] Busse (2013), here: p. 73.

[85] Foucault (1970), p. 18.

[86] Emil Durkheim defines the concept of institution from the perspective of sociology as collectives of individuals that persist beyond the individuality of the individual but have a retroactive effect on the "individual practice of action" (Diaz-Bone 2013, here: p. 88). Cf. Durkheim (1964), pp. 28 ff.

[87] Foucault (1970), pp. 9 ff.

[88] Diaz-Bone (2008), here: p. 31.

[89] Cf. Wedl et al. (2014), pp. 541–542.

conditions they are produced, and how they relate to each other.[90] Naturally, this is no longer about researching subjective meaning in the sense of Friedrich Schleiermacher's hermeneutics, because the subject is already "constituted in discursive practice."[91] For literary scholars, this means searching for rules or, as Jonas Wieschollek pointedly puts it, searching for recurring language patterns.[92] It is interesting, in this context, that the discipline of literary studies is increasingly turning away from textual hermeneutics and towards discourse analysis in order, as Jürgen Link comments, to no longer focus on the interpretation of texts but to describe the external processes of cultural production.[93] The aim is to capture the subliminal discourse in social structures, from which diffuse writing and speaking about certain statements emerge. When these new statements follow common conventions, formats, and rules, a novel 'discipline' emerges. For example, a legal statement can only constitute jurisprudence if it corresponds to certain disciplinary conventions, such as specialised vocabulary, normative references, certain symbols (e.g. §), etc.[94] Foucault's subjective level of institutionalised speech acts and rituals must be distinguished from this 'implicit' subject driven, subliminal discourse, which requires a detective-like approach, and corresponds to the dogmatics of certain groups that seek to consolidate their position of power in society through doctrinal authority (discourses):[95]

> Doctrine binds individuals to certain types of enunciation and consequently forbids them all others; but it uses, in return, certain types of enunciation to bind individuals among themselves, and to differentiate them by that fact from all others. Doctrine brings about a double subjection: of the speaking subjects to discourses, and of discourses to (at least virtual) group of speaking individuals.[96]

From a legal perspective, one example of the idea of the institutionalised and ritualised speech act of certain groups of people is the Inquisition, whose members defended and fertilised a doctrine and simultaneously submitted to it. Similarly, one could speak of today's judicial apparatus, whose representatives follow certain rituals, make specific statements in a certain way, and adhere to the 'code' of the institution of 'justice'.

However, in the context of the counterfactual investigation of legal discourses in literature, which is the focus of this work, Foucault's discourse as a theory of power plays only a subordinate role and will thus not be examined in further detail herein. Instead, the focus lies on the fruitfulness of Foucault's authorless text and discourse theory for the linguistic-textual-discursive regularities and particularities of legal discourses in literature. Ralf Konersmann's attempt to grasp Foucault's diffuse

---

[90] See Wrana (2014), here: pp. 521–522.

[91] Ibid., p. 522.

[92] Wieschollek (2024), here: pp. 170–171. Cf. Foucault (1972), pp. 13; 27.

[93] Link (1983), p. 10.

[94] Cf. ibid., pp. 18–25.

[95] Cf. Foucault (1970), p. 12.

[96] Ibid.

concept of discourse as a form of knowledge production aptly ties in with this priority:

> The concept of discourse asks about the very 'zone du non-pensé' that defines the conditions and contours of thought. What, the question is, are the conditions that finally decide what [...] is actually said at a certain time and in a certain place? The concept of discourse gains its indeterminacy, which is both a weakness and a strength, from the fact that it describes not only the organisation of knowledge, i.e. a form, but also its production, i.e. a practice [...].[97]

Konersmann's remarks not only highlight Foucault's interest in the 'visible' discourse of linguistic regularities and practices,[98] but also his search for the relevant but 'invisible' discourse of the 'unsaid', both of which are constitutive for the emergence of knowledge systems, as Foucault keeps emphasising by indicating that discourse "is as much about what we don't say as it is about what is marked by gestures, attitudes, ways of being, patterns of behaviour and spatial arrangements."[99] These diverse dimensions of discourse, speech, practice and invisible gestures, behaviours, and 'forms of being' form epistemes, i.e. knowledge systems that confront each other in the struggle for social power, dominance, and supremacy: "*Discours bataille et non discours reflet*."[100] Dietrich Busse understands Foucault's concept of episteme in this sense as going beyond scientific knowledge,[101] as the "regularities in the occurrence of discourse elements"[102] or the "set of statements that belong to the same formation system"[103] are linked to knowledge elements via general language and not just via scientific jargon. Language, knowledge, and discourse strategies thus form an interdependent triangle.[104] Rainer Diaz-Bone understands episteme as "a socially shared structure of perception that has a socialising effect: as a socio-episteme, it organises the individual experiences and perceptions of the individual members of the collective."[105] In this sense, for Foucault discourse analysis means to search

> the unity of discourse in the objects themselves, in their distribution, in the interplay of their differences in their proximity or distance – in short, in what it is given to the speaking subject; and, in the end, we are sent back to a setting-up of relations that characterizes discursive practice itself; what we discover is [...] a group of *rules* that are immanent in a practice, and define it in its specificity.[106]

---

[97] Konersmann (1991), here: p. 77.

[98] From a linguistic perspective, 'discourse' represents the level that goes beyond the sentence and, as Roland Barthes puts it, becomes discourse linguistics: "As we know, linguistics stops at the sentence: this is the last unit it thinks it has the right to deal with; [...] And yet it is obvious that the discourse itself (like the set of sentences) is organised, and that through this organisation it appears as the message of another language, superior to the language of linguists [...]: the discourse would be a great 'phrase' [...]." (Barthes 1966, here: p. 3).

[99] Foucault (2017), pp. 123–124.

[100] Ibid., p. 124. See also: Foucault (2002), pp. 669–792.

[101] Cf. on this Busse (2013), p. 65.

[102] Busse (2018), here: p. 3.

[103] Ibid., p. 4.

[104] Ibid., p. 5.

[105] Diaz-Bone (2013), p. 83.

[106] Foucault (1972), p. 46.

According to Busse, discursivity presupposes four essential core elements, namely the "*event*", the "*series*", the "*regularity*", and the "*condition of possibility.*"[107] Discourse research therefore opens up interesting opportunities to track down knowledge-relevant events in their supra-individual, social context and to analyse their processes and interactions with other disciplines, manifestations, and epistemic effects.[108] As an example of a suitable object of investigation, Busse cites the specialisation tendency of knowledge in our society, whose individual areas can be examined for their triggering event, for epistemic and cognitive schemata and frames, for epistemic interactions and the regularity of recurring epistemic and linguistic phenomena. In addition to the linguistic approach, Busse represents the strongly social approach of Foucault's discourse theory, which is taken up and deepened by Reiner Keller when he interprets Foucault's concept of discourse as socio-historical attempts to "institutionalise binding orders of knowledge and practice in social collectives",[109] whereby "the 'objective reality' is socially constructed via institutionalisation processes and appropriated as 'subjective reality' via socialisation processes."[110] In the social sense, discourses are therefore the result of a multitude of individual actions that are neither individually 'willed' nor artificially created by people but rather lead in their entirety to social and epistemic processes.[111] According to Thomas Luckmann, language, which is to be understood as a store of knowledge, constructs and mediates social reality.[112] In this sense, the sociological analysis of discourse "treats discourses as practices which form the objects they deal with: Discourses are something that is actually carried out in statements by speakers, and the knowledge constituted therein in linguistic or sign form is the way in which (a specific) reality of world relations is given to us."[113] From this linguistic store of knowledge, Charles Morris also develops the idea of a discourse, which he explains by way of example and which differs from other types of discourse depending on the field of knowledge:

> In the course of time various specializations of this common language have appeared in order that certain purposes may be more adequately met. Such specializations of language will be called *types of discourse*. Books, for example, are classified as scientific, mathematical, poetic, religious, and the like; and within these larger classifications subdivisions and overlappings occur almost without limit.[114]

George Mead supplements the linguistic dimension with the social dimension insofar as he understands 'discourse' not only as a linguistically but also as a socially

---

[107] Busse (2013), p. 65.

[108] Cf. Ibid., pp. 68–70.

[109] Keller (2018), here: p. 199.

[110] Keller (2013), here: p. 23.

[111] Cf. Busse (2013), p. 73.

[112] Luckmann (1980), p. 117.

[113] Ibid., p. 44.

[114] Morris (1995), p. 123.

systemically bound "system of meaning that is produced by a group of individuals participating in a social process of experience and behaviour."[115]

Willy Viehöver explains the sociolinguistic understanding of discourse research by stating that certain *formation rules* delimit the various fields of discourse from one another and that this is precisely where the work of the discourse researcher lies: "The discourse researcher should, however, start from the empirical data, from what is recorded in written form, or from what is spoken and documented using appropriate techniques."[116] The essential working basis is the written text, which must be interpreted where "discourse-generating formations of objects, concepts, strategies and modes of expression" already exist, or where new "discourse objects and concepts" need to be uncovered. If one is guided by the distinction between 'internal', subliminally (in)visible and external discourses, one could recognise Foucault's statement that discourses are "practices that systematically form the objects of which they speak"[117] as an indication that discourse research not only implies an interpretative work of what has already been 'said', but also performs a creative-positivist work of 'finding' new discourse objects.[118] In this sense, Viehöver aptly summarises the challenge for textual discourse research: "He himself [the discourse researcher, author's note], must interpretively identify the 'traces' of the formation rules in 'texts' or 'actions' and formulate their existence and mode of action as a hypothesis."[119]

To summarise the discourse investigation of law in literature, it should be noted that Foucault's text- and proposition-oriented discourse theory offers a particularly interesting methodological approach in contrast to discourse as an instrument of power, which has especially been further developed in sociolinguistic research. It explains the special research approach to literary texts, which can be analysed in terms of explicit and implicit legal discourses. The disclosure of implicit legal phenomena can constitute new knowledge in the sense of Foucault's episteme approach and thus simultaneously delimit or connect literature and law. This is not an aporia, but the thesis that the disciplinary boundaries between 'what is law' and 'what is literature' must first be drawn to then search for those points of contact that best bring the two fields of knowledge together. Such an exploration of interdisciplinary docking possibilities can be achieved by linking different epistemic discourses in the interdiscourse. Interdiscourse as a method of linking disciplines will therefore be examined in more detail in the following section, whereby the focus remains on legal and literary studies in this context.

[115] Keller (2013), p. 40. See also Mead (2015).

[116] Viehöver (2012), here: p. 83.

[117] Foucault (1972), pp. 48–49.

[118] Cf. Viehöver (2012), pp. 83–84.

[119] Ibid., p. 84.

3.2.2 Discourse as a Link Between Law and Literature: Interdiscourse

Rolf Parr assumes that interdiscursive work presupposes differentiation, i.e. the delimitation of the various fields of knowledge from one another. For this reason, Foucault's concept of discourse as a theory of the development of different epistemes in society appears to be a suitable starting point for the development of interdiscursive working methods for interdisciplinary links. In this context, Parr also points to interesting affinities between Foucault's discourse theory and Niklas Luhmann's systems theory,[120] insofar as both aim to understand society as a complex structure of differentiated systems that are characterised by their respective special discourses.[121] Following Luhmann, it could be argued that although the literary system and the legal system differ from one another, i.e. that each of the two systems is operationally self-contained and sees itself as an environment that is distinct from the other system, they are nevertheless able to communicate with each other due to their mutual openness to shifting external contexts. Based on Luhmann's example of the relationship between social and psychological systems, which operate separately but are dependent on each other, it can be assumed that even if two systems 'operate' in varied ways, i.e. function differently, they can still be in an interdisciplinary relationship with each other.[122] Luhmann illustrates this with the concept of the 'nesting of systems': Actions, as selective processes, can belong simultaneously to a plurality of systems. They can take their orientation from a number of distinct system/environment references. Social systems, in other words, are not necessarily mutually exclusive […]".[123] In order to enable this nesting process, the difference between the 'system' and its 'environment' must be clearly established. In other words, for each individual system, it must be clear which

---

[120] Luhmann's systems theory understands society as a composite of operating systems. A system is created through external and self-observation, which only constitutes the system through its differentiation from its environment. Systems always produce themselves through autopoiesis, i.e. they are operationally closed but open to the environment in that they react to external irritations (cf. Berghaus 2022, pp. 11–60). Following this brief explanation, Tobias Peter's reference to the semantic constitutiveness of social systems in Luhmann should be reproduced here, whereby the close relationship that Parr establishes between Luhmann and Foucault's discourse theory is made plausible: "Nevertheless, the function and the order of the functional systems among themselves is not predetermined by the social system, but is formed communicatively in the course of mutual observation along reference problems" (Peter 2014, here: p. 48). Within these fluctuating systems, Foucault sees the formation of meaning through discourse and Luhmann sees systemic communication, whereby both are mutually dependent (ibid., pp. 52–54). Matthias Leanza further elaborates the essential discursive similarities between Foucault and Luhmann, which can be located, above all, in the semantics constituting knowledge and subject (Foucault) and system (Luhmann) (Leanza 2010, pp. 119–146).

[121] Cf. Parr (2015), here: p. 289. Cf. also Reinhardt-Becker (2020), pp. 246–250.

[122] Cf. Luhmann (2013), pp. 105–106. For deepening Luhmann's theory about the functioning of social systems cf. Luhmann (1982).

[123] Luhmann (1982), p. 86.

elements belong to the system, and which belong to the environment. With these system-specific boundary and environment definitions in place, the boundaries of different systems can overlap, opening the way to interdisciplinary connections.

If one attempts to transfer Luhmann's concept of 'internal system closure/external system openness' to law and literary studies, it is evident that both law and literary studies are guided internally by autonomous, discipline-specific rules and functional mechanisms, i.e. they differ significantly from each other in their mode of operation, without such a differentiation excluding the possibility of common points of intersection and methods. In other words, different methods and terminologies do not prevent the development of methodological and conceptual commonalities.

A similar, but primarily literary approach to interdiscourse analysis, and therefore particularly interesting for our purposes, is Jürgen Link's proposal to understand literature as a connecting mediator between specialised discourses via shared linguistic symbols. In this sense, Link understands literary discourse as interdiscursively interspersed with other sub-areas, such as medicine, law, economics, etc.:[124]

> Modern societies based on the division of labour tend to form specialised discourses (e.g. medical, legal and economic), which […] are integrated in literature through elementary literary elements. These include, for example, 'figures, clichés, stereotypes' (Link 1988, p. 289) and, above all, collective symbols […]. In the sense of Foucault's archaeological approach, interdiscourse analysis understands literary texts as the intersection of different discourses, as so-called interdiscourses […].[125]

Link attempts here to compensate for the lack of an explicitly formulated theory of literary discourse, which Foucault could not bring himself to formulate,[126] with the help of semantic symbolism and to show how literature can facilitate communication between different fields of knowledge (epistemes) through interdiscourse so that it can be understood "*as a socially institutionalised processing of interdiscourse.*"[127] Link therefore proposes making Foucault's discourse theory fruitful for the interdiscursive function: "We propose labelling every historically specific 'discursive formation' as a 'special discourse' in Foucault's sense and then call all interfering, coupling, integrating, etc. cross-relationships between several special discourses 'interdiscursive'."[128] The interdiscourse theorised in this way functions—via collective symbolism, the knowledge of which can be attributed to general knowledge as the matrix of all people in a particular cultural group—as a kind of 'translator' between the representatives of different fields of knowledge. In

---

[124] Link (1988), pp. 284–307.

[125] Preisinger et al. (2014), pp. 133–134. See also: Link (1988), p. 289.

[126] Link and Link-Heer (1990), here: p. 91. Cf. Geisenhanslüke (2020), here: p. 377.

[127] Link (1988), p. 300.

[128] Link and Link-Heer (1990), p. 92. See Oliver Sill's comment: "By insisting on the necessity of a discourse analysis that relates different discourses to each other in a synchronic and diachronic perspective, or more precisely: reconstructs their interrelationships with each other and analyses them as meaning-forming patterns, this approach enriches the spectrum of existing concepts of literary sociology" (Sill 2001, here: p. 35).

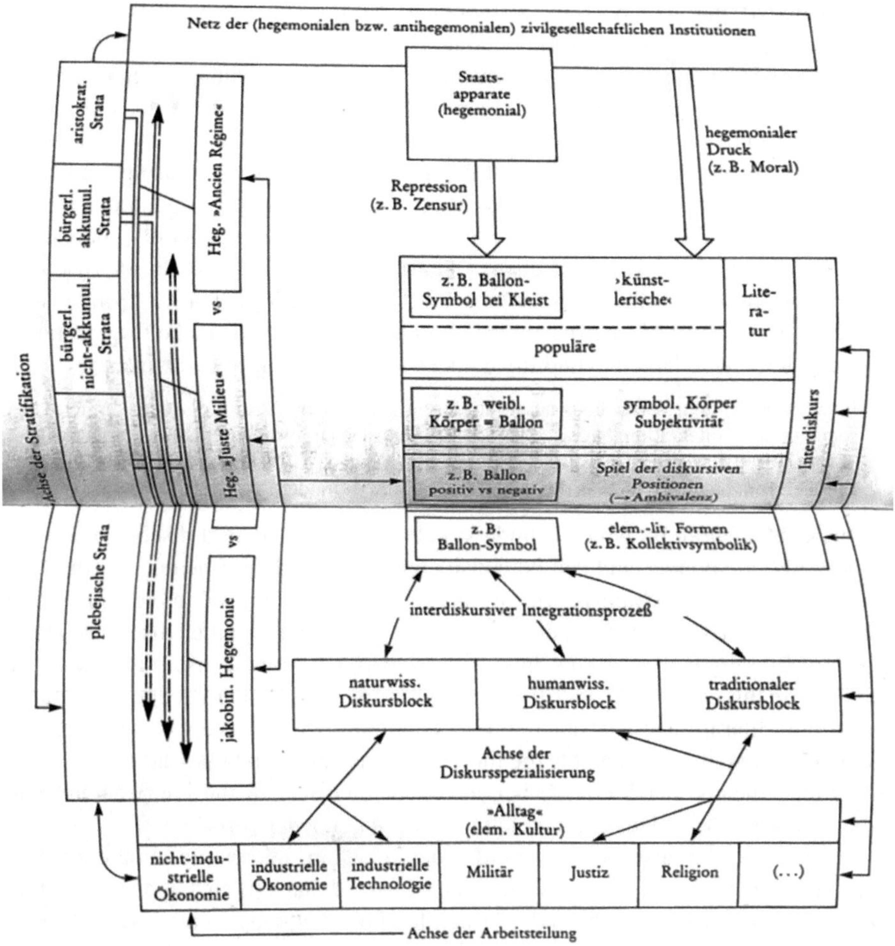

Fig. 3.1 Scheme 'Interdiscourse' from: Link, *Literaturanalyse als Diskursanalyse*, pp. 298–299

Fig. 3.1, Link illustrates how the representatives of different specialised fields, who are each familiar with specific specialist discourses such as economics, technology, the military, justice, religion, etc., can assign the same semantic meaning to the term 'balloon' based on their general knowledge.

Link's symbolism as an example of a unifying communication signifier aims to illustrate the potentially interdisciplinary function of literature: "Literature is a particular form of linking knowledge from other discourses; its special function, which at the same time distinguishes it significantly from other specialised discourses, consists in the transformation of knowledge into subjectively applicable specifications."[129] In this understanding, literature becomes the carrier and mediator

[129] Link and Link-Heer (1990), p. 133.

of knowledge that goes beyond its (innocent) ontology as fiction. It is precisely to bring such different fields of knowledge as the natural sciences, humanities and social sciences to a common communication denominator that such interdiscursive language elements are required, which are generally understandable and have a connecting effect between the disciplines. As Rolf Parr also emphasises, this is achieved "most simply by making one specialised area of society the structuring medium of another in the form of analogy relations."[130] Put more simply, it is about making highly specialised discourses comprehensible by resorting to generally understandable metaphors, symbols, or narratives.[131] Parr thus ties in with Link's interdiscourse theory and shows how the "popular presentation of complex scientific problems and contexts in the form of interdiscursive speech" is designed to make them connectable and understandable beyond the boundaries of specialised discourses:

> Interdiscourses thus form the general interdiscursive framework of a discourse system, a social bond of integration that provides a reservoir of visual forms for the necessary coding of specialised discursive facts, especially for current events. The totality of these procedures can therefore be understood as the integrating culture of modern societies.[132]

In this sense, literature, which is understood as a distinct field of discourse, absorbs society like a 'sponge' and can be considered particularly permeable to other specialised discourses, which is why it "assumes the function of interdiscursive re-integration to a very special degree."[133] If the reception of other discourses takes place in literature, it fulfils its interdiscursive function as a discipline-mediating medium. In this context, Anabel Ternès aptly summarises the knowledge-constituting function of literature as a bridge to other disciplines: "The concept of intertextuality as interdiscursivity understands the literary text as one social discourse among others, which means that literature is constituted precisely in the interweaving with other discursive practices from which it draws its knowledge."[134]

Dietrich Busse also views interdiscourse as an interesting methodological approach for interdisciplinary work: "As a form of analysis that spans disciplines and methods, discourse analysis in principle applies equally to all potential object levels (events, elements, structures/relations, constraints, processes/procedures) and should do so with the same intensity. The sociality of knowledge is reflected at all levels and shapes the episteme."[135]

While there is a certain consensus on the applicability of Foucault's discourse theory to literature, its suitability for literary analysis cannot be asserted with absolute certainty—despite Link's attempts to develop a plausible interdiscourse theory for literature—as it has not yet been clarified, according to Achim Geisenhanslücke, "what exactly the mediation of literary interpretation and discourse analysis should

[130] Parr (2015), p. 290.

[131] Cf. Jürgen Link's comments on symbolism in: Link (1988), pp. 284–307.

[132] Parr (2020b), here: pp. 234–235.

[133] Ibid., p. 236.

[134] Ternès (2016), p. 41.

[135] Busse (2013), p. 69.

look like."[136] Clemens Kammler is similarly sceptical since Foucault's suppression of signifiers "blunts the tools of discourse analysis in relation to the wealth of meaning that characterises literary texts."[137]

From the perspective of making law understandable in literature and thus paving the way for an interdisciplinary understanding between law and literary studies, however, it seems worthwhile to utilise the potential of the interdiscursive idea, despite all its vagueness and partial contradictions. Perhaps it is precisely in the grey areas of Foucault's discourse theory that the opportunity lies to develop new perspectives and approaches and to reflect on the approaches of Luhmann and Link. In this sense, Bernhard Greiner also refers to Foucault's discourse theory as an interesting interdisciplinary 'binding agent' between law and literature, because "law and literature can be related to each other in the horizon of Foucault's discourse theory in the light of a common third party [...]. At the same time, discourse analysis provides a methodological approach that encompasses both fields of research [...],"[138] which is intended to bring about "the *changing influence of* one discourse on the other."[139] The common 'third' can refer to a so-called interfering 'third discourse'[140] that arises from other subject areas, such as religion, medicine, psychiatry, aesthetics, justice, etc. On the one hand, legal contexts, problems, questions, issues, grievances and oral or codified legal sources can be illuminated, illustrated, explained or criticised through literature. On the other hand, the analysis of legal texts, if it follows the criteria of literary hermeneutics, aesthetics and linguistics, opens new perspectives for understanding texts and leads to "asking about the effectiveness of literary rules in the creation, codification and interpretation of law."[141]

Regardless of the perspective taken, Rolf Parr sees the technique of interdiscursive text integration as an interesting method of linking disciplines:

> The first step in interdiscourse theory is always a reconstruction of the discourse system or discursive formation within which a text to be analysed (or another media or cultural object in the broadest sense) is to be situated in its specificity. [...] The second step is to analyse which areas of practice are integrated in each case and how this integration project relates to the discourse subject of the time.[142]

According to Parr, the function of interdiscourse as an interdisciplinary integrator in a complexly organised society fundamentally fulfils the same integrative function as intertextuality in literary studies: "Beyond the narrower subject area of literature, interdiscourse theory thus not only provides a model for the complex functional

[136] Geisenhanslüke (2020), p. 381.

[137] Kammler (2006), here: p. 238.

[138] Greiner (2010), p. 10.

[139] Ibid., p. 22.

[140] Ibid.

[141] Ibid., p. 20. Klaus Lüderssen counters this mutual entanglement by arguing that the interpreters of legal texts must subordinate themselves to the intention of the legislator, which is why literary openness is inadmissible for them.

[142] Parr (2020b), p. 236.

context of literature, special discourses and overall culture but also makes a contribution to the debate on intertextuality, which would then merely be understood as a special case of interdiscursivity."[143]

Ternès agrees with the 'near-equation' of interdiscursivity and intertextuality insofar as the only essential difference between interdiscourse and intertextuality lies in the lack of authorial reference in interdiscourse.[144] In contrast to Parr's and Ternès' equivalent view, Jürgen Link understands interdiscourse as a necessary precursor of intertextuality: "Before intertextuality can emerge, interdiscursivity must always have already existed."[145] Ternès counters this contingency condition by arguing that nothing speaks against the equation of interdiscourse and intertextuality if Link's view is seen as an "interference game between the individual social texts or discourses."[146] In this sense, intertextuality as interdiscursivity can be explained by Julia Kristeva's postulate that "the literary structure is not, but is only created from the relationship to another structure", without the criterion of authorship.[147] If one follows this approach, the necessary referentiality to the author is dispensed with and attention can solely be focused on the texts, which influence, penetrate, and condition each other, as Ternès goes on to explain: "Every text builds itself up as a mosaic of quotations, every text is an absorption and transformation of another text. The concept of intersubjectivity is replaced by the concept of intertextuality."[148] It follows that every text is created in the totality of the texts produced, which Jan Assmann refers to as cultural memory,[149] whereby according to Ternès, this has two consequences: "Firstly, every text is only a fragment of the *texte général* [spelling based on Roland Barthes,[150] emphasis added by the author], as it contains the traces of the textual past and present. Every text is therefore an intertext, i.e. an 'intertextually organised text'."[151]

From the perspective of the interdiscourse between the disciplines, it is now obvious to ask not only about the *literary* discourse function but also about the discourse in law. In this context, Jürgen Habermas raises the question of the 'correct' decision-making by the judicial authority, and this requires discourse:

> Hence interpretations of the individual case, which are formed in the light of a coherent system of norms, depend on the communicative form of a discourse whose socio-ontological constitution allows the perspectives of the participants and the perspectives of uninvolved members of the community (represented by an impartial judge) to be transformed into one another.[152]

[143] Ibid., pp. 234–237.

[144] Ternès (2016), pp. 35–37.

[145] Link (1988), p. 301.

[146] Ternès (2016), p. 36.

[147] Kristeva (1972), here: p. 346.

[148] Ternès (2016), p. 14.

[149] Assmann (1988), here: p. 15.

[150] Cf. Barthes (1974), p. 5.

[151] Ibid., pp. 5–20.

[152] Habermas (1996), p. 229.

Habermas understands this to mean procedural norms that derive their legitimisation from the "democratic procedure intended to guarantee a rational treatment of political questions"[153] and regulate both the procedural process up to the judicial decision and the finding of evidence. In this way, a consensual 'legal discourse' develops between society, the litigants, and the court, which makes the 'correctness' of judicial decisions plausible.[154] The 'legal discourse', Habermas continues, arises precisely from this standardised procedural logic, which determines the relationship between the accuser and the accused, regulates the right to defence and the gathering of evidence, and subjects the court decisions of the first instance to review by higher instances. In addition to the procedural legal and discourse order, which are to be understood as a sequence *of discussions*, the Supreme Court case law enriches the discourse as a whole. As Habermas explains, the resulting *legal discourse* programmes a logical and generally accepted course of proceedings up to the judicial decision: "Rules of court procedure institutionalize judicial decision-making in such a way that the judgement and its justification can be considered the outcome of an argumentation game governed by a special program."[155] Only the judicial discourse at the end of the trial, insofar as it is based on the standardised logic of the chain of reasoning and the presentation of evidence, is located in "a procedural-legal vacuum, so that reaching a judgement is left up to the judge's professional ability."[156] One could argue here that even the judge's freedom of decision, as found by Gadamer, is perhaps not completely conditioned by the discursive laws of judicial training, but at least guided by them. Habermas' legal discourse can then be understood as an 'outflow' of positivist legal norms (in continental law) or judicial practice (in common law), which determines decision-making in accordance with a democratic society.

To summarise, it should be noted that discourses are specific to knowledge and disciplines and therefore have a demarcating effect. At the same time, determining the contours of an epistemological field (Foucault) or of a system (Luhmann) is a prerequisite for interdiscursive work. Even if Foucault did not develop a specific discourse theory for literature, it can be assumed, despite some divergent positions, that literature offers a suitable medium for interdiscursive links between disciplines. Julia Kristeva's theorisation of intertextuality, reinforced by Roland Barthes, already suggests literary connectivity. An analogously extended reference to interdiscourse, as a disciplinary open linking method between literature and other disciplines, seems quite plausible and is therefore increasingly being advocated (Link, Parr, Ternès). In particular, Jürgen Link's suggestion that literature should be recognised

[153] Ibid., p. 170.

[154] "The legitimacy of legal statutes is determined not only by the rightness of moral judgements but, among other things, by the availability, cogency, relevance, and selection of information; by how fruitful such information proves to be; by how appropriately the situation is interpreted and the issue framed; by the rationality of voting decisions; by the authenticity of strong evaluations; and above all by the fairness of compromises involved" (ibid., pp. 232–233).

[155] Ibid., p. 234.

[156] Ibid., p. 237.

as a unifying medium of communication between different disciplines thanks to symbolic semantics is an interesting methodological approach that is also taken up by Rolf Parr. If literature can function as an interdiscursive catalyser, then this possibility must apply equally to the inclusion of legal discourse in literature. While Foucault stylises the concept of discourse in general, and ostensibly in the context of historical research, Jürgen Habermas attempts to develop a theory of discourse that is specifically suitable for law as a product of the process that culminates in the judicial decision. According to this state of research, the recourse to interdiscourse as an interdisciplinary method of investigation forces itself upon us for the purposes of the counterfactual investigation between law and literature and, as will be shown later, will find its way into the method of legal counterfactuals.

In this section, discourse and interdiscourse were discussed concerning a potential (and certainly interesting) method for analysing legal discourse in literature. The transition to hermeneutics seems justified insofar as hermeneutics appears suitable for identifying common conceptual points of intersection between law and literature. Even if hermeneutics has lost its position of primacy as a scientific approach in today's literary studies in favour of discourse studies, it continues to play an important role in the interpretation and application of legal texts in jurisprudence. These considerations lead to the question of the extent to which hermeneutics can be used, if not necessarily as a technique for accessing texts, then at least as an interdisciplinary connecting criterion between law and literature.

3.3 Hermeneutics

Even if, as previously indicated, research in literary theory—in contrast to legal studies—seems to be turning away from hermeneutics in favour of discourse theory,[157] an in-depth comparative study of literary and legal hermeneutics still seems sensible, if not necessary, for interdisciplinary-methodological reasons. For the development of a legal counterfactual as a *method*, the greatest possible denominator of methodological points of contact between literature and law must be sought as a priority, and this denominator includes not only discourse theory but also hermeneutics, which, as will be shown below, provides several common interfaces between the disciplines.

As Winfried Hassemer explains in his introduction to legal hermeneutics, the term 'hermeneutics' refers generally and across disciplines to

> a method of scientific approach to objects […]; it is a […] phenomenon that demands attention for every kind of scientific activity, it precedes and underlies the individual sciences. **This easily explains that the dimensions of hermeneutics have nothing to do with the boundaries of science** [my emphasis], that hermeneutics […] influences and epistemologically co-founds the individual sciences: from history to theology and literary studies […].[158]

[157] Preisinger et al. (2014), p. 139.

[158] Hassemer (1986), here: pp. 195–196.

Hassemer's disciplinary de-limitation of hermeneutic processes seems to offer a good starting point for the search for common methodological and structural points of contact between law and literature. In the following, the discipline-specific hermeneutics of law and literature are first discussed to then bring together the insights gained in Sect. 3.3.3 and make them fruitful for interdisciplinary links.

3.3.1 Literary Hermeneutics

While the concept of discourse refers to the meaningful forms of expression of signs, speeches, and practices, literary hermeneutics seeks to fully understand the meaning behind such forms of expression. Its guiding concepts are, to paraphrase Oliver Scholz, 'understanding' and 'interpretation',[159] based on the reading of a text.[160] It thus turns to the triad of understanding - interpreting - applying a text,[161] whereby, according to Axel Bühler, the interpreting activity becomes necessary "when it is not possible to understand linguistic utterances (or other signs [...] more or less clearly at first go)."[162] While, as Ingolf Dalferth explains, 'understanding' is to be considered as a stand-in for immediate successful comprehension, the term 'interpreting' stands for the process of realisation, as it requires intellectual effort.[163] Hermeneutics as a practical process and as a methodology of understanding and interpreting[164] 'pushes' itself between the author and the text, so to speak, and deals with the understanding of the latter and/or the intention of the former. As Andreas Mauz emphasises, its reference instances are "generally and with varying degrees of emphasis 'the author', the 'text', 'the reader' and the 'context', and it revolves around the ideal of better understanding."[165] In this context, Manfred Frank recalls Hamlet's ironic answer to Polonius' question "What do you read my lord?"[166] with "Words, words, words":[167] Hamlet only reads words, not a text, while Friedrich Schleiermacher ascribes the endeavour to hermeneutics to "understand the speech of the other, because "speaking is the medium of communality of thought, and for this reason rhetoric and hermeneutics belong together and both are related to dialectics".[168] Schleiermacher's basic attitude concerning the necessity of methodi-

[159] Scholz (2015), pp. 778–784.

[160] Weimar (2020), pp. 79–85.

[161] Jauß (1981), here: p. 461.

[162] Bühler (2003), here. p. 4.

[163] Dalferth (2000), here: p. 57.

[164] In the praxeological view of hermeneutics, theory and practice should complement each other by testing the theory for its practical suitability in the reality of life. Cf. Mauz (2021), here: pp. 5–21.

[165] Ibid., p. 1.

[166] Shakespeare (2004), here p. 1092 (2.2.).

[167] Ibid., p. 1093 (2.2.).

[168] Schleiermacher (1977), p. 97.

cally analysing texts is later taken up by Paul Ricœur when, as Manfred Frank explains, he assumes that no text understands itself but always requires interpretative work.[169]

The hermeneutic development in literary studies has progressed from a strongly subjective hermeneutics based on the author, which was initiated by Friedrich Schleiermacher, to a combination of author-related subjectivity and textual objectivity, to objectivist authorless text interpretation, as postulated by Michel Foucault, Roland Barthes, Paul Ricœur, and Roman Ingarden.

The beginning of the historical development of literary hermeneutics can be traced back to Friedrich Schleiermacher's unification of the originally separate categories of theological and secular hermeneutics into a unified specialised hermeneutics for texts:[170] "At present there is no general hermeneutics as the art of understanding but only a variety of specialized hermeneutics."[171] Thus, as Schleiermacher himself emphasises, "the task of hermeneutics is to reproduce the whole internal process of an author's way of combining thoughts […]."[172] To perfect the interpretative approach, however, it is not enough to concentrate on the text itself, its genesis and the author's environment, if Schleiermacher is to be followed, but it is also necessary to empathise with the reader's canon of understanding at the time of the historical reception of the text, i.e. "to establish the same relationship between oneself and the author as between him and his original address."[173] According to this view, the triangle of author - text - reader is closed by perfecting the process of empathy, in that the interpreter, as Karl Lachmann concludes, empathises with "obedient devotion the thoughts, intentions and feelings of the poet as they were in him and as they must have appeared to his contemporaries",[174] as faithfully as possible. Wilhelm Dilthey, Fritz Hermanns, and Siegfried Jäger all agreed with Friedrich Schleiermacher's strongly subjective hermeneutics. Even more than Schleiermacher, Dilthey emphasises the inner life of the author as a hermeneutical criterion, because, according to Dilthey, every utterance must be examined for its 'inner life', insofar as every work is to be understood as a "true expression" of the author's soul life.[175] Similarly, Fritz Hermanns examines how a text conveys speaking intentions and points of view, and what intentions, emotions,

[169] Frank (1982), here: p. 123.

[170] For a synthesis of the historical genesis of the concept of hermeneutics, see: Albrecht and Danneberg (2021), here: pp. 23–39.

[171] Schleiermacher (1977), p. 95. Oliver R. Scholz accuses Schleiermacher of having—by establishing a specialised literary hermeneutics—destroyed the originally promising attempts to develop a general philosophically-based hermeneutics, a *hermeneutica generalis*, which was founded on Aristotle'*s Peri hermeneias*. According to Scholz, a general hermeneutics based on the logical reconstitution of thought in word and writing could have functioned as a trans- and interdisciplinary foundation. Cf. Scholz (2024), pp. 18–25.

[172] Schleiermacher (1977), p. 188.

[173] Ibid., p. 104. Cf. also: Dalferth (2018), pp. 293–294.

[174] Lachmann (1843), here: p. III. Cf. also: Gärtner (2023), pp. 37–52.

[175] Dilthey (1990), here: p. 318.

and cognitions are expressed,[176] while Siegfried Jäger looks for the linguistic means and the message of the text as well as the basic attitude of the author.[177]

August Boeckh criticises Schleiermacher's strongly subjectively oriented textual hermeneutics through deep psychological empathy with the inner life of the author as a difficult undertaking:

> If the task [...] were completely solvable, one would have to be able to reproduce the entire work, with consciousness and reflection; this would be the final test of individual understanding. For this, however, it would be necessary to enter completely into a foreign individuality, which can only be achieved by approximation.[178]

The vagueness of hermeneutics, Boeckh continues, solely arises in this case from the fact that "the foreign individuality can never be fully understood", which is why "hermeneutics can only be solved through infinite approximation, i.e. through gradual, point-by-point, but never complete approximation."[179] Boeckh therefore proposes supplementing Schleiermacher's complex author-related subjectivity with objective conditions of knowledge of scripture and language as well as the historical embedding of the text. However, this supplemented view of hermeneutics differs only slightly from Schleiermacher's in essence, if one considers that text and author remain closely linked to the extent that a thorough understanding of a text in the sense of Boeckh's concept of the interpreter requires the ability to empathise with the authors and to understand the genesis of their work beyond the linguistic and grammatical aspects.[180] In this understanding, the proof of the complete decoding of a text would be the ability to reconstruct the work by 'dismembering' and 'reassembling' it, and not only that because, as Goethe insists, one must also understand the life of the author himself and go to the place where he lived: "Whoever wants to understand the poet / Must go to the poet's country."[181] A more balanced position between the subjectivity of the author and the objectivity of the text is taken by Friedrich Ast, a contemporary of Schleiermacher, who favours a three-stage interpretation that takes into account "the historical understanding, which relates to the content, the grammatical understanding, which relates to form, language and delivery, and the spiritual understanding, which relates to the spirit of the individual writer and that of the epoch."[182]

At the end of the 1960s, Roland Barthes and Michel Foucault took an extreme counter-position to Schleiermacher's subjective hermeneutics by denying the author any relevance as a reference instance for text interpretation in favour of the reader.[183] While Barthes emphasises intertextuality and reception by the reader instead of the

---

[176] Hermanns (2007), here: p. 197.

[177] Jäger (1999), pp. 184–185.

[178] Boeckh (1886), p. 140.

[179] Ibid., p. 86.

[180] Cf. ibid., pp. 82–83.

[181] von Goethe (2005), here: p. 126. For more details, see Danneberg (2015), here: pp. 416–421.

[182] Szondi (1975), p. 158.

[183] Cf. Schiesser (2007), here: p. 21.

author,[184] Foucault postulates the 'authorless' discourse'[185] as a liberation for the reader and author, whereby both thinkers detach themselves from the attributions of the text.[186] Barthes' about-turn took place a few years later when he wrote in *The Pleasure of the Text*: "But in a text, in a way, I desire the author: I need his figure [...], as he needs mine [...]."[187]

Roman Ingarden can also be located in the lineage of Foucault and the 'early' Barthes when he turns his gaze away from the author towards the intention and meaning of the text as a sufficient criterion for understanding:

> The process of [...] finding the intention of meaning is basically nothing other than an actualisation of this intention. In other words: by understanding a text, I think the meaning of the text I read. I take it from the text, so to speak, and transform it into the current intention of my understanding act of thought, into an intention that is identical with the intention of the word or sentence that appears in the text. Then the text is really 'understood'.[188] [...] Only when we succeed in using and actualising all the factors provided by the text, and in constituting the organised meaningful whole of the work in question in accordance with the intentions of meaning contained in the text itself, in its layer of meaning, do we really understand the content of the work.[189]

Since Ingarden, it seems, leaves the author out of the hermeneutic process and relies in principle on the text in its verbalised form, he realises that several interpretations can be possible for the same text, whereby it is up to the interpreter to decide in favour of one of the possible interpretation variants:

> The work is only recognised well in its language when the reader is not only sensitive enough to the mere presence of ambiguities but also recognises which different interpretations of the text are permitted by the text and which are eliminated by the other parts of the text. And he must also orientate himself as to which of these interpretations permitted by the ambiguity have priority over other possible significances or whether all of them may be considered equally in the final interpretation of the text.[190]

Like Ingarden, Paul Ricœur understands hermeneutic activity as a decision-making process between the diverse semantic possibilities of a text. For Ricœur, understanding a text results from grasping the linguistically linguistic structure *and* explaining the text through appropriation: "To explain is to bring out the structure, that is, the internal relations of dependence that constitute the statics of the text; to interpret is to follow the path of thought opened up by the text [...]."[191] This appropriation of the text is only possible after going through a structured procedure, which Ricœur calls a 'hermeneutic arc or circle', not to be confused with Gadamer's

---

[184] Barthes (1974), p. 151. See also: Jannidis et al. (2000), pp. 185–193.

[185] Foucault (1998), pp. 205–222.

[186] Cf. Breu (2020), p. 75.

[187] Barthes (1975), p. 27.

[188] Ingarden (1968), p. 30.

[189] Ibid., p. 33.

[190] Ebd., p. 366.

[191] Ricœur (1991), p. 122.

'hermeneutic circle':[192] The first phase of the intuitive attempt at understanding or 'naive understanding' is followed by the phase of explanation, which revises, modifies, and corrects the first understanding with the 'logic of probability'. Finally, the process of understanding takes place in the appropriation of the text by the recipient by grasping, as Veronika Hoffmann comments, the "world that the text designs 'in front of' itself."[193] By this, Ricœur does not mean the world that the author intends, but the world as it emerges from the text for the reader: "For what must be interpreted in a text is a proposed world that I could inhabit and wherein I could project one of my own most possibilities. That is what I call the world of the text, the world proper to this unique text."[194] According to Ricœur, the text consists of a structure of words that are made to speak through language. The reader must extract the language, the meaning, and the discourse from this structural framework of words: "the object is the text itself; the sign is the deep semantics disclosed by structural analysis; and the series of interpretants is the chain of interpretations produced by the interpreting community and incorporated into the dynamics of the text, as the work of meaning upon itself."[195] In this sense, Ricœur continues, semantic ambiguity requires the ability of the interpreter to recognise which interpretation of a text is most appropriate on the basis of the general lexical understanding: "This activity of discernment is properly called interpretation; it consists in recognizing what relatively univocal message the speaker has constructed on the polysemic basis of the common lexicon."[196] It is interesting at this point that Boeckh, more than a century before Ricœur, already points to the "infinite number of relations"[197] in the hermeneutic, text-related process, which makes it impossible to achieve discursive clarity. Whether one can (or may) here assume a first origin of Michel Foucault's concept of diffuse discourse in a space of dispersion (*l'espace de dispersion*),[198] remains as open as the question of whether, as Jørgen Sneis asks, there can in principle be "such a thing as correct interpretations of a literary text."[199] According to Sneis, Imgarden's demand for a 'sensitive' reader as a criterion for hermeneutic practice seems particularly nebulous in this context, insofar as 'sensitivity' is difficult to grasp and define.[200] When is an interpreter sensitive? What qualifications characterise him as such? Does 'sensitivity' require certain prior knowledge? Ingarden ultimately leaves all of these questions unanswered. In this sense, Dirk Werle also criticises the 'sponginess' of 'sensitivity' as a hermeneutical guideline.[201]

---

[192] Ibid., pp. 69; 124.

[193] Hoffmann (2024), here: p. 1230.

[194] Ricœur (1991), p. 86.

[195] Ibid., p. 124.

[196] Ibid., p. 55.

[197] Boeckh (1886), p. 86.

[198] Foucault (1972), p. 10.

[199] Sneis (2015), here: p. 478.

[200] Ibid., p. 476.

[201] Werle (2015), here: p. 350.

Beyond the development of a unified hermeneutics of literary studies, Friedrich Schleiermacher argued in favour of viewing the previously separately understood moments of understanding and interpretation as two sides of the same 'coin': "understanding is the reverse side of an act of speaking, and one must grasp the thinking that underlies a given statement. 3. Dialectics relies on hermeneutic and rhetoric because the development of all knowledge depends on both speaking and understanding"[202] In this sense, understanding is part of the process of interpretation, just as interpretation is part of the process of understanding. Hans-Georg Gadamer receives Schleiermacher's coupling of understanding and interpretation in a unified process[203] when he defines interpretation as an "explicit form of understanding."[204] As Emil Anghern explains, interpretation in this sense is "as it were the inner articulation of an understanding, its actual realisation, which sets apart the potential meaning of an object, clarifies its content and makes it present to others."[205] In other words, understanding is realised through interpretation, which leads to full understanding and to the unfolding of what may be hidden.

According to Peter Zima, Hans-Georg Gadamer brings the historical context of the text's origin into the focus of the hermeneutic approach, insofar as it is to be understood as an answer to "certain questions that arose in its historical context of origin"[206] and which, in a second step, relates it to the reader's own historical situation.[207] In this context, Zima continues, Gadamer's hermeneutic centrepiece lies in the *hermeneutic circle*, i.e. in the reconstruction of the reader's horizon of expectation at the time of the work's publication,[208] whereby it is no longer a matter of 'putting oneself in the author's mental state', as with Schleiermacher, but rather trying "to transpose ourselves into the perspective within which he has formed his views."[209] In order to arrive at an understanding of the text, the interpreter must take previous opinions into account, i.e. research conducted on the matter, and open up to them. With this attitude of traditional prior knowledge, which especially applies to the humanities, the understanding of texts is modified by the subjectivity of prior understanding, i.e. the 'pre-judgement' as an expectation of those who read a text with an understanding, whereby it must be emphasised that for Gadamer such an understanding is not even possible without prior knowledge.[210] Gadamer formulates the principle of the hermeneutic circle as follows:

---

[202] Schleiermacher (1977), p. 97.

[203] Gadamer (1982), p. 184. Original German publication: *Wahrheit und Methode* (1960).

[204] Ibid., p. 307.

[205] Anghern (2021), here: p. 51.

[206] Zima (2020), p. 242.

[207] Cf. also Jauß (1981), pp. 467–468.

[208] Cf. ibid., *Literarische Ästhetik*, p. 473.

[209] Gadamer (1982), p. 292.

[210] Cf. ibid., p. 267.

> A person who is trying to understand a text is always projecting. He projects a meaning for the text as a whole as soon as some initial meaning emerges in the text. Again, the initial meaning emerges only because he is reading the text with particular expectations in regard to a certain meaning. Working out this fore-projection, which is constantly revised in terms of what emerges as he penetrates into the meaning, is understanding what is there.[211]

In Gadamer's conception, text and recipient—"movement of tradition and movement of the interpreter"[212]—face each other, and approach each other spirally, step by step, until the greatest possible agreement, ideally[213] until a perfect congruence of text and understanding is obtained. The recipients' first approach is determined by their prior knowledge, i.e. their expectations of the text. As Gadamer emphasises, the anticipation of meaning that guides the understanding of the text does not arise from a subjective action, but "proceeds from the commonality that binds us to tradition", whereby this 'commonality' emerges from a process that is "constantly being formed in our relation to the tradition."[214] Between expectation and understanding, there is thus a gradual convergence between the recipient's anticipation of meaning and the actual meaning of the text (anticipation of perfection), eliminating incongruent meaning results, until the greatest possible congruence between the actual meaning and the recipient's anticipation of meaning is achieved. As Gadamer explains, the development of this actual meaning always starts from the whole and returns to parts of the whole, in a kind of back-and-forth movement:

> This means, then, that the expectation changes and that the text unifies its meaning around another expectation. Thus the movement of understanding is constantly from the whole to the part and back to the whole. Our task is to expand the unity of the understood meaning centrifugally. The harmony of all the details with the whole is the criterion of correct understanding. The failure to achieve this harmony means that understanding has failed.[215]

Consequently, as Gadamer goes on to explain, "the only 'objectivity' here is the confirmation of a fore-meaning in its being worked out."[216] To put it simply, according to Ralph Sichler, the concept of the hermeneutic circle originally meant "that the part can only be understood from the whole and the whole only from the part."[217] In this sense, partial and whole meanings are mutually dependent, whereby, Sichler continues, "with a profound knowledge of the overall context, the meaning of the partial elements can be easily deciphered."[218] As Ulla Fix explains, the process of interaction between parts of the text and the whole text, the expectations with which the text is approached, and the change in the horizon of expectations through the

[211] Ibid., p. 267.

[212] Ibid., p. 293.

[213] Susanne Bleich, however, doubts the possibility of complete congruence between the actual meaning of the text and the recipient's understanding of it. Cf. Bleich (1992), pp. 7–20.

[214] Gadamer (1982), p. 293.

[215] Ibid., p. 291.

[216] Ibid., p. 267.

[217] Sichler (2020), here: p. 135.

[218] Ibid.

text ultimately result in the hermeneutic spiral,[219] a concept that, as Siegfried Lamnek notes, was already known to Schleiermacher.[220] Moritz Baßler explains that this involves 'rubbing one's own knowledge' against the resistance of the text, i.e. against "that which is always already understood",[221] to arrive at a complete understanding of the text in this way. However, this 'rubbing against' does not only take place against the 'previously understood' of a text but, as Gadamer adds, also against the historical-temporal distance between the text and its interpreters: "We saw that to understand a text always means to apply it to ourselves and to know that, even if it must always be understood in different ways, it is still the same text presenting itself to us in these different ways."[222] In this view, the understanding and interpretation of a text depend not only on prior knowledge, i.e. on one's own knowledge of the state of research, personal knowledge, and familiarity with other texts but also on the relationship between the historical time of origin of the text and the historical present of the hermeneutist. The fact that Gadamer's hermeneutic circle, as Matthias Klatt emphasises, has also found its way into legal hermeneutics will be examined in more detail in the following chapter as an essential point of connection between law and literature.[223]

In literary studies, Gadamer's hermeneutic circle is reflected above all as a method of text interpretation, as Susanne Bleich, in agreement with Peter Szondi[224] and Karlheinz Stierle,[225] explains: "Assuming that hermeneutics and method coexist [which Gadamer denies, author's note], the relationship between the two in general, and thus also in the particular case of literary hermeneutics and literary method, is a hierarchical one: it is regulated inclusively, insofar as hermeneutics encompasses method – and that means at the same time: the individual methods."[226] According to this view, which distinguishes between hermeneutics and method, interpretation (hermeneutics) is epistemologically orientated in that it examines the mechanism of understanding, while the method specifically aims at the application of hermeneutics to the text.

In terms of literary theory, Hans Robert Jauß builds on Gadamer's theory but extends it from the text to the reception and thus incorporates the social function of the work into the hermeneutic process. In this sense, Jauß is concerned with "understanding the work from its effect and reception, the history of an art as a process of communication between author and audience, past and present."[227] According to Jauß, the first reading of the text must be dedicated to aesthetic perception before

[219] Fix (2021), here: p. 696.

[220] Lamnek (2005), p. 64.

[221] Baßler (2021), here: p. 856.

[222] Gadamer (1982), p. 398.

[223] Cf. Klatt (2021), here: p. 233.

[224] Cf. Szondi (1975), pp. 7–192.

[225] See Stierle (1985), pp. 340–354.

[226] Bleich (1992), p. 47.

[227] Jauß (1991), p. 20.

Gadamer's 'questioning'—'understanding means understanding something as a response'—takes place in a second step, insofar as this 'understanding' can only follow "the primary act of perceptive understanding, which introduces and constitutes the aesthetic experience of the poetic text."[228] Jauss formulates the concept of 'aesthetic experience' as a relationship between self-enjoyment and the enjoyment of others: "In aesthetic behaviour, the subject always enjoys more than just itself: it experiences itself in the appropriation of an experience of the meaning of the world that both its own productive activity and the absorption of the experience of the other can open up to it [...]. Aesthetic pleasure [...] is a way of experiencing oneself in the experience of the other."[229] For the recipient—and here lies the core of Jauß' reception theory—aesthetics is thus combined with *poiesis* as a "process in which the recipient becomes a co-creator of the work",[230] who performs active hermeneutic 'work' through questions and reflection. In Jauß' understanding of 'aesthetic experience', Susanne Bleich sees both the pleasure in the reception of the text and that in oneself as a recipient, whereby a dialectical relationship "of self-enjoyment in the enjoyment of others" arises.[231] Following the principle of *aisthesis*,[232] according to Jauß, the recipient should try to perceive the work of art as impartially as possible, i.e. avoid a hasty identification of the real world with the fiction: "Anyone who wants to perceive a painting aesthetically, i.e. arrive at new knowledge by seeing, must resist the tendency to hastily identify or recognise [...]."[233] Author and recipient thus participate together in the completion of the artwork through poiesis (author and recipient) and aisthesis (recipient). Tobias Klauk, Niels Klenner, and Tilmann Köppe believe that the aesthetic appreciation of a text is the basis of literary hermeneutics, which also guides the way it is interpreted, as they demonstrate through several examples: for example, the assessment of whether the main character in the fiction is the murderer guides the way it is interpreted.[234]

Finally, in the 1990s, attempts were made to introduce concepts, structures, and methods from a field of knowledge foreign to literature into literature through analogical procedures and to make them fruitful for literary-theoretical work. In his defence of pragmatic case-by-case hermeneutics as the best possible technique for finding the law, guided by equivalence and Kantian reason, François Ost cites the

[228] Jauß (1981), p. 475.

[229] Jauß (1991), p. 85.

[230] Ibid., p. 117.

[231] Cf. Bleich (1992), p. 78.

[232] The distinction between *aesthetics*, as the feeling and perception of beauty (theory of the arts), and *aesthetics*, as the cognitive performance of the perception of art, goes back to Kant's third critique, in which the aesthetic, alongside the teleological power of judgement, is defined as the "ability to judge formal expediency (otherwise also called subjective) through the feeling of pleasure and displeasure [...]." See Kant (1974), p. A XLVIII; see also Witte (2020), here: S. 67–68.

[233] Jauß (1991), p. 292.

[234] Klauk and Klenner (2021), here: p. 802. The authors cite the example of Annette Droste-Hülshoff's *The Jew's Beech Tree: A Moral Portrait from Mountainous Westphalia* (2014), orig. *Die Judenbuche* (1842).

analogical method of reasoning, also known as abduction. Such a procedure makes it possible to solve unknown facts by imaginatively tracing them back to the known: "Abduction is the form of analogical reasoning required when moving from the known to the unknown."[235] In Umberto Eco's novel *Der Name der Rose* (1980), William formulates the principle of analogy as a reasoning that relates different facts to each other to find a solution for the unknown: "'It means, rather, facing one or two or three particular data apparently with nothing in common, and trying to imagine whether they could represent so many instances of a general law you don't yet know, ad which perhaps has never been pronounced."[236] Ost describes the analogical approach as a horizontal rhizome-like process of searching for acceptable equivalences, similarities, and functional commonalities that are able to establish a connection, as he explains by way of example, between the swimming fin of a fish and the wing of a bird via a functional commonality (locomotion):

> Abduction, on the other hand, which takes seriously everything that thwarts uniformity, focuses on functional equivalences; it accommodates obvious differences but also points to similarities (of function), it 'judges' the acceptable equivalence, it 'constructs' the common measure. For example, in questioning this 'thing' on the fish's body, it assumes that it is related to a motor function, and, taking part in the known (the bird's eye), it risks going into the unknown by establishing the relation of analogy: 'what the wing is to the bird, X (the fin) is to the fish'.[237]

Karin Knorr-Cetina takes up this idea of functional equivalence when she defines an analogue approach as the transfer of knowledge "from an investigated, well-known case to a less known, unclear situation [...]. Since the knowledge mobilised by the metaphor or analogy has already proven itself in a similar context, it seems likely that it can also be made to 'function' in the new situation, provided that appropriate modifications are made."[238] There are now attempts to transfer scientific methods to literary studies in an analogous way, as Andrea Albrecht explains. As an example, she cites the attempt to make the mathematical concept of the attractor fruitful for literary hermeneutics,[239] whereby it should be noted that the hermeneutic method derived from this comes very close to Gadamer's idea of the hermeneutic circle in that it is also an organised process of reading and re-reading in search of meaning and delimitation, taking the knowledge and experience of others into account.[240]

In recent research on praxeological hermeneutics, which focuses specifically on the concrete application of hermeneutics, the act of interpreting implies the creative

---

[235] Ost (2014), here: p. 120. François Ost refers here to Papaux (2003).

[236] Eco (2004), p. 295.

[237] Ost (2014), p. 121.

[238] Knorr-Cetina (2016), p. 107.

[239] Albrecht (2015), here: pp. 285–292.

[240] Cf. ibid., pp. 285–286.

production of objects and meaningful realities.[241] There appear here to be strong similarities with Foucault's discourse, insofar as both active interpretation and discourse constitutively access our world in this view.

Klaus Birnstil believes that the concept of literary hermeneutics in general must be understood differently and more openly with the entry of literature into the digital era, as literature now goes far beyond the printed book and manifests itself in social media, like "the rustle in the forest of leaves."[242] The dynamic fleetingness of the present—which interjects itself between the regularly recalled past and a hopeless future[243]—compels a new understanding of contemporary literature: "Anyone who wants to engage with it appropriately must move through it by reading laterally and discard his or her old braided categories of author, work and reader in the university archive."[244] The triangular relationship between author-text-reader, which Birnstil criticises as a "caricature" of poor hermeneutics,[245] seems to have to give way to a ubiquitous concept of literature,[246] which has to take into account the paradigms of the pluralistic-digital world.[247]

Annette Gerok-Reiter also touches on the question of hermeneutic plurality which, due to the historical context, cannot come to a definitive end, which is why every understanding implies "the admission of non-understanding."[248] Ursula Christmann indicates that the understanding of a text arises from the interweaving of the surface of the text (wording and grammar), the propositional textual basis (facts in the text in connection with subjective prior knowledge), and the textual statement of meaning.[249] According to Fix, the interpretation of the text itself, be it literary or legal texts, is a "special kind of understanding that one resorts to if one wants to penetrate deeper into the contexts in the service of interpretation",[250] whereby text analysis as a consciously reflected methodological approach and interpretation as the attribution of meaning are linked.

In summary, the attempt to provide an overview of the very complex hermeneutics research relevant to the present study provides in three main findings: the difficulty of theoretical pluralism,[251] the interest of Gadamer's hermeneutic circle as a possible methodological docking point between literature and law, and the neglect of hermeneutics in favour of discourse theory in literary studies.

---

[241] Anghern (2021), p. 53.

Lenk (1993) and Abel (2022), should be mentioned as radical representatives of application-orientated hermeneutics.

[242] Birnstiel (2021), here: p. 791.

[243] Cf. Gumbrecht (2010); Gumbrecht (2004).

[244] Birnstiel (2021), p. 794.

[245] Ibid., p. 790.

[246] See also: Schulze (2020).

[247] Birnstiel (2021), p. 795.

[248] Gerok-Reiter (2021), here: p. 756.

[249] Cf. Christmann (2008), here: p. 1093.

[250] Fix (2021), p. 698.

[251] Cf. Jauß (1997), here: p. 334.

Access to previous hermeneutics research is complicated by the strong pluralism of theoretical approaches and their heterogeneous changes over time. Starting with Schleiermacher's subjective-psychological anchoring of the interpretative approach in the person of the author, followed by Dilthey, Lachmann, Hermanns, and Jäger, research has arrived at the objective radicality of the text via mediating positions between subjectivity and objectivity (Boeckh, Ast) with Foucault, Barthes, Ricœur, and Imgarden, thereby eliminating subjective factors.

The approaches diverge less strongly than in the area of determining criteria concerning the hermeneutic application process, which since Schleiermacher has generally been understood as a binary relationship between understanding and interpretation. If there is a relative consensus that understanding and interpretation are not separate moments, there are, however, variations in the role of the recipient, who for Gadamer is limited to the understanding reception of the text, while Jauß ascribes to the reader an active participatory function in the hermeneutic process.

Of particular interest in the search for methodological similarities between law and literature is Gadamer's philosophical concept of the hermeneutic circle, which recognises positive 'prior knowledge' as decisive for the interpretation of texts and thus comes irritatingly close to the literary concept of intertextuality. From a legal perspective, Gadamer's imperative of 'prior knowledge' as a positive 'prior judgement' immediately triggers associations with the legal concepts of systematic and historical interpretation, which will be discussed in more detail in the following section. Equally interesting is the idea of 'wandering back and forth' between the general and the particular—which can also be imagined as a gradual narrowing of the radius of the circle—because to understand and interpret literary texts, it will usually be necessary to move from an initial general grasp of the text via detailed observations and analyses to a deeper understanding of the text. In the same way, the legal practitioner must break down the general abstractness of legal norms until they can be applied to the specific individual case. Interestingly, in the context of the various possible interpretations, literary studies can also resort to analogous procedures that are a matter of course for jurisprudence and have always been an integral part of legal hermeneutics. In more recent literary research, however, the notion of hermeneutic 'rulelessness' seems to have prevailed since the dawn of the digital age.

Finally, it is worth highlighting the tendency in current literary theory research to replace hermeneutics with discourse as a method of accessing texts. Both literary and legal texts can be understood as discourses, as has already been explained at some length, and can enter dialogue with each other via the interdiscourse. For an investigation of possible points of connection between law and literature, it also seems appropriate to (sub)examine both hermeneutic and discursive approaches for both disciplines, because while the former emphasises understanding, the latter provides information about epistemic peculiarities or commonalities.

The following section will provide a more profound insight into legal hermeneutics because, without knowledge of it, it will not be possible to recognise the points of contact between literary and legal interpretation.

3.3.2 Legal Hermeneutics

While the goal of literary hermeneutics is limited to the attempt to understand texts as profoundly as possible, legal hermeneutics also strives to understand texts but does so with regard to the stringent goal of practical effect, which unfolds when a certain situation is regulated through the pragmatic application of the law. In this respect, legal hermeneutics is conditioned by the dialectic between the claim to validity and application of the law: legal texts are normative because (in democracies) they have undergone a certain process of finding the law; they demand an abstract 'ought'. The possibility of applying the abstract 'ought' must be examined by interpreting it to the specific individual case (subsumption).[252] In this context, Martin Kriele recalls the three-stage process of a legal decision: "1. clarification of the facts, 2. hermeneutic clarification of the legal norms, 3. subsumption of the facts under the relevant norm", whereby the difficulties lie "in point 2."[253] The peculiarity of legal interpretation and application fundamentally lies in the challenging discrepancy between the normative abstractness of legal norms and their practical application to a concrete situation- and person- specific context. This process of norm subsumption requires the linguistic endeavour of interpreting written (in *continental law*) or orally transmitted (in *common law*) legal texts. As Dieter Grimm and Christoph König emphasise, it is not the aesthetics of the normative text but its clarity that is decisive in supporting this transition from the normatively abstract to the actually concrete as far as possible.[254] Matthias Klatt aptly formulates the central problem of legal hermeneutics: "At the centre of the interest of legal hermeneutics are the problems of the relationship between norm and fact and the openness of language",[255] which can be solved through prior knowledge as a possibility of understanding, i.e. through tradition, and individual prior understanding (general and specific knowledge of language, knowledge of the facts, legal texts, and case law, etc.).[256] The development of modern legal hermeneutics, as already indicated in the previous section, owes much to Hans-Georg Gadamer's theory of prior knowledge and prior judgement. This is already recognised by Josef Esser when he states that, in addition to a 'correct' sense of values, legal interpretation requires, above all, social practical experience and learning processes as well as prior legal knowledge acquired through training.[257] It has also already been pointed out that the process of norm subsumption corresponds to the mechanism of Gadamer's hermeneutic circle, as described by Wolfgang Fikentscher under the concept of *case norm theory*: "The formation of the case norm[258] is achieved when the hermeneutic circle

[252] Cf. Möllers (2023), pp. 126–131.

[253] Kriele (1981), here: p. 149.

[254] Grimm and König (2020), here: pp. 7–12.

[255] Klatt (2021), p. 234.

[256] Cf. Gizbert-Studnicki (1987), here: p. 481 and p. 484.

[257] Cf. Esser (1972), p. 10.

[258] By the 'case norm', Fikentscher means the norm applicable to the specific case as it has been isolated from the abstract norm or from a combination of abstract norms through the process of interpretation.

'ascends and descends' only once between the norm and the facts of the case and there is no further question to be answered positively as to whether the facts of the case also provide the correct norm for its judgement."[259] Gadamer's hermeneutic circle is recognisable here insofar as, as Matthias Klatt points out, prior knowledge of language and content is a prerequisite for drawing conclusions from the general to the specific, from the abstract norm to the individual case, i.e. assigning a concrete fact to one or more norms.[260] In this respect, Karl-Ludwig Kunz and Mona Martino confirm Gadamer's 'circularity' between prior knowledge of the law and its application to the concrete case: "One cannot understand the case in its legal meaning without a prior understanding of the law; the law, however, requires a case-related concretisation in order to be understood."[261] For Reinhold Zippelius, circularity consists in the 'self-referential' regulation of the interpretation of the law by the law, "insofar as criteria for the interpretation of the law are taken from the law itself, which in turn serve to clarify and develop the law."[262] However, Zippelius' view of circularity cannot be understood in the sense of Gadamer's hermeneutic circle. Rather, one could perhaps—and this is a conjecture that cannot be pursued further here—draw parallels between Zippelius' logic and Luhmann's systemic coherence.[263]

The analogy procedure already mentioned in the previous chapter on literary studies is also based on Gadamer's principle of prior knowledge,[264] whereby it is necessary to bridge the gaps in the law that are contrary to plan, arising from the diversity of situations in everyday life, and which the legislator's imagination cannot cope with *a priori*. The Austrian Civil Code therefore expressly provides for analogy:

> If a legal case cannot be decided either from the words or from the natural meaning of a law, consideration must be given to similar cases that have been decided in the law and to the grounds of other related laws. If the legal case remains doubtful, it must be decided according to the natural principles of law with regard to the carefully collected and carefully considered circumstances (§ 7 ABGB).

To solve the problem of applying the law to facts that are neither covered by legal norms nor by case law, the judge can analogously fall back on precedents (previous case law) by referring to the similarity of precedents. Möllers describes the process of legal analogy as the application of a general idea that is derived from

---

259 Fikentscher (1977), pp. 201–202.

260 Cf. Klatt (2021), p. 236.

261 Kunz and Martino (2006), p. 175.

262 Zippelius (2006), p. 58.

263 Cf. Sect. 3.2.2, footnote 120.

264 According to G. Ipseu, *analogy* refers to the similarity of relationship between two objects, as a 'similarity that is not based on individual properties or parts of these objects, but on the mutual relationship between properties and parts. The properties or parts of two objects can all be very different, and yet there can be a similarity in the relationship between their properties or their parts'. See Ipseu (1927), p. 320.

an existing, legally regulated situation (*induction*) and correlated with the non-regulated situation (*deduction*).[265] The similarity between the normative facts referred to and the facts to be assessed must be justified, for which the interpreter can rely on the purpose of the applicable norm and the correspondence of certain elements in both facts or on the commonality of a general legal concept.[266] The analogue procedure of legal interpretation is, of course, only considered secondarily as an aid to filling gaps if the statutory canon of interpretation proves to be inadequate. In principle, therefore, the applicability of the four canons derived by Friedrich von Savigny,[267] which the German Federal Constitutional Court has summarised as follows, must first be examined in any application of the law: "The interpretation from the *wording* of the norm (grammatical interpretation), from its *context* (systematic interpretation), from its *purpose* (teleological interpretation) and from the legislative materials and the legislative *history* (historical interpretation) serve this purpose of interpretation."[268] Here, the High Court has succeeded in summarising the essential principles of legal hermeneutics in one sentence.

The grammatical interpretation, to begin with the first reference of the German Federal Constitutional Court, is therefore based on the interpretation of the wording, whereby it must be assumed "that the legislator uses the words in the sense in which they are commonly understood."[269] In cases of doubt, the Duden dictionary or etymological dictionaries are consulted for linguistic determination.[270] The linguistic or textual understanding that stands between the normative text (norms, laws, court decisions, contracts, declarations of intent, etc.) and its concrete application must always be scrutinised and, in most cases, forces the interpreters to choose between several "possible interpretations",[271] although they must justify the choice with arguments.[272] For the grammatical interpretation, Austrian law refers to the *peculiar meaning of the words*: "In principle, no other meaning may be attributed to a law in its application than that which emerges from the peculiar meaning of the words in their context and from the clear intention of the legislator" (§ 6 ABGB). Here, grammatical criteria are combined with systematic and teleological interpretation criteria and the aim is to move on to systematic interpretation.

---

[265] Cf. Möllers (2023), p. 258.

[266] Cf. ibid., pp. 253–258.

[267] Savigny already presented the systematisation of the canon of legal interpretation in a lecture in 1802/1803, which Jakob Grimm (!) wrote down (Möllers 2023, p. 132, fn. 31). Law and literature meet here at eye level. See also: von Savigny (1951). See also: von Savigny (1840), pp. 213 ff.

[268] BVerfG 17 May 1960–2 BvL 11/59 and others, BVerfGE 11, 126 (130) – Nachkonstitutioneller Bestätigungswille (post-constitutional will of confirmation).

[269] Larenz (1991), p. 320.

[270] Cf. Hamann (2017), here: pp. 182–183.

[271] Klatt (2021), p. 234.

[272] Cf. ibid., pp. 238–239.

Systematic interpretation refers to the embedding of the legal text in the "overall context of the law"[273] and actually in the "legal system as a whole",[274] particularly taking into account the interrelationships and interdependencies of the hierarchy of the law (hierarchy of norms) and the legal conflict rules between norms of equal rank (earlier-later, particular-general).[275] The rules of systematic interpretation have a logical meaning-forming function, which can also be attributed to literary intertextuality. Here, too, the German Federal Constitutional Court has found an illustrative short formula:

> Systematic interpretation must be based on the fact that individual legal sentences that the legislator has placed in a factual context must generally be interpreted in such a way that they are logically compatible with each other. This is because it must be assumed that the legislator has regulated factually related matters in such a way that the entire provision makes consistent, comprehensible sense.[276]

When Section 6 ABGB requires that a legal text is to be interpreted as it "emerges from the clear intention of the legislator", this means that "the *ratio legis*, i.e. the meaning and purpose" of a norm[277] is enquired into to give it concrete legal force. Within this purpose-bound nature of legal interpretation, the subjective theory, which is based on the will of the legislator, and the objective theory, which prioritises the criteria of reason and the meaning of words, are opposed to each other. Both the subjective and the objective interpretation variants can be based on the actual will of the historical legislator (subjective or objective theory of origin) or the hypothetical will of the present legislator (subjective or objective theory of interpretation). None of the theories excludes the other.[278] The objective interpretation theory allows the new factual and legal situation to be given preference in the specific interpretation of the law, even if this is contrary to the wording of the law. An example of this would be the excuse of ignorance of the law, contrary to the generally recognised principle that "ignorance is no defence against punishment", in order to take account of the strong inflation of the law, which today makes complete knowledge of all legal norms impossible.[279] Ralph Christensen's and Hans Kudlich's objection that teleological interpretation runs the risk of becoming susceptible to subjectively coloured interpretations[280] is strongly reminiscent of the literary-theoretical debate on the relationship between author and text, between subjective and objective text interpretation.

---

[273] Möllers (2023), p. 153.

[274] Christensen and Kudlich (2004), pp. 74–83.

[275] Cf. Möllers (2023), pp. 153–164.

[276] BVerfG 9 May 1978–2 BvR 952/75, BVerfGE 48, 246 (257) - Ehrenamtliche Richter (honorary judges).

[277] Möllers (2023), p. 182.

[278] Klatt (2021), p. 235.

[279] Cf. Kriele (1981), p. 150.

[280] Christensen and Kudlich (2004), p. 80. See also: Dworkin (2001), pp. 33–57.

However, the historical interpretation, which primarily refers to the interpretation of the Basic Law,[281] will not be discussed in detail here.

Jürgen Habermas decisively denied the question of whether legal interpretation should also include moral judgements to fill gaps: "But the more complex validity dimension of legal norms prohibits one from assimilating the legitimacy of legal decisions to the validity of moral judgements. To this extent one should not conceive legal discourse as a special case of moral discourses (of application)."[282] Against Habermas' separation of law and morality, Robert Alexy developed the 'special case thesis', according to which "legal discourse can be understood as a special case of general practical discourse."[283] In this sense, recourse to moral and ethical questions is permissible if the practical applicability of the norm, i.e. the "reasonableness of the law"[284] in relation to a specific legal situation, requires this. In general, as Möllers emphasises, it is now "quite undisputed that the constitution as a value system has an impact on all areas of life and thus also on the various areas of law."[285]

To summarise, it can be emphasised that the primary task of law is the concrete enforcement of the 'ought', 'must', or 'must not'. To fulfil this task, law is naturally—and in contrast to literature—characterised by an intrinsically normative character. The abstract, generally valid 'you should', 'you must', or 'you must not' can only be conveyed via the medium of the normative text, whereby the problem is that legal texts can only be drafted *a priori* in the abstract for a hypothetical and limited series of circumstances, insofar as the legislator cannot foresee every specific individual case that will occur in the future. This is precisely where the hermeneutic process comes in as the link between abstract norm and concrete 'case' by determining how and whether a particular real-life situation can be subsumed under one or a combination of several legal norms. In other words, the legal practitioner must use the canon of interpretation to determine whether (and which) norms apply to a particular set of facts. In doing so, the legal text must be examined concerning its semantic meaning, which is generally recognised in a certain cultural area, its coherent-logical relationship to the overall legal structure, and its practical purpose. The subsumption procedure described in this way finds its equivalent in Gadamer's idea of the hermeneutic circle as an ever tighter circular movement between the prior knowledge of abstract norms and the gradual breaking down of their possible meanings and applications by eliminating options that are out of the question until, ideally, the abstract norm and the concrete facts finally coincide. Where the legislator has failed to establish the law, i.e. where there is a gap in the law, Gadamer's hermeneutic circle once again takes effect in the analogy procedure, in the search for elementary or ideal similarities between precedents or norms and the concrete

[281] Cf. von Savigny (2004).

[282] Habermas (1996), p. 233.

[283] Alexy (1989), pp. 179–180.

[284] Neumann (2021), here: p. 248.

[285] Möllers (2023), p. 187.

facts that must be resolved. Judgemental interpretations are also available to the hermeneuticist, as it is always a question of the pragmatic-practical application of the law for the legally effective resolution of real 'cases'. Whichever interpretation criteria the interpreters choose to fulfil the imperative of pragmatic case resolution, they must always give appropriate reasons for their interpretation decision, which is why legal interpretation, as the German Federal Constitutional Court has stated, "has the character of a discourse (cf. BVerfGE 82, 30 (38)",[286] "in which, even with methodologically flawless work, not absolutely correct statements that cannot be doubted among experts are presented, but reasons are asserted, other reasons are put forward against them and ultimately the better reasons should prevail."[287]

In this sense, the practitioner of the law (usually the judge) can be ascribed a creative function by 'thinking ahead' of the law,[288] as Philipp Heck explains:

> From this point of view, the judge must not only fill in the blank but also supplement and possibly correct the existing precepts in accordance with the interests at stake. The judge is not merely a subsumption apparatus, an automaton into which the facts and legal norm are incorporated and from which the judgement then jumps out without any evaluation on the part of the judge. Rather, he is himself a *creator of applicable norms*, an assistant to the legislator, albeit a subordinate one.[289]

After reading legal hermeneutics and the previous section on literary hermeneutics, some points of contact between the two disciplines can already be surmised. Even if their aims are not the same, since law must fulfil a pragmatic social function (social order), whereas literature is not subject to purpose-bound imperatives, methodological similarities in the process of interpretation can be identified. As the following chapter will show, Gadamer's hermeneutic circle has found its way into both literary studies and jurisprudence.

3.3.3 Similarities and Differences Between Literary and Legal Hermeneutics

As indicated in Sect. 3.1 on interdisciplinarity, common methods are required for truly interdisciplinary work beyond the specialist areas. In this context, Oliver Jahraus proposes using hermeneutics as a link between law and literary studies,[290] insofar as both disciplines deal with language in the text and thus the written word is a central element for both lawyers and literary scholars. With regard to the

---

[286] Neumann (2021), p. 239.

[287] BVerfG, decision 05.04.1990–2 BvR 413/88 - Besorgnis der Befangenheit eines Bundesverfassungsrichters, p. 2458 (Concerns about the impartiality of a Federal Constitutional Court judge).

[288] Cf. Kriele (1981), pp. 151–152.

[289] Heck (1958), p. 473.

[290] Cf. Jahraus (2013), p. 376.

interdisciplinary working basis, Rolf Gröschner points out that for the legal hermeneuticist, language is always at the centre of his effort, as it is language that "conveys a matter to the lawyer, makes it understandable", insofar as everything in the world of law is language, since legal relationships or disputes can only be understood through the word and understanding itself is owed to language: "All legal understanding is linguistic understanding of a matter in dispute – constituted by language – with the – linguistically constituted – means of law, in short: is mediation between law and language."[291] Consequently, both legal and literary studies operate in relation to text and language and are therefore, as Gideon Stiening emphasises, *ipso facto* in need of interpretation: "Furthermore, it is true for both subject areas of legal and literary hermeneutics that law and literature are both *possible* to interpret and in *need* of interpretation, i.e. there is a need for interpretation in both fields."[292] The fact that this is possible, but not always easy, is shown by Eric Hirsch's 'self-praise' towards the writer, which seems like a competition between law and literature for the same method, where he states the following:

> A lawyer normally interprets the law better than a literary scholar not because he applies special rules for the interpretation of laws, but because he possesses a greater degree of directly relevant knowledge. To put it more precisely, Aristotle's thesis, when applied to hermeneutics, should therefore be that every interpretative problem can only be solved within a context of specific relevant prior knowledge.[293]

The significance of Gadamer's hermeneutic circle for interpretation in both disciplines cannot be overlooked here. Gadamer himself assumes the close affinity that originally linked *philological* hermeneutics with *juridical* hermeneutics: "The split runs through legal interpretation also, in that discovering the meaning of a legal text and discovering how to apply it in a particular legal instance are not two separate actions, but one unitary process."[294] He sees, indeed, the common ground between literary and juridical hermeneutics in the fact that for both, understanding the text also simultaneously enables "its application in the concrete moment of interpretation:"[295] "The meaning of a law that emerges in its normative application is fundamentally no different from the meaning reached in understanding a text."[296] According to Gadamer, pre-understanding and the transmission of texts, which must be understood differently in each new context, form the general, which is why "understanding, then, is a special case of applying something universal to a particular situation."[297] With this view, Gadamer departs from Schleiermacher by recognising the supremacy of the text. The text is always the central object of legal hermeneutics, even if it is interpreted teleologically or, as can be the case with

---

[291] Gröschner (1982), here: p. 623.

[292] Stiening (2024), here: p. 7.

[293] Hirsch (1972), p. 7.

[294] Gadamer (1982), p. 310.

[295] Ibid., p. 309.

[296] Ibid., p. 311.

[297] Ibid., p. 312.

foundational texts, historically. Legal and philological hermeneutics thus meet here in the idea of contextualisation through prior knowledge and embedding in 'pre-existing and contemporaneous knowledge'.

Susanne Bleich puts forward the following thesis on hermeneutics as a possible point of interlinkage between law and literature: "When interpreting 'their' texts, literary scholars and lawyers are basically doing the same thing. The essential hermeneutic procedures of literary and legal hermeneutics are the same."[298] According to Bleich, both disciplines share the method of text interpretation, even if the goals cannot be identical due to the different practical claims of law and literature: "The differences between literary and legal hermeneutics all stem from the special nature of legal interpretation results, which are legally binding for the citizens concerned and thus have a direct (and possibly massive) impact on the reality of people's lives."[299] The only difference, according to Bleich, is that the writer is only confronted with *one* text, which is completed in the reception process, whereas the lawyer is confronted with *two* texts: that of the norm and that of the practical case, which is to be subsumed under the norm. The freedom of interpretation is therefore much broader for literature than for law, which remains bound to the contingency of the concrete application of the law.[300] In other words, legal interpretation, in contrast to literary interpretation, is significantly restricted by its purposefulness, i.e. by its imperative of 'shall' or 'may not'.

Sebastian Speth objects to Bleich's juxtaposition of two texts in legal interpretation and a single text in literary hermeneutics, arguing that Bleich's analysis ignores the aesthetic aspect brought into play by Hans Robert Jauß, namely that of the genre conventions of literature.[301] This 'two-track approach' to literary interpretation is also defended by Manfred Frank, who argues that it must include "the entirety of the socio-cultural codes of an epoch" in the interpretation process.[302]

A contribution by Reinhart Herzog entitled "Zum Verhältnis von Norm und Narrativität in den applikativen Hermeneutiken" summarises the reflections of the ninth colloquium of the research group 'Poetik und Hermeneutik' ('Poetics and Hermeneutics'), which took place from 25 to 27 May 1978 in Bad Homburg, about the overlapping of legal and literary hermeneutics in the form of a comparative triad (Table 3.1).[303]

This triad shows once again that both disciplines are concerned with making texts accessible, albeit with different aims and effects.

Bernhard Schlink, himself a writer and lawyer, refers to this when he points to the obvious common denominator of literature and law, which arises from the fact that both disciplines deal with texts that consist of words and require interpretation.

---

[298] Bleich (1989), here: p. 3197.

[299] Ibid.

[300] Ibid., p. 3198.

[301] Speth (2024), here: pp. 240–241.

[302] Frank (1982), p. 123.

[303] Herzog (1981), here: p. 436.

Table 3.1 Hermeneutics law/literature (Alexandra Juster)

	Subject of interpretation	Standard	Application
Law	Case	Legal norm	Judgement
Literature	Literary work	Aesthetic norm	Aesthetic judgement

He notes the following: "The interest in the interpretation of standardised texts, as if they were literary texts, starts with the obvious fact that both are texts that require interpretation."[304] Oskar Pfeiffer, Ernst Strouhal, and Ruth Wodak agree with Schlink's analysis when they state that legal interpretation means "equating the reality conveyed by everyday language with the linguistic reality in the law."[305] According to Schlink, a further methodological similarity lies in grammatical and teleological hermeneutics, which in law refers to the wording of the text and the intention of the legislator, while in literature the difference between author-related and text-related interpretation is emphasised:

> The arguments for and against the idea associated with the concept of formalism that the meaning of a text lies in its words, and for and against the idea associated with the concept of intentionalism that it lies in the motives and intentions of the author, correspond to each other, whether they are put forward by legal scholars or literary scholars.[306]

In the spirit of Schlink, Christian Hiebaum refers to interdisciplinary points of intersection which—in contrast to subjective intentionalism that refers to the intentions of the author or the legislator—primarily refer to the text, taking into account linguistic conventions, cultural parameters, and intertextual correlations.[307] Klaus Röhl explains the parallels between author-related text interpretation and subjective legal interpretation, between text-related hermeneutics and objective legal interpretation, as well as between reception-oriented text interpretation and the view in structuring legal theory that the legal text is comparable to an incomplete form to be filled in by the user of the law.[308] In a similar way, Denis Thouard establishes the connection between law and literature by assuming that both disciplines conduct "discussions about a specific case or text."[309] What they have in common is the judgement that both the judge and the literary scholar make about a case or a text, taking into account subjective (legislative and authorial intention) and objective (textual/grammatical) criteria. The purpose and temporal contingency of judgements are to be evaluated differently: legal texts are interpreted in this sense to the effect that they are to be applied concretely and empirically to a specific case as soon as possible in response to a real need. In contrast, literary texts are discussed again and again, interpreted and categorised in an endless series of successive judgements.

---

[304] Schlink (2013), p. 277.

[305] Pfeiffer et al. (1987), p. 15.

[306] Cf. Schlink (2013), p. 278.

[307] Hiebaum (2015), here: pp. 155–162.

[308] Röhl (2020), here: pp. 416–417. Cf. in more detail: Augsberg (2009), pp. 100–101; Schmidt (1973), pp. 150 ff; Müller et al. (1997), pp. 31–36.

[309] Thouard (2020), here: p. 255.

Jurisprudence is contingently orientated towards the practical resolution of cases, while literature is conjecturally orientated towards indefinite further development. What law and literature have in common is the further development of the norm through the emergence of subsequent practical cases (jurisprudence) and the further development of textual judgements through the series of subsequent textual interpretations and criticisms.[310]

All these reflections on the relationship between law and literature show that Gadamer's triad of *understanding - interpretation - application* underpins both disciplines: the interpretation of a text presupposes its understanding, and understanding is already the beginning of interpretation as a prerequisite for application: in law, it is about the application of the norm to the concrete 'case', about the process of understanding both the facts or the course of events and the abstract norm; in literature, it is about understanding and interpreting a text to evaluate it. In both disciplines, the success of the hermeneutic process of understanding is determined by prior knowledge, which for Gadamer results from the questions the interpreter asks of the text. For Rudolf Bultmann, this means that "literary hermeneutics [must] now also question itself through the text in questioning the text."[311] Contrastingly to legal hermeneutics, however, the first preparatory aesthetic reading of a literary text can, according to Jauß, take place entirely free of any questioning contingency.[312] However, Jauß' presupposition of a first aesthetic 'passage' for literature does not alter the hermeneutic similarities between law and literature.

For Schlink, however, a clear difference between the two disciplines can be seen in the gradation of possible social consequences of the interpretation of texts, because while the literary interpretation is at best surprising or alienating, a "new, surprising, idiosyncratic interpretation of the criminal law"[313] could land someone in prison. The responsibility for the possible consequences of subjective interpretation, for the choice and application of the hermeneutic canon and the method of interpretation, is therefore much greater for the lawyer than for the writer, insofar as it has concrete social consequences. In this sense, as Karl-Ludwig Kunz and Mona Martino emphasise, the danger of judicial interpretation of the law lies in the inaccuracy of human decisions, which is difficult to eliminate due to the inevitable interference of feeling, emotion, and psychology: "It is therefore conscious and unconscious prejudices, convictions and intuitions that lead the court to judge in one way and not in another. A certain proximity between this understanding of the psychology of judicial decision-making and hermeneutics as a method of judicial decision-making is obvious."[314] It is evident to assume that literary interpretation is possibly subject to even greater subjective influences than legal hermeneutics due to the imprecision of the hermeneutic canon. However, the consequences of literary

---

[310] Cf. ibid., pp. 255–269.

[311] Bultmann (1961), p. 228.

[312] Cf. Jauß (1981), p. 475.

[313] Schlink (2013), p. 278.

[314] Kunz and Martino (2006), p. 134.

subjectivity cannot be given the same weight as legal errors of interpretation. Pierre Bourdieu refers to this fact when he emphasises the limited autonomy of legal hermeneutics as a purpose-bound practice compared to the greater freedom of literature: “Unlike literary or philosophical hermeneutics, the theoretical practice of interpreting legal texts is not an end in itself; it is directly oriented towards practical goals and capable of determining practical effects, but it pays for its effectiveness by limiting its autonomy.”[315] Contrastingly, legal systems are strictly hierarchically structured and subject to the interpretation of the law, which in turn is regulated by legal norms and hierarchical control to enforce the highest degree of legal certainty.[316] According to Bourdieu, the purpose-bound imperatives of law also affect the division of roles between the doctrinaire legal hermeneutics, which tend to focus on the syntax of legal texts (legal theorists and professors), and the judges, who are concerned with the pragmatics of the concrete application of the law: “There is every reason to believe that the tendency to emphasise the syntax of the law is more likely to be found among theorists and professors, while attention to pragmatics is more likely to be found among judges.”[317] In comparison, literary hermeneutics appears to be much more open and indeterminate, as it is not orientated towards normative guidelines and therefore finds it difficult to arrive at a uniform practice. As Bourdieu notes, however, judicial arbitrariness cannot be ruled out despite the normative narrowing of legal interpretation practice: “Given the extraordinary elasticity of the texts, sometimes to the point of indeterminacy or ambiguity, the hermeneutic operation of the *declaratio* has immense freedom.”[318] The polysemy of legal texts often forces the judge to *extensio*, *restrictio* or analogy in order to solve a specific case,[319] which is why, according to my thesis, a space of hermeneutic blurring opens up for the interpretation of both legal and literary texts, which connects both disciplines.

Finally, reference should be made to Hans Müller-Seidl’s examination not only of the theoretical question of the common points of intersection between law and literature, but above all the practical linking of literary and legal knowledge in texts, which will be of particular importance for the further investigation. According to Müller-Seidl, to understand interdisciplinary intersections in their entirety, the focus must not only be on the text itself but must also be directed towards the “historical side of the ‘matter’,” i.e. *the text must be related to the corresponding background knowledge*, whereby it is important to plausibly “link knowledge about the text with the background knowledge in question. This cannot mean anything other than providing the justification for what you are bringing together, and that can be many things.”[320] The linking and integration of ‘other knowledge’ “remains to be done on

[315] Bourdieu (1986), here: p. 4.

[316] See Zippelius’ concept of ‘circularity’: Zippelius (2006), p. 58.

[317] Bourdieu (1986), p. 6.

[318] Ibid., p. 8.

[319] Cf. ibid.

[320] Müller-Seidl (1986), pp. 88–89.

a case-by-case basis, indeed, almost from sentence to sentence."[321] This is precisely where my thesis comes in: it is not possible to analyse a literary text profitably in terms of legal discourse if the legal knowledge necessary for a better understanding is not concurrently conveyed.

If one now attempts to summarise the essential similarities and differences between law and literature from a hermeneutical point of view, it becomes apparent that the differences essentially lie at the level of reception and function, while a considerable number of similarities can be emphasised at the methodological level.

The main divergences lie in the different social functions of law and literature, namely, in the fact that the person applying the law must apply abstract norms to real-life situations with concrete effects while ensuring the greatest possible legal certainty (subsumption). It is about doing justice to the duty to preserve social peace and responsibly assessing the consequences of the concrete application of the law. In this respect, the judicial decision has a far greater responsibility than literary scholars, who have greater freedom of interpretation simply because they can decide between subjective and objective canons of interpretation. The literary interpretation offered is one of many in a long chain of earlier interpretations. There is no objection to a possible, in individual cases even radical, contradiction to earlier or future interpretations. On the other hand, the requirement of legal certainty demands the preservation of standardised interpretation guidelines by tying the interpreter to precedents and a strongly binding canon of interpretation. The evaluation criteria for a 'good' or 'bad' hermeneutic achievement will lie in the success or failure of the concrete case solution for the legal decision, while aesthetic and literary-theoretical criteria will be in the foreground for literature.

As already emphasised, the differences between law and literary studies just listed are contrasted by essential methodological similarities in text interpretation, which can be made fruitful for interdisciplinary work. The cornerstone of this interdisciplinary connection is Hans Gadamer's concept of the hermeneutic circle if the hermeneutic process is viewed objectively in relation to the text. The triad of *understanding - interpreting - applying* applies to law as well as to literature. The prior knowledge and judgement of the legal interpreter correspond to the intertextual references and prior knowledge of the literary text interpreter. The text as the basic building block of both disciplines cannot be understood in isolation from its historicity and from other texts. Likewise, the process of textual meaning formation through the conclusion from the whole or general to the particular through the increasing narrowing and filtering of meanings as well as through back-and-forth reading processes is common to law and literature. If we consider the subjective dimension of interpretation, i.e. the relationship between author/text and norm/intention of the legislator, it becomes clear that both disciplines recognise this and perceive it as problematic.

As has already been emphasised several times, interdisciplinary counterfactual work requires knowledge of both disciplines to be effective at all. Hence, before we

[321] Ibid., p. 90.

get to the actual 'counterfactual' investigation as a method, we must first clarify what 'counterfactual' actually *is* and how 'counterfactual thinking' works. This is the focus of the following section.

3.4 Counterfactuality

Based on the 'counterfactual' representation of history in literature as a *deviating historical narrative*, "terms such as 'uchrony', 'uchronian fiction', 'alternative history', 'parahistorical' novel'"[322] or 'thought experiment' also circulate alongside the term 'counterfactual'.[323] In his volume, *Kontrafaktik der Gegenwart* (2021), Michael Navratil attempts to test the concept of counterfactuality in contemporary political literature and arrives at a literature-specific re-adaptation of the term as "[…] significant variations of real-world factual material within fictional media."[324] In order to give meaning to this formula and to work out the concept of counterfactuality, the concept of *fictionality* must first be defined as a literary-theoretical concept to be able to determine the relationship between fiction and reality—both in the relationship between text and reality and in the relationship between text and reader.

3.4.1 On the Relationship Between Fiction and Fact

In the German Duden, fiction is equated with 'invention' or 'false assumption'.[325] In the lexicon of the humanities, the same term is associated with 'pure invention' or 'erroneously false assumption'.[326] The concept of fiction in literary studies does not coincide with the colloquial equation of fiction with lies or false invention but attempts to place the artistic imagination in an appropriate relationship to reality and the recipient, i.e. the reader. Fictions attempt to "contradict the underlying reality in their own world"[327] and ask how the reader can recognise the fiction or how the fiction relates to reality without, however, being considered a 'lie'. Put simply, it could also be argued that poets do not lie as long as they do not falsely claim to be telling the truth.[328] Franck Zipfel poses the question of what is meant by 'reality' and refers in this regard to Nelson Goodman and Umberto Eco, who subsume our everyday experiences and expert knowledge under the term '*everyday reality*':

[322] Widmann (2009), pp. 14–15.

[323] Danneberg (2015), p. 422.

[324] Navratil (2021), p. 85.

[325] Dudenredaktion (2020), p. 452.

[326] Reinalter and Brenner (2011), p. 181.

[327] Albrecht (2020), p. 148.

[328] Cf. Sidney (1971), p. 52.

> According to Goodman, everyday reality is what is considered real or actual by the members of a society. The knowledge of what is considered real is made up of knowledge about different parts of different versions of the world. An extended world version of this everyday reality includes not only our active experiential knowledge that has emerged from our life experiences, but also the so-called expert knowledge that is passively available to us in the sense of the linguistic division of labour. U. Eco calls this comprehensive knowledge an 'encyclopaedia'.[329]

Aristotle attempts to solve the fiction/reality dilemma with the assumption of literary mimesis, i.e. the writers imitate reality, whereby they are not "bound by the law of historical truth, but by the law of poetic probability."[330] In fact, Aristotle formulated the difference between fiction and reality as early as the fourth century BC as follows: "For the historian and the poet do not differ from each other in that the one communicates in verse and the other in prose […]; they differ rather in that the one communicates what really happened, the other what might have happened."[331] According to Aleida Assmann, Aristotle's concession of poetic freedom assures the writer "the right to the independent legality of his work and yet guarantees the close reference to reality of the imitation."[332] In contrast to currents that look for linguistically linguistic characteristics as signs of fictionality,[333] current literary scholarship favours the reception-specific thesis on the one hand—according to the principle of convention that authors do not lie as long as they do not claim to be telling the truth—and on the other hand attempts to determine the correlation between fiction[334] and reality, a concern that is particularly evident in contemporary literature, which often deals with real-world situations.[335] Gil Charbonnier and Franck Petit confirm this growing tendency in contemporary literature to incorporate real facts into the diegesis: "Literary fiction tends to incorporate more reality, stretching the conventional procedures of the novel and modifying the contribution made by the imagination."[336] If one follows Christine Künzel, two key points of the concept of fictionality must be emphasised in view of the necessary definition of the fiction/fact relationship:

> 1. the thesis, based on Iser's considerations, that reality and fiction are by no means to be regarded as opposing concepts, but rather that fiction stands in a relational relationship to reality and 2. the concept of the so-called fiction contract, which describes a pact between text and reader in which the question of truth status is suspended.[337]

---

[329] Zipfel (2001), p. 75.

[330] Cf. Assmann (1980), here: p. 9.

[331] Martínez and Scheffel (2019), p. 13.

[332] Cf. Assmann (1980), pp. 9–10.

[333] Cf. Hamburger (1977).

[334] Cf. on this Martínez and Scheffel (2019), pp. 11–22 and pp. 184–186 (bibliographical references).

[335] See in particular Michael Navratil's volume on contemporary political literature: Navratil (2021).

[336] Charbonnier and Petit (2023), p. 25.

[337] Künzel (2015), here: p. 174.

In particular, Wolfgang Iser's relational understanding of fictionality can be made fruitful for explaining the concept of counterfactuality by understanding the relationship between fiction and reality not as mutually exclusive but, on the contrary, as correlating with one another: "Therefore, the fictional could be qualified as a peculiar transitional form that always shoves between the real and the imaginary for the purpose of their mutual connectivity."[338] Iser understands this to mean that real facts are 'faked' in fiction, while non-real facts are imagined in fiction. This creates a correlation between fiction and reality through fabrication on the one hand and between fabrication and fiction through imagination on the other.[339] Iser's view corresponds with Michael Navratil's explanations of the concept of the counterfactual, which will be discussed in more detail later, as a 'reflection' of real facts in fiction. To illustrate this counterfactual relationship between "real object and object of the narrative",[340] Christoph Rodiek presents a striking example based on Napoleon, which is also useful for our purposes:

> The name 'Napoleon' refers in principle to the real person Napoleon, i.e. to that individual of empirical reality who belongs to the reader's encyclopaedic knowledge base. Where the counterfactual Napoleon (Nk) appears incompatible with the real Napoleon (Nr) in terms of certain characteristics, the corresponding Nr characteristics are neutralised during the reading in such a way that a homogeneous Nk is created as a fictional figure. On the one hand, the 'fusion' of Nk and Nr is only an as-if fusion; on the other hand, it is only valid for the duration of the reading. *In fact, the real and counterfactual Napoleon coexist in the reader's consciousness as clearly distinguishable entities* [author's emphasis].[341]

However, this *awareness of clearly distinguishable real and counterfactual variables* can only arise in the readers if they are aware of the real facts as only then is it possible for them to recognise any counterfactual deviations from this reality in the fiction. In other words, to be able to recognise counterfactual law in fictional texts at all, the reader must be given knowledge of real law.

Relatedly, Ralf Klausnitzer distinguishes between the possible coexistence in fiction of genuinely *fictional* (e.g. Gregor Samsa in Kafka's *The Metamorphosis*), *real-world*, or *pseudo-real* objects[342] (e.g. attributes that alienate a real person but still allow them to be recognised, such as the character Henrik Högens in Klaus Mann's *Mephisto: Roman einer Karriere* (1936) [engl. *Mephisto: Story of a rising star*] which is recognisable as an alienation of the real actor Gustaf Gründgen). Literary fiction does not exist in a vacuum far removed from reality, but rather, as Frank Zipfel points out, incorporates elements of the real world: "Fictional stories are never entirely fictional",[343] they are "always related to the real world in one way or another."[344] In addition to being entirely fictional, they can also refer to real or

[338] Iser (1983a), here: p. 150.

[339] Cf. Henrich and Iser (1983), pp. 121–125.

[340] Zipfel (2001), p. 101.

[341] Rodiek (1993), p. 273.

[342] Klausnitzer (2008), pp. 217–218.

[343] Zipfel (2001), p. 79.

[344] Klausnitzer (2008), p. 82.

pseudo-real objects or people.[345] Nathalie Jacoby sees the integration of fictional *and* factual elements as a general characteristic of literature.[346]

Paul Ricœur reminds us that the world of fiction is the world of the text, which in turn projects the world, whereby fiction necessarily 'refers' to it: "the power that the work possesses to project itself outside itself and to give birth to a world that would truly be the 'thing' referred to by the text. This internal dynamic and external projection constitute what I call the work of the text."[347] Käthe Hamburger seems to use the terms 'reality' and 'truth' synonymously when she postulates that the real world naturally flows into the fictional poiesis:

> As the opposite of fiction, in the sense of literary fiction, this concept of truth contains the sense of reality, it signifies the truth of reality. It is the relationship between poetry and reality that has always ex- or implicitly underpinned theoretical considerations of poetry and has largely determined discussions of poetic truth.[348]

Michel Foucault, as Arne Klawitter comments, explains the relationship between fiction and fact using his concept of discourse as a mechanism for producing things through language: "For Foucault, [...] the condition for things to appear (in language) is the organising principle of fiction."[349] Klawitter goes on to explain that Foucault sees literature, on the one hand, as a space of possibility in which the boundaries of the unspeakable can be transgressed, and on the other hand, as a medium that has the ability to undermine the blind spots of 'non-discourse'.[350] Even if there is a relative consensus that both real and fictional facts can flow into fiction without calling into question the status of fiction itself, the difficulty of drawing the line between fiction and reality is by no means a thing of the past, as Aleida Assmann aptly summarises: "Fiction and reality: in literary studies there is hardly a more vague, common and at the same time more controversial pair of terms. Both are closely dependent on each other; the problem of fiction cannot be thought, described or evaluated without reference to an image of reality, however concealed it may be."[351] Wolfgang Iser and Dieter Henrich are also aware of the indeterminacy of the concept of fiction when they attempt to define it: "Fiction, it seems, cannot be isolated, but must be made comprehensible in the context of other basic terms. These include above all 'imagination' and 'reality', but also hallucination, dream, illusion and deception."[352] Apparently, fiction is here to be negatively defined, that is, defined by what it is not.

---

[345] Zipfel understands pseudo-real objects as "objects borrowed from reality but significantly modified" (Zipfel 2001, p. 98).

[346] Jacoby (2005), p. 18.

[347] Ricœur (1991), pp. 17–18.

[348] Hamburger (1979), p. 94.

[349] Klawitter (2020), here: p. 113.

[350] Ibid., pp. 113–118.

[351] Assmann (1980), p. 7.

[352] Henrich and Iser (1983), here: p. 9.

On the side of the reception and acceptance of literature as fictional, without devaluing it as a brazen lie, the view has prevailed in literary theory that it is a matter of a certain "mode of reception and communication",[353] on the basis of which a tacit (fictitious) agreement is reached between text and reader to recognise the fictional text as such,[354] without accusing it of being deceptive. The act of reception itself, which Rainer Warning understands as a "confrontation of the recipient with a model of reality",[355] is supplemented by a conscious 'so-doing-as-if' on the part of the reader to recognise a text as fictional, but not as a lie. Dieter Henrich compares this approach with Kant's postulate of awareness that it is not about truth, but about how we deal with it.[356] John Searle made an important contribution to the development of conventional theories of fictionality—i.e. to the assumption of a convention between author and reader according to which fiction is not an act of knowing deception—with his thesis that the author of a fictional text does create the appearance of an illocutionary act—"the author of a work of fiction pretends to perform a series of illocutionary acts, normally of the representative type"[357]—but does not in fact perform them, and therefore cannot be assumed to have the intention to lie: "What distinguishes fiction from lies is the existence of a separate set of conventions which enables the author to go through the motions of making statements which he knows to be not true even though he has no intention to deceive."[358] To describe the state of the reader who participates in the 'trick' of fiction, Kendall Walton later develops the so-called 'make-believe' theory, according to which the recipient plays with the fictional truth as if in a game according to implicit rules. He formulates his basic idea as follows:

> In order to understand paintings, plays, films, and novels, we must first look at dolls, hobbyhorses, toy trucks and teddy bears. The activities in which representational works of arts are embedded, and which give them their point are best seen as continuous with children's games of make-believe. Indeed, I advocate regarding these activities as games of make-believe themselves, and I shall argue that representational works function as props in such games, as dolls and teddy bears serve as props in children's games.[359]

Without relying on Walton's 'make-believe' theory, Frank Zipfel assumes that the reader "believes the text to be true for the time of its reception."[360] While Walton argues in favour of a permanent assumption and acceptance of fiction, Zipfel advocates a temporary assumption of truth, limited to the duration of reading. Samuel Coleridge and Umberto Eco advocate a similar correspondence between text and

353 Anderegg (1983), here: p. 155.

354 See also Warning (2013), here: pp. 194–206.

355 Ibid., p. 205.

356 Henrich (2013), here: p. 516.

357 Searle (1975), here: p. 329.

358 Ibid., p. 326.

359 Walton (1990), p. 11. See also Currie (1990). For more detail on Walton's make-believe theory, see Bareis (2008), pp. 19–48.

360 Zipfel (2001), p. 277.

recipient by assuming that readers consciously suspend their disbelief in the fiction—"willing suspension of disbelief" (Coleridge)[361]—or that it is a "fictional agreement" (Eco), based on which the author and reader make an agreement for the duration of the reading that the former will indicate the fiction to the reader through textual, paratextual, or contextual signals and the latter will not question it for its truth value.[362]

Umberto Eco also brings into play the idea that the recipient should regard fictions as closed worlds that are not dissimilar to the real world, but ontologically reflect only a small part of the real world: "In reality, fictional worlds *are* parasites of the actual one, but they are in effect 'small worlds' which bracket most of our competence of the actual world and allow us to concentrate on a finite, enclosed world, very similar to ours but ontologically poorer."[363] Nursan Celik explains Eco's concept of the 'contractual relationship' between reader and author as the '*reality principle*', according to which "for a fictional text, everything that is not described within the text as deviating from reality or even fundamentally different is unspokenly taken for granted and completed."[364] For Kendall Walton, Eco's concept of contract has the advantage of freeing the author from the obligation to explain "what is assumed to be fictionally true […] in a fictional narrative without this having to be explicitly stated at the textual level."[365] For John Searle, however, the fictional character of the reading already results from the author's speech act, which deviates from the usual rules: "Now, what makes fiction possible, I suggest, is a set of extralinguistic, non-semantic conventions that break the connection between words and the world."[366]

Lutz Danneberg now attempts to reduce the multitude of theories and modes of reception highlighted above to a simpler denominator: "A representation classified as non-fictional on the basis of a certain knowledge can in principle […] also be treated as fictional – and vice versa",[367] thus fulfilling the tacit agreement between text and reader.

Although there appears to be a relatively broad consensus that authors do not have to justify to readers whether literary fiction is true or not, the greater difficulty seems to lie in defining the term itself. In fact, there is no standardised ontological definition of the term 'fiction'. Attempts to define it oscillate between the pragmatic approach of a use-specific contextualisation to characterise the fictional and the understanding of fictionality as an intellectual transgression that enables human thought to go beyond ontological reality.[368] In this sense, the concept of fiction

---

[361] Engell and Bate (1983), p. 6.

[362] Eco (1994), p. 75.

[363] Ibid., p. 85.

[364] Celik (2024), p. 188.

[365] Ibid., p. 189. Cf. also Walton (1990), p. 144.

[366] Searle (1975), p. 326.

[367] Danneberg (2006b), here: p. 40.

[368] Cf. Iser (1983b), pp. 547–557.

serves to conceptually outline the transfer of the ontologically real into the imagined and the thought and enables access to what Kant seeks to grasp with the concept of the postulate of pure practical reason, namely the statement that no confirmation by empirical evidence can be expected for the "existence of supersensible objects and states."[369]

When Alexander Bareis limits fictional truth to the intradiegetic reference to truth, he overlooks the essential question of the relationship between extradiegetic reality and intradiegesis, which will particularly concern us in the following counterfactual investigation: "Fictional truth denotes the relationship of statements about the represented world to the represented world, and not to non-fictional reality."[370] Michael Navratil counters this apparent shortcoming with Marc Chinca's pragmatic approach, which can be made fruitful for the counterfactual analysis insofar as he defines fictionality "from its 'seat in life', as a function of the relation between the speech act and its situation of use. This situation, and not linguistic characteristics of the text, is ultimately decisive."[371] Navratil celebrates Chinca's pragmatic understanding of fiction as particularly suitable for texts that "combine fictionality with a clear reference to the world [...]",[372] as will be the case with the texts to be examined in this work, since the ultimate aim is to relate the real-world, extradiegetic law to the intradiegetic law in order to recognise the counterfactual 'delta' (Δ), i.e. the degree of divergence between narrated and real law.

This raises the question of whether the same factuality can be claimed for legal norms and legal systems as for other real-world 'facts', whereby this question seems even more justified as legal norms are usually analysed in terms of their *normative* effect rather than their factual effect. Or, should we rather claim that the question is wrong, and that the *normative nature* of law also means its factuality? Considerations on this question will now be made in the following section.

3.4.2 On the Factuality of the Law

Concerning the reception of real law in a fictional text, the question arises as to whether the law is to be regarded as 'real' or whether, due to its written nature, it shares the debate about fictionality and reality with literature. The law has an inherently normative character with the function of regulating factually real conditions and situations. Hence, it is not without reason that the difference between the norm—which is strictly bound to reality and its concrete enforceability—on the one hand, and polymorphous literature, which is open to the imagination, on the other, is often emphasised. Philippe Ségur confirms this when he ascribes to law the

[369] Guyer (1997), here: p. 9.

[370] Bareis (2008), p. 65.

[371] Chinca (2003), p. 313.

[372] Navratil (2021), pp. 89–90.

function of producing truth, while literature produces illusion: "If literary fiction creates illusion, the law seems to create reality."[373] Kristin Albrecht denies, with a few exceptions, the fictional character of law, insofar as legal norms are abstract and normative and are also intended to have a real effect. The fact that the legislator nevertheless resorts to fictional legal texts in certain cases results, on the one hand, from its freedom to enact rules regardless of whether "something has really happened and is therefore true or not",[374] and, on the other hand, from the imperative of certain legal needs. In this sense, the legislator may issue regulations that do not correspond to reality. In such cases, the legislator generally uses the term 'deemed' to characterise the fictional nature of a legal norm. As an example of this, Möllers cites Section 1923 (2) of the German Civil Code, which also grants the right of inheritance to unborn children: "Anyone who was not yet alive at the time of the inheritance but was already conceived is deemed to have been born before the inheritance."[375] Here, the legislator uses the fiction of (not yet) birth for the unborn life to enable the application of the law at all. In such cases, according to Angela Condello and Tiziano Toracca, they resort to fiction without being accused of lying.[376] According to the two authors, both literary and legal texts elude the parameters of truth or lies because they create another, a third reality: "In other words, they are not judged on the basis of truth or falsehood, but construct another reality."[377] As in Möllers' example, the law produces a concrete effect because, as Michele Spanò and Massimo Vallerani explain, it assumes something false (namely that unborn life is alive) as true: "If it produces effects by creating an alternative reality, it is because the false is taken as true."[378]

Normally, however, the aim is not to create a self-created world but to prescribe reality *as it should be* by means of abstract norms, i.e. norms that can be applied to as many situations as possible. Similarly, the legal subject is not expected to co-operatively adhere to an unspoken agreement with the legal text, but rather to compulsorily comply with the legal norm, the statement of which implies a concrete reality-based will.[379] In other words, reality, i.e. the factuality of law (in democracies), is created through the process of positive *norm production,* which itself is based on a constitution adopted and recognised by a majority and at the same time presupposes its enforceability. According to Habermas, the facticity of law is therefore artificially created: it arises through the enforceability of norms, which obtain their legal validity through "the socially integrative force of the 'concurring and united will of all' free and equal citizens."[380] However, this common will is not just

[373] Ségur (2017), here: p. 110.
[374] Möllers (2023), p. 140.
[375] Ibid., p. 141.
[376] Cf. Condello and Toracca (2021), here: p. 207.
[377] Ibid., p. 208.
[378] Spanò and Vallerani (2016), here: p. 10.
[379] Albrecht (2020), pp. 156–160.
[380] Habermas (1996), p. 32.

any will, but "the legitimate will that stems from presumptively rational self-legislation of politically autonomous citizens."[381] Here, Habermas addresses the legitimacy[382] of positive law,[383] which is 'true' in the sense of 'valid' because it is validly 'set' by democratically appointed authorities according to certain rules: "The validity of positive law is in the first instance characterized tautologically, in that the law is considered to be whatever acquires the force of law on the basis of legally valid procedures and retains its legal force for the time being [...]."[384] In his legal figure of the *normative power of the factual*, Georg Jellinek describes this legal validity as resulting from the coincidence of three characteristics of legal norms: 1. they determine the external behaviour of people towards each other; 2. they emanate from external authority; and 3. their binding force is guaranteed by external powers.[385] For Jellinek, norms are factually normative, i.e. binding, "if their existence and validity is affirmed by both the rulers and the ruled."[386] Hans Kelsen also emphasises *the validity as proof of the factuality* of the norm: "In this sense, law is a normative coercive order. *Its specific existence is its validity.*"[387] In agreement with Jellinek and Habermas, for Kelsen legal facticity, i.e. validity, arises from the fact that norms are established under certain conditions and develop binding effectiveness: "One is that the law is *established* through acts qualified in a certain way (*ius positivum*), the other is that the law must be *effective* to a certain degree. This is the only sense in which one can speak of a 'normative force of the factual'."[388] Legal norms must therefore, as Tim König summarises, "simultaneously be able to bring about a willingness to follow through factual coercion and insight through legitimate validity."[389] *Only when the coercion of norms, i.e. their enforceability, is legally secured and institutionalised we can speak of de facto law.*[390] Judith Hahn aptly summarises this idea of legal effectiveness: "A norm is effective if it is obeyed or if its breach is sanctioned. A norm is ineffective if it is not observed, but this remains without consequences insofar as its violation does not result in sanctions."[391]

---

[381] Ibid., p. 33.

[382] König (2012), p. 10.

[383] From a positivist-legalist perspective, state authority has a monopoly "on law-making and the development of law in relation to social regulatory systems such as religion, morality, custom and practice" (Wieacker 1985, here: p. 355). In this sense, the law is *legal* if, as Raiser explains, "it has been correctly enacted by a competent body with the power to legislate and has not been revoked and is compatible with higher-ranking law" (Raiser 2007, p. 237). However, legality does not yet mean legal validity: for this, the law must be effective, i.e. enforceable.

[384] Habermas (1996), p. 29.

[385] Jellinek (1921), here: p. 333.

[386] Ibid., p. 337. Cf. also: Grimmer (1971), pp. 11–17.

[387] Kelsen (1965), here: p. 465.

[388] Ibid.

[389] König (2012), p. 11.

[390] Cf. Habermas (1996), pp. 171–172 (*principle of binding the judiciary to existing law*).

[391] Hahn (2019b), here: p. 190.

In other words, for a norm to be effective, actual compliance is required, which can either occur spontaneously or be enforced.

Customary law can be seen as a special form of applicable law that acquires *de facto factuality* through legitimisation. As early as the nineteenth century, Friedrich Carl von Savigny and Georg Friedrich Puchta explained customary law as a phenomenon of the 'spirit of the people', as a kind of tacit social agreement on the normative character of certain actions or rites.[392] In connection with customary law, Georg Jellinek speaks of the "normative power of the factual",[393] whose effect is based on the long-lasting repeated factual existence: "All law in a people is originally nothing but factual practice. Continuous practice generates the idea of the normative nature of this practice, and the norm itself thus appears as an authoritative commandment of the community, i.e. as a legal norm."[394] Hans Kelsen confirms the possible validity of customary law resulting from the "voluntarism" of a legal community.[395] In this sense, customary law acquires normative force through *factual existence*, which establishes its factuality. The factual 'being' of actions or circumstances thus generates, under certain conditions, 'normativity' as an expression of the factual 'existence' of a legal norm, i.e. its factuality. According to today's understanding, customary law has "a supplementary, gap-filling function in relation to codified law"[396] and derives its validity from the common conviction of the legal community (*consensus omnium*) over a longer period (*longa consuetuo*) of the binding nature of a given practice (*opinio necessitatis*). Many national legal systems and international law recognise customary law as a legitimate source of law.[397]

Both positive and customary law norms can therefore 'be', 'be there', and 'be true', in a word they *exist factually* as soon as they *apply*. Gustav Radbruch aptly summarises the principle of legal validity as an expression of *factual existence* for positive law and customary law by also clarifying that it is not the origin of the norm that is decisive, but its *concrete observation in the reality of life*, which can take place either through state coercion or through voluntary social adhesion:

> It is generally recognised today that there is no other than 'established, 'positive' law. But if the established law is to fulfil its purpose, […] the establishment of the law must belong to a will that is also able to enforce it against any opposing view of the law: *society, which speaks in customary law*, the *state, which speaks in statute law* [author's emphasis]. Even every single legal command of society or the state can only be regarded as 'valid' law if it is not 'merely on paper', but has become a rule of life, even if perhaps exceptionally broken by offences. Only that, but also everything that will be called upon to legislate sets and enforces, is valid law.[398]

---

[392] See also: Puchta (1828), pp. 139 ff. Lahusen (2019).

[393] Jellinek (1921), p. 338.

[394] Ibid., p. 339.

[395] Kelsen (1965), p. 466. Kelsen refers here to Erim (1939), p. 64.

[396] Geis (2021), here: p. 28.

[397] Cf. ibid., pp. 28–31.

[398] Radbruch (1925), pp. 33–34.

Radbruch thus makes it clear here that *the factual existence of law* and the validity of law always coincide when legal norms are effectively enforced in real life. In this context, Hans Kelsen draws an even more subtle dividing line between the validity and effectiveness of the law, since it is only the effectiveness and not the validity that confirms the existence of the norm: “It is also not superfluous to emphasise emphatically that the effectiveness of the law is not its validity. That the law is ‘valid’ means that it *is to* be obeyed or applied; that it is effective means that it *is* obeyed or applied.”[399] Kelsen’s subtle distinction between legal validity and legal effect can be well understood for the purpose of counterfactual contrasting, because for its possibility it is not relevant whether a norm is obeyed, but whether it factually *exists* or whether it *is* factual. After all, counterfactual work is about the *factual existence of legal norms* and not about the fact of norm-compliant or norm-violating behaviour. When Manfred Rehbinder claims that “normativity without factuality [...] is dead law”,[400] his incorrect use of the term factuality here contradicts the idea of the factual *existence of a legal norm*, as Hans Kelsen also seems to understand it when he separates legal validity and legal effect as two different phenomena. In this sense, Kelsen’s differentiation criterion does not refer to the factual existence of legal norms, but to their different effectiveness. Rehbinder’s statement should also be understood to mean that it is not normativity without factuality, but rather normativity without effectiveness that produces dead law.

For the sake of completeness, it should be noted that the question of the factuality of legal norms, as Judith Hahn explains, is also taken up by sociology, albeit “in a descriptive sense”,[401] in that Niklas Luhmann links legal legitimacy to the convictions of the addressees of the law. Thus, legitimacy, in the sociological sense is to be understood as the “disseminated factual conviction in the validity of law or of principles and values upon which binding decisions are based.”[402] The sociological approach excludes legal normativity as a validity factor in favour of factual acceptance in a particular legal community and is thus functionally closer to legal customary law, but without adopting its normativity. It is replaced by social acceptance, as Klaus Röhl comments: “In recent years, the term acceptance is increasingly being used for legitimacy [...] in a purely factual sense.”[403] The voluntary acceptance of rules excludes their normative character from the outset. Their compliance therefore cannot be enforced, but it can be promoted through plausibility, as Manfred Rehbinder explains: “In order to achieve factual effectiveness and not just legal validity on paper, the norm generally cannot do without appearing plausible to the norm addressees.”[404]

---

[399] Kelsen (1965), p. 467.

[400] Rehbinder (2014), p. 2.

[401] Hahn (2019a), here: p. 148.

[402] Luhmann (1985), p. 199.

[403] See Röhl (1987), p. 177.

[404] Rehbinder (2014), p. 93.

In conclusion, it can be stated that legal norms as real facts cannot be understood in the same sense as other real facts. This is because legal norms are initially abstract and at best formulated in writing in this primary state and are not 'suitable for the world'. They only enter the real world, or to put it another way, they only leave tangible traces in the space of the real world when they enter the state of actual legal validity. Only then do they acquire, as Georg Jellinek puts it, the power of the factual, only then are they *factually there* and come into question for the counterfactual contrasting of fact and fiction. In democratic state systems, the process that leads from the codification of legal norms *that do not yet exist* (which even ceases to exist in the case of customary law) to the legally binding, *de facto* (valid) norm must fulfil certain criteria for a norm to be enforceable: It must pass through a prescribed legislative procedure (e.g. adoption by parliament and the senate, according to certain quorums, etc.) by constitutionally established legislative bodies in order to regulate matters with legal force at the end of this procedure and after it has been promulgated. This also implies that the norm *must* be complied with, and that compliance can be enforced if necessary. For the purposes of the counterfactual analysis, it is irrelevant whether the real-world legal norms that are juxtaposed with the diegetic legal discourse are legally effective, i.e. whether they are actually followed. Rather, the legal validity is sufficient as an external sign of the factuality of the law. As briefly mentioned, the same conditions of factuality also apply to customary law, which differs from positive law in the way it is created: It is not positively set by legally legitimised authorities in a prescribed procedure but results from the general conviction of a legal community over a given period that certain unwritten norms are to be followed. In contrast to the sociological concept of acceptance without legal effect, a long-standing *custom* (*usage*) can acquire legal effect and form the basis of a judicial decision. However, this usually happens subordinately, namely when legal loopholes cannot be closed by positive law.

The section on the facticity of law concludes the theoretical groundwork for the planned elaboration of legal counterfactuality: the concepts of interdisciplinarity, discourse, hermeneutics, and counterfactuality have been presented in detail in preparation for interdisciplinary considerations on legal and literary studies. They were examined in more detail because their combination seems to not only be necessary but also fruitful for the methodological development that I will discuss in the following section. The aim is to develop a structured and reproducible method of counterfactual investigation and exposure of the legal discourse in literary texts, based on the conviction that knowledge of the real-world legal system referred to in the literary diegesis is a prerequisite for both a deeper understanding of the literary work itself and counterfactual contrasting in general. If no relevant knowledge is conveyed in this sense, an essential parameter of comparison is missing, which robs the process of counterfactual contrasting of its meaning. The following section therefore introduces the concept of counterfactual work, which should now be facilitated by the prior theoretical knowledge already imparted—this is intriguingly reminiscent of Gadamer's hermeneutic circle (sic!).

3.4.3 *The Concept of Counterfactuality*

When examining the concept of 'counterfactuality', one must begin by looking to counterfactual historiography. It is *the* discipline that practises the reference of fiction to non-diegetic real facts, whereby the distance between historical and fictional truth can vary. In this context, Jürgen H. Petersen emphasises the special position of the historical novel among literary genres: "Such intermediate areas, such as those occupied by the historical novel, are of course special cases, which in turn are due to the fact that one and the same language can name both fictional and real objects."[405] Despite the decided focus of his counterfactual investigation on contemporary literature, Michael Navratil therefore does not fail to point out that it is historical research that is particularly well suited to counterfactual experiments, as it has at its disposal

> a high degree of conventionality, i.e. familiarity and intersubjective commitment. Accordingly, if there is a deviation from historical facts, it can be reasonably reliably assumed that this deviation will be recognised as such and that the specific reception process of the counterfactual – i.e. the comparison between the fictional and real world regarding specific individual elements – will be initiated.[406]

Erhard Schütz is succinct when he defines the phenomenon of counterfactuality in historical fiction as a story that takes "a different turn from that known in historiography."[407] Johannes Dillinger speaks of alternative "speculations about history that did not happen",[408] which can also be called counterfactual stories because they are invented and contradict the historically proven facts.[409] According to Karlheinz Steinmüller, an account is counterfactual if it clearly contradicts the historical facts and this "deviation from normal history" is also recognisable to the recipient.[410] Riccardo Nicolosi illustrates the technique of the counterfactual approach using the fictional thought experiment *ad absurdum*, which is deliberately used in contradiction to reality in order to invalidate illogical postulates. For Richard Ned Lebow, counterfactual thinking offers the possibility of distancing oneself from reality, thereby asking the right questions and thus making historical leaps (of thought) in historical research.[411] According to Lebow, this can be achieved through the counterfactual connection between fiction and fact: "Historical counterfactuals have the potential to build bridges between history and fiction. They may be used to interrogate and offer critical perspectives on history and social science or their intellectual foundations."[412] To shed further light on the counterfactual mechanism,

[405] Petersen (1994), p. 9.

[406] Navratil (2021), p. 71.

[407] Schütz (2013), here: p. 468.

[408] Dillinger (2015), p. 15.

[409] Cf. ibid., p. 16.

[410] Steinmüller (1999), here: pp. 45–46. Cf. also Ritter (1999), here: p. 13–16.

[411] Lebow (2009), here: pp. 57–58.

[412] Ibid., p. 69.

Nicolosi cites Malthus' thought experiment of a possible world with exponential population growth to show that this is not possible due to the earth's limited resources. Counterfactual thinking is used here as a formula of proof through thinking *a contrario*,[413] which Lutz Danneberg calls "counterfactual imaginations."[414] He points out that counterfactual ideas about "alternative historical constellations" can rewrite the course of historical events or reveal coincidences and apparent trivialities in the course of history. As an example of such a historical counterfactual imagination, Danneberg cites Blaise Pascal's thought experiment on the course of world history, in which one imagines what would have happened if Cleopatra had had a shorter nose:[415] "If Cleopatra's nose had been shorter, the face of the world would have changed."[416] It is important, as Christoph Rodiek emphasises, that this is not "an arbitrarily created 'imaginary' history", but "a 'hypothetical' past that is as plausible as possible."[417] According to Widmann, however, the criterion of plausibility is problematic for literary studies insofar as "the adaptation of the standards of historical research that endeavours to be exact" cannot apply to novelists.[418] It must be countered that the obligation to historical accuracy only applies to academic historiography, but not to the historical novel, which is allowed to vary and alienate historical data to a greater or lesser extent in its diegesis. It is therefore a confrontation between a real-scientific episteme, historiography, and a more or less fictional work, the historical novel.

Michael Navratil confirms my analysis in this context when he emphasises *that the preferred approach for historiography by no means excludes "other types of facts as the basis of counterfactuals."*[419] This sets the tone that also determines my investigation, namely that the technique of counterfactuality can also find its way into areas of knowledge other than historical research, insofar as it is always about the tension between fact and fiction, whereby neither the fact nor the fiction necessarily has to be of a historical nature in order to legitimise counterfactual reasoning. Navratil's somewhat confusing reference elsewhere that the transfer of the theory of the counterfactual from historical studies to literary studies is problematic is only seemingly contradictory to the thesis that counterfactual thinking is not limited to historical novels, as Navratil explains in an apparently contradictory manner:

> However, the orientation of a theory of counterfactuality towards historical science entails a series of problems. These problems have their common vanishing point in the fundamental dubiousness of the attempt to transfer the conditions and validity claims of a scientific-epistemic discourse to an artistic-aesthetic discourse […].[420]

---

[413] Nicolosi (2013), here: pp. 55–66.

[414] Cf. Danneberg (2006a), pp. 73–100.

[415] Danneberg (2015), p. 423.

[416] Pascal (n.d.), pp. 487-5 (internet-link in the bibliography).

[417] Rodiek (1997), p. 25. See also on the plausibility of counterfactual representations: Rusch (2012), here p. 88. Hellekson (2001), p. 1.

[418] Widmann (2009), p. 95.

[419] Navratil (2021), p. 72.

[420] Ibid., p. 65.

Eva-Maria Konrad counters this assertion by correcting that if the plausibility criterion of historical counterfactuality is asserted as an indicator of the quality of academic counterfactual historical research,[421] Navratil's rejection of a methodological point-by-point transfer of historical counterfactuality to literature is understandable, but not applicable to all projects. Even if, as Navratil argues, methodological disciplining is difficult to reconcile with the claim to autonomy of art in general and literary art in particular,[422] this is unlikely to apply to interdisciplinary work between law and literature. This assumption is supported by the fact that, if one restricts oneself to exchanging historical facts for legal ones, the claim to methodological stringency and coherence for qualitative work should in any case be upheld. For the specific purpose of counterfactual work with legal facts in the literature, Konrad's analysis not only provides supporting arguments for its legitimacy but also valuable information on how to proceed with counterfactual work, which is also transferable to non-historical epistemes and is divided into three phases: "The deviation (and thus the counterfactual antecedent), the consequences or conclusions from this deviation and the overall conception."[423] Konrad outlines a basic methodological framework that can be applied in many ways without losing any of its epistemic rigour. Considering the so-called 'minimal-rewrite-rule', according to Konrad, the deviation of the counterfactual representation appears all the more justified and "epistemically relevant" the less it deviates from the 'original' and the more logical the 'fit' of the proposed variation to the original data appears. The decisive factor here is that the overall conception of the counterfactual approach is scientifically structured and reflexive, such that relevant, new epistemic insights are produced.[424] Danneberg also refutes Navratil's fear of a lack of stringency in counterfactual work by pointing out that counterfactual imaginations, especially when they are based on epistemic knowledge sharing, are not necessarily subject to the suspicion of arbitrariness. Indeed, according to Danneberg, "it is even possible to find quality criteria that allow such imaginings to be regarded as more or less appropriate in given epistemic situations."[425] In other words, counterfactual thought experiments can lose their obvious falsity and be systematised for certain areas of knowledge. Danneberg claims this—as already explained for the facticity of law—for law, among other things, insofar as it can feign legal qualifications or effects without being recognised as obviously false, and gives some examples: "For example, one could legally treat someone born in slavery as a 'freeborn', or one could regard illegitimate children as legitimate. The law cannot bring a dead person back to life, but it can treat him as if he were still alive – *ius fingit contra factum.*"[426] Luigi Viola makes a very interesting observation on the operativity of the counterfactual in the legal field with regard to

[421] Konrad (2023), here: p. 153.

[422] Cf. Navratil (2021), p. 70.

[423] Konrad (2023), p. 154.

[424] Ibid., pp. 155–158.

[425] Danneberg (2015), p. 422.

[426] Ibid., p. 423.

the fact that court judgements necessarily speak about a past fact or set of facts, i.e. they retrospectively reconstruct past facts or sets of facts by replacing the subjective narrative of the trial participants with the legal narrative. According to Viola, this leads to a 'rewriting' of past facts: While the writer in the uchronia describes the historical events as they did not happen but could have happened, the judge rewrites the facts as they did not happen but could have happened: "Whereas the writer of an uchronia rewrites the past 'as it was not, as it could have been', the judge rewrites the disputed fact 'as it was not, as it should have been'."[427] This discrepancy between the actual facts in the past and their 'rewriting' in the judgement, taking into account the interpretation and application of the law, results in the counterfactual variation.[428] Here lies the core of the experimental idea that Danneberg and Viola assert beyond the literary-historical uchronia, and which Klausnitzer also seeks to clarify in his explanation of the concept of the counterfactual. However, the counterfactual can also be managed without experimentation by incorporating external facts into the fictional diegesis without any claim to variation, as I have tried to show using the example of Juli Zeh's novel *About People* (2023).[429] Here, the counterfactual seems like a faithful reflection of the real outside world.

The interest in counterfactual research approaches is repeatedly confirmed in science. Jon Elster, for example, argues that the counterfactual reference to possible worlds facilitates the description of the real world.[430] Hayden White points to the interest of counterfactual work on a cognitive level, namely the "realisation […] that we only recognise the *actual* when we contrast and compare it with the *imaginable*."[431] White's emphasis on contrasting the real with the imaginable as a means of cognition effectively illustrates the mechanism of counterfactual work, which Ansgar Nünning outlines as interacting referentiality of varying degrees between fiction and fact and which is characterised by the fact that "they cross the ontological boundary between fiction and reality by integrating references to real elements into a fictional context", whereby "variable mixing ratios can exist between the two."[432] At this point, reference should repeatedly be made to the concept of fiction in connection with the tension between real, semi-real, or fictional facts, which was discussed in detail in the previous chapter. Incidentally, Andreas Kablitz refers to this potential mixed relationship in fiction mentioned by Nünning when he states that in literary fiction there is a correlation between the "fictionality of the speech and the

---

[427] Viola (2023), here: p. 748.

[428] Cf. ibid., pp. 739–749.

[429] Zeh (2023).
Cf. Juster (2023).

[430] Elster (1981), p. 23.

[431] White (1991), here: p. 120.

[432] Nünning (1995), p. 46.

potential fictionality or factuality of the facts" about which statements are made.[433] As a reminder: A fictional text can describe fictional (non-existent), factual (existing in reality and sensually and empirically perceptible), or semi-real things and circumstances, whereby in case of doubt the reality or fictionality of things or circumstances is decided in favour of the latter.[434] According to Nursan Celik, semi-real objects or persons as variations of the real, which move between fiction and fact, are particularly difficult to categorise.[435] As Celik goes on to explain, the author's release from the obligation to write truth makes it possible for fiction and fact to coexist, whereby "counterfactual statements that are contrary to fact [...] can be categorised as false or true counterfactuals."[436] Kablitz comments: "Wherever persons, things or facts have to be regarded as unknown, we seem to be entitled to regard them as fictitious. The denser the references to fact become, just think of the historical novel, the more difficult it is to make the relevant decision."[437] According to Kablitz, this involves a gradual distinction between the real and historical world, "and the continuing dominance of factual reality is nowhere more evident in the fact that the knowledge we have of this world also applies in fictional texts wherever it is not explicitly questioned. (*Not least for this reason, correspondences to the factual world are also of legal relevance*, my emphasis)."[438]

However, as Andreas M. Widmann rightly emphasises, in order to be able to identify this real world as such, the reader must have knowledge of the historical facts to recognise the divergence or correspondence between fact and fiction in the story: "The references to reality made by historical novels demand that the fictional narrative plot be related back to extra-literary knowledge [...] by specifically referring to it."[439] Widmann cites the historical novel as an example here, although the divergence to be recognised between fact and fiction can also be applied to non-historical novels. What is decisive is not the type of episteme, but the type of contrast between fact and fiction, which is always possible when fictional text and the real world meet. The question to be asked here is what happens to the reference values of reality-factuality in fiction. Wolfgang Iser provides a suggestion on how to articulate the correlation between fiction (text) and reality (world), namely

---

[433] Kablitz (2014), here: p. 96. Kablitz refers here to the distinction between *fictionality* as a "characteristic of a speech for which both true and untrue claims are permissible" and *fictiveness* as a designation of the "characteristic of the objects and facts that a text contains" (Kablitz 2014, pp. 95–96).

[434] Cf. ibid., pp. 95–97.

[435] Cf. Celik (2024), pp. 171–172. By problematising semi-real things, Celik alludes to the more or less strong alienation of facts in fictions, which prove to be particularly relevant for the case law on literary artistic freedom.

[436] Ibid., p. 194.

[437] Kablitz (2014), p. 97.

[438] Kablitz (2012), p. 167.

[439] Widmann (2009), p. 31.

> as the extra-textual world […], which precedes the text as a given and generally forms its fields of reference. These can be systems of meaning, social systems and world views as well as other texts in which a specific organisation or interpretation of reality is achieved. Consequently, the real is defined as the diversity of discourses to which the author's world-orientation through the text applies.[440]

Iser identifies the 'diversity of discourses' as an indication of reality, which, as Keller points out, gives the concept of 'reality' a very elastic breadth, since everything that human society talks about can be considered real. In this sense, language is ascribed a constitutive effect insofar as the things that make up the real world are constituted through language.[441] At this point, it is easy to recognise the interface between Foucault's discourse and the fictional text, namely where real facts flow into the fictional text.[442]

To define the complex relationship between fact and fiction in literature in more detail, Carl D. Malmgren speaks of fictional and factual modes of statement and internal and external fields of reference. According to Malmgren, fictional statements can be made in texts with a purely diegetic claim to truth or factual statements with a verifiable claim to reality or a mixture of both (*factual/fictional sign vehicles*). The combination of these different intradiegetic statement modes creates a frame *of* reference that is either perceived as factually 'true' or as 'fictitiously coherent' (*frame of reference*).[443] This textual frame of reference is in turn assigned external, real-world or internal diegetic frames of reference (*fields of reference*).[444] Malmgren draws here on the theory of *frame semantics* by Marvin Minsky and Charles Fillemore, which shows how the reader deals cognitively—i.e. in the function of his previous knowledge and his individual life experience (here Gadamer is ghosting around again!)—with fact and fiction in the diegesis and how he relates them to the real world.[445] Dietrich Busse explains the nature of this *frame semantics* as follows:

> A frame/knowledge framework is a structure of knowledge in which a certain constellation of knowledge elements is grouped with reference to a structural frame core, which can also be understood as the 'object' or 'topic' of the frame, which in this perspective […] function as frame-constituting frame elements. These knowledge elements (or frame elements) are not epistemically completely 'filled' with concrete data, but function as connection points (*slots*) to which concrete ('filling', concretising) knowledge elements (so-called 'fillings', 'values' or attributions) are assigned in an epistemic contextualisation (embedding, 'filling') of the frame.[446]

---

[440] Iser (1983a), p. 123, footnote 2.

[441] See Keller (2013), pp. 26–29.

[442] Cf. Foucault (1972), pp. 22; 183.

[443] The term 'frames', derived from frame theory or frame semantics, refers to context- and situation-specific knowledge that is stored in human memory and can be retrieved as required. Frames are structures of knowledge that are based on experience, are characterised by life history, and form an individual thesaurus of precedent traps. Cf. Fraas (2000), pp. 31–45 and Busse (2012) (see especially pp. 305 ff.).

[444] Cf. Malmgren (1985), p. 27.

[445] Minsky (1992), pp. 92–134. Cf. in detail Busse (2012).

[446] Ibid., p. 563.

Jochen Strobel, Jan de Vries, and Friederike Wißmach refer to the function of these *frames* as knowledge structures that initiate the replacement, completion, supplementation or modification of prior knowledge at the moment of confrontation with the text.[447] The readers will ask themselves whether certain intradiegetic facts conform to reality or not, or what discrepancies exist between fact and fiction, and they will attempt to fill or modify the open 'gaps' with their own values and knowledge. To give a simple example, when reading Zeh's novel *About People*, the readers could ask themselves whether "Trump, Höcke and the Brexit people" are really "completely crazy" in the real world (extradiegetic truth)[448] or whether they are only to be regarded as really 'crazy' in fiction (fictional truth) and will relate their previous knowledge to this, associate values and compare the diegetic statement with their own knowledge, if necessary renew their knowledge, and consolidate or modify views they have already acquired.

Malmgren's theory also makes the extension of the counterfactual principle from the historical novel to literature plausible insofar as it explains the relationship between statements in texts that refer to real-world information, data, persons, contexts, events, etc. and their modification possibilities in the diegesis. In this context, Andreas Widmann attempts to explain the principle of counterfactuality with reference to Malmgren's theory of reference as follows:

> Counterfactuality results [...] from a specific procedure of text-internal reference to facts external to the text, which results in counterfactual statements. Such counterfactual propositions in literary texts are fictional statements of a special kind, since they, like all fictional statements, by definition have no claim to verifiability beyond the text, but within it they are externally referential in their direction and refer to facts that belong to an external field of reference and thereby deviate decidedly and deliberately from the generally recognised knowledge about these facts.[449]

While Widmann understands counterfactuals as a special form of textual pragmatics, Ralf Klausnitzer looks at counterfactual representation in literature from the perspective of experimentation, which utilises the idea of friction between fiction and imagination to open new perspectives:

> Literary texts imagine actions in fictional spaces and thus, as it were, on trial; they play out counterfactual assumptions and develop scenarios in which differentiated plans can be made, assumptions tested, and experiences formulated. In a symbolic way, they express the absent, make the invisible visible and thus allow observations that remain closed to other perspectives.[450]

While Klausnitzer sees the counterfactual as a means for representation, i.e. an instrument for gaining knowledge, Widmann describes its functional mechanism from a literary-pragmatic perspective. At this point, one may assume that Navratil is referring to Malmgren and Widmann when he states that "[...] real-world facts are

---

447 Strobel et al. (2019), here: pp. 144–146.

448 Cf. Juster (2023), pp. 78–94.

449 Widmann (2009), p. 355.

450 Klausnitzer (2008), p. VII.

used in a very specific way within the framework of a fictional medium in order to achieve aesthetic, affective or normative effects",[451] i.e. in plain language, that the real facts appear in a "significantly varied way."[452] According to Navratil, however, whether real facts that are varied or faithfully depicted in the diegesis are true cannot be assessed in general terms, but must be examined on a case-by-case basis for specific text genres or even for individual texts.[453] Lutz Danneberg proposes the technique of multidirectional access to determine whether real facts are actually counterfactually varied real facts, i.e. real facts can be viewed and interpreted from several different perspectives, while fictional worlds can only be accessed via the text itself.[454] It should be noted that for the counterfactual examination of a text, not only the distinction between 'real' and 'fictional' is important, but it is also always a matter of determining how real facts are varied in the fictional diegesis, which is why, as Navratil explains, the examination of a double reference imposes itself:

> When interpreting a counterfactual work, both its direct references to elements of the fictional world (what is stated in the work itself) and its indirect references to an extratextual reality (what these statements deviate from or conflict with in the event that they were applied to the real world) must be considered. It is precisely this tension between explicit fictional and implicit real-world reference that sets the specific counterfactual interpretation process in motion.[455]

In other words, there are two opposing areas: the fictional narrative world on the one hand, and the real outside world on the other. Between the *narrative* and the *real world* is the *text*, which can explicitly or implicitly refer to real facts. Within the diegesis, there may be fictional elements that are considered true or false within the diegesis or real facts of extradiegetic origin. These real facts can be varied in the diegesis to varying degrees, i.e. they can diverge more or less from the external world real facts. The spectrum of modulation ranges from the faithful, unaltered incorporation of real facts into the diegesis to such a strong degree that the worldly original is barely recognisable.

In my estimation, one can always speak of counterfactuality when a minimal correlation between extradiegetic real fact and the corresponding intradiegetic fact is recognisable, whereby this minimal correlation can also flourish to the maximum correlation, i.e. to the congruence of real and interdiegetic fact. In this coexistence of diegetic self-reference and external reference lies Navratil's double reference, which, as Wolfgang Künne notes, generates transfictionality,[456] i.e. a correlation, as Navratil explains, "between a fact in the real world and a fact within the diegesis."[457]

---

[451] Navratil (2021), p. 96.

[452] Ibid., p. 102.

[453] Ibid., p. 94.

[454] Danneberg (2006b), p. 65. Navratil cites the Alps as an example of multidirectional access to real facts: "For example, you can climb the real Alps yourself, read about them, look at them in photographs, etc." (Navratil 2021, p. 106).

[455] Navratil (2021), p. 117.

[456] Künne (1983), p. 295.

[457] Navratil (2021), p. 118.

To summarise, it should be noted that the principle of counterfactuality has primarily found its way into historical research under the concept of uchronia as a technique of alternative historical narrative. The interest of historians in the technique of counterfactual writing is explained by the assumption that certain historical facts are generally known and that deviations and variations from these facts are therefore easily recognisable in historical novels. However, as Eva-Maria Konrad and Lutz Danneberg show, nothing stands in the way of transferring counterfactual contrasting to other areas of knowledge, as it is to be understood as an experimental technique of representation which, if applied correctly, certainly satisfies the rigour of epistemic quality. In this context, the following three moments must be identified: enunciation in the diegesis, fact in the real world, and the recognisable relationship between enunciation in the diegesis and real-world fact. If the recipient has no knowledge of the real-world facts, the correspondence function between enunciation and real fact is disturbed and the counterfactual effect cannot occur. Real prior knowledge—and here associations with Gadamer's hermeneutic circle repeatedly come to mind—is therefore an absolute prerequisite for counterfactual operations. If this is the case, counterfactual writing can also be used confidently in other areas of knowledge, as Andreas Kablitz explicitly asserts for *correspondences between fact and law*.[458]

On a literary-theoretical and linguistic-pragmatic level, two points of reference are relevant for the counterfactual: the *real extradiegetic fact and its varied adoption in the diegesis*. As Wolfgang Iser and Michael Foucault argue, the attribution of information to the real world takes place via the constitutive power of language, which determines the attribution of the fact to the world generally perceived as real. In the diegetic dimension, a distinction must be made between two reference spaces: the space in which statements are only true or false internally (without reference to the outside world), and the space into which real-world facts penetrate, which correlate in some way with the outside world. With reference to the distinction between the dimension of inner diegesis and its variation possibilities on the one hand, and the overlapping of diegesis and the external world on the other, Carl D. Malmgren speaks of different levels of reference, while Michael Navratil refers to double reference.

From a teleological point of view, 'playing' with the counterfactual offers an interesting space for experiments that are fuelled by imaginations that diverge from reality and can open new insights and spaces for reflection through the question 'What if reality were like this or would have looked like this?'

Applied to law in literature, the counterfactual perspective—always under the condition, which cannot be emphasised enough, that the real-world law is sufficiently known to be recognised—allows scientific access to the legal discourse in the diegesis and the examination of its stringency (or not) in comparison to real-world law, whereby the experimental rather than the linguistic-pragmatic orientation of the counterfactual will herein come into play.

[458] Cf. Kablitz (2012), p. 167.

In the following, a potential approach to making the theoretical aspects that were presented fruitful for practical application to the study of legal discourses in literary texts is outlined. To this end, a working method is presented which will be tested on the basis of five very different texts to draw conclusions about methodological secants between law and literature. The aim of such an approach is, as already emphasised several times, to develop a reproducible working method when it comes to recognising and examining law in literature. At the same time, it is hoped that this work will make plausible, consolidate, and expand the possibilities of interdisciplinary research between law and literature.

References

Abel, Günter. 2022. *Interpretationswelten. Gegenwartsphilosophie jenseits von Essentialismus und Relativismus*. Frankfurt am Main: Suhrkamp.

Achermann, Eric, and Klaus Stierstorfer. 2022. Squaring Law and Literature: Materiality – Comparativity – Constitutivity. *Law & Literature* 35 (3): 457–489.

Achermann, Eric, and Klaus Stierstorfer. 2023. Einleitung: Materialität – Komparativität – Konstitutivität. In *Literatur und Recht: Materialität. Formen und Prozesse gegenseitiger Vergegenständlichung*, ed. Eric Achermann, Andreas Blödorn, Corinna Norrick-Rühl, and Petra Pohlmann, 3–43. Berlin/Heidelberg: J. B. Metzler.

Agresti, Jean-Philippe. 2023. Préface. In *Quand la littérature moderne (ré)invente le droit. Œuvres choisies du XXe siècle à aujourd'hui*, ed. Gil Charbonnier and Franck Petit. Paris: LexisNexis.

Albrecht, Andrea (2015): "Analogieschlüsse und metaphorische Extensionen", in: Andrea Albrecht, Lutz Danneberg, Olav Krämer, Carlos Spoerhase (eds.), *Theorien, Methoden und Praktiken des Interpretierens*, Berlin/Munich/Boston: De Gruyter, 271–299.

Albrecht, Kristin. 2020. *Fiktionen im Recht*. Baden-Baden: Nomos.

Albrecht, Andrea, and Lutz Danneberg. 2021. Verstehen, Auslegen,Darstellen und Vermitteln. Literaturwissenschaftliche Interpretationstexte in praxeologischer Perspektive. In *Doing Interpretation. Perspektiven praxeologischer Hermeneutik*, ed. Johannes Corrodi Katzenstein, Andreas Mauz, and Christiane Tietz, vol. 2, 23–50. Paderborn: Brill Schöningh.

Alexy, Robert. 1989. *A Theory of Legal Argumentation: The Theory of Rational Discourse as Theory of Legal Justification*. Oxford: Clarendon Press.

Anderegg, Johannes. 1983. Das Fiktionale und das Ästhetische. In *Funktionen des Fiktiven*, ed. Dieter Henrich and Wolfgang Iser, 153–172. Munich: W. Fink.

Angermüller, Johannes. 2014. Einleitung. In *Diskursforschung. Ein interdisziplinäres Handbuch. Theorien, Methodologien, Kontroversen*, ed. Johannes Angermüller, Martin Nonhoff, Eva Herschinger, et al., vol. 1, 16–36. Bielefeld: transcript.

Anghern, Emil. 2021. Interpretation, Konstruktion, Praxis. Zur Hermeneutik der Selbstverständigung. In *Doing Interpretation. Perspektiven praxeologischer Hermeneutik*, ed. Johannes Corrodi Katzenstein, Andreas Mauz, and Christiane Tietz, vol. 2, 51–63. Paderborn: Brill Schöningh.

Assmann, Aleida. 1980. Die Legitimität der Fiktion. In *Theorie und Geschichte der Literatur und der schönen Künste. Texte und Abhandlungen*, ed. Max Imdahl, Wolfgang Iser, Hans Robert Jauß, et al., vol. 55, 3–194. Munich: Fink.

Assmann, Jan. 1988. Kollektives Gedächtnis und kulturelle Identität. In *Kultur und Gedächtnis*, ed. Jan Assmann and Tonio Hölscher, 9–19. Frankfurt am Main: Suhrkamp.

Augsberg, Ino. 2009. *Die Lesbarkeit des Rechts. Texttheoretische Lekti- onen für eine postmoderne juristische Methodologie*. Weilerswist: Velbrück Wissenschaft.

Bacon, Francis. 2006. In *Über die Würde und die Förderung der Wissenschaften*, ed. Hermann Klenner. Freiburg: Haufe.

Balsiger, Philipp. 2005. *Transdisziplinarität. Systematisch-vergleichende Untersuchung disziplinübergreifender Wissenschaftspraxis*. Munich: W. Fink.

Bareis, Alexander. 2008. *Fiktionales Erzählen. Zur Theorie der literarischen Fiktion als Make-Believe*, 19–48. Gothenbourg: Acta Universitatis Gothoburgensis.

Barthes, Roland. 1966. Introduction à l'analyse structurale des récits. *Communications* 1966 (8): 1–27.

Barthes, Roland. 1974. *S/Z*. New York: Noonday Press.

Barthes, Roland. 1975. *The Pleasure of the Text*. New York: Hill and Wang.

Baßler, Moritz. 2021. Verstandenhaben. *Zeitschrift für Literaturwissenschaft und Linguistik* 2021 (51): 855–860.

Berghaus, Margot. 2022. *Luhmann leicht gemacht. Eine Einführung in die Systemtheorie*. Cologne/ Vienna: Böhlau.

Birnstiel, Klaus. 2021. Lateral lesen. Für eine dezentrierte Hermeneutik der Gegenwart. *Zeitschrift für Literaturwissenschaft und Linguistik* 2021 (51): 789–795.

Bleich, Susanne. 1989. Die literarische und die juristische Hermeneutik – Ein Vergleich. *NWJ* 1989 (50): 3197–3203.

Bleich, Susanne. 1992. *Der hermeneutische Prozess: Autor – Text – Rezipient. Von der Fiktionalisierung des juristischen Diskurses zur Rezeption literarischer Werke*. Bonn: Romanistischer Verlag.

Boeckh, August. 1886. In *Encyclopädie und Methodologie der philosophischen Wissenschaften*, ed. Ernst Bratuscheck. Leipzig: B. G. Teubner.

Bourdieu, Pierre. 1986. La force du droit. Éléments pour une sociologie du champ juridique. *Actes de la Recherche en Sciences Sociales* 1986 (64): 3–19.

Breu, Clarissa. 2020. *Autorschaft in der Johannesoffenbarung: Eine postmoderne Lektüre*. Tübingen: Mohr Siebeck.

Bühler, Axel. 2003. *"Grundprobleme der Hermeneutik", in: Axel Bühler, Hermeneutik*, 3–19. Heidelberg: Synchron.

Bultmann, Rudolf. 1961. *Glauben und Verstehen*. Vol. 2. Tübingen: Mohr Siebeck.

Busse, Dietrich. 2012. *Frame-Semantik. Ein Kompendium*. Berlin/Boston: De Gruyter.

Busse, Dietrich. 2013. Linguistische Diskursanalyse. Die Macht der Sprache und die soziale Konstruktion der Wirklichkeit aus der Perspektive einer linguistischen Epistemologie. In *Diskurs – Sprache – Wissen. Interdisziplinäre Beiträge zum Verhältnis von Sprache und Wissen in der Diskursforschung*, ed. Willy Viehöver, Reiner Keller, and Werner Schneider, 51–77. Wiesbaden: Springer.

Busse, Dietrich. 2018. Diskurs und Wissensrahmen. In *Handbuch Diskurs*, ed. Ingo Warnke, 3–29. Berlin: De Gruyter.

Celik, Nursan. 2024. *Das Recht der Fiktion. Zu den Lizenzen und juristischen Implikationen fiktionalen Schreibens*. Berlin: J. B. Metzler.

Charbonnier, Gil, and Franck Petit. 2023. *Quand la littérature moderne (ré) invente le droit. Œuvres choisies du XXe siècle à aujourd'hui*. Paris: LexisNexis.

Chinca, Mark. 2003. Mögliche Welten. Alternatives Erzählen und Fiktionalität im Tristanroman Gottfrieds von Straßburg. *Poetica* (35): 307–333.

Christensen, Ralph, and Hans Kudlich. 2004. Die Kanones der Auslegung als Hilfsmittel für die Entscheidung von Bedeutungskonflikten. *Juristische Arbeitsblätter* 2004 (1): 74–83.

Christmann, Ursula. 2008. Rhetorisch-stilistische Aspekte moderner Verstehens- und Verständlichkeitsforschung. In *Rhetorik und Stilistik. Ein internationales Handbuch historischer und systematischer Forschung*, ed. Ulla Fix, Andreas Gardt, and Joachim Knape, 1092–1106. Berlin/New York: De Gruyter.

Condello, Angela, and Tiziano Toracca. 2020. *A Theory of Law and Literature. Across Two Arts of Compromising*. Leiden/Boston: Brill.

Condello, Angela, and Tiziano Toracca. 2021. La finzione giuridica e la finzione letteraria. In *Fiction e non-fiction. Storia, teorie e forme*, ed. Riccardo Castellana, 207–227. Rome: Carocci editore.

Currie, Gregory. 1990. *The Nature of Fiction*. Cambridge: Cambridge University Press.

Dalferth, Ingolf U. 2000. Die Phänomene des Verstehens und die Praxis des Interpretierens. Prolegomena zu einer theologischen Hermeneutik. In *Verstehen und Interpretieren. Zum Basisvokabular von Hermeneutik und Interpretationstheorie*, ed. Andreas Mauz and Christiane Tietz, 57–78. Paderborn: Brill Schöningh.

Dalferth, Ingolf U. 2018. *Die Kunst des Verstehens. Grundzüge einer Hermeneutik der Kommunikation durch Texte*. Tübingen: Mohr Siebeck.

Danneberg, Lutz. 2006a. Überlegungen zu kontrafaktischen Imaginationen in argumentativen Kontexten und zu Beispielen ihrer Funktion in der Denkgeschichte. In *Imagination und Innovation*, ed. Toni Bernhart and Philipp Mehn, 73–100. Berlin/Boston: De Gruyter.

Danneberg, Lutz. 2006b. Weder Tränen noch Logik. Über die Zugänglichkeit fiktionaler Welten. In *Heuristiken der Literaturwissenschaft. Disziplinexterne Perspektiven auf Literatur*, ed. Uta Klein, Katja Mellmann, and Steffanie Metzger, 35–83. Paderborn: Mentis.

Danneberg, Lutz. 2015. Das Sich-Hineinversetzen und der sensus auctoris et primorum lectorum. Der Beitrag kontrafaktischer Imaginationen zur Ausbildung der *hermeneutica sacra* und *profana* im 18. und am Beginn des 19. Jahrhunderts. In *Theorien, Methoden und Praktiken des Interpretierens*, ed. Andrea Albrecht, Lutz Danneberg, Olav Krämer, and Carlos Spoerhase, 407–458. Berlin/München/Boston: De Gruyter.

de Spinoza, Baruch. 1901. In *A Study of the Ethics of Spinoza (Ethica ordine geometrico demonstrate)*, ed. Harold Henry. Oxford: Oxford Clarendon Press.

Diaz-Bone, Rainer. 2008. Die französische Epistemologie und ihre Revisionen. Zur Rekonstruktion des methodologischen Standortes der Foucault'schen Diskursanalyse. *Historical Social Research* 33 (1): 29–72.

Diaz-Bone, Rainer. 2013. Sozio-Episteme und Sozio-Kognition. Epistemologische Zugänge von Diskurs und Wissen. In *Diskurs – Sprache – Wissen. Interdisziplinäre Beiträge zum Verhältnis von Sprache und Wissen in der Diskursforschung*, ed. Willy Viehöver, Reiner Keller, and Werner Schneider, 79–96. Wiesbaden: Springer.

Dillinger, Johannes. 2015. *Ungeschehene Geschichte von der Antike bis zum Steampunk*. Paderborn: F. Schöningh.

Dilthey, Wilhelm. 1990. Die Entstehung der Hermeneutik. In *Gesammelte Schriften*, ed. Wilhelm Dilthey, vol. V, 317–338. Göttingen: Vandenhoeck & Ruprecht.

Dudenredaktion, ed. 2020. *Duden. Die deutsche Rechtschreibung*. Vol. 1. 28th ed. Berlin: Dudenverlag.

Durkheim, Émile. 1964. *The Rules of Sociological Method*. New York: The Free Press.

Dworkin, Ronald. 2001. *A Matter of Principle*. Oxford/New York: Oxford University Press.

Eco, Umberto. 1994. *Six Walks in the Fictional Woods*. Cambridge/Massachusetts: Harvard University Press.

Eco, Umberto. 2004. *The Name of the Rose*. London: Vintage.

Elster, Jon. 1981. *Logik und Gesellschaft. Widersprüche und mögliche Welten*. Frankfurt am Main: Suhrkamp.

Engell, James, and W. Jackson Bate, eds. 1983. *The Collected Works of Samuel Taylor Coleridge. Biographia Literaria or Biographical Sketches of My Literary Life and Opinions*. Princeton: Princeton University Press.

Erim, Ismail N. 1939. *Le positivisme juridique et le droit international*, Doctoral thesis, 22.2.1939, University of Paris, Paris: Les Presses modernes.

Esposito, Elena. 2012. Kontingenzerfahrung und Kontingenzbewusstsein in systemtheoretischer Perspektive. In *Politik und Kontingenz*, ed. Katrin Toens and Ulrich Willems, 39–48. Wiesbaden: Springer.

Esser, Josef. 1972. *Vorverständnis und Methodenwahl in der Rechtsfindung. Rationalitätsgrundlagen richterlicher Entscheidungspraxis*. Frankfurt am Main: Fischer.

Fikentscher, Wolfgang. 1977. *Methoden des Rechts in vergleichender Darstellung*. Vol. IV. Tübingen: J.C.B. Mohr.

Fix, Ulla. 2021. Wir entkommen der Hermeneutik nicht! *Zeitschrift für Literaturwissenschaft und Linguistik* 2021 (51): 695–702.

Fohrmann, Jürgen, and Harro Müller. 1988. Einleitung: Diskurstheorien und Literaturwissenschaft. In *Diskurstheorien und Literaturwissenschaft*, ed. Jürgen Fohrmann and Harro Müller, 9–21. Frankfurt am Main: Suhrkamp.

Foucault, Michel. 1970. *The Order of Discourse*, The Anarchist Library (theanarchistlibrary.org).

Foucault, Michel. 1972. *The Archeology of Knowledge*. New York: Pantheon Books.

Foucault, Michel. 1977. *Discipline and Punish: The Birth of the Prison*. New York: Pantheon Books.

Foucault, Michel. 1998. What is an Author? In *Michel Foucault, Essential Work of Foucault 1954-1984*, ed. James D. Faubion, vol. 2, 205–222. New York: The New Press.

Foucault, Michel. 2002. Die Wahrheit und die juristischen Formen. In *Schriften in vier Bänden. Dits et Ecrits, Bd. II: 1970–1975*, ed. Michel Foucault, Daniel Defert, and François Ewald, 669–792. Frankfurt am Main, Suhrkamp.

Foucault, Michel. 2017. Le discours ne doit pas être pris comme…. In *Dits et écrits II: 1976–1988*, ed. Michel Foucault, Daniel Defert, and François Ewald, 123–124. Paris: Gallimard.

Fraas, Claudia. 2000. Begriffe – Konzepte – Kulturelles Gedächtnis. Ansätze zur Beschreibung kollektiver Wissenssysteme. In *Sprache und Kultur*, ed. Horst D. Schlosser, 31–45. Frankfurt am Main/Vienna: Peter Lang.

Frank, Manfred. 1982. Textauslegung. In *Erkenntnis der Literatur. Theorien, Konzepte, Methoden der Literaturwissenschaft*, ed. Dietrich Harth and Peter Gebhardt, 123–160. Stuttgart: J. B. Metzler.

Fürbeth, Frank. 1999. Was heißt, wozu dient und wohin führt uns Interdisziplinarität. *Zeitschrift des Mediävistenverbandes* 4 (1): 7–16.

Gadamer, Hans-Georg. 1982. *Truth and Method*. New York: Crossroad.

Gärtner, Kurt. 2023. Karl Lachmann als Grundleger textkritischer Verfahren: Die Iwein-Ausgabe. In *Geschichte der altgermanistischen Edition*, ed. Judith Lange and Martin Schubert, 37–52. Berlin/Boston: De Gruyter.

Geis, Max-Emmanuel. 2021. Gewohnheitsrecht. In *Handbuch Rechtsphilosophie*, ed. Eric Hilgendorf and Jan C. Joerden, 27–31. Berlin/Heidelberg: J. B. Metzler.

Geisenhanslüke, Achim. 2008. *Gegendiskurse. Literatur und Diskursanalyse bei Michel Foucault*. Heidelberg: Synchron.

Geisenhanslüke, Achim. 2020. Literaturwissenschaft. Diskursanalyse und Literaturwissenschaft. In *Foucault Handbuch. Leben – Werk – Wirkung*, ed. Clemens Kammler, Rolf Parr, and Ulrich J. Schneider, 376–384. Berlin: J. B. Metzler.

Gerok-Reiter, Annette. 2021. Lektüren des Ästhetischen – Ästhetische Lektüren. Alte und neue Hermeneutik. *Zeitschrift für Literaturwissenschaft und Linguistik* 2021 (51): 751–758.

Gizbert-Studnicki, Tomasz. 1987. Der Vorverständnisbegriff in der juristischen Hermeneutik, *Archiv für Rechts- und Sozialphilosophie / Archives for Philsophy of Law and Social. Philosophy* 73 (4): 476–493.

Gräfrath, Bernd. 2005. Disziplin. In *Enzyklopädie Philosophie und Wissenschaftstheorie*, ed. Jürgen Mittelstraß, vol. 2, 237–238. Stuttgart: J. B. Metzler.

Greiner, Bernhard, Barbara Thums, and Wolfgang Graf Vitzthum, eds. 2010. *Recht und Literatur. Interdisziplinäre Bezüge*. Heidelberg: Winter.

Greshoff, Rainer. 2000. Interdisziplinarität und Vergleichen. In *Vergleichende Wissenschaften. Interdisziplinarität und Interkulturalität in den Komparatistiken*, ed. Peter V. Zima, 29–45. Tübingen: Narr.

Grimm, Dieter, and Christoph König. 2020. Lektüre und Geltung – Einleitung. In *Lektüre und Geltung. Zur Verstehenspraxis in der Rechtswissenschaft und in der Literaturwissenschaft*, ed. Dieter Grimm and Christoph König, 7–23. Göttingen: Wallstein.

Grimmer, Klaus. 1971. *Die Rechtsfiguren einer 'Normativität des Faktischen'*. In *Untersuchungen zum Verhältnis von Norm und Faktum und zur Funktion der Rechtsgestaltungsorgane*, vol. 24. Berlin: Duncker & Humblot.

Gröschner, Rolf. 1982. Das Hermeneutische der juristischen Hermeneutik. *JuristenZeitung* 37 (18): 622–626.

Gumbrecht, Hans U. 2004. *Diesseits der Hermeneutik. Die Produktion von Präsenz*. Frankfurt am Main: Suhrkamp.

Gumbrecht, Hans U. 2010. *Unsere breite Gegenwart*. Berlin: Suhrkamp.

Guyer, Paul. 1997. In praktischer Absicht: Kants Begriff der Postulate der reinen praktischen Vernunft. *Philosophisches Jahrbuch* 104 (I): 1–18.

Habermas, Jürgen. 1996. *Between Facts and Norms. Contributions to a Discourse Theory of Law and Democracy*. Cambridge/Massachusetts: MIT Press.

Hahn, Judith. 2019a. Rechtgeltung und Legitimität. In *Grundlegung der Kirchenrechtssoziologie. Zur Realität des Rechts in der römisch-katholischen Kirche*, ed. Judith Hahn, 147–188. Wiesbaden: Springer.

Hahn, Judith. 2019b. Wirksamkeit des Rechts. In *Grundlegung der Kirchenrechtssoziologie. Zur Realität des Rechts in der römisch-katholischen Kirche*, ed. Judith Hahn, 189–233. Wiesbaden: Springer.

Hamann, Hanjo. 2017. Strukturierende Rechtslehre als juristische Sprachtheorie. In *Handbuch Sprache im Recht*, ed. Ekkehard Felder and Andreas Gardt, 175–186. Berlin/Boston: De Gruyter.

Hamburger, Käthe. 1977. *Die Logik der Dichtung*. Stuttgart: Klett- Cotta.

Hamburger, Käthe. 1979. *Wahrheit und ästhetische Wahrheit*. Stuttgart: Klett-Cotta.

Hassemer, Winfried. 1986. Juristische Hermeneutik. *Archiv für Rechts- und Sozialphilosophie/ Archives for Philosophy of Law and Social Philosophy* 72 (2): 195–212.

Heck, Philipp. 1958. *Grundriß des Schuldrechts*. Aalen: Scientia.

Hellekson, Karen. 2001. *The Alternate History. Refiguring Historical Time*. Kent (Ohio)/London: Kent State University Press.

Henrich, Dieter. 2013. Versuch über Fiktion und Wahrheit. In *Diskurs – Sprache – Wissen*, ed. Willy Viehöver, Reiner Keller, and Werner Schneider, 511–519. Wiesbaden: Springer.

Henrich, Dieter, and Wolfgang Iser, eds. 1983. *Funktionen des Fiktiven*. Munich: W. Fink.

Hermanns, Fritz. 2007. Diskurshermeneutik. In *Diskurslinguistik nach Foucault*, ed. Ingo Warnke, 187–210. Berlin: De Gruyter.

Herzog, Reinhart. 1981. Zum Verhältnis von Norm und Narrativität in den applikativen Hermeneutiken. In *Text und Applikation: Theologie, Jurisprudenz und Literaturwissenschaft im hermeneutischen Gespräch*, ed. Manfred Fuhrmann, Hans R. Jauß, and Wolfhart Pannenberg, 435–455. Munich: W. Fink.

Hiebaum, Christian. 2015. Literatur, die verpflichtet. Über die Interpretation von Rechtstexten. In *Recht und Literatur im Zwischenraum / Law and Literature In-Between. Aktuelle inter- und transdisziplinäre Zugänge / Contemporary Inter- and Transdisciplinary Approaches*, ed. Christian Hiebaum, Susanne Knaller, and Doris Pichler, 155–170. Bielefeld: transcript.

Hilgendorf, Eric. 2021. Interdisziplinarität. In *Handbuch Rechtsphilosophie*, ed. Eric Hilgendorf and Jan C. Joerden, 491–496. Berlin/Heidelberg: J. B. Metzler.

Hirsch, Eric D. 1972. *Prinzipien der Interpretation*. Munich: W. Fink.

Hitzig, Julius E., and Willibald Alexis. 1842. *Der neue Pitaval: eine Sammlung der interessantesten Criminalgeschichten aller Länder aus älterer und neuerer Zeit*. Leipzig: Brockhaus.

Hoffmann, Veronika. 2024. Interpretationen im Konflikt. In *Grundfragen hermeneutischer Anthropologie. Paul Ricœurs Werk im historischen Kontext: Existenz, Interpretation, Praxis, Geschichte*, ed. Burkhard Liebsch, 1221–1236. Baden-Baden: Karl Alber.

Ingarden, Roman. 1968. *Vom Erkennen des literarischen Kunstwerks*. Tübingen: Niemeyer.

Ipseu, G. 1927. Der Begriff der Analogie. *Indogermanische Forschungen* 44 (s1): 320.

Iser, Wolfgang. 1983a. Akte des Fingierens. Oder: Was ist das Fiktive im fiktionalen Text? In *Funktionen des Fiktiven*, ed. Dieter Henrich and Wolfgang Iser, 121–151. Munich: W. Fink.

Iser, Wolfgang. 1983b. Das Fiktive im Horizont seiner Möglichkeiten. In *Funktionen des Fiktiven*, ed. Dieter Henrich and Wolfgang Iser, 547–557. Munich: W. Fink.

Jacoby, Nathalie. 2005. *Mögliche Leben. Zur formalen Integration von fiktiven und faktischen Elementen in der Literatur am Beispiel der zeitgenössischen fiktionalen Biographie*. Frankfurt am Main: Peter Lang.

Jäger, Siegfried. 1999. *Kritische Diskursanalyse. Eine Einführung*. Duisburg: DISS.

Jahraus, Oliver. 2013. Inter- und Transdisziplinarität. Wissenschaftspolitik und Wissenschaftssystematik. In *Handbuch Literaturwissenschaft. Methoden und Theorien*, ed. Thomas Anz, vol. 2, 373–378. Stuttgart/Weimar: J. B. Metzler.

Jannidis, Fotis, Lauer, Gerhard, Martinez, Mathias, Winko, Simone (eds.) (2000): *Texte zur Theorie der Autorschaft*, Stuttgart: Reclam.

Jauß, Hans R. 1981. Zur Abgrenzung und Bestimmung einer literarischen Hermeneutik. In *Text und Applikation: Theologie, Jurisprudenz und Li- teraturwissenschaft im hermeneutischen Gespräch*, ed. Hans R. Jauß, Manfred Fuhrmann, and Wolfhart Pannenberg, 459–481. Munich: W. Fink.

Jauß, Hans R. 1991. *Ästhetische Erfahrung und literarische Hermeneutik*. Frankfurt am Main: Suhrkamp.

Jauß, Hans Robert. 1997. Der Leser als Instanz einer neuen Geschichte der Literatur. *Poetica* 3 (4): 325–344.

Jellinek, Georg. 1921. Staat und Recht. In *Allgemeine Staatslehre*, ed. Georg Jellinek, 332–379. Berlin/Heidelberg: Springer.

Juster, Alexandra. 2022. *Neurezeption und juristische Dystopie: Eine Untersuchung des Romans Corpus Delicti: Ein Prozess von Juli Zeh*. Berlin: Peter Lang.

Juster, Alexandra. 2023. *Eine kontrafaktische Lektüre von Juli Zehs Roman Über Menschen. Gesellschaft, Politik, Ethik*. Berlin: Peter Lang.

Käbisch, Markus. 2001. Sprachlogische Einheitskonzeptionen der Wissenschaft und Sprachvielfalt der Disziplinen. Überlegungen zu theoretischen und praktischen Ansätzen von Interdisziplinarität. In *Interdisziplinarität. Chancen – Risiken – Konzepte*, ed. Holger Maaß and Sarah Schmidt, 13–31. Leipzig: Leipziger Universitätsverlag.

Kablitz, Andreas. 2012. *Kunst des Möglichen. Theorie der Literatur*. Freiburg: Rombach litterae.

Kablitz, Andreas. 2014. Referenz und Fiktion. In *Linguistics and Literary Studies / Linguistik und Literaturwissenschaft. Interfaces, Encounters, Transfers / Begegnungen, Interferenzen und Kooperationen*, ed. Monika Fludernik and Daniel Jacob, 93–125. Berlin/Boston: De Gruyter.

Kafka, Franz. 1995. *The Judgement and the Penal Colony*. New York: Penguin Books.

Kähler, Lorenz. 2018. Die asymmetrische Interdisziplinarität der Rechtswissenschaft. In *Der Erkenntniswert von Rechtswissenschaft für andere Disziplinen*, ed. Markus Rehberg, 105–151. Wiesbaden: Springer.

Kammler, Clemens. 2006. Die Abwesenheit der Theorie. In *Die Abwesenheit des Werkes. Nach Foucault*, ed. Klaus-Michael Bogdal and Achim Geisenhanslüke, 231–241. Heidelberg: Synchron.

Kant, Immanuel. 1974. *Kritik der Urteilskraft, hrsg. v. Wilhelm Weischedel*. Frankfurt am Main: Suhrkamp.

Kastner, Klaus. 2004. Literatur und Recht – eine unendliche Geschichte. In *Dichter als Juristen*, ed. Hermann Weber, 1–18. Berlin: Berliner Wissenschaftsverlag.

Keller, Reiner. 2013. Das Wissen der Wörter und Diskurse. Über Sprache und Wissen in der Wissenssoziologischen Diskursanalyse. In *Diskurs – Sprache – Wissen. Inter- disziplinäre Beiträge zum Verhältnis von Sprache und Wissen in der Diskursforschung*, ed. Willy Viehöver, Reiner Keller, and Werner Schneider, 21–49. Wiesbaden: Springer.

Keller, Reiner. 2018. Diskurs/Diskurstheorien. In *Handbuch Wissenssoziologie und Wissensforschung*, ed. Rainer Schützeichel, 199–213. Köln: Halem.

Kelsen, Hans. 1965. Was ist juristischer Positivismus? *JuristenZeitung* 20 (15): 465–469.

Kelsen, Hans. 2017. *Reine Rechtslehre*. Vol. 2. (study edition of the 2nd ed. 1960). Tübingen: Mohr Siebeck.

Kirste, Stephan. 2016a. Globalisierung und Interdisziplinarität in den Rechtswissenschaften. In *Wissenschaft und globales Denken*, ed. Franz Gmainer-Pranzl and Angela Schottenhammer, 131–150. Frankfurt am Main: Peter Lang.

Kirste, Stephan. 2016b. Voraussetzungen von Interdisziplinarität der Rechtswissenschaften. In *Interdisziplinarität in den Rechtswissenschaften. Ein interdisziplinärer und internationaler Dialog*, ed. Stephan Kirste, 35–85. Berlin: Duncker & Humblot.

Kirste, Stephan. 2021. Literatur und Recht. In *Handbuch Rechtsphilosophie*, ed. Eric Hilgendorf and Jan C. Joerden, 351–362. Berlin/Heidelberg: J. B. Metzler.

Klatt, Matthias. 2021. Juristische Hermeneutik. In *Handbuch Rechtsphilosophie*, ed. Eric Hilgendorf and Jan C. Joerden, 233–239. Berlin/Heidelberg: J. B. Metzler.

Klauk, Tobias, and Niels Klenner. 2021. Tilmann Köppe (2021) Literarische – Hermeneutik – Verstehen. *Zeitschrift für Literaturwissenschaft und Linguistik* 51:797–806.

Klausnitzer, Ralf. 2008. *Literatur und Wissen. Zugänge – Modelle – Analysen*. Berlin: De Gruyter.

Klawitter, Arno. 2020. Schriften zur Literatur. In *Foucault Handbuch. Leben – Werk – Wirkung*, ed. Clemens Kammler, Rolf Parr, and Ulrich J. Schneider, 108–118. Berlin: J. B. Metzler.

Knorr-Cetina, Karin. 2016. *Die Fabrikation von Erkenntnis. Zur Anthropologie der Wissenschaft*. Berlin: Suhrkamp.

Konersmann, Ralf. 1991. Der Philosoph mit der Maske. Michel Foucaults *L'ordre du discours*. In *Die Ordnung des Diskurses*, ed. Michel Foucault, 53–91. Frankfurt am Main: Fischer.

König, Tim. 2012. *In guter Gesellschaft? Einführung in die politische Soziologie von Jürgen Habermas und Niklas Luhmann*. Wiesbaden: Springer.

Konrad, Eva-Maria. 2023. Zur Plausibilität kontrafaktischer Szenarien in Geschichtswissenschaft und Literatur. In *Plausibilisierung und Evidenz. Dynamiken und Praktiken von der Antike bis zur Gegenwart*, ed. Antje Flüchter, Birte Förster, Britta Hochkirchen, and Silke Schwandt, 149–168. Bielefeld: Bielefeld University Press.

Kriele, Martin. 1981. Juristische Hermeneutik am Beispiel der 'Mephisto'-Entscheidung. In *Theologie, Jurisprudenz und Literaturwissenschaft im hermeneutischen Gespräch*, ed. Manfred Fuhrmann, Hans Robert Jauß, and Wolfhart Pannenberg, 149–162. Munich: W. Fink.

Kristeva, Julia. 1972. Bachtin, das Wort, der Dialog und der Roman. In *Literaturwissenschaft und Linguistik. Ergebnisse und Perspektiven, vol. 3: Zur linguistischen Basis der Literaturwissenschaft*, ed. Jens Ihwe, 345–375. Frankfurt am Main: Athenäum.

Krüger, Lorenz. 1987. Einheit der Welt – Vielheit der Wissenschaften. In *Interdisziplinarität: Praxis – Herausforderung – Ideologie*, ed. Jürgen Kocka, 106–128. Frankfurt am Main: Suhrkamp.

Künne, Wolfgang. 1983. *Abstrakte Gegenstände: Semantik und Ontologie*. Frankfurt am Main: Suhrkamp.

Kunz, Karl-Ludwig, and Mona Martino. 2006. *Rechtsphilosophie, Rechtstheorie, Rechtssoziologie. Eine Einführung in die theoretischen Grundlagen der Rechtswissenschaft*. Berne/Stuttgart/Vienna: Haupt Verlag.

Künzel, Christine. 2015. Imaginierte Fakten. Zur Bedeutung von Fiktion(en) in der richterlichen Urteilsbildung. In *Recht und Literatur im Zwischenraum / Law and Literature In-Between. Aktuelle inter- und transdisziplinäre Zugänge / Contemporary Inter- and Transdisciplinary Approaches*, ed. Christian Hiebaum, Susanne Knaller, and Doris Pichler, 171–187. Bielefeld: transcript.

Lachmann, Karl. 1843. Vorrede. In *Iwein. Eine Erzählung von Hartmann von Aue*, ed. Georg F. Benecke and Karl Lachmann, III–X. Berlin: Reimer.

Lahusen, Benjamin. 2019. *Alles Recht geht vom Volksgeist aus. Friedrich Carl von Savigny und die moderne Rechtswissenschaft*. Weilerswist-Metternich: Dittrich.

Lämmert, Eberhard. 1999. Zurück zu den Anfängen? Die kulturwis- senschaftliche Weite der Germanistik von 1846. In *Zur Geschichte und Problematik der Nationalphilologien in Europa. 150 Jahre Erste Germanistenversammlung in Frankfurt am Main (1846–1996)*, ed. Frank Fürbeth, Pierre Krügel, Ernst E. Metzner, and Olaf Müller, 7–22. Tübingen: Niemeyer.

Lamnek, Siegfried. 2005. *Qualitative Sozialforschung. Lehrbuch*. Weinheim: Beltz.

Larenz, Karl. 1991. *Methodenlehre der Rechtswissenschaft*. Berlin/Heidelberg: Springer.

Leanza, Matthias. 2010. Semantik und Diskurs. Die Wissenskonzeptionen Niklas Luhmanns und Michel Foucaults im Vergleich. In *Zwischen Sprachspiel und Methode: Perspektiven der Diskursanalyse*, ed. Robert Feustel and Maximilian Schochow, 119–146. Bielefeld: transcript.

Lebow, Richard N. 2009. Counterfactuals, History and Fiction. *Historical Social Research* 34 (2): 57–73.

Lenk, Hans. 1993. *Interpretationskonstrukte. Zur Kritik der interpretatorischen Vernunft*. Frankfurt am Main: Suhrkamp.

Link, Jürgen. 1983. *Elementare Literatur und generative Diskursanalyse*. München: W. Fink.

Link, Jürgen. 1988. Literaturanalyse als Interdiskursanalyse. Am Beispiel des Ursprungs literarischer Symbolik in der Kollektivsymbolik. In *Diskurstheorien und Literaturwissenschaft*, ed. Jürgen Fohrmann and Harro Müller, 284–307. Frankfurt am Main: Suhrkamp.

Link, Jürgen, and Ursula Link-Heer. 1990. Diskurs, Interdiskurs und Literaturanalyse. *Zeitschrift für Literaturwissenschaft und Linguistik* 77:88–99.

Löhr, Kathrin. 2022. Dimensionen der Vergegenständlichung von Recht im Pitaval. Zur Einführung: 'Was ist der Pitaval'? In *Literatur und Recht: Materialität. Formen und Prozesse gegenseitiger Vergegenständlichung*, ed. Eric Achermann, Andreas Blödorn, Corinna Norrick-Rühl, and Petra Pohlmann, 249–256. Berlin/Heidelberg: J. B. Metzler.

Luckmann, Thomas. 1980. *Lebenswelt und Gesellschaft. Grundstrukturen und geschichtliche Wandlungen*. Paderborn: F. Schöningh.

Luhmann, Niklas. 1982. *The Differentiation of Society*. New York: Columbia University Press.

Luhmann, Niklas. 1985. *A Sociological Theory of Law*. London/Boston: Routledge & Kegan Paul.

Luhmann, Niklas. 2013. *Introduction to Systems Theory*. Cambridge: Polity Press.

Lyotard, Jean-François. 1988. *The Differend: Phrases in Dispute*. Minneapolis: University of Minnesota Press.

Malmgren, Carl D. 1985. *Fictional Space in the Modernist and Post-modernist American Novel*. London/Toronto: Associated University Press.

Martínez, Matías, and Michael Scheffel. 2019. *Einführung in die Erzähltheorie*. Munich: C. H. Beck.

Mauz, Andreas. 2021. Doing Interpretation. Einleitende Hinweise zur praxeologischen Hermeneutik. In *Doing Interpretation. Perspektiven praxeologischer Hermeneutik*, ed. Johannes Corrodi Katzenstein, Andreas Mauz, and Christiane Tietz, vol. 2, 1–22. Paderborn: Brill Schöningh.

Mead, George H. 2015. *Mind, Self, and Society. The Definitive Edition*. Chicago/London: University of Chicago Press.

Minsky, Marvin. 1992. Eine Rahmenstruktur für die Wissensrepräsentation. In *Kognitionswissenschaft. Grundlagen, Probleme, Perspektiven*, ed. Dieter Münch, 92–134. Frankfurt am Main: Suhrkamp.

Mittelstraß, Jürgen. 1989. *Der Flug der Eule. Von der Vernunft der Wissenschaft und der Aufgabe der Philosophie*. Suhrkamp: Frankfurt am Main.

Mittelstraß, Jürgen. 2005. Methodische Transdisziplinarität. *TATup* 14 (2): 18–23.

Mittelstraß, Jürgen. 2012. Transdisziplinarität oder: von der schwachen zur starken Interdisziplinarität. *GEGENWORTE. Hefte für den Disput über Wissen* 2012 (28): 10–13.

Mittelstraß, Jürgen. 2018. Forschung und Gesellschaft. Von theoretischer und praktischer Transdisziplinarität (Reaktion auf W. Krohn & al. in *GAIA* 26/4 2017). *GAIA* 27 (2): 201–204.

Mölk, Ulrich, ed. 1996a. *Literatur und Recht. Literarische Rechtsfälle von der Antike bis in die Gegenwart*. Göttingen: Wallstein.

Mölk, Ulrich. 1996b. *Literatur und Recht. Literarische Rechtsfälle von der Antike bis in die Gegenwart*. Göttingen: Wallstein.

Möllers, Thomas M. J. 2023. *Juristische Methodenlehre*. Munich: C. H. Beck.

Morris, Charles. 1995. *Signs, Language, and Behavior*. New York: G. Braziller.

Müller, Friedrich, Ralph Christensen, and Michael Sokolowski. 1997. *Rechtstext und Textarbeit*. Berlin: Duncker & Humblot.

Müller-Dietz, Heinz. 1990. *Grenzüberschreitungen. Beiträge zur Beziehung zwischen Literatur und Recht*. Baden-Baden: Nomos.

Müller-Seidel, Walter. 1986. *Die Deportation des Menschen. Kafkas Erzählung 'In der Strafkolonie' im europäischen Kontext*. Stuttgart: J. B. Metzler.

Navratil, Michael. 2021. *Kontrafaktik der Gegenwart*. Berlin: De Gruyter.
Neumann, Ulfrid. 2021. Juristische Argumentationstheorie. In *Handbuch Rechtsphilosophie*, ed. Eric Hilgendorf and Jan C. Joerden, 244–249. Berlin: J. B. Metzler.
Nicolosi, Riccardo. 2013. Kontrafaktische Überbevölkerungsphantasien. Gedankenexperimente zwischen Wissenschaft und Literatur am Beispiel von Thomas Malthus' *An Essay on the Principle of Population* (1798) und Vladimir Odoevskijs *Poslednee samoubijstvo* (Der letzte Selbstmord, 1844). *Scientia Poetica* 17 (1): 50–75.
Nossack, Hans Erich. 1968. *Das Verhältnis der Literatur zu Recht und Gerechtigkeit*. Wiesbaden: Steiner.
Nünning, Ansgar. 1995. *Von historischer Fiktion zu historiographischer Metafiktion, vol 1: Theorie, Typologie und Poetik des historischen Romans*. Trier: Wissenschaftlicher Verlag Trier.
Ost, François. 2014. Penser par cas: la littérature comme laboratoire expérimental de la démarche juridique. *Revue interdisciplinaire d'études juridiques* 2014 (2): 99–131.
Papaux, Alain. 2003. *Essai philosophique sur la qualification juridique: de la subsomption à l'abduction. L'exemple du droit international privé*. Brussels/Paris: Bruylant/L.G.D.J./ Schulthess.
Parr, Rolf. 2015. Autorität und Geltung zwischen Spezial- und Interdiskursen. In *Erzählung und Geltung. Wissenschaft zwischen Autorschaft und Autorität*, ed. Safia Azzouni, Stefan Böschen, and Carsten Reinhardt, 289–302. Weilerswist: Velbrück Wissenschaft.
Parr, Rolf. 2020a. Diskurs. In *Foucault Handbuch. Leben – Werk – Wirkung*, ed. Clemens Kammler, Rolf Parr, and Ulrich J. Schneider, 274–277. Berlin: J. B. Metzler.
Parr, Rolf. 2020b. Interdiskurstheorie / Interdiskursanalyse. In *Foucault Handbuch. Leben – Werk – Wirkung*, ed. Clemens Kammler, Rolf Parr, and Ulrich J. Schneider, 234–237. Berlin: J. B. Metzler.
Pascal, Blaise. n.d. Les pensées de Pascal, Dossier de travail 31 (Laf. 413– Sel. 32), In *Recueil des originaux*, 487-5, http://www.penseesdepascal.fr/RO-extraits/RO487-5.pdf.
Peter, Tobias. 2014. Politisierte Systeme – Grenzen der Politik und Entgrenzung des Politischen bei Niklas Luhmann. In *Spurensuche: Konstruktivistische Theorien der Politik*, ed. Renate Martinsen, 45–61. Wiesbaden: Springer.
Petersen, Jürgen. 1994. *Erzählsysteme. Eine Poetik epischer Texte*. Stuttgart: J. B. Metzler.
Pichler, Doris. 2015. Law and Literature: Some Reflections upon the Nature of its Interdisciplinarity. In *Recht und Literatur im Zwischenraum / Law and Literature In-Between. Aktuelle inter- und transdisziplinäre Zugänge / Contemporary Inter- and Transdisciplinary Approaches*, ed. Christian Hiebaum, Susanne Knaller, and Doris Pichler, 15–33. Bielefeld: transcript.
Preisinger, Alexander, Pascale Delormas, and Jan Standke. 2014. Diskursforschung in der Literaturwissenschaft. In *Diskursforschung. Ein interdisziplinäres Handbuch, vol. 1: Theorien, Methodologien, Kontroversen*, ed. Johannes Angermüller, Martin Nonhoff, Eva Herschinger, et al., 130–139. Bielefeld: transcript.
Puchta, Georg F. 1828. *Das Gewohnheitsrecht, part 1*. Erlangen: Palm'sche Verlagsbuchhandlung.
Radbruch, Gustav. 1925. *Wissenschaft und Bildung: Einzeldarstellungen aus allen Gebieten des Wissens*. Leipzig: Quelle & Meyer.
Raiser, Thomas. 2007. *Grundlagen der Rechtssoziologie*. Tübingen: UTB.
Rehbinder, Manfred. 2014. *Rechtssoziologie. Ein Studienbuch*. Munich: C. H. Beck.
Reinalter, Helmut. 1993. Einleitung. In *Vernetztes Denken – Gemeinsames Handeln. Interdisziplinarität in Theorie und Praxis*, ed. Helmut Reinalter, 9–13. Thaur/Vienna/Munich: Kulturverlag.
Reinalter, Helmut, and Peter Brenner, eds. 2011. *Lexikon der Geisteswissenschaften: Sachbegriffe – Disziplinen – Personen*. Vienna: Böhlau.
Reinhardt-Becker, Elke. 2020. Niklas Luhmann. In *Foucault Handbuch. Leben – Werk – Wirkung*, ed. Clemens Kammler, Rolf Parr, and Ulrich J. Schneider, 246–250. Berlin: J. B. Metzler.
Ricœur, Paul. 1991. *From Text to Action. Essays in Hermeneutics II*. Evanston: Northwestern University Press.

Ritter, Hermann. 1999. Kontrafaktische Geschichte. Unterhaltung versus Erkenntnis. In *Was Wäre Wenn. Alternativ- und Parallelgeschichte: Brücken zwischen Phantasie und Wirklichkeit*, ed. Michael Salewski, 13–42. Stuttgart: Franz Steiner.

Rodiek, Christoph. 1993. Prolegomena zu einer Poetik des Kontrafaktischen. *Poetica* 1993 (25): 262–281.

Rodiek, Christoph. 1997. *Erfundene Vergangenheit. Kontrafaktische Geschichtsdarstellung (Uchronie) in der Literatur*. Frankfurt am Main: Vittorio Klostermann.

Röhl, Klaus F. 1987. *Rechtssoziologie. Ein Lehrbuch*. Cologne/Berlin/Bonn/Munich: Heymann.

Röhl, Klaus F. 2020. Literaturwissenschaft und Rechtstheorie. In *Rechtstheorie*, ed. Athanasios Gromitsaris, Rainer Schröder, and Martin Schulte, vol. 51/4, 413–432. Berlin: Duncker & Humblot.

Rusch, Kristine K. 2012. Alternate History: Worlds of What if. In *Strange Divisions and Alien Territories. The Sub-Genres of Science Fiction*, ed. Keith Brooke, 83–96. Chippenham/ Eastbourne: Red Globe Press.

Schiesser, Giaco. 2007. Autorschaft nach dem Tod des Autors. Barthes und Foucault revisited. In *Autorschaft in den Künsten: Konzepte – Praktiken – Medien. Zürcher Jahrbuch der Künste*, ed. Corina Caduff and Tan Wälchli, 20–33. Zürich: Museum für Gestaltung.

Schleiermacher, Friedrich. 1977. In *Hermeneutics: The Handwritten Manuscripts*, ed. Heinz Kimmerle. Missoula (Montana): Scholars Press for the American Academy of Religion.

Schlink, Bernhard. 2013. Das Bilderbuch des Rechts. In *Rechtsgeschichten. Über Gerechtigkeit in der Literatur*, ed. Richard Weisberg, 275–289. Berlin: Suhrkamp.

Schmidt, Siegfried J. 1973. *Texttheorie*. Munich: W. Fink.

Scholz, Oliver R. 2015. Art. Hermeneutics. In *The International Encyclopedia of Social and Behavioral Sciences*, ed. James D. Wright, vol. 10, 778–784. Oxford: Elsevier.

Scholz, Oliver R. 2024. Die Idee einer Hermeneutica generalis und die vielen Bereichshermeneutiken. Plädoyer für eine vergleichende Hermeneutik. In *Rechtsnorm und ästhetische Reflexion. Studien zum Verhältnis zwischen den Hermeneutiken des Rechts und der Literatur*, ed. Gideon Stiening, 13–29. Berlin: J. B. Metzler.

Schulte, Joachim. 2022. Sprachspiel. In *Wittgenstein-Handbuch. Leben – Werk – Wirkung*, ed. Anja Weiberg and Stefan Majetschak, 387–392. Berlin/Heidelberg: J. B. Metzler.

Schulze, Holger. 2020. *Ubiquitäre Literatur. Eine Partikelpoetik*. Berlin: Matthes & Seitz.

Schütz, Erhard. 2013. Kontrafaktische Geschichtsschreibung zum NS in Romanen nach 1945. In *Der historische Roman zwischen Kunst, Ideologie und Wissenschaft*, ed. Ina U. Paul and Richard Faber, 467–485. Würzburg: Königshausen & Neumann.

Searle, John. 1975. The Logical Status of Fictional Discourse. *The New Literary History* 6 (2): 319–332.

Ségur, Philippe. 2017. Droit et littérature. Éléments pour la recherche. Éléments pour la recherche. *Revue Droit & Littérature* 2017 (1): 109–123.

Shakespeare, William. 2004. Hamlet. In *William Skahespeare, The Complete Works of William Shakespeare*, ed. David Bevington, 1091–1149. New York: Pearson Longman.

Sichler, Ralph. 2020. Hermeneutik. In *Handbuch Qualitative Forschung in der Psychologie, vol. 1: Ansätze und Anwendungsfelder*, ed. Günter Mey and Katja Mruck, 126–143. Wiesbaden: Springer.

Sidney, Philip. 1971. In *A Defence of Poetry*, ed. Jan A. Dorsten. Oxford: Oxford University Press.

Sill, Oliver. 2001. *Literatur in der funktional differenzierten Gesellschaft. Systemtheoretische Perspektiven auf ein komplexes Phänomen*. Wiesbaden: Springer.

Sneis, Jørgen. 2015. Rekonstruktion als Interpretation. Überlegungen zu Roman Ingardens Versuch einer erkenntnistheoretischen Grundlegung der Literaturwissenschaft. In *Theorien, Methoden und Praktiken des Interpretierens*, ed. Andrea Albrecht, Lutz Danneberg, Olav Krämer, and Carlos Spoerhase, 459–479. Berlin/Munich/Boston: De Gruyter.

Spanò, Michele, and Massimo Vallerani. 2016. Avvertenza. In *Fictio legis: la finzione romana e i suoi limiti medievali*, ed. Yan Thomas, 7–14. Macerata: Quodlibet.

Speth, Sebastian. 2024. Gattungskonvention und Heteronomie. Zur intentionsadäquaten Interpretation von Böhmermanns Schmähkritik und der Pitavalgeschichte des Rechtsstreits zwischen Saurin und Rousseau. In *Rechtsnorm und ästhetische Reflexion. Studien zum Verhältnis zwischen den Hermeneutiken des Rechts und der Literatur*, ed. Gideon Stiening, 233–250. Berlin: J. B. Metzler.

Steinmüller, Karlheinz. 1999. Zukünfte, die nicht Geschichte werden. Zum Gedankenexperiment in Zukunftsforschung und Geschichtswissenschaft. In *Was Wäre Wenn. Alternativ- und Parallelgeschichte: Brücken zwischen Phantasie und Wirklichkeit*, ed. Michael Salewski, 43–54. Stuttgart: Franz Steiner.

Stiening, Gideon. 2022. Materialität als Begriff und Kategorie der Korrelation von Recht und Literatur. In *Literatur und Recht: Materialität. Formen und Prozesse gegenseitiger Vergegenständlichung*, ed. Eric Achermann, Andreas Blödorn, Corinna Norrick-Rühl, and Petra Pohlmann, 45–68. Berlin/Heidelberg: J. B. Metzler.

Stiening, Gideon. 2024. Zur Einführung: Rechtsnorm und ästhetische Reflexion. Zum Verhältnis zwischen Hermeneutiken des Rechts und der Literatur. In *Rechtsnorm und ästhetische Reflexion. Studien zum Verhältnis zwischen den Hermeneutiken des Rechts und der Literatur*, ed. Gideon Stiening, 1–9. Berlin: J. B. Metzler.

Stierle, Karlheinz. 1985. Für eine Öffnung des hermeneutischen Zirkels. *POETICA* 1985 (17): 340–354.

Strobel, Jochen, Jan de Vries, and Friederike Wißmach. 2019. Leserkognition und Wissensemergenz bei kontrafaktischem Erzählen aus Sicht der Frame-Semantik. Der 'Wenderoman' als Alternativweltgeschichte. *Zeitschrift für Literaturwissenschaft und Linguistik* 2019 (49): 139–162.

Strouhal, Ernst, and Ruth Wodak. 1987. *Recht auf Sprache. Verstehen und Verständlichkeit von Gesetzen*. Wien: Orac.

Szondi, Peter. 1975. *Einführung in die literarische Hermeneutik*. Frankfurt am Main: Suhrkamp.

Ternès, Anabel. 2016. *Intertextualität. Der Text als Collage*. Wiesbaden: Springer.

Thouard, Denis. 2020. Urteilen und Verstehen. Über Nähe und Differenz von Recht und Philologie. In *Lektüre und Geltung. Zur Verstehenspraxis in der Rechtswissenschaft und in der Literaturwissenschaft*, ed. Dieter Grimm and Christoph König, 255–269. Göttingen: Wallstein.

Van Dyk, Silke, Antje Langer, Felicitas Macgilchrist, et al. 2014. Discourse and Beyond? In *Diskursforschung. Ein interdisziplinäres Handbuch, vol. 1: Theorien, Methodologien, Kontroversen*, ed. Johannes Angermüller, Martin Nonhoff, Eva Herschinger, et al., 347–363. Bielefeld: transcript.

Viehöver, Willy. 2012. 'Menschen lesbarer machen': Narration, Diskurs, Referenz. In *Erzählungen im Öffentlichen. Über die Wirkung narrativer Diskurse*, ed. Markus Arnold, Gert Dressel, and Willy Viehöver, 65–132. Wiesbaden: Springer.

Viola, Luigi. 2023. Emmanuel Carrère, l'uchronie et le juge. *Les cahiers de la justice* 2023 (4): 739–749.

von Goethe, Johann W. 2005. Noten und Abhandlungen zu besserem Verständnis des west-östlichen Divans. In *Werke, vol. 2: Gedichte und Epen II*, ed. Johann W. von Goethe, 126–267. Munich: C. H. Beck.

von Savigny, Friedrich C. 1840. *System des heutigen Römischen Rechts*. Vol. 1. Berlin: Veit und Comp.

von Savigny, Friedrich C. 1951. In *Juristische Methodenlehre. Nach der Ausarbeitung des Jakob Grimm*, ed. Gerhard Wesenberg. Stuttgart: K. F. Koehler.

von Savigny, Friedrich C. 2004. *Vorlesungen über juristische Methodologie 1802–1842*. Vol. 2. Frankfurt am Main: Vittorio Klostermann.

von Schirnding, Albert. 1990. *Recht und Richter im Spiegel der Literatur*. München: Boorberg.

Walton, Kendall. 1990. *Mimesis as Make-Believe: On the Foundations of the Representational Arts*. Cambridge/Massachusetts: Harvard University Press.

Ward, Ian. 1995. *Law and Literature. Possibilities and Perspectives*. Cambridge: Cambridge University Press.

Warning, Rainer. 2013. Der inszenierte Diskurs. In *Diskurs – Sprache – Wissen*, ed. Willy Viehöver, Reiner Keller, and Werner Schneider, 183–206. Wiesbaden: Springer.

Wedl, Juliette, Eva Herschinger, and Ludwig Gasteiger. 2014. Diskursforschung oder Inhaltsanalyse? In *Diskursforschung. Ein interdisziplinäres Handbuch, vol. 1: Theorien, Methodologien, Kontroversen*, ed. Johannes Angermüller, Martin Nonhoff, Eva Herschinger, et al., 537–563. Bielefeld: transcript.

Weimar, Klaus. 2020. Hermeneutica in nuce. In *Verstehen und Interpretieren. Zum Basisvokabular von Hermeneutik und Interpretationstheorie, Hermeneutik und Interpretationstheorie 1*, ed. Andreas Mauz, Christiane Tietz, and Tilmann Köppe, 79–85. Paderborn: F. Schöningh.

Weingart, Peter, and Nico Stehr, eds. 2000. *Practising Interdisciplinarity.* Toronto/Buffalo/London: University of Toronto Press.

Werle, Dirk. 2015. 'Unvollständiges Verstehen' am Beispiel einer Goethe-Parodie in Daniel Kehlmanns Roman *Die Vermessung der Welt.* Ein Beitrag zur Erforschung interpretatorischer Praxis. In *Theorien, Methoden und Praktiken des Interpretierens*, ed. Andrea Albrecht, Lutz Danneberg, Olav Krämer, and Carlos Spoerhase, 345–365. Berlin/München/Boston: De Gruyter.

White, Hayden. 1991. Der historische Text als literarisches Kunstwerk. In *Auch Klio dichtet oder die Fiktion des Faktischen. Studien zur Tropologie des historischen Diskurses*, ed. Hayden White, 101–122. Stuttgart: Klett-Cotta.

Widmann, Andreas M. 2009. *Kontrafaktische Geschichtsdarstellung. Untersuchungen an Romanen von Günter Grass, Thomas Pynchon, Thomas Brussig, Michael Kleeberg, Philip Roth und Christoph Ransmayr.* Hei- delberg: Winter.

Wieacker, Franz. 1985. Konstituenten der okzidentalen Rechtskultur. In *Römisches Recht in der europäischen Tradition*, ed. Okko Behrends, Malte Diesselhorst, and Wulf E. Voss, 355–364. Ebelsbach: Gremer.

Wieschollek, Jonas. 2024. Wie und warum zitieren Gerichte Gerichtsentscheidungen? Eine Typologie gerichtlicher Zitationsweisen auf diskurstraditioneller Grundlage. In *Rechtsnorm und ästhetische Reflexion. Studien zum Verhältnis zwischen den Hermeneutiken des Rechts und der Literatur*, ed. Gideon Stiening, 163–196. Berlin: J. B. Metzler.

Witte, Egbert. 2020. Aisthesis. In *Handbuch Bildungs- und Erziehungsphilosophie*, ed. Gabriele Weiß and Jörg Zirfas, 67–75. Wiesbaden: Springer.

Wrana, Daniel. 2014. Diskursanalyse jenseits von Hermeneutik und Strukturalismus. In *Diskursforschung. Ein interdisziplinäres Handbuch, vol. 1: Theorien, Methodologien, Kontroversen*, ed. Johannes Angermüller, Martin Nonhoff, Eva Herschinger, et al., 511–536. Bielefeld: transcript.

Zeh, Juli. 2014. *The Method.* New York: Vintage.

Zeh, Juli. 2023. *About People.* New York: World Editions.

Zima, Peter V. 2020. *Literarische Ästhetik. Methoden und Modelle der Literaturwissenschaft.* Tübingen: Narr Francke Attempto.

Zipfel, Frank. 2001. *Fiktion, Fiktivität, Fiktionalität: Analysen zur Fiktion in der Literatur und zum Fiktionsbegriff in der Literaturwissenschaft.* Berlin: Schmidt.

Zippelius, Reinhold. 2006. *Juristische Methodenlehre.* Munich: C. H. Beck.

Chapter 4
Method of Legal Counterfactuals

As repeatedly stressed, this work focuses on developing a *counterfactual method* for researching legal discourses in literary texts. The term *counterfactual method* implies *method* and *counterfactuality*: the former is the object of the attempt to open *methodological* perspectives for interdisciplinary work between law and literature, and the latter was dealt with in detail as a *concept in* the previous chapter and is now further developed here as a *method*. The development of a novel approach should serve to strengthen the interdisciplinary connection between law and literary studies by demonstrating common methodological approaches: I refer in this respect to the Sect. 3.1 on interdisciplinarity, in which it is made clear that viable interdisciplinary work is not possible without methodological and conceptual commonalities. Counterfactuality as a method focuses on the juxtaposition of real-world law and intradiegetic legal discourse as a prerequisite for counterfactual thinking and cognition on the one hand, and on a deeper understanding of legal discourses in literature as well as literature in a broader sense on the other hand.

For the purposes of this study, it is useful to draw on the non-empirical method, which is commonly used in the humanities and which Hans-Bernd Brosius, Alexander Haas, and Friederike Koschel define in contrast to the empirical method commonly used in the social sciences: "To proceed non-empirically means to understand and systematically categorise a singular fact on the basis of one's own experience and the theoretical, general knowledge of a science."[1] This definition could not be more apt for the present research project: the aim here is to develop a method suitable for interdisciplinary use, building on and starting from both the current state of research on 'law and literature' and the theoretical building blocks of interdisciplinarity, discourse, hermeneutics, and counterfactuals. My own interdisciplinary experiences of a legal, literary, and scientific nature will certainly prove helpful in this endeavour. It will have to be clarified to what extent a literary-legal

[1] Brosius et al. (2016), here: p. 3.

A. Juster, *Law, Literature and Legal Counterfactuals*, Law and Visual Jurisprudence 16, https://doi.org/10.1007/978-3-032-03792-3_4

investigation can draw on common interdisciplinary working methods and how the relationship between law and literature can be organised: Can a separate discipline develop from this, or must it remain a more or less deepened 'parallel-disciplinary' coexistence, limited to a few common interfaces? And what could such a 'deepening' look like?

My approach is orientated towards Edmund Husserl's phenomenological method, from which three advantages, in particular, can be derived for the present study: 1) its strictly science-critical character, with which it strives for the "uncovering and investigation of all basic assumptions and presuppositions"[2] of different fields of knowledge, 2) its unprejudiced and undogmatic approach to the latter, 3) its discipline-specific correlation, 4) its multiperspectivity, and 5) its search for essential structures of a phenomenon. On the fifth point, Bojan Godina explains the extent to which the phenomenological method is particularly suitable for interdisciplinary work:

> By recognising the essential structures of a phenomenon, it is easier to create transferable knowledge and higher-level concepts. In the current scientific landscape (including the social sciences and humanities) there are many specialists, but also generalists. It is likely that in the future, great insights will be less and less likely to come from generalists or specialists, but rather from *scientists working synthetically, who are able to translate between the individual scientific disciplines and who are able to develop higher-level concepts* [...]. *It is interesting to observe that researchers who have been trained in two or more disciplines tend to recognise phenomenal essential structures much more quickly than they tend to get lost in details* [author's emphasis].[3]

Interesting elements can be taken from Husserl's phenomenological method and made fruitful for literary-legal research insofar as phenomenology deals with science as subjective knowledge in a specific relationship to a certain object (phenomenon).[4] It approaches the object of research as impartially as possible (without prejudice) by consciously describing a phenomenon (intention). This transition from mere perception to deliberate scientific investigation takes place from diverse perspectives (eidetic variation) and in different ways (correlation),[5] with the aim of grasping the ultimate essence of a phenomenon.

4.1 Observation of the Research Process (*First Epoch*)

At the last stage before the highest level of absolute consciousness (*second epoch*),[6] which has no practical value here, phenomenological consciousness (*first epoch*) forms the highest level of research experience (Fig. 4.1): Husserl understands this to

[2] Godina (2012), p. 52.

[3] Ibid., pp. 52–53.

[4] Cf. Szilasi (1959), p. 7.

[5] Cf. Husserl (2023), pp. 80–87.

[6] Godina (2012), p. 50.

Fig. 4.1 "The first epoch through pausing for introspection." Godina, *Die phänomenologische Methode*, p. 44

be "a meta-level of consciousness above the acts of consciousness."[7] This refers to the ability to observe one's own act of research neutrally, as Husserl explains: "He [the human being, author's note] keeps himself out of the relationship that takes place between himself as a naturally experiencing human being and the objects that appear to this human being as existing."[8]

The observation of the methodological procedure is useful in that it firstly illustrates the main features of Husserl's methodological phenomenology on the basis of the concrete procedure in the context of the present research project. Secondly, it provides preliminary considerations for the development of a practically applicable counterfactual working method for interdisciplinary research between law and literature. The following meta-observation of observation will therefore be orientated towards the core points of methodological phenomenology, namely scientificity, impartiality, correlation, eidetic variation, and essence theory.

The *scientific character of the phenomenological method* (point 1) is considered by the stringent foundation of the research on the theoretical 'building blocks' of interdisciplinarity, discourse, hermeneutics, and counterfactuality. The first three 'building blocks' were studied to derive common methodological approaches for interdisciplinary work between legal and literary studies from their combination. The following considerations will show whether a new hybrid discipline of literature/law can emerge from this attempt or whether it is just sufficient to develop more sustainable and robust interdisciplinary paradigms.

Unprejudiced phenomenological description (point 2) seeks to perceive the structures of phenomena as well as differences and connections between

---

[7] Cf. ibid., p. 43.

[8] Held (1998), p. 35.

phenomena through "reflective and descriptive seeing"[9] to draw conclusions. The starting points are one's own experience of the world as it is (a world "before all theory"),[10] the objective approach to the previous experience of others, and the endeavour to gain meaningful insights from it that transcend individual subjectivity. Edmund Husserl explains how he understands this lack of prejudice in the sense of an unbound, free acquisition of knowledge:

> Nature must therefore be directly given to us as existing reality before all theory, before all indirect cognition [...]. But the immediate given of existing nature is sensory perception, the primal form of experience. To go back to experience [...] means nothing other than not speaking about real reality from above, from preconceptions, from vague opinions, from unseen traditions, but to see it for oneself [...].[11]

Husserl's view here is that good research must approach the object of research 'rich in ideas', uninfluenced by previous theories, dogmas, authoritarian opinions, etc., and is reminiscent of Gadamer's hermeneutic circle. According to Husserl, ideas must be able to unfold freely in everyday life as well as in science: "Everything is full of ideas, and our thinking is constantly interspersed with idea thinking and also idea views, both in everyday, pre-scientific thinking and even more so in scientific thinking."[12] In this sense, Maren Wehrle interprets the unprejudiced description as a process of improving knowledge: "It is a conscious methodological attitude that brackets the current theoretical methods and assumptions in order to thematise them and examine their legitimacy. The aim must be to arrive at a better theory, i.e. a theory with which the things to be analysed can be grasped more adequately, more effectively."[13] To achieve this goal, the cognising person must deal with the matter itself with the conscious intention of scientific knowledge and, in doing so, put aside their own 'pre-opinions' (Gadamer's hermeneutic circle repeatedly breaks through here) (eidetic reduction),[14] insofar as good scientific work presupposes theoretical impartiality.

In addition to the prerequisite of an unbiased openness, the methodological approach of the phenomenologist, as Werner Marx emphasises, requires the subjective decision to place oneself in the 'existing' world. In doing so, it is necessary to appropriate the peculiar 'theoretical practice' to approach the object of investigation step by step. According to Werner Marx, it is precisely the development of the subject area that determines the choice of how to approach research, i.e. the research method.[15] Helmut Danner refers to Husserl's concept of intentionality, according to

[9] Cf. Wehrle (2022), p. 29.

[10] Husserl (1998), p. 136.

By the world "before all theory", Husserl means the natural world as it surrounds us and as we experience it subjectively, without a research focus, empirically, psychologically, and imaginatively (cf. Godina 2012, p. 25).

[11] Husserl (2023), p. 10.

[12] Ibid., p. 11.

[13] Wehrle (2022), p. 141.

[14] Cf. Zahavi (2007), pp. 17–20.

[15] Marx (1987), p. 21.

which the natural 'contemplation' of an object only becomes a *phenomenon* through consciously intended description, investigation, and observation.[16] It is precisely this intentionality of consciousness that determines which object, which part of an object, and from which perspective an object is investigated.

Following Husserl's and Gadamer's postulates of prior knowledge and impartiality, I endeavour to direct my research gaze towards the subject of 'law *in* literature' in a scientifically 'unprejudiced' but consciously intentional way. By this I mean an open approach to the research subject of 'law *in* literature', without being disadvantageously predetermined by previous opinions, theories, theses, or assumptions of existing research. Disadvantageous here means a conditional predetermination of the research result based on previous opinions, which, however, can certainly be invalidated or modified with sufficient openness and thus lead to a new research result. However, in this context, a lack of prejudice is not to be understood in the sense of ignorance, on the contrary: the attempt to take a new look at the research field of law *in* literature requires solid prior knowledge of both the relevant theory and previous research achievements in the field of 'law *in* literature'. Furthermore, it seems sensible to utilise my own empirical and theoretical knowledge, which I have acquired in several disciplines, for the present work. In this sense, I would like to do justice to Husserl's phenomenological method in the first two points (scientificity and impartiality) by attempting to draw unconditionally on both my own and others' prior knowledge of literature and law. Therefore, Husserl's conception of an open approach to a research object appears essential for innovative research.

Further important methodological insights of Husserl relate, as already mentioned, to the principles of *correlation* (point 3) and *multiperspectivity* (point 4). The successful investigation of a phenomenon depends on the choice of a suitable approach to the object of research, i.e. on the correct *correlation*,[17] as Held explains: "There is a reciprocal relationship, a correlation, between the self-evidence of the objects and their subjective situation-bound mode of existence, the concrete character of which depends on the type of objectivity."[18] Diverse correlation possibilities (doubt, certainty, memory, etc.)[19] open up mental variation possibilities for the researchers, which they can, as Husserl writes, continue "and so on at will"[20] or not (eidetic variation), as long as the object does not lose its identity.[21] The phenomenon, i.e. the object of research, then emerges from the consciousness that concentrates intentionally on an object in a suitable way (correlation), as Bojan Godina illustrates in Fig. 4.2.

---

[16] Cf. Danner (1998), p. 125.

[17] Werner Marx compares this correlation with the "rules of the game" that govern the relationship between access mode and object (Marx 1987, p. 21).

[18] Held (1998), p. 15.

[19] Cf. Husserl (1973), pp. 36–37.

[20] Ibid., p. 217.

[21] Cf. Godina (2012), p. 37.

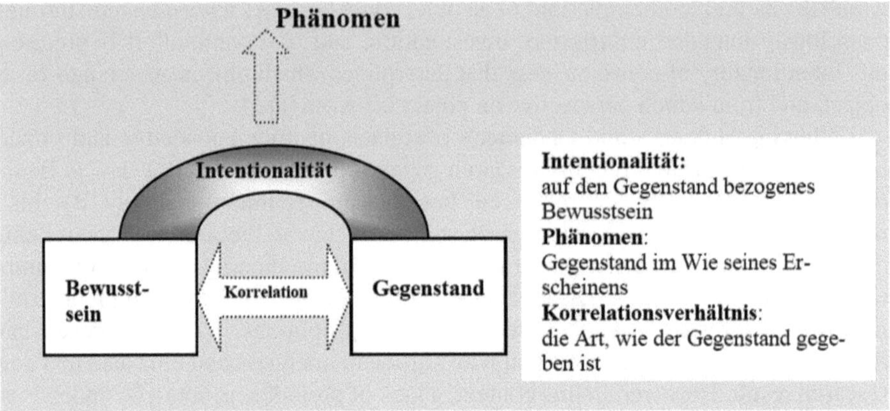

Fig. 4.2 "Act of research." Godina, *Die phänomenologische Methode*, p. 33

Correlation and eidetic variation play a special role here for interdisciplinary research between law and literature insofar as each of the two disciplines must be approached differently in both theoretical and practical terms. To illustrate this, I would like to highlight the relationship between literature and society in comparison to the relationship between law and society from the multitude of possible examples. It would make little sense to analyse the relationship between literature and society according to principles of legal theory or the relationship between law and literature according to the sole principles of literary or legal theory. For law, this would mean assuming the fictional character of literature and losing its normative character. For literature, on the other hand, this would mean understanding every sentence as a normative 'should' or 'you-may-not' and losing its fictional character. Such misguided *correlations*, to paraphrase Husserl, would lead to a falsified, meaningless research result: the law would lie and, in its function as a social seismograph, predict what literature will prescribe. Novels would become normatively binding for the reader, while legal texts could be read as entertaining fiction. This example clearly demonstrates the meaning of Husserl's call for an approach appropriate to the specificity of the object of research. The relevance of Husserl's possibilities of intellectual variation should also be pointed out, in the sense of the scientific interest in viewing an object of research from different perspectives, 'walking around' it, illuminating it from different angles, etc. To explain the interest of Husserl's eidetic variation for interdisciplinary work, the text will be used as an example, whereby the very understanding of what a text it is depends on the perspective of the observer/researcher: the literary theorist will define the term 'text' differently from the linguist, the lawyer, the sociologist or the cultural scientist.[22] The research perspective can also vary within the same epistemic field. By way of example, it can be argued that the text of the novel *La décision* by Karine Tuil would be analysed from the perspective of the

[22] Cf. Adamzik (2018), pp. 26–51.

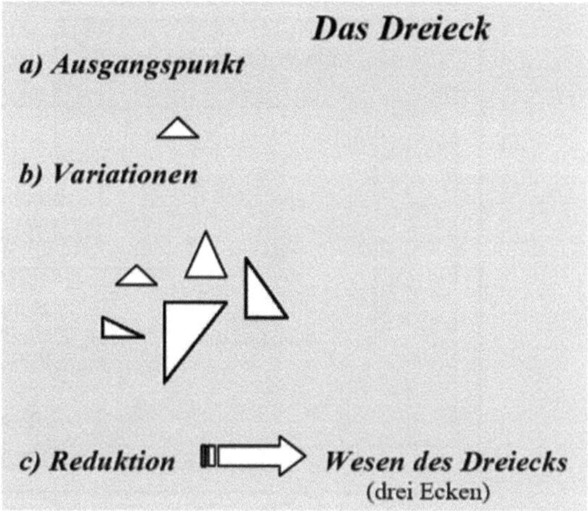

Fig. 4.3 "*The essence* of things." Godina, *Die phänomenologische Methode*, p. 41

literary scholar in terms of narrative perspectives and modes of expression, the alternation between inner monologue and outer narrative perspective, intertextual references to other works, etc. The legal scholar, on the other hand, would take interest in the same work for the depiction of the investigating judge's tasks in the 'counter-terrorism' department, for the legal plausibility of the descriptions, for the question of whether the terrorism legislation mentioned exists in this form or in a form other than that described in the story, etc. As this example shows, the same text can be 'circled' by several observers in a knowledge-specific way, or the same observer can decide to focus on the same text in different ways. For the interdisciplinary work here between law and literature, the concentration of literary and legal expertise in the same person therefore certainly offers the advantage of being able to perform this 'textual circumnavigation' from the perspective of the same observer.

According to Husserl, the interest of the 'qualitative researcher' lies not only in finding the right correlation to the object of research and viewing it from multiple perspectives but also in getting to the *essence* of things (point 5), i.e. the basic property or structure that remains the same in all variations. Godina illustrates Husserl's idea of essence pictorially (Fig. 4.3) using a triangle whose basic structure is determined by three corners, regardless of how the variation turns out[23] (because if the variation cancels out this basic triangular shape, the research object 'triangle' would lose its identity).

What is the essence of the 'intersection' between law and literature? Are there basic structures as the lowest denominators that law and literature have in common? In my investigation to derive answers to these questions, I concluded that the lowest denominator underlying both disciplines as an irreducible nature is the written text: without text, there is neither literature nor law nor, strictly speaking, neither literary studies nor jurisprudence. Law and literature as disciplines can at best be conveyed and passed on orally, but science cannot do without written fixation and

[23] Cf. Godina (2012), pp. 38–41.

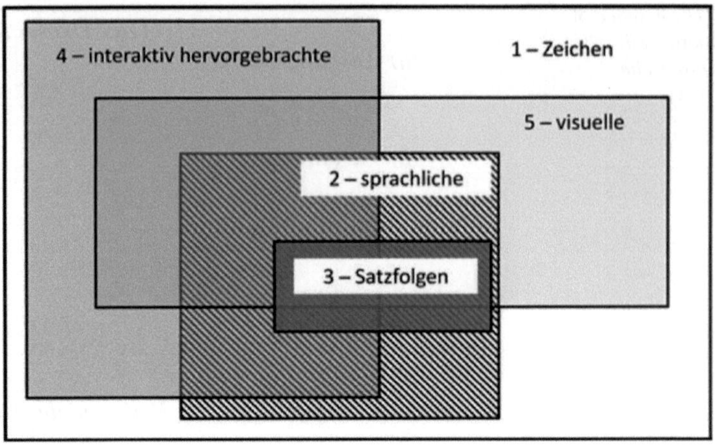

Fig. 4.4 "Definition areas of the term 'text'." Adamzik, "Was ist ein Text?", p. 29

transmission. How else can it draw on previous knowledge to update existing knowledge and develop new knowledge?

The text as the basis of interdisciplinary research between law and literature can be expanded, reduced, changed, and corrected, but it cannot be replaced by anything other than text. If this were the case, the essence, i.e. the unchangeable minimal structure, would be lost to be recognised as a 'text'. But what must this minimal structure of the text be like to be suitable for interdisciplinary literature/law research?

As already indicated, today the definitions of what a text is, diverge widely and range from the narrowest linguistic-grammatical definition of a "coherent sequence of sentences"[24] to the most extensive definition, which subsumes "signs of any kind (including odours, for example)"[25] under the term 'text', as Kirsten Adamzik illustrates with the following diagram (Fig. 4.4).

For our purposes, we can confidently assume that the smallest unit, i.e. the grammatically coherent sequence of sentences (no. 3), can be regarded as the *essence* of the object of research since the required 'material for investigation' can be the text, and only the text, and neither the linguistic interactions (no. 4) nor the visual or other signs (nos. 1, 2, 5). The research will therefore concentrate on the text in the narrow sense, i.e. on the sequences of sentences in the literary text that refer to legal relationships, and on the sequences of sentences in the legal text that provide information about the nature of the real-world legal system.

To summarise, in the chapters and sections leading up to this section, the *self-observational function at the meta-level of the observation process* has been explained through the methodological analysis of the research process to date on the research phenomenon of *legal counterfactuals: a method of contrastive discourse analysis between law and literature*.

[24] Brinker et al. (2018), p. 15.

[25] Adamzik (2018), p. 29.

In the state of *being in the natural world*, to use Husserl's words, I encountered law and literature in various situations and contexts, in literature lessons at grammar school, in law studies at university, in my work as a translator of legal texts, and as an employee of a legal publishing house, in my professional experience as a lawyer, etc. In all these activities, however, I acquired non-specific, non-research-oriented knowledge that prepared and built up my interdisciplinary prior knowledge. The additional acquisition of specific knowledge related to the planned object of research led to the precise formulation of the research intention in the form of the research project entitled *Law, Literature and Legal Counterfactuals: A Method of Contrastive Discourse Analysis Using the Example of Contemporary Literature*. To paraphrase Husserl, this was a conscious approach to the object of research, which through this *intentionality* was lifted out of the general, amorphous natural world and elevated to the status of a *phenomenon*. *Free from the dogmatic constrictions* of the existing state of research, guided by my own and previous scientific knowledge, approached with *openness*, with the joy of 'trying things out', of 'feeling', of a wide-ranging 'search'. This conscious 'searching' process led to my decision to precede the study with a historical-comparative overview of research in the field of law and literature and to base it on the theoretical pillars of interdisciplinarity, discourse, hermeneutics, and counterfactuality in an attempt to develop an interdisciplinary working method between law and literature on this basis. This theoretically conceived methodological approach will be empirically tested on the basis of five literary works. As indicated, adequate *correlation* as a suitable research approach considers the respective characteristics of law and literature, at the intersection of which is the search for a minimal common *essential structure* that appears to lie in the text as a coherent sequence of sentences. The text can be analysed from different perspectives (*eidetic variations*), i.e. in this specific case from both a literary and a legal perspective.

This retrospective, self-reflective meta-analysis of the previous research path, based on Husserl's methodological phenomenology, should now pave the way for further considerations on a *practically applicable and repeatable method* of counterfactual investigation of law *in* literature. The aim of these endeavours is, on the one hand, to lead to a better understanding of literary works with legal references and to a more trusting approach to law, also for literary scholars, through counterfactual contrasting and, on the other hand, to attempt to offer methodological approaches that enable robust, interdisciplinary work.

4.2 Draft of a Method for the Counterfactual Analysis of Legal Discourses in Literature

For the practical application of Husserl's phenomenology, Gerhard Kleining proposes a 'qualitative heuristic' methodology that provides for the combined observance four basic rules:

Rule 1: openness of the researcher (openness to new concepts and findings),

Rule 2: openness of the object of investigation (modulability of the object of research during the research),
Rule 3: maximum structural variation of perspectives, and
Rule 4: analyse for commonalities (similarities between the different perspectives).[26]

Rules 1–3 have already been explained and require no further comment here, they are assumed.

Rather, attention should be drawn to rule no. 4, whereby it should be noted that an analysis of the similarities presupposes an awareness of the differences. As Gerhard Kleining explains, the "comparison of differences [...] leads to an infinite number of possible combinations and requires the legitimisation of the – ultimately subjective – selection made in each case", while "the analysis of commonalities aims to trace complex data sets back to their structure in a comprehensible way."[27] In this sense, the concepts of interdisciplinarity, discourse, and hermeneutics are used to analyse the differences between law and literature and to derive commonalities from them. The selected basic theoretical concepts thus serve here as relevant parameters for differentiation and at the same time unification. Differentiation and commonality therefore appear to be two sides of the same coin, i.e. one cannot be thought of without the other. This process of differentiation/common ground must first be preceded by a clear delineation of where the points of separation between law and literary studies lie, to then be able to draw conclusions about common intersections that could be suitable for the construction of common methodological working techniques. Table 4.1 provides an overview of the 'intersections' between law and literature on the one hand, and the differences between the two disciplines on the other.

From the tabular overview of the differences and similarities between law and literary studies, it is indeed possible to identify a common matrix for law and literature. Michel Foucault had already supported this idea, as mentioned previously, calling for a link between the humanities and law.[28] This *common matrix* is the written TEXT, which in its generally accepted lexical-semantic meaning unites law and literature in that it is able to describe human behaviour in the Zeitgeist of society in all its breadth and forms the basis of the process of interpretation. Understanding and interpretation, coupled with prior knowledge, are to be considered closely together and lead from an imprecise overall picture through gradual filtering and sorting out of inappropriate interpretations to an adequate detailed interpretation, whereby the interpreter actively participates in the process of developing the hermeneutic 'history'.

My *methodological proposal* for analysing literary texts that include legal discourses is based on the realisation that the text as a basic unit is common to law and literature and undoubtedly represents the lowest common denominator of both disciplines. It is always a text, be it a literary diegesis, treatises on literary theory, literary or jurisprudential research contributions, legal texts, court judgements, legal

[26] Kleining (2010), p. 68.
[27] Ibid., p. 67.
[28] Foucault (1977), p. 23.

Table 4.1 Synthesis of commonalities and divergences between Law and Literature (Aexandra Juster)

Literature	Law	Intersection of literature/law
Interdisciplinarity		
Limit of the representability of normativity	Normativity	Human behaviour as an object
Representation of 'everything that is and is not'	Representation of external human actions	Representation of human actions
		Relative thematic delimitation
Fiction	Real world (actual state)	Factuality
Seismograph and mirror of human society	Mirror of human society, feedback on predictions	Mirror of human society and the Zeitgeist
		TEXT
		Intertextuality, coherence
Freedom of design	Contingency	
Language until the limits of its possibilities	Finality and form condition the language	Language as an organ of communication
literary-theoretical jargon/ theoretical cacophony, literary concepts	Legal terminology/ normative over-complexity, legal concepts	Object adequacy
Illustration, criticism, explanation, invention	Standardisation and legislation	
Discourse		
Constitutive function	Normative constitutive function	The constitution of reality and the world through statements
		Special research approach to words and meaning, context and linguistic regularities
Specialised literary vocabulary, subject-specific signs and phrases	Legal vocabulary, normativity, subject-specific symbols and formulas, procedural rules, finding evidence, level system	The constitution of epistemes through visible and invisible discourses
		Self-contained episteme, but open to the environment and capable of communicating with other disciplines
		Subjective or objective author/text reference
Interdiscursive function as knowledge mediator and 'translator' between disciplines		
Substitution of hermeneutics by discourse research	Clear separation between discourse and hermeneutics	

(continued)

Table 4.1 (continued)

Literature	Law	Intersection of literature/law
Hermeneutics		
Indeterminacy of hermeneutic rules due to changing or diverging theories	The strictest possible hermeneutic rules in the interest of legal certainty, hierarchical control	hermeneutic imprecision due to human subjectivity
One text	Two texts: the abstract norm and the specific individual case (subsumption)	Understanding/interpretation/ application
Independence of the interpretation	Earmarking of the interpretation (practical effectiveness)	
Text aesthetics	Clarity of the text	TEXT as a hermeneutic reference
Intertextuality	Step structure Collision rules	Grammatical (objective), teleological (subjective) and systematic interpretation (intertext)
Author-text-reader context	Legislator-text-judge/ lawyer-context	Creative function of the interpreter
Interpretation without time constraints in an endless series of interpretations	Interpretation in a timely manner and adapted to the specific case	Interpretation
Reception-related (readers and literary scholars), relevance of aesthetics	Subject-related (lawyer, judge) Relevance of practical effectiveness	Hermeneutic circle: prior knowledge, overall and partial context, text meaning through progressive 'sorting out', participation in the creative process of further development
	Value-orientated interpretation, the impact of the Basic Law	
		Central role of the general lexical meaning
Interpretation without concrete social impact	Interpretation with concrete consequences (prison sentence or fine, etc.)	

doctrine or legal fragments, terms and commentaries that flow into the literary text. As indicated, the written text is an ideal medium for the absorption and fusion of different discourses, as is the case here for law and literature. My proposal is derived from this realisation to approach the selected literary texts from a discourse-theoretical perspective and, on this basis, to open the texts through interpretation in order, in the next step, to contrast the legal discourse in the fiction and the legal real-world text counterfactually.

In practical application, the *process of understanding* will therefore be divided into the following steps:

1. first reading to gain a general aesthetic impression.
2. second reading focussing on the explicit legal discourse in the literary text (explicit mention of legal institutions, terms and concepts, legal paragraphs, procedural acts, etc.).

According to Gadamer's hermeneutic circle, interpretation, as already mentioned several times, presupposes understanding, or, to put it another way: understanding takes place in interpretation. The process of interdisciplinary understanding and interpretation can therefore not function without knowledge of the real-world legal text that corresponds to the literary text, which is why in the third step:

3. The real-world law, which correlates with the literary text, is identified by analysing the explicit legal discourse in the diegesis.

If, for example, the text of the novel refers to Talmudic law, this is to be understood as an indicator that knowledge of real-world Talmudic law will be essential for perfecting the process of understanding, and hence the approach focuses on:

4. Acquisition of knowledge of the real-world law that correlates with the literary text.

At this point, I would like to refer once again to Walter Müller-Seidl, who emphasises that a text must be linked to the corresponding background knowledge, whereby it is important to plausibly "link knowledge about the text with the background knowledge in question."[29] I especially agree with Müller-Seidl that "it must be made clear what the one has to do with the other. This cannot simply be left to the reader. The linking and integration of the other must be done on a case-by-case basis, actually from sentence to sentence."[30] It is in this sense that I am convinced that the interdisciplinary scholar must acquire the interdisciplinary knowledge necessary to deepen the text: The literary scholars must be prepared to familiarise themselves with legal texts, and the legal scholars must be interested in questions of literary theory. The combination of textual and legal knowledge in interdisciplinary discourse then makes it possible to achieve a deeper understanding of the text through the process of interpretation:

5. Third reading, enriched with prior legal knowledge, which also makes it possible to recognise any implicit legal references in the literary text.

The understanding deepened in this way ultimately enables an appropriate interpretation of the work and sets the professional course for a meaningful counterfactual contrast, i.e. for the identification of differences (and their extent) or similarities between the legal discourse in the diegesis and the real legal discourse. As already emphasised several times, counterfactual thinking is only possible with knowledge of the two comparison parameters fictional world/real world. *Counterfactual thinking* always implies the juxtaposition of the real and fictional world, insofar as it

[29] Müller-Seidel (1986), pp. 88–89.

[30] Ibid., p. 90.

concerns the relationship between the real and possible world as a counterfactual alternative world to the real world.[31] As Keith Markman & al. explain, the method of counterfactual thinking implies the idea of alternative events or occurrences to those that have actually taken place: "An imagination of alternatives to reality is called counterfactual thinking."[32] According to Roland Wenzlhuemer, Markman & al. refer here to the human reaction that tends to draw conclusions about the current situation from the occurrence of alternative unforeseen events: "When the thinkers compare the actual result or situation with the alternative 'what might have been'-result, this also leads to a reassessment of the actual situation in the light of the alternative outcome. Roese calls this the 'contrast effect'."[33] It is precisely this contrast between 'what is' and 'what is imaginable' that must be made fruitful for the 'legal counterfactual', i.e. the contrast between the law 'that is' and the law that is presented as an alternative in narrative fiction. The law 'that is' is correlated here through the hermeneutic procedure with the law that is 'imagined' in the diegesis. In this context, Wenzlhuemer refers to the interest of contrasting as a scientific method, especially to overcome boundaries and constrictions and to develop innovative research paths: "Counterfactual thoughts can help researchers to overcome traditional, established boundaries and pathways of enquiry. They can allow us to zoom out, refocus and contemplate a fresh perspective, when in danger of becoming professionally blinkered."[34] Moreover, Wenzlhuemer continues: "Developing counterfactual scenarios in research can constitute an opportunity for the researcher to think about a problem in unorthodox ways."[35] New, previously unconsidered perspectives for investigation and thought can be opened up in this way through counterfactual contrasting: And this is precisely the intention of the legal counterfactual experiment: *it should open up a 'new' view of the relationship between literature and law and demonstrate possibilities for closer interdisciplinary approaches.*

The process of contrasting what is with what could have been, but ultimately is not, paradoxically increases the understanding of what is. Wenzlhuemer illustrates this assumption using the historical example of the Second World War, the outcome of which (victory of the Allied powers) can only be truly understood if the possible alternative (victory of the Axis powers) is also included. In this sense, counterfactual contrasting enables a better understanding of the object of research since "counterfactuals are applied to reveal contrasts and the creation of meaning."[36] This statement can also be extended to law and literature; if one assumes that contrasting the law in fiction as a hypothesis of what could be or could have been with real-world law as a fact of what is leads to a better understanding of law and literature as a subject of research. In this way, the contrastive approach places legal reality and

[31] Zipfel (2001), p. 84.

[32] Markman et al. (1993), here: p. 88.

[33] Wenzlhuemer (2009), here: p. 29.

[34] Ibid., p. 30.

[35] Ibid., p. 35.

[36] Ibid. See also Birke et al. (2011), here: p. 2.

the deviating representation of law in literature in a reciprocal relationship that can lead to a better understanding of both sides.

At this point, Alexander Demandt refers to the historical counterfactual when he emphasises that what did not happen is also relevant for understanding what 'happened':

> Certainly, the objection that what has not happened has no meaning remains correct. The possibilities that have not occurred have no relevance themselves but provide us with the necessary backdrop against which we can recognise the significance of what has actually happened. Unreality is no more an argument for irrelevance than reality is an argument for relevance.[37]

The same considerations can be applied to law in literature: even if not all law in fiction is real law, there are still meaningful references or food for thought about current legal relationships that only come into their own when contrasted with real law. A similar function of opening up perspectives is performed by '*counterfictionality*',[38] which retells fictions that have already been told, as Richard Saint-Gelais explains: "A counterfiction, as I define it, is a text that sets out to modify the diegesis of a former fictional narrative."[39] The mechanism is similar to that of the counterfactual, with the difference that instead of contrasting two fictional media (fiction A and fiction B as a variation of fiction A), a fictional medium is contrasted with a factual one. The legal counterfactual can therefore be explained analogously to counterfiction: Here, the *factual* law is varied in the *fictional* diegesis, while in counterfiction a fiction A is transformed into a fiction B.

Finally, the following programme summarises the practical, methodical steps as a working aid:

1.	Reading to gain a general aesthetic impression.
2.	Reading with a focus on explicit legal discourses in literary texts.
3.	Identification of the real-world legal system to which the literary text refers.
4.	Acquiring knowledge of this real-world right.
5.	Final reading to recognise possible implicit legal references through legal interpretation.
6.	Counterfactual contrast.

From this theoretical-methodological part of the work, which has now been completed, we will now move on to the practical examination of five literary works to empirically test the conceptual and methodological knowledge gained in the first part and at the same time attempt to (pre-)demonstrate the methodological procedure in practice. Only this practical step will make it possible to verify the suitability of the draft of a legal counterfactual method and to modify it if necessary. It will also indicate whether this method is suitable for bringing about a closer interdisciplinary link between law and literature or whether it is generally applicable to the study of law *in* literature and can thus become a method common to literary and legal studies.

---

[37] Demandt (1986), p. 39.

[38] Cf. Hills (2003), pp. 436–455.

[39] Saint-Gelais, here: p. 244.

References

Adamzik, Kirsten. 2018. Was ist ein Text? In *Handbuch Text und Gespräch*, ed. Karin Birkner and Nina Janich, 26–51. Berlin/Boston: De Gruyter.

Birke, Dorothee, Michael Butter, and Tilmann Köppe. 2011. Introduction: England Win. In *Counterfactual Thinking –Counterfactual Writing*, ed. Dorothee Birke, Michael Butter, and Tilmann Köppe, 1–11. Berlin/Boston: De Gruyter.

Brinker, Klaus, Hermann Cölfen, and Steffen Pappert. 2018. *Linguistische Textanalyse. Einführung in Grundbegriffe und Methoden*. Berlin: Erich Schmidt.

Brosius, Hans-Bernd, Alexander Haas, and Friederike Koschel. 2016. Was sind Methoden, was ist Empirie? In *Methoden der empirischen Kommunikationsforschung*, ed. Hans-Bernd Brosius, Friederike Koschel, and Alexander Haas, 1–31. Wiesbaden: Springer.

Danner, Helmut. 1998. *Methoden geisteswissenschaftlicher Pädagogik*. Munich: Ernst Reinhardt.

Demandt, Alexander. 1986. *Ungeschehene Geschichte. Ein Traktat über die Frage: Was wäre geschehen, wenn ...?* Göttingen: Vandenhoeck & Ruprecht.

Foucault, Michel. 1977. *Discipline and Punish: The Birth of the Prison*. New York: Pantheon Books.

Godina, Bojan. 2012. *Die phänomenologische Methode Husserls für Sozial- und Geisteswissenschaftler. Ebenen und Schritte der phänomenologischen Reduktion*. Wiesbaden: Springer.

Held, Klaus. 1998. Einleitung. In *Die phänomenologische Methode. Ausgewählte Texte I*, ed. Edmund Husserl and Klaus Held. Stuttgart: Reclam.

Hills, Matt. 2003. Counterfiction in the Work of Kim Newman: Rewriting Gothic SF as 'Alternate-Story Stories'. *Science Fiction Studies* 2003 (30): 436–455.

Husserl, Edmund. 1973. *Experience and Judgement; Investigations in a Genealogy of Logic*. Evanston: Northwestern University Press.

Husserl, Edmund. 1998. In *Die phänomenologische Methode. Ausgewählte Texte I*, ed. Klaus Held. Stuttgart: Reclam.

Husserl, Edmund. 2023. In *Einleitung in die Phänomenologie. Vorlesung 1912*, ed. Thomas Vongehr. Wiesbaden: Springer.

Kleining, Gerhard. 2010. Qualitative Heuristik. In *Handbuch Qualitative Forschung in der Psychologie*, ed. Günter Mey and Katja Mruck, 65–78. Wiesbaden: VS Verlag für Sozialwissenschaften.

Markman, Keith D., Igor Gavanski, Stephen J. Sherman, and Matthew Mc-Mullen. 1993. The Mental Simulation of Better and Worse Possible Worlds. *Journal of Experimental Social Psychology* 1993 (29): 87–109.

Marx, Werner. 1987. *Die Phänomenologie Edmund Husserls*. Munich: Fink.

Müller-Seidel, Walter. 1986. *Die Deportation des Menschen. Kafkas Erzählung 'In der Strafkolonie' im europäischen Kontext*. Stuttgart: J. B. Metzler.

Szilasi, Wilhelm. 1959. *Einführung in die Phänomenologie Edmund Husserls*. Tübingen: Max Niemeyer.

Wehrle, Maren. 2022. *Phänomenologie. Eine Einführung*. Berlin: J. B. Metzler.

Wenzlhuemer, Roland. 2009. Counterfactual Thinking as a Scientific Method. *Historical Social Research* 34 (2): 27–56.

Zahavi, Dan. 2007. *Phänomenologie für Einsteiger*. Paderborn: W. Fink.

Zipfel, Frank. 2001. *Fiktion, Fiktivität, Fiktionalität: Analysen zur Fiktion in der Literatur und zum Fiktionsbegriff in der Literaturwissenschaft*. Berlin: Schmidt.

Chapter 5
Counterfactual Analyses in Practice

The practical investigation will be preceded by a brief theoretical explanation of the normative theory narrative, which is particularly suitable for texts with legal references, before moving on to the practical investigation. The following literary works will be analysed here:

(1) Karine Tuil's novel *La décision* (2022) introduces the reader to the work of an investigating judge in the French anti-terrorism department and to French anti-terrorism legislation.
(2) Elvira Dones' novel *Sworn Virgin* (2014) thematises the disenfranchisement of women according to the canon of Albanian customary law 'Kanun', which Hana tries to escape by swearing eternal virginity.
(3) Deborah Feldman's autobiographical novel ~~Unorthodox~~ (2012) describes the author's condition as a woman and her forced marriage in the ultra-orthodox Jewish Satmar community in New York (Jewish-Talmudic law).
(4) Claude Chossat's equally autobiographical novel *Repenti* (2017), in which the author explains the unwritten rules of blood revenge (*vendetta*) in French Corsica that are still in force today.
(5) Abbas Khider's *A Slap in the Face* (2016) guides the reader through the administrative and bureaucratic jungle that asylum seekers face in Germany.

The selection of these five works is explained, on the one hand, by the fact that the interactions between law and society that they portray are of particular interest for an interdisciplinary counterfactual investigation and, on the other hand, by the endeavour to transcend criminal law—which is traditionally overrepresented in the literature—by including new areas of law such as the fight against terrorism, family and asylum law, Talmudic law, and customary law.

The examination of each of the five works will follow the working method described in detail in Sect. 4.2 to test the practical applicability of the outlined method of legal counterfactuals.

A. Juster, *Law, Literature and Legal Counterfactuals*, Law and Visual Jurisprudence 16, https://doi.org/10.1007/978-3-032-03792-3_5

5.1 Narratives Between Fact and Fiction

All five novels analysed below refer explicitly to very different factual-legal contexts of the real world, which are varied, i.e. 'narrated', in literary fiction counterfactually to our real world. According to Willy Viehöver, the term 'narrative' should be understood as the "linguistic representation of an event, i.e. a temporally organised sequence of events", whose contexts are meaningful and can, under certain circumstances, be classified in certain superordinate narratives,[1] whereby this can also concern legal relationships, for example. Matías Martínez and Michael Scheffel define the term 'narrative' in a similar way as "a type of oral or written speech in which someone communicates something special to someone else; leaving aside a meaning in the broader sense of 'to communicate, to say in confidence' [...], a speech is obviously called a 'narrative' if this speech visualises a process preceding it in time, which can be defined as an 'event' or 'occurrence'."[2] The two authors distinguish between the narration of real (factual) or invented (fictional) events and between literary fiction and non-literary everyday speech.[3]

In this sense, the works selected for the study are fictions whose referentiality to real legal relationships will have to be analysed. It will be necessary to clarify how real-world legal facts are represented in fiction and modified in relation to legal reality. In doing so, the possibility of mixing factuality and fictionality in fiction will have to be worked out. It thus makes sense to ask about the narrative form that can access this legal reality, i.e. of combining legal facts and fiction. Christian Klein and Matías Martínez coin the term "*reality narrative*" for narratives that refer to concrete reality and make "statements with a specific claim to validity."[4] Such a claim to reality can refer to the actual state of the 'as-is' (descriptive reality narrative), the target state of the 'should-be' (normative reality narrative), or the predicted state of the 'will-be' (predictive reality narrative).[5] For narratives that refer to legal relations, the sub-genre of the *normative reality narrative* is particularly tautological in this context. The fact that the concept of reality narrative can also be applied to literary texts confirms Klein and Martínez's view that a mixture of fictional and factual references can also occur on a narrative level:

> At the level of the *histoire* (the level of the narrative), not only real events are sometimes described, but also, for example, fictional case histories (e.g. in economic or legal discourse). However, since these fictional elements are functionalised in the sense of regulating practice or defining general structural features with reference to extra-linguistic reality, we understand them as *narratives of reality*.[6]

---

[1] Klein (2013), pp. 17–21, here: p. 18.

[2] Martínez and Scheffel (2019), pp. 11-12.

[3] Ibid., p. 12. See Sect. 3.4.1 "Zum Verhältnis zwischen Fiktion und Fakt".

[4] Klein and Martínez (2009), pp. 1–13, here: p. 1.

[5] Ibid., pp. 6–7.

[6] Ibid., p. 7.

The fact that the occurrence of factual references in fictional texts is quite common beyond the specifics of the young narratological concept of the 'truth narrative', without detracting from literary fiction, has already been explained in more detail in Sect. 3.4.1 on the relationship between fiction and fact.

5.2 *La décision* (2022) by Karine Tuil[7]

According to Gerhard Wild, "literature and public life" are more "intertwined" in France than in other European countries.[8] Karine Tuil confirmed this statement in her inaugural speech on 14 September 2023 on the occasion of taking up the traditional one-year chair reserved for a selected author and writer at the Institute of Political Sciences in Paris (*Sciences Po Paris*), which she introduced with the following sentence: "Literature is the last pocket of resistance in a world that is collapsing."[9] She emphasises the social commitment of her writing as a means of finding the truth through the word, just as the law obliges the judge to find the truth. According to Tuil, literature, like law, is an act of defence, it is freedom in the service of freedom. The French author has an experienced perspective on this matter, as she studied law herself. Literature and law, she argues, can change society, draw attention to certain issues and change perspectives. Literature opens contradictory, democratic debates by asking questions, seeking answers, and focusing on problems that affect society.[10] One of these current debates in France concerns the fight against Islamist terror, which has been shaking the public since 1985, with brief interruptions.

Tuil's novel *La décision* should be read against the backdrop of the renewed threat of Islamist terrorism, which, after a somewhat calmer phase since the series of attacks in the 1990s, has been plaguing France again,[11] particularly since 2015, as Wild explains: "Since the beginning of 2015, France has been experiencing an unprecedented series of Islamist terrorist attacks, to which the state has responded with the state of emergency."[12] A special criminal law was introduced in France as early as 1986 (loi n° 86–1020 du 9 septembre 1986), which was intended to take the severity and peculiarities of the terrorist act into account. Every successive attack occasioned amendments and additions to the law, until most recently in June 2017 (loi n° 2017–1510 du 30 octobre 2017).[13] Tuil's focus in this context, as Marion Mas points

[7] Tuil (2022). For citation purposes, the original French version is used under the siglum 'LD' with the page number in the running text. No English translation of the novel is currently available, all translations are mine.

[8] Wild (2017), p. 9.

[9] Tuil (2023) (internet-link in the bibliography).

[10] Tuil (2023).

[11] See also Trévidic (2011), pp. 24–25.

[12] Wild (2017), p. 10.

[13] Status on 12/06/2024.

out, is on the difficulty of making the right decision between releasing and imprisoning suspected terrorists who have not yet committed a provable offence: "For the aim […] the reader is to place at the centre of the difficulties inherent in the act of judging, exposing him or her to the polyphony […] of different judgements."[14] The principle of the presumption of innocence on the one hand, and concern for public safety on the other, are in conflict with each other, a conflict that is difficult to resolve, whereby the presumption of terrorist intentions is evident when French followers of Islam travel to Syria to be trained by the Islamic State (IS). As will be shown, the question of the correctness of the investigating judge's decision is complicated by subjective influencing factors. According to Rémy Cabrillac, Karine Tuil skilfully points to the dilemma between the overwhelming responsibility of the investigating judge (in the French criminal proceeding the so called *juge de l'instruction*). A fallibly rendered judgement can cost human lives or change them to the point of unbearableness; preservation of humane life is why the novel, as a form, is important to the legal profession, as stated below: "This fictional but remarkably well-documented account of the legal world will be of particular interest to legal scholars."[15]

With *La décision*, Tuil proves how closely law and literature, legislation and emotions are linked. For her, as Sophie Tardy-Joubert notes, literature is a place of transgression and overcoming taboos: "Literature must be a place of transgression, of breaking taboos and denials. A place where everything can be said about society. To be a novelist is to claim this freedom."[16] As Marc Trévidic, himself a former prosecutor and now an anti-terrorism judge at the Paris Court, confirms, it also aptly captures the difficult and at the same time responsible role of the investigating judges in the search for the truth, in that they not only know how to incriminate the accused but also how to exonerate them: "For my part, I have always appreciated the notion of instruction for and against, a difficult task entrusted to the investigating judge. But also, the nobility of his function. What greater satisfaction can there be than that, for a judge, of investigating the truth? This satisfaction reaches its peak when the investigation exonerates a suspect."[17] As Tuil makes clear in *La décision* in agreement with Marc Trévidic, it must also be the judge's concern to grant the suspect the possibility of innocence and probation, because true satisfaction lies not in the guilty verdict, but in the acquittal.

5.2.1 La décision*: Content*

Alma Revel, investigating judge and coordinator of the French counter-terrorism department in Paris, is, among many other cases, in charge of investigating the case of 'Abdeljalil Kacem', a case that she is overseeing in the binomial with her

[14] Mas (2023), p. 3. See also Rolle (2024), pp. 42–43.

[15] Cabrillac (2022), p. 141.

[16] Tardy-Joubert (2020), pp. 27–29, here: p. 29.

[17] Trévidic (2011), p. 140.

colleague François Vasseur. This case is one of many centered on the radicalisation of French citizens, as they travel to Syria to be trained by the Islamic State (IS), and return to France as trained terrorists and murderers. Abdeljalil Kacem also travelled to an IS training camp with his wife Sonia Dos Santos in 2014 and returned to France 2 years later. However, it cannot be proven that he has already committed an offence, and only the suspicion that his return did not harbour peaceful intentions is obvious. Alma Revel's investigations should shed light on whether Kacem can and should be released from custody without endangering the public. Under French criminal law, special anti-terror legislation allows suspects to be charged preventively and, if necessary, punished based on proven criminal *intent.* Alma Revel's work is overshadowed by the breakdown of her marriage to Ezra Halevi, by the great psychological pressure of her work in constant confrontation with the violence of the perpetrators and the endless suffering of the victims, as well as by the constant fear for her own life and that of her three children. In a state of personal fragility and against the commandment to avoid conflicts of interest—she falls in love with Abdeljalil Kacem's defence lawyer, Emmanuel Forest. The latter is defending Kacem and his wife Sonia, who claim to have travelled to Syria with peaceful intentions to live there according to the laws of the Islamic religion. On their return to France via Turkey, they were caught there, interned in a camp and extradited to France shortly afterwards. Suspected of having actively participated in the IS, they were immediately placed under police surveillance (Sonia) or remanded in custody (Abdeljalil) (LD 118–119). At the end of her investigation, Alma Revel, influenced by her lover Emmanuel Forest and Kacem's seemingly positive behaviour, decides to grant him conditional freedom, with the condition of that he wears an electronic bracelet and undergoes regular police checks. This decision soon (dramatically) proves to be wrong: a few days later, Kacem carries out an attack on the Parisian nightclub *L'Entrepôt*, killing eleven people, including Ali, the partner of Revel's daughter Milena.[18]

After this brief description of the background and plot, attention will now be drawn to the *explicit legal discourse in the narrative*, as it is accessible to the reader even without legal background knowledge of specific French anti-terrorist criminal law. Legally relevant information is obtained from the discourse analysis of the text, which results in a preliminary overall legal picture within the framework of the fiction. In the second step, the special criminal law currently in force in France to combat terrorism will be presented and contrasted counterfactually with the fictional overall picture. Only the combination of the diegetic legal discourse with the real-world legal-historical background knowledge about particular terrorism legislation in France will fully open up Tuil's novel and decisively enhance understanding through interpretation.

[18] Cf. Charbonnier and Petit (2023), pp. 72–79.

5.2.2 *Explicit Legal Discourse in the Diegesis*

Tuil's fiction depicts the very real world of French special criminal law and its protagonists—public prosecutors, investigating magistrates, defence lawyers, prison judges, and criminal police—but without completely renouncing the freedom of literary fiction, insofar as the novel's characters and their dialogues, emotions, fears, and hopes are of fictional origin. Rémy Cabrillac confirms, as already mentioned, that Tuil's fiction paints a seriously researched picture of French anti-terrorist justice.[19] To paraphrase Foucault, it brings to life the practice of the anti-terrorism department of a Parisian Court by describing both its actors and the rules of criminal procedure in the diegesis.[20] In line with this judicial practice, Tuil outlines the conventions of French special criminal law in *La décision* by adhering very closely to the legal terms, the specialised vocabulary, and the normative provisions.[21] Beyond the explicitly comprehensible rules of criminal law, the fiction attempts to reconstruct and clearly portray invisible behaviours, attitudes, and practices in the special criminal justice system. As a text, *La décision* produces the 'back and forth' between the real law and the medium of the literary text as an imaginary force, which Philippe Agresti describes as follows: "The text. Always the text as a source of reflection [...]. The authors emphasise the constant movement of texts between the legal discipline, which is rooted in reality, and the literary discipline, which appeals to the imaginary [...]."[22] In this way, the legal discourse appears to be embedded in a fictional, imaginary plot that pursues two goals: Firstly, to clarify and explain the functions of the criminal law institution, the course of the criminal trial, the operation of the court, and the functions and interactions of the individual actors in this process. Secondly, the psychological and human processes, difficulties, and conflicts that these actors go through and with which they must struggle, especially when it comes to making the right decision. The professional-looking interrogations and questioning of the accused Kacem, which enforce the narrative, do not allow Revel to gain a clear picture of Kacem's intentions, either favourable or unfavourable. The reader, on the other hand, suspects that Kacem's statements are most likely not entirely credible. The question of the 'right' decision arises for Revel both in her fictional private life and in her professional work as an investigating judge. In doing so, she not only continually refers to the reality of French anti-terror legislation, but also to the critical potential of literature.

In the following, the aim is to separate the two fictional spheres, the fictional and the factual-real, to expose the legal discourse. In this context, it is worth recalling the possible relationship between fictionality and reality in fiction, which Wolfgang Iser understands as not mutually exclusive: "Therefore, the fictional could be qualified as a peculiar transitional form that always shoves between the real and the

[19] Cf. Cabrillac (2022), p. 141.

[20] Cf. Foucault (1972), pp. 48–49.

[21] Cf. Link (1983), pp. 18–25.

[22] Agresti (2023).

imaginary for the purpose of their mutual connectivity."[23] Connectivity instead of exclusivity: precisely this connection, to which Iser refers, determines the relationship between fictional and factual discourse in the novel *La décision* insofar as real law on the one hand, and imagined actions and actors on the other, correlate in the text. In other words: literature and law, fiction and fact meet in the text without being mutually exclusive. To paraphrase Michel Foucault, the question at this point is how French anti-terror legislation is expressed in the text and how it relates to the imaginary fiction of the characters.[24] In the process of interpreting the text, it will be a matter of gradually sorting out the inapplicable in the sense of Gadamer's hermeneutic circle until what is relevant for the present study is narrowly circumscribed, namely the legal discourse with reference to French anti-terror legislation.

The sentence on the first page "As an anti-terrorist judge [...]" (LD 13) provides an immediate introduction to the world of special French anti-terrorist criminal law. The simultaneous question posed by the first-person narrator and investigating judge in the anti-terrorism department, Alma Revel, as to whether she will be up to her task of showing the victims the horror of the detailed recordings of the attacks, makes the criminal law context clear (LD 13). By mentioning her fellow judge François Vasseur, who has joined the department since the attack on the satirical magazine *Charlie Hebdo*, Revel refers to the judicial investigative work in binomial, in cooperation with the chief judge Éric Macri, who was entrusted with the case (LD 14).

The fact that Alma Revel deals with cases of terrorism is clear from the list of what she has already seen in the course of her career: "videos of executions, [...] extracts from surveillance cameras, decapitations [...]" and self-recordings of kamikaze attacks, who are not only concerned with the act of terror but above all with its mediatisation: "They use a harness to hold the camera to their torso and switch it on when they're ready to kill. It's not enough for them to kill, they want to show how they did it [...]" (LD 15–16). Revel provides more detailed information about her work as a specialised investigating judge when she describes how she took up her position in the anti-terrorism department in Paris in 2009 and was promoted to coordinator of eleven judges in 2012 (LD 21). Her area of expertise extends to attacks without geographical limits as soon as they claim victims. Regarding the status of the investigating judge, she states that she conducts investigations, interrogates the accused and their accomplices, and receives the families of the victims. The task of the investigating judge is not to prove guilt, but to collect objectively ascertainable evidence. Three services work together with the investigating magistrates and the judge in charge of the case: the French Domestic Security Service (DGSI),[25] the anti-terrorist sub-department of the judicial police (SDAT),[26] and the

[23] Iser (1983), p. 150.

[24] Cf. Foucault (1972), pp. 22; 183.

[25] DGSI = *Direction Générale de la Sécurité Intérieure*. It was established on 30 April 2014 and has since taken over the tasks of the DCRI. It reports directly to the Ministry of the Interior (cf. Yves Mayaud 2020a, p. 22).

[26] SDAT = *Sous-Direction Anti-Terroriste* (Trévidic 2011, p. 15).

anti-terrorist department of the judicial police. The daily work consists of regular meetings and the commissioning of experts and investigative assistants with numerous expert reports: DNA analyses, computer data, and psychological reports. As Revel explains, her daily work also includes preparing and conducting interrogations, often carrying out dangerous field missions in areas where jihadist troops operate, and drafting resolutions (LD 21–24).

According to Revel, after the traumatic experience of a long series of terrorist attacks in the 1990s,[27] retributive justice turned into preventive justice from 2015 onwards. It even became possible to prosecute a terrorist's intention without an actual offence having been committed: "Today, when it comes to terrorism, we have a preventive offence, we arrest as far in advance as possible, we charge a simple intent…." (LD 184). As soon as people travelled to Syria, they are investigated on suspicion of preparing a terrorist attack and sentenced to prison, sometimes wrongly (LD 33).

In this context, Revel meticulously explains the procedure for Syrian returnees: as soon as they get off the plane at Orly airport, they are met by three search agents on the runway, undergo an identity check, are taken to the border police at Orly airport and informed of their rights. The DGSI is informed to appoint a public defender and a doctor. After identifying and sealing the luggage at the airport, the arrivals are taken into police custody in Levallois, where the interrogation begins the next morning in the presence of three investigators: one agent conducts the interrogation, another agent examines the sealed luggage, and a third agent takes care of the rest (files, presence in social networks, etc.).

Against the background of the comments on the problem of Syrian returnees and how to deal with them, the incidental insertion on the case of 'Nadia Karmouche' and the central case of Abdeljalil Kacem and his wife Sonia should be understood: When Anna Revel spends a weekend on holiday with her husband to make one last attempt to save their marriage, she is informed by a DGSI investigator that Nadia Karmouche—who had been apprehended by the police in Turkey during her attempt to cross into Syria and is currently under judicial control in France—has not dutifully reported to the police station. Revel immediately feared that Karmouche had disregarded her court order to commit an assassination: "Such moments are pure horror. You are convinced that the person in question is not fulfilling her duty to report, with the intention of carrying out an assassination" (LD 78). Revel justifies her decision not to remand Nadia Karmouche in custody by stating that she had been sent back before she had even set foot on Syrian soil. At the same time, however, she warns that Karmouche had sworn allegiance to the IS and should therefore be categorised as dangerous (LD 78–81).

[27] Between 1985 and 1987, Paris was shaken by a series of attacks on metro stations (Saint-Michel, Orsay, Maisons-Blanches, Port-Royal), department stores (Publicis Drugstore, Marks & Spencer, Galéries Lafayette, Fnac, Gibert-Jeunes), and in the street (rue Copernic, rue de Rosiers, rue de Rennes) (see Trévidic 2011, pp. 19–25). This was followed in 2012 by attacks in Toulouse and Montauban, on 7 January 2015 on the *Charlie Hébdo* newspaper editorial office in Paris, on 13 November 2015 on Le Bataclan theatre in Paris, and on 14 July 2016 on the *Promenade des Anglais* in Nice (DGSI).

The central case of Abdeljalil Kacem and his wife Sonia should be understood as contextually the same as the criminal prosecution of Syrian returnees: The moment they returned to France after spending several weeks in Syria, Revel imposed electronic bracelet police checks on Sonia and pre-trial detention on Abdeljalil (LD 118–119). Since then, Revel has been trying to establish the truth and decide whether the evidence she has is sufficient to refer the defendants to Judge Eric Macri. This is the central question that Revel constantly asks herself: Is she making the right decision? "Am I making the *right* decision? And what is the right decision? Right for whom? The accused? The society? My conscience?" (LD 127).

The description of the interrogations of the defendant Abdeljalil reveals clear norms of criminal procedure: It is about establishing the truth according to strict rules, whereby the court officer is an indispensable companion of the investigating judge, responsible for taking care of procedural matters, being present during interrogations, advising, listening and recording the interrogation. The accused have the right to remain silent, but this rarely happens, as they know that the punishment in this case is usually more severe (LD 95–96).

Revel's investigations are made more challenging by her adulterous love affair with the lawyer Emmanuel Forest, who is defending Abdeljalil Kacem in the investigation proceedings she is conducting. Subjective-emotional factors harbour the danger that in this situation she does not adhere to the precept of avoiding conflicts of interest between judges and lawyers: "Conflicts of interest can arise when dealing with the same cases" (LD 58). In fact, Forest tries to influence his lover and judge Revel regarding the outcome of the investigation into the Abdeljalil Kacem case by arguing that she has no solid evidence that his client was involved in assassinations (LD 183–185). In a conversation with Revel and her binomial François Vasseur, Forest repeatedly urges that Kacem should be released and backs up his demand with the decision of the detention review judge, according to whom there is no danger of Kacem being released. Furthermore, all material requirements for his release had been met: His mother had agreed to take in her son, his wife was in the process of finding a job, and the result of the feasibility check was positive (LD 220–225). The reports from the probation service (*service de probation et de l'insertion pénitentiaire*) (LD 229), psychologists, psychiatrists (LD 234), experts, and the prison administration were positive (LD 230). Kacem's personality is categorised as less impressionable, with the will to integrate into society (LD 234). Forest's skilful argumentation and Revel's emotional bias lead to Revel granting Forest's request and applying to the public prosecutor's office for Kacem's release from pre-trial detention (LD 235). Unsurprisingly, the application is rejected. Revel then decides to exercise her right to make her own decision (LD 238–238). As expected, the prosecution appeals (LD 240), but the first President of the Court of Appeal upholds Revel's decision on appeal and Kacem is now free on condition that he wears an electronic bracelet and reports to the police every day (LD 243).

To make matters worse, Revel is summoned by the wife and law firm partner of Emmanuel Forest as a witness in the trial against the terrorist Mohammed Abdallah, against whom she has conducted preliminary investigations, a situation that rarely occurs and is very unpleasant for the judge. She is threatened with death by Abdallah and attacked and injured in the toilet by one of Abdallah's suspected accomplices (LD 101–102).

Above all, Revel fears the moment that the investigating judges must publicly inform the lawyers and civil plaintiffs about the outcome of the investigation against each defendant and give an account of it: "I had to summarise a month's work in three hours. I presented the facts of the development of the investigation, named the responsible parties, described their paths—I didn't dissimulate anything. I read the extracts of text message transcripts, of conversations of the people who were called into question [...]. I posed the questions raised by the enquiry" (LD 193).

Shortly after his release, Kacem obtains weapons and carries out a bloody attack on the Parisian nightclub *L'Entrepôt*, killing 11 people. When he barricades himself in the nightclub's office, he negotiates with DGSI employees by telephone who try to persuade him to give up, thus avoiding another bloodbath. Kacem knows that if he turns himself in, he risks the maximum prison sentence of 30 years with an incompressible security period of 22 years under French criminal law (LD 266).

This analysis of the legal discourse in *La décision* yields the following overall legal picture: The Paris anti-terrorism department is tasked with initiating an investigation about charges against terrorists, jihadists, and assassins whose attacks have victimised French citizens worldwide to decide whether the accused should be released or referred to the chief judge. It consists of twelve investigating judges who work in binomials according to the four-eyes principle. The special French criminal law allows the preventive prosecution and punishment of terrorist intentions, even if no material terrorist offence has yet been committed. The return of French citizens from Syria who are suspected of having terrorist intentions therefore falls within the scope of this preventive criminal law competence. On arrival at the airport, the suspects are immediately taken into custody, their identity is checked, and their luggage is sealed. They are questioned by the police and either placed under police control—with the obligation to wear an electronic bracelet and report daily to the responsible guard post—or they are transferred to pre-trial detention. To gather evidence, the investigating judges rely on partner institutions such as the DGSI, the SDAT, the specialised criminal investigation department, psychologists, psychiatrists, and experts as part of the investigation procedure. They carry out field operations, collects evidence of all kinds, and interrogate the accused, in compliance with strict rules and in the presence of a court officer. The accused have the right to remain silent, but any refusal to testify will be interpreted against them. Any decision to release the accused will be based on the reports of the prison review judge, probation service, psychologists, psychiatrists, experts, and the prison administration.

Personal proximity between investigating judges and lawyers in the same criminal case is not prohibited by law but should be avoided if possible and may lead to disciplinary proceedings against the judge (LD 302). Examining magistrates may be called to the witness stand in criminal proceedings in which they have been entrusted with the investigation of evidence, even if this is rarely the case.

The following section contrasts the above description of the criminal law and criminal procedure discourse in *La decision* with the actual French anti-terror legislation, selectively touching on the legal issues that Karine Tuil particularly addresses in her novel to show that the real French anti-terror legislation has been very carefully and truthfully incorporated into the diegesis regarding the aspects covered. As will be shown, the counterfactual variation (Δ) between the fictional and real-world criminal law is negligible; on the contrary, it can be argued that the law in the fiction is almost identical to real law. However, the very sober legal discourse in the real world is permeated by Revel's strongly emotional fictional profile, which may make it somewhat more difficult to separate the legal discourse from the overall fictional picture. The overemphasis on Revel's fictional feelings, thoughts, and inner struggles in both her professional and private life may blur the line between factuality and fictionality and thus complicate the work of interpretation focusing exclusively on the law *in* literature.

5.2.3 *Counterfactual Contrast: French Anti-Terror Legislation vs Legal Discourse in Diegesis*

In the forefield of the actual contrastive examination of the diegetic criminal law discourse with the real-world French anti-terror legislation, the factuality of the latter must first be established. If the factuality of this law were not assured, it would not be possible, as has already been emphasised several times, to contrast the diegesis (fiction) with the real-world law (fact).[28] It should be recalled here that one of the most common criteria for distinguishing between law and literature refers to the dividing line between the literary illusion and the factual truth of law.[29]

5.2.3.1 Factuality of French Anti-Terrorism Legislation

The law should fulfil the function of concretely regulating 'cases' and for this, it must be valid and effective to unfold its practical effect. Legal facticity can be derived from this requirement, which, as Habermas emphasises, is artificially created by the positive production of norms together with the enforceability of the latter.[30] Habermas summarises this artificial facticity, as already explained, as follows: "For an empirical approach, the validity of positive law is in the first instance characterized tautologically, in that the law is considered to be whatever acquires the force of law on the basis of legally valid procedures […]."[31] If we now apply Habermas' artificial production of law to French special anti-terrorist criminal law, it is evident that this is a series of legal acts passed by parliament that supplement

[28] See Sect. 3.4 on Counterfactuality.

[29] Cf. on this Ségur (2017), p. 110.

[30] Cf. Habermas (1996), p. 32.

[31] Ibid., p. 29.

the French Criminal Code FCC (*Code pénal*) and the French Code of Criminal Procedure FCPC (*Code de procédure pénale*), which was initiated with Act No. 86-1020 of 9 September 1986. In the years that followed, the Act was amended and tightened in line with the series of attacks.[32] The factual-normative 'being',[33] i.e. the validity of French anti-terror legislation, results precisely from this series of binding Acts that have been passed by the French parliament in accordance with the law.[34]

5.2.3.2 Historical Preliminary Remarks on French Anti-Terrorism Legislation

The reason for the adoption of such a special legal regulation in the fight against terrorism was initially rooted in the seemingly never-ending series of bloody terrorist attacks that began in France in 1985: it started on 23 February 1985 in Paris with an attack on the *Marks & Spencer department store*, followed by the *Rivoli-Beaubourg* cinema on 9 March 1985, and the *Printemps Haussmann department store* 9 months later on 7 December 1985. The bloody year of 1985 was followed by an even bloodier 1986, which was heralded by an attack on 3 February 1986 in the shopping mall of the *Claridge Hotel*, followed the next day by explosions in the *Gibert-Jeune* bookshop and the *Fnac Forum des Halles department store*. However, this was not all: on 17 March 1986, an attack was carried out on a high-speed train (TGV) near the town of Brunoy, and on 20 March 1986 a Parisian shopping street on the *Champs Elysées* was again the target of terrorism, while on the same day, another attack at the *Châtelet* underground railway station (RER) claimed several lives. On 8 September 1986, the post office of the Paris City Hall, on 12 September 1986 the Casino *Coffee* in the *La Défense* shopping centre, on 14 September 1986 the *Renault pub* on the *Champs-Elysées*, and on 15 September 1986 the police prefecture *rue de Rennes* were the scenes of attacks. In total, no fewer than thirteen terrorist attacks were carried out in France in 1985 and 1986 alone.[35]

In 1995 and 1996, the country experienced another series of attacks: On 25 July 1995, a bomb exploded in the *Saint-Michel* RER station in Paris, causing eight deaths and injuring one hundred and fifty people. This was followed by further attacks on the *Maison Blanche* metro station on 6 October 1995, the *Musée d'Orsay* on 17 October 1995,[36] and the *Port Royal* RER station on 3 December 1996, which left four people dead and ninety-one injured.[37] France was not spared in the 21st

---

[32] Cf. Malabat (2022), p. 655. This was followed by a series of legal acts: loi n° 96-647 du 22 juillet 1996, loi n° 2001-1062 du 15 novembre 2001, loi n° 2014-1353 du 13 novembre 2014, loi n° 2016-731 du 3 juin 2016, loi n° 2016-987 du 21 juillet 2016, and loi n° 2017-1510 du 30 octobre 2017.

[33] Cf. Jellinek (1921), pp. 333–337.

[34] Kelsen (1965), p. 465.

[35] See also Trévidic (2011), pp. 24–25.

[36] Gas (2002), in : *Rfi*, 30/09/2002 (internet-link in the bibliography).

[37] INA (2021) (internet-link in the bibliography).

century either: on 19 March 2012, Mohamed Merah carried out an attack on a Jewish school in Toulouse.[38] On 15 March 2012, the same Merah attacked the paratrooper unit stationed in Montauban.[39] Moreover, just 3 years later, the deadliest year for France began: on 7, 8, and 9 January 2015, the bloody attack on the *Charlie Hebdo* newspaper editorial office took place, and on 9 January 2015, hostages were taken in a kosher supermarket near the *Porte de Vincennes*. On 26 June 2015, a businessman was beheaded in *Saint Quentin-Fallavier*, on 21 August 2015 there was an attack on the Paris-Amsterdam high-speed train (Thalys), and on 13 November 2015 one of the deadliest terrorist attacks France has ever experienced took place: The packed *Le Bataclan* theatre in Paris became the scene of one of the bloodiest massacres, leaving eighty-six dead and three hundred injured. In 2016, the bloody series continued with the double murder of a police couple in Magnanville and the massacre on the sea promenade *des Anglais* in Nice during the National Day celebrations on 14 July 2016, in which eighty-six people were killed and four hundred and thirty-four injured. On 26 July 2016, a priest was brutally murdered in the church of Saint-Étienne-de-Rouvray. The year 2017 saw an increase in attacks on soldiers and police officers.[40] On 16 October 2020, secondary school teacher Samuel Paty fell victim to Islamist fanaticism by beheading,[41] on 13 October 2023, secondary school teacher Dominique Bernard succumbed to the fatal stab wounds of his attacker.[42] The horrifying list seems endless and explains France's endeavour to not only fight terrorism on the ground but also to adapt the legal situation to the need to protect the population as effectively as possible.

5.2.3.3 Counterfactual Contrasting

Beyond the historical premises, another reason for the special French legislation is the realisation that French citizens who turn to Islam and are often radicalised under the influence of Islamist preachers in the numerous French mosques usually travel to Syria or similar countries to learn the 'craft' of terrorism there. The aim of this training is almost invariably to return to France to put what they have learnt into practice locally in the name of Jihad.

French anti-terrorism legislation takes this realisation into account by introducing the preventive principle instead of the usual principle of presumption of innocence, which establishes a presumption of guilt with regard to terrorist intentions for French citizens returning from areas where terrorists are demonstrably being trained, such as Syria in particular.

---

[38] Thomas and Taveira (2022) (internet-link in the bibliography). See also Chetrit (2022).

[39] Abela (2022) (internet-link in the bibliography).

[40] Cf. Yves Mayaud (2020b), p. 23. For an overview in German, see Hegemann (2023), pp. 79–80; 95–97; 100–101.

[41] Simon and Kebbas (2023).

[42] Gubert (2023) (internet-link in the bibliography).

In this sense, the French anti-terrorism legislation provides for the preventive imposition of administrative and/or judicial control or detention measures for such returnees as soon as they set foot on French soil, according to the motto 'first secure, then check'. This means that the mere presumption of intent, even before the actual commission of a criminal offence has taken place or can be proven, justifies the imposition of administrative or judicial measures pending further investigation of the evidence.

At the administrative level, Section L. 225-1 of the French Internal Security Code (French ISC) authorises the French Minister of the Interior, after informing the competent public prosecutor's office, to restrict the geographical freedom of movement of returnees from designated terrorist areas by imposing residence requirements, weekly reporting to the police, or wearing an electronic bracelet. The maximum duration of these administrative measures is 3 months.[43] Section 78-3-1 of the French Criminal Procedure Code (FCPC) makes it possible to detain persons suspected of terrorist links for up to 4 h to carry out an in-depth identity check and consult the data in the electronic register of persons.[44]

In terms of criminal law, the Paris Court is responsible for the criminal prosecution of returnees from terrorist areas. In principle, it has concurrent national jurisdiction for all terrorist offences (Art. 113-2 French Criminal Code [FCC]; Art. 706-16 FCPC[45]), which in practice is exclusive, with the exception of the offence of glorification of terrorism (Art. 421-2-5 FCC), as the regional courts generally cede their jurisdiction to the Paris court.[46] Its material and geographical jurisdiction extends to all criminal offences in connection with terrorist acts in France and abroad, with or without victims, regardless of their nationality, committed by French citizens or other persons with their habitual residence in France (Art. 113-6; Art. 113-7 FCC). The imposition or execution of sentences is also centralised for the whole of France from Paris (Art. 706-11-1; Art. 706-16 FCPC).

In *La décision*, the national and international jurisdiction of the investigating judge is established: "I am in charge of investigating all attacks in the world that have claimed French victims [...]" (LD 24). Alma Revel describes the place of her work as the *Galérie*, which is in a highly secured wing of the Paris Court (*Palais de Justice*) (LD 21). Marc Trévidic, former public prosecutor and now investigating judge in the anti-terrorism department of the Paris Court, confirms that the Paris anti-terrorism department is housed in the *Galérie Saint Éloi* of the *Parisian Palais de Justice*: "THE STAGE: the Galerie Saint Eloi. This long corridor [...] is located at the top of the *Palais de Justice* in Paris, in the heart of the *Île de la Cité*."[47]

---

[43] Mayaud (2020a), pp. 158–160.

[44] Ibid., pp. 156–157.

[45] French Criminal Code = FCC (*Code pénal*); FCPC = French Criminal Procedure Code (*Code de procédure pénale*).

[46] Mayaud (2020b), pp. 184–185.

[47] Trévidic (2011), p. 7.

As Mayaud explains, the anti-terrorism legislation enables the preventive prosecution of French returnees from areas suspected of training terrorists in training camps, even if they have not (yet) committed a criminal offence on French soil:

> Any terrorist crime or offence committed abroad by a French citizen can therefore be prosecuted in France. [...] French citizens who travel abroad to attend training camps or receive indoctrination are particularly targeted. They can be prosecuted even if they have not committed a crime on French territory.[48]

The Paris Criminal Court may detain returnees for up to 96 h (4 days, Art. 706-73 FCPC) pursuant to Section 62-2 FCC as described in *La décision*, or in exceptional cases, for up to 144 h (6 days) (Art. 706-88-1 FCPC) to grant the judicial police the necessary time for preliminary investigations and questioning in cases of *suspected* offences punishable by imprisonment.

> A stop notice is a measure of offence decided by a judicial police officer under the supervision of the judicial authority, by which a person in whose presence there are one or more plausible reasons for suspecting that he or she has committed or attempted to commit a crime or offence punishable by a penalty of imprisonment is kept at the disposal of the investigators (Art. 62-2FCPC).

At this point, the insertion 'offence punishable by imprisonment' needs to be explained in more detail: The French anti-terrorism legislation does not provide for any new offences but borrows the offences from general criminal law and qualifies them as individual or collective acts of terrorism if they are committed intentionally to cause terror and panic to the public (Art. 421-1 FCC). For example, an 'ordinary' murder that is intentionally committed to cause terror and panic among the public is an act of terrorism. According to Yves Mayaud, the qualification of a punishable offence as an 'act of terrorism' arises precisely from the programmatic planning of the act, the public proclamation of the act of revenge, and the deliberate 'disturbance of the public peace' through intimidation and terror—"with the aim of seriously disrupting public order through intimidation or terror"—whereby it is about something greater than individual fear: "Intimidation can be defined as the physical fear that paralyses the individual, while terror is the psychological fear that grips the community."[49] The decisive factor is therefore a shock to the public that transcends the individual and gives rise to a collective feeling of fear, powerlessness, and helplessness in the face of this phenomenon of violence:

> What is at stake is the impact of the terrorist enterprise, which must be manifested by a destabilisation of the community, after having created fears and anxieties in it, the first effect of which is to paralyse the spirit of initiative, to counteract mutual confidence and to deny public authorities the opportunity to react.[50]

---

[48] Ibid., pp. 205–206.

[49] Colcombet (1991), p. 93.

[50] Mayaud (2020b), p. 88.

As Mayaud goes on to explain, deadly terrorists usually knowingly and consciously aim to target as many victims as possible to traumatise society as a whole:[51] "Intent presupposes that everything that contributed to the commission of the crime or offence was fully known to the accused or defendant [...]."[52] In other words, the turn to terrorist ideology must accompany the offence, it must be its motivation and cause a pre-programmed collective trauma through violence.[53]

After this explanatory insertion, I will return to the possibility of imposing preventive control or detention measures against returnees from known terrorist-orientated areas: After the (usually) 96 h of detention, the court can order pre-trial detention for up to 6 months (Art. 421-1 - 421-6 FCC), which, by decision of the detention review judge (*juge des libertés et de la détention*), can be extended to a maximum of 2 years, and in the case of involvement in the preparation of an act of organised crime (Art. 421-2-1 FCC), up to 3 years.[54]

This is where Alma Revel's role in *La décision* comes into play because as an investigating judge in the Paris anti-terrorism department, she is responsible for gathering evidence against qualified returnees who have been remanded in custody.

From the very first page of Tuil's novel, it becomes clear that the central figure is an investigating judge in the terrorism division of the Paris Court, who is leading the investigation against Abdeljalil and Sonia Kacem. As Yves Mayaud points out, she corresponds to the figure of the isolated investigating judge in the French criminal process, who is granted very far-reaching—perhaps too far-reaching—powers, which is why her position appears problematic: "The examining magistrates are currently in a weak position, acting alone with exorbitant powers [...]."[55] They often work in coordination with their colleagues in the anti-terrorist section of the Paris Court and have exclusive jurisdiction over the judicial criminal investigation, which is intended to shed light on whether or not charges should be brought against the accused (*prévenu*), and whether the accused should be released or remain in custody. The president of the court can assign two or more investigating judges to a criminal terrorism case, whereby the work is coordinated but not collegial.

Tuil refers to this when Alma Revel is entrusted with the function of coordinating the anti-terrorism department (LD 21) and when she investigates the Kacem case in binomial with François Vasseur (LD 14). In her role as investigating judge, she conducts investigations to gather evidence for or against the filing of charges against Kacem, the outcome of which will determine whether he is released from custody or referred to Chief Judge Macri. Revel's investigations are based on the assistance of the DGSI, the SDAT, the criminal investigation department, and expert reports.

---

[51] Cf. ibid., pp. 88–89.

[52] Ibid., p. 94; cf. also pp. 96–97.

[53] Cf. ibid., p. 94; p. 97.

[54] Cf. ibid., p. 294.

[55] Ibid., p. 179.

As Marc Trévidic explains, the most important partner and informant for the anti-terrorism judge is the Domestic Counter-Intelligence Service (DCRI[56]), which later became the DGSI. It acts on the one hand as an information body (a kind of French FBI) and on the other as a criminal investigation department. This dual role enables the investigating judge to access information directly from the DCRI, with the exception of official telephone taps.[57] The DGSI can tap and analyse telephones, intercept electronic correspondence and communications, shadow internet activities, search computers and storage systems, etc.[58] All investigations must be authorised in advance by the Minister of the Interior after consultation with the *Commission nationale de contrôle des techniques de renseignement* (CNCTR) and may not last longer than 4 months.[59] Conversely, the DGSI benefits from all information gathered by the investigating judge during the investigation process: telephone taps, acoustic surveillance, internet surveillance, house searches, confiscations, interrogations, questioning, computer analyses, etc.[60]

In *La décision,* the focus is placed on the problematic interference with the principle of the presumption of innocence through preventive prosecution and punishment on the one hand, and on the difficulty for the investigating judge to come to a correct decision based on presumptions of intent through conclusive evidence on the other. This dilemma is illustrated by the example of the Kacem couple, who travelled to Syria, were taken in and allegedly mistreated by members of the IS and returned to France via a Turkish detention camp. Immediately after landing at Paris airport, they are taken into custody by the police and interrogated for 4 days by DGSI officers (LD 118–119). As a result of these preliminary investigations, Sonia Kacem is fitted with an electronic bracelet and placed under police surveillance, while Abdeljalil Kacem is placed in provisional pre-trial detention (LD 119).

This is where Revel's investigative work begins. It is based on the interrogation according to section 116-1-120 FCPC as well as on the SDAT[61] and the DGSI[62] (LD 22). Tuil regularly inserts fictitious interrogations into the story, which Revel conducts with Abdeljalil Kacem according to the model of the interrogation pursuant to section 116-1-120 FCPC. Using these fictitious questions and answers, she shows the opacity of Kacem's personality to the extent that seemingly peaceful intentions are at odds with untruths that shine through. This highlights the full extent of the difficulty for the judge to make the right decision when there is no solid evidence. To mislead Judge Revel, Kacem builds his strategy on apparent naivety, ignorance (LD 75-76), and rejection of violence:

[56] DCRI: *La direction centrale du renseignement intérieur* (Trévidic 2011, p. 14). It has been replaced by the DGSI since 2014 (Mayaud 2020a, p. 22).

[57] Cf. Trévidic (2011), pp. 244–247.

[58] Mayaud (2020a), pp. 53–54.

[59] Ibid., pp. 27–28.

[60] Trévidic (2011), p. 252.

[61] SDAT = *sous-direction antiterroriste*. It is a subdivision of the French judicial police (Trévidic 2011, p. 15).

[62] DGSI = *Direction Générale de la Sécurité Intérieure* (General Directorate for Internal Security).

When asked by Revel why he left France so quickly, Kacem claims that he wanted to live in an Islamic country to practise his faith in an appropriate environment and at the same time help the Syrian population. He consistently denies any intention of wanting to join the Jihad (LD 51), claims ignorance of the terrorist activities of the IS (LD 52; 186–188; 200–202; 232–233), and asserts the rejection of violence (LD 55). However, his statement that he knew that IS was committing atrocities but was naïve enough not to believe it until he saw it with his own eyes, casts doubt on his sincerity (LD 64; 91). His remark to his wife that he had only expressed his admiration for IS and for videos showing beheadings as a joke invites suspicious clairaudience (LD 104). The atrocities he admits to having seen would have shocked him to the core (LD 189). In response to Revel's question as to whether he had renounced Islamist ideology, Kacem answers with a seemingly resolute 'yes' (LD 250).

As Valérie Malabat emphasises, the preventive punishment of preparatory acts, especially when they are individual initiatives unrelated to a group, remains a controversial issue.[63] Revel has little concrete evidence of Kacem's intentions, and he appears to have acted alone. The only information that is available to her includes some text messages and conversations between Kacem and his wife (LD 104), a video on his phone with a beheading scene (LD 54), some videos with Islamist propaganda on his computer, and an execution scene of a young Israeli (LD 201), the fact that Kacem deleted his Facebook account (LD 53), the interrogation protocols, and expert reports and psychological findings on the person of the accused. As indicated, Tuil very clearly highlights the problems of preventive justice here. In addition, she portrays a love affair between Revel and Kacem's defence lawyer Emmanuel Forest, which raises the question of judicial bias and compromises the judge's impartiality in the decision-making process.

In this context, the professional ethics of the French judiciary is based on a double principle: the preservation of credibility and trust in the judiciary and the interest of the accused or defendant to be defended by the same defence lawyer throughout the trial. To preserve the reputation of the judiciary, judicial ethics also require that there be no conspicuous proximity between judges and defence counsel in and around the courtroom: "Members of the judiciary must not appear to be in close proximity to any of the parties or their counsel at any place, in particular in the vicinity of the courtroom and in the courtroom itself" (Art. 6 Rodm[64]).[65] If personal and official interests conflict and the objective exercise of the office is impaired as a result, judges are obliged to admit this openly and to declare themselves biased:

> **21.** Judges have a duty of vigilance to avoid any conflict between the duties of their office and their personal interests or those of their relatives.
>
> **22.** A conflict of interest is any situation of interference between a public interest and public or private interests which is likely to influence, or appear to influence, the independent, impartial and objective exercise of a function.

---

[63] Cf. Malabat (2022), p. 659.

[64] 'Rodm' for *Recueil des obligations déontologiques des magistrats* (Code of Ethics for Judges).

[65] Conseil Supérieur de la Magistrature (2019), p. 22 (internet-link in the bibliography).

> **23.** With a view to the defence, magistrates shall sincerely enquire into any situation that may arise in such a way as to create a conflict of interests. To this end, they consider all its interests as well as the interests or activities of its neighbours.
>
> **24.** They shall, without awaiting an eventual recusation, deport themselves each time a situation may give rise to a legitimate doubt in the minds of the parties or of the public as to their impartiality with regard to the existence of a conflict of interests.
>
> **25.** In their personal engagements, the magistrates shall endeavour to reconcile the legitimate exercise of their rights as a citizen with the duties attached to their judicial functions. They comport or express themselves in public with prudence and moderation (Art. 22–25 Rodm).[66]

As Frederick Dupuis comments, it is inappropriate in terms of the required 'decency' to show obvious familiarity when dealing with a litigant or a defence lawyer in the public sphere of the courtroom and its surroundings. According to Dupuis, the professional and trustworthy image of the judiciary as an institution must be preserved.[67] However, this does not mean that personal human relationships are excluded, but simply that public displays thereof should be avoided.[68] The most pragmatic and sensible approach is to be as discreet as possible and, in the event of excessive intimacy, to honestly declare oneself biased (the judge, author's note), while the defence lawyer should continue to defend his client: "The most intelligent solution is to take certain precautions. That a judge who has too obvious/substantial links with a party's lawyer should recuse himself on his own initiative. That a lawyer should avoid highlighting his links, whatever they may be, with a judge when they have a case in common."[69] Even if one of the parties to the court can in principle challenge the judge on the grounds of bias (Art. L 111-6 COJ[70]), it is always difficult to prove that closer human relationships are in play, which is why it seems most reasonable to appeal to the pragmatic honesty of the judges themselves.

In this sense, the diegetic legal discourse deviates from the real law, as there can be no doubt that Revel should have declared herself biased against Emmanuel Forest and entrusted the investigation of Kacem's case to a colleague. That this was a serious omission is demonstrated by the fact that Revel's decision to release Kacem from prison is strongly influenced by Forest's efforts to secure his client's release. Forest argues that his client has not yet committed any offence: "It's completely unfair to label someone who hasn't done anything a terrorist, that's all" (LD 183–185). Forest is even more insistent in his treatment towards his lover Revel as towards her binomial François Vasseur, as he tries to convince her that nothing in the documents, reports, and expert statements indicates that Kacem could be dangerous: "He won't do anything! He is not dangerous! He hasn't made a single wrong move; he hasn't been described by the prison service as radicalised" (LD 222). Forest also goes on to try to dispel the concerns of the two judges by appealing to

[66] Ibid., p. 24.

[67] See Cass. soc., 18 novembre 1998, n° 94-43.840.

[68] Frederick Dupuis (2021), p. 1 (internet-link in the bibliography).

[69] Ibid., p. 2.

[70] COJ: *Code de l'organisation judiciaire* (Code of Judicial Organisation).

their humanity: "You have to give him a chance to rebuild his life outside, to rebuild his life with his wife and child, away from bad influences, you have to set him free" (LD 222). The defence counsel's arguments are supported by the positive reports of the Probation and Prison Integration Service (*probation and prison insertion service*) (LD 229), the psychologists, psychiatrists (LD 234) and experts as well as the prison administration (LD 230).

Revel's decision was to prove wrong, as Kacem carried out an attack on the Parisian nightclub *L'Entrepôt* immediately after his release, killing people and injuring others.

The case of Abdeljalil Kacem sheds light on the criminal law definition of a terrorist offence in the sense of section 421-1 FCC, which can be punished preventively in accordance with section 421-2-1 and section 421-2-6 FCC: An act of terrorism can be committed individually or as part of organised crime and is then punishable under section 421-1 FCC if the intention to prepare such an act is expressed through the *possession, procurement or manufacture of dangerous objects or substances* in connection with *one* of the following acts: 1. Obtaining information about places or persons against whom a terrorist act is to be committed, or 2. Training in the handling or manufacture of weapons and explosives or training in the operation of aircraft and ships, or 3. Regularly visiting websites or possessing documents that incite or glorify terrorism, or 4. *Being abroad in an area of terrorist movements*.[71] As mentioned, to qualify as an 'act of terrorism', an act must also aim to seriously disturb public peace through intimidation or terror. In this context, intentional injury to life and limb, intentional destruction and damage, the intentional use of explosives, and the intentional use of weapons are relevant. It is also crucial that the planned act was deliberately prepared and organised, regardless of whether the criminal act was successful or not.[72] Here also, the criterion of intent becomes clear, which enables preventive prosecution. The French legal doctrine even goes one step further in distancing itself from the principle of innocence when it states that French case law does not even presuppose the personal intention to commit a terrorist act, but already incriminates a loose, temporary connection or proximity to a terrorist organisation: "The doctrine has also shown that the jurisprudence considers any kind of membership of the group, possibly temporary, such as a close relationship maintained with a member of the group[73] and that it does not require that the defendant personally pursues a terrorist aim, or even that he actively participates in a terrorist group."[74]

---

[71] Cf. ibid., p. 655. Art. 421-1 French Criminal Code: "Constituent des actes de terrorisme, lorsqu'ils sont intentionnellement en relation avec une entreprise individuelle ou collective ayant pour but de troubler gravement l'ordre public par l'intimidation ou la terreur, les infractions suivantes: 1° Les atteintes volontaires à la vie, les atteintes volontaires à l'intégrité de la personne, l'enlèvement et la séquestration ainsi que le détournement d'aéronef, de navire ou de tout autre moyen de transport, définis par le livre II du présent code."

[72] Crim. 10 janvier 2017, n° 16-84596, Dr. Pénal 2017, comm. 35, note P. Conte (case called 'de Tarnac').

[73] Poncela (2016), pp. 7–26, here: pp. 18–20.

[74] Cahn (2017), pp. 127–138, here: p. 130. See also: Alix (2017), p. 79.

Originally, the viewing and retrieval of texts, representations, or images depicting or encouraging acts of terrorism were also to be criminalised (repealed Article 421-2-5-2 FCC). However, following two judgements by the French Constitutional Court—which were reconfirmed 3 years later[75]—this provision was repealed on the grounds that it disproportionately restricted freedom of communication.[76] Observance of the principle of proportionality prompted the French Constitutional Court to protect the fundamental right of freedom of communication from excessive preventive interference.

Abdeljalil Kacem's attack on the Paris nightclub *L'Entrepôt* is to be classified as an act of terrorism under section 421-1 FCPC, as it was premeditated and strategically planned, committed with armed force and with the deliberate intention of spreading fear and terror. All the criteria required by French special law for subsumption under section 421-1 FCPC are met here: Kacem scouts out the neighbourhood of the nightclub, procures weapons, and storms the premises to kill as many persons as possible and injure them incidentally, with the decided aim of achieving a high media impact through public panic. The premeditated and planned murder of people is punishable as qualified intentional homicide *(assassinat)* under section 221-3 FCC. The collateral consequences of the violence exercised or threatened by Kacem, i.e. injured or mutilated persons, are to be qualified as intentional or threatened bodily harm and fall under sections 222-7 to 222-16-3 FCC (violence) and sections 222-17 to 222-18-3 FCC (threat).[77] The unauthorised acquisition and use of weapons falls under the prohibitions of sections 222-52 FCC and 222-54 FCC.[78] Against this background, Kacem's intention to disturb the public peace through intimidation and terror by means of common criminal offences gives his attack on the nightclub *L'Entrepôt* all the characteristics of an act of terrorism.

The penalty for acts of terrorism is also based on general criminal law: the prison sentence of 30 years for offences under general criminal law (murder) is increased to life imprisonment for acts of terrorism. Section 421-5 FCC punishes the direction of the preparation of acts of organised crime with life imprisonment and a fine of 500,000 euros; section 421-6 FCC punishes the preparation of acts of terrorism within the framework of organised crime with 30 years' imprisonment and a fine of 450,000 euros. Section 421-5 FCC penalises the preparation of the same terrorist acts on one's own with 10 years' imprisonment and a fine of 225,000 euros.[79]

---

[75] Conseil Constitutionnel décision n° 2020-845 QPC du 19 juin 2020.

[76] Conseil Constitutionnel décision n° 2016-611 QPC du 10 février 2017.
Conseil Constitutionnel décision n° 2017-682 QPC du 15 décembre 2017.

[77] Cf. Mayaud (2020b), p. 29.

[78] Cf. ibid., p. 31.

[79] Cf. Malabat (2022), p. 660.

In a slight departure from French special criminal law, Kacem surmises that if he voluntarily surrenders to justice, he risks a maximum sentence of 30 years imprisonment with an incompressible security period of 22 years under French criminal law (LD 266).

To summarise, it can be said that in *La décision*, Tuil reproduces French anti-terror legislation in the diegesis very realistically. In this sense, the diegetic discourse makes use of legal jargon, even if it refrains from naming exact legal sections, and outlines the legal framework of the preventive fight against terrorism, which is to a certain extent embellished by imagined persons, interrogations and conversations between the actors in the criminal proceedings (accused, defendants, judges, defence lawyers, civil parties, police agents, etc.). The fictional case of Abdeljalil Kacem serves to illustrate the real criminal law proceeding reserved for returnees from terrorist areas. French anti-terrorism legislation provides for a preventive presumption of guilt, with the aim of preventing acts of terrorism before they are committed. The long and bloody series of terrorist attacks carried out on French soil since 1986 explains this deliberate circumvention of the principle of the presumption of innocence, which remains problematic in that it is a matter of deciding guilt or innocence even when there is no solid evidence of an actual offence. On the problematic subject of the 'right' decision, between individual human fate and responsibility for public safety, Tuil provides a sketch of the real legal discourse, which she perfects with fictional characters, dialogues, feelings, and emotions. The legal conventions and practices as well as the corresponding vocabulary reflect the real anti-terror legislation. The factuality of real law meets the fictional legal discourse, whereby the two almost completely coincide, i.e. no significant counterfactual 'delta' (Δ) can be recognised, with the exception of the missing paragraph designation of the criminal law and criminal procedure provisions, as well as the professional ethical obligation for judges to declare themselves biased if they are in an inadmissibly close relationship with a litigant (here with the lawyer Forest). In contrast, the legal discourse in the diegesis is disproportionately supplemented by an emotionally charged imaginary component that real law does not recognise. In other words, the diegetic legal discourse in *La décision*, which adopts the real law almost congruently, establishes a close connection between law and literature, while the strong fictionality of the plot maintains the epistemic separation without, however, impairing interdisciplinary understanding. While this complicates the work of interpretation if it is to focus on the legal discourse, in general, however, the focus here is less on the hermeneutical question of legal interpretation and more on the ethical question of the right decision in the context of preventive criminal law. Alma Revel fights less against a possible hermeneutical vagueness of criminal law than against the ambiguity of the facts of the case and the personality of the accused: not the interpretation of the law, but the unclear evidence, in the conflict between legal certainty and public safety, is the focus in *La décision*.

5.3 *Sworn Virgin* (2014)[80] by Elvira Dones

Elvira Dones first wrote the original version of the novel *Sworn Virgin* in Italian,[81] after thoroughly researching the phenomenon of the sworn virgin and personally meeting some of these still-living 'man-women' in northern Albania.[82] As Karol Karp explains, she belongs to the generation of Albanian writers who, after the collapse of the communist dictatorship under Enver Hoxha in 1991, wrote not only in their native Albanian language but also in Italian.[83] The fact that Albanian writers also write in Italian can be explained by the close relationship between Albania and Italy. Albanian Arbëreshë *communities* settled in southern Italy as early as the fifteenth century. Much later, between 1939 and 1943, Albania was the target of Mussolini's colonisation efforts and was occupied by Italian soldiers in the Axis alliance with Hitler's Germany. During the harsh communist regime under Enver Hoxha from 1944 onwards, Italian radio stations essentially constituted the only form of access to information about the Western world outside Albania's hermetically sealed borders, due to the country's geographical proximity to Albania,[84] which explains why Italian became a second language for many. With the end of the communist era in 1991, the close ties between the two countries manifested themselves in a strong wave of emigration to Italy.[85] The fact that the close cultural ties continue to this day is demonstrated by the contributions in the field of Italian and Romance studies to Albanian literature and thus also to the novel *Sworn Virgin*.

After the fall of the communist regime in 1991, there was a state of legal anarchy, with the simultaneous revival of the old customary law of the *Kanun*, which had never ceased to be effective in northern Albania and was now also reawakening in the peripheral areas of the cities of southern Albania, as well as an increased interest in its diverse effects and manifestations beyond the better-known feudal law. One of these lesser-known phenomena is that of the 'Burrnesha', the man-women. In Albanian, the term *Burrnesha* or *Burrneshë* aptly describes a woman who is courageous and strong, like a man.[86]

As Laura Gherlone emphasises, Dones' novel *Sworn Virgin* is entirely devoted to this phenomenon of the *Burrnesha*, which has been little researched to date and therefore seems alien: "a social 'eventuality' completely alien to the culture of

[80] Dones (2014). For citation purposes, the sigle 'SV' is used with the page number in the running text. The original Italian edition was published in 2007 under the title *Vergine giurata* by the Feltrinelli editor in Milan. The film of the same name, directed by Laura Bispuri, was released in 2015.

[81] Frei-Tomic (2018) (internet-link in the bibliography).
See also: Anastasi and Martini (2023), pp. 428–439, here: p. 430.

[82] Goldsmith (2019) (internet-link in the bibliography).

[83] Karp (2015), pp. 147–157, here: p. 147.

[84] Romeo (2019), pp. 79–86, here: pp. 79–80.

[85] Cf. Bond and Comberiati (2013), pp. 2–27.

[86] Mazzon (2018), p. 49.

Western Europe, but present in the neighbouring Balkans […].”[87] Florian Kienzle emphasises Dones' bilingualism in Albanian/Italian as well as her engagement with Albanian customary law, whereby Dones can be assigned to Albanian and not Italian literature.[88]

While the commentaries and research on *Sworn Virgin* focus predominantly on the gender issue of female identity and freedom,[89] Karp's essay is one of the few contributions that thematise the *Kanun* as a cultural phenomenon in *Sworn Virgin*, even if here the *Kanun* is considered a cultural phenomenon from a gender perspective and not from the perspective of customary law:

> This work takes us into the vision of the cultural code, the so-called Kanun, which governs the life of the Albanian community described in it. It is a set of laws handed down from generation to generation and is therefore strongly rooted in tradition. The presence of a code, as the Polish philosopher Leszek Kołakowski notes, characterises any conservative world (KOŁAKOWSKI 1967: p. 163), and the one outlined by Dones is certainly one.[90]

According to these rules, a woman has no rights; she is only created to bear children and do housework. To exist in society, she must be married, because without a husband, to whom she owes absolute obedience, she is worth nothing, as Uncle Gjergj admonishes Hana: “A woman who is not married is worth nothing” (SV 133). As will be explained in more detail later, the *Kanun* actually defines the woman “as a sack, made to endure as long as she lives in her husband's house” (Art. XXIX Kanun).[91] One is inclined to compare the lawlessness of women in the *Kanun* with the lawless figure of *homo sacer* in Giorgio Agamben,[92] an outlawed being floating defencelessly in a lawless space, too unworthy to be a subject of law, but equally unworthy to be killed. In the following, however, this strictly regulated and extremely restricted social role that the *Kanun* assigns to women will not be analysed from the usual gender perspective, but from the perspective of customary law. As Franca Pellegrini emphasises, an orphan like Hana has only two alternatives in this legal system: either she accepts marriage or she becomes a ‘man’ and takes on his social characteristics: “An orphaned girl […] can accept an arranged marriage or become a ‘man’ and assume his social role.”[93] As Elvira Dones explains at a presentation of her novel, Hana loses her outward femininity and the right to sexuality but gains the advantages of the social status of a man, which allows her to move freely without being raped, to carry a gun, and drink liquor and smoke with other men.[94] In his

---

[87] Gherlone (2019), pp. 7–24, here: p. 16.

[88] Cf. Kienzle (2020), p. 6.

[89] Cf. Kalo and Shella (2024), pp. 276–290; Romeo (2023), p. 44; Romeo and O'Healy (2022), pp. 1–21; Romano-Martín (2011), pp. 199–212; Pozo Sánchez (2022), pp. 151–159; Xhaho (2013), pp. 112–125.

[90] Karp (2015), pp. 147–148.

[91] I refer here and in the following to the text of the *Kanun* as it is printed in the Albanian English edition of 1989, according to Gjeçovi (1989), translation by Leonard Fox.

[92] Cf: Agamben (1998).

[93] Pellegrini (2013), pp. 149–166, here: p. 151.

[94] Feltrinelli Editore (2007) (internet-link in the bibliography).

novel *BESA - an Albanian rescue* (2023), Wolfgang Wagner describes Paul's encounter with a *Burrnesha*, a sworn virgin, whom he meets while fighting with the Albanian partisans against the Germans during the Second World War and who explains to him:

> that there had been no male head of the family in her family when she was fifteen years old. [...]. The family urged her to take a vow to renounce the traditional role of a woman, any sexual relationship, marriage and children. She had taken the vow before the elder of the tribe and from then on was considered a man. The Kanun had regulated this ritual precisely. Since then, she has worn men's clothing and weapons and assumed the position of head of her family.[95]

Jean-Christophe Boccou makes the phenomena of the *Kanun* and the *Burrnesha* the subject of the contemporary thriller *La vierge jurée* (2021), in which Irina can only avenge her mother's murderer by renouncing her vow of virginity and transforming herself into *Skander*.[96] In Rene Karabash's novel *Vierge jurée* (2022), Bekia becomes the virgin Matia to ward off her husband's revenge after a rape before the wedding, should he find out that she has already been deflowered.[97]

In this context, it should be emphasised that the phenomenon of the *Burrnesha* is not a gender issue, but rather a change in social status, as the *Burrnesha* remains a woman in terms of gender, but takes on the status of a man by adopting the external characteristics of a man (clothing, lifestyle, male work), with a few exceptions.[98] Nor do the *Burrnesha* feel attracted to the opposite sex or even to the male or female sex; rather, they are to be understood as asexual, because they close themselves off to reflections on sex or sexual needs, which they have never been allowed to try out. This consideration becomes clear in *Sworn Virgin* when Hana emphasises her original gender status: "I'm not a transvestite, or a transsexual, and I'm not gay. I've never been any of these things" (SV 233). She has merely improved her social status as a woman. Barbara Mazzon also *cites* the novel *Sworn Virgin* as a vivid example of the status of *Burrnesha*, which offers women the only socially accepted way out of their unfree, lawless role: "Becoming a sworn virgin is therefore the only socially acceptable means of rebellion to gain greater freedom and respect."[99]

It is precisely this change in social status provided for by customary law in the *Kanun* that is the subject of the following examination of the novel *Sworn Virgin*.

---

[95] Wagner (2023), p. 146.

Wagner's novel outlines the role of the customary *Mikëpritja* (cf. Qerimi 2022, pp. 30–33), the sacred hospitality of the *Kanun* – "The house of the Albanian belongs to God and the guest" (§ 602 *Kanun*) – for the fact that many Jews were saved from deportation to concentration camps during the German occupation of Albania in the Second World War. Cf. Elsie (2014a), p. 136.

[96] Boccou (2021).

[97] Karabash (2022).

[98] The sworn virgin is not only a theme in literature, but also in films. See: *Luanas Schwur* (Luana's Oath) by Bujar Alimani, 2023.

[99] Mazzon (2018), p. 15.

5.3.1 Sworn Virgin: *Contents*

Since her parents were killed in a bus accident (SV 66), Hana Doda has been an orphan and is being raised by her uncle Gjergj and his wife Katrina in the northern Albanian mountain village of Rrnajë. She is passionate about literature and manages to study literature at the university in Tirana: "She was the only girl in the village enrolled in college. She hadn't wanted children, all she had wanted was books" (SV 55). Shortly before the end of her first year at university, she learns that her uncle is terminally ill with cancer and has only a short time to live. When his wife Katrina, who has been caring for her sick husband, unexpectedly dies of a heart attack before him, Hana decides to abandon her studies and stay with her now single uncle. To avoid being forced into marriage without disgracing her uncle with disobedience, Hana decides at the age of 19 (SV 68) to take the vow of virginity and adopt the male name 'Mark Doda' (SV 144). Now, as a sworn virgin, she can care for her uncle alone, without male paternalism, until his death and also look after the remaining property. Fourteen years later, Hana follows her cousin Lila's repeated requests to emigrate to the USA, where she undergoes a slow and arduous process of rediscovering her original female identity.

Antonia Young, who has intensively studied the phenomenon of *Burrnesha* in Albania, sees Hana's emigration as *Burrnesha* less as a liberation from her man-woman status and more as a submission to the pressure of Western culture by trying to return to her original female identity:

> In Albania an additional factor which is likely to erode the determination of 'sworn virgins' to keep their vow is the increasingly wide desire to emigrate. When this eventually affects them, they may find that they can no longer retain their male status abroad but are forced by their exposure to Western culture to make compromises to adjust to their new surroundings.[100]

The rules of the *Kanun*, which give women the opportunity to 'become men' to acquire a social status almost equal to that of men, are of a customary law nature, i.e. they were originally passed down orally. Against this background, the following section will focus on the *explicit customary law discourse in the narrative*, as it is presented to the reader without background knowledge of the real-world Albanian *Kanun*. Based on this customary law discourse in the narrative, the relevant information is worked out and brought together to form a preliminary overall legal picture as it emerges from the text. In a second step, the customary law of the *Kanun* still in force in northern Albania today will be explained and put into perspective with the overall diegetic picture.

[100]Young (2000), pp. 126–127.

5.3.2 *On the Explicit Customary Law Discourse (*Kanun*) in the Diegesis*

Hana's life, from her youth with her uncle and aunt in a northern Albanian village to her brief period of study in Tirana and her vow of lifelong chastity to accept the social status of the sworn virgin (*Burrnesha*), is presented against the background of the *Kanun*.[101] The term 'Kanun' refers to Albanian customary law, which is discussed in more detail in the following section. To separate the customary law discourse according to the *Kanun* in *Sworn Virgin*, it should only be briefly recalled that customary law, as Friedrich Puchta explains, is to be understood as an unwritten law that is a form of tacit social agreement on the normative character of certain actions or rites,[102] which, as Robert Elsie emphasises, enjoyed priority over other legal systems in the remote mountains of Albania and, in some cases, still does today.[103]

The austere, gloomy Albanian mountain landscape forms the backdrop in *Sworn Virgin*: "Mountains made of eyes that observe and forbid, mountains made of silence…" (SV 25). When Hana travels to visit her cousin Lila in the United States, people in the village of Rrnajë know that she has left on a regular female passport. For her, there is no going back to the Albanian past (SV 13; 46; 68), i.e. to the world of the *Kanun*, in which.

> all the menfolk in the clan of one of the women live permanently locked inside their kulla, under the threat of an ancient blood feud. Only she can leave the house without risk of being shot and killed. The Kanun says that women, children and priests are not targets. The old woman's clan is in a blood feud with a clan from Bogë. […] What must it be like to live with ten men shut up in your kulla, the only thread of hope for so much frustrated virility? The history of blood spilt between the two families goes back a hundred years, relieved only by a brief truce imposed by the communists. Hakia had a hundred years of death in her memories. (SV 199)

For 14 years, Hana has lived like a man in this world (SV 31; 56), from which there is no turning back because according to the laws of the *Kanun*, breaking an oath can be punished with death (SV 68). Hana had to take care of the *kulla*[104] and the cattle

[101] Reference is made here to the *Kanun* of Lekë Dukagjini (1410–1481), which is the best-known collection of Albanian customary law. It was first written down and published by the Franciscan priest Shtjefën Gjeçovi (1874–1929). Cf. Elsie (ed.), *Der Kanun*, pp. V–VI).

[102] Puchta (1828), p. 139 ff.

[103] Elsie (2014b), pp. V–XI, here: p. V.

[104] "The term *kulla* refers to the stone-built houses typical of northern Albania. They serve both as dwellings and for protection" (H 43, footnote 4). Fulvio Cordignano describes the 'kulla' in the words of Padre Pasi as a kind of fortified building that only the wealthier families could afford and which served as protection against blood feuds: "[…] The kind of dwelling that only the wealthiest families can afford to build, called kulla, places of refuge and defence, especially in blood feuds. For this reason, in addition to one or two small windows measuring about 25 by 30 centimetres, they also have slanting holes in the wall, like loopholes, to shoot at the enemy and defend themselves from his blows." (Cordignano 1933, p. 262).

while her uncle Gjergj laid terminally ill in bed and her aunt Katrina had already died (SV 97). "She was the only girl in the village enrolled in college. She hadn't wanted children, all she had wanted was books. But in the mountains you couldn't say these things if you were born a girl" (SV 55). There were no books in the *kulla*, except "a well-hidden Bible and a history of Skanderbeg, the national hero " (SV 74). The illness of her uncle Gjergj forced Hana to bid farewell to her student life in Tirana, which she did in accordance with traditional custom: "Hana liked using the *tungjatjeta* goodbye. Hand on heart, solemn gaze, the fleeting touch of foreheads to seal the sacred nature of the farewell. *May your life grow longer*!" (SV 73). For a single woman like Hana, it is dangerous to fetch medicine for her uncle from the town of Scutari, as the village nurse explains to her: "'Hana, my girl, [...] 'You need to go down to Scutari to pick up your uncle's drugs. I can't do everything, and anyway it's dangerous, a woman all alone...I'm married and my husband won't allow it'" (SV 111). To be able to care for her uncle alone and unmarried, Hana had to become 'Mark Doda': "'Then Uncle Gjergj got a cancer. I had to go to the city to get his drugs once a month. I couldn't go if I was a woman. It was a matter of honour, morality, a woman's inviolability' [...] 'So I just started dressing like a man'" (SV 68). "She had men's clothes and a flask of raki in her pocket [...]" (SV 54). Hana thus became a man in the eyes of Albanian society by swearing never to marry:

> It's a tradition that exists only in the north of the country. [...] when there are no boys in a family, one of the girls swears to behave like a man and to remain a man for the rest of her life. From that moment on, she has to play all the roles and take over all the tasks of a man. [...]. Only a man can be the head of a family. Men are free to go where they like, to give orders, buy land, defend themselves, attack if need be, kill or order someone else to be killed. Men get freedom and glory along with their duties. Women are left to obedience. (SV 67)

All that remains for a married woman is obedience. "There is no discussion" (SV 116), the woman has to serve her husband and bear him children (SV 133). In this image of society, "a woman who is not married is worth nothing" (SV 133), she is not allowed to enter a premarital relationship with any man, as the village doctor Artan, who pursues Hana, knows very well: "I know that in these parts there's no other way to have a relationship with a girl, so I'll ask him for your hand in marriage" (SV 110). Women are also forbidden to receive male visitors, as Hana explains to her fellow student Arben Leska: "'In the mountains don't come and visit girls they're not engaged to. It's just not done!'" (SV 127). To spare Hana the fate of the 'outlaw' wife, Uncle Gjergj wants to find her a suitable husband before he dies: "If I don't marry you off now while I'm still alive, you'll end up without a husband and you know only a man can take care of everything" (SV 131). If Hana remains alone, she will be "undefended" (SV 133) after his death and will "be left alone" (SV 133). Against Hana's wishes, Uncle Gjergj is therefore in the process of getting Hana engaged to an elementary school teacher (SV 139): "The wedding will be at the end of the year" (SV 140). Hana counters this with her transformation into Mark Doda, which she finally decides to do after narrowly escaping being raped (SV 142–143):

> When she goes downstairs and presents herself to Gjergj dressed as a man, her uncle is struck dumb. [...] It's November 6, 1986. Hana scratches the date on the wall of the guest room. [...]. When she has finished, she goes back to Gjergj. He passes her his rifle [...]. 'Are you sure you want to take this step, dear daughter?' 'My name will be Mark. Mark Doda' (SV 144).

Karol Karp points out that the handing over of the rifle as a symbol of male power symbolises Gjergj's agreement that Hana is now outwardly recognised as Mark.[105] "The next day the news spreads around Rrnajë and the village is alive with gossip. The men will greet her as a man, and the women will avoid her eye" (SV 144). Hana/Mark is now a man in the eyes of the community, a sworn virgin, a *Burrnesha*. She is not a lesbian, not a transvestite, not a transsexual (SV 233)—"Mark Doda has been a product of her iron will" (SV 178)—she is a woman who represses her femininity and this includes renouncing the charms of the female body: "You did whatever the Doda family code of honor required you to do, and looking at your own naked body was simply wrong. That was the ancient code of the mountains. The Kanun inspired the greatest fear of all. It was as powerfully outlined and yet obscure as a recurring nightmare" (SV 178). Hana thus becomes a sworn virgin of her own free will in accordance with the unwritten laws of the *Kanun* (SV 233).

Elvira Dones' *Sworn Virgin* primarily focuses on the phenomenon of the sworn virgin in the Albanian customary law of the *Kanun*, whereby the numerous other rules of the *Kanun* regulating the positions of women, blood feuds, feudal laws, social symbolism *(tungjatjeta)*, and the institution of the *kulla* are not dealt with in detail. The following section will therefore focus on those rules of the real *Kanun* that correlate most closely with Dones' customary law discourse, i.e. primarily on the figure of the *burrnesha* as a way out of the lawless position of women. In addition, as in the novel *Sworn Virgin*, the *Kanun*'s right to feud is addressed in passing.

5.3.3 Counterfactual Contrast: Albanian **Kanun**[106] *vs Customary Law in the Diegesis*

For a counterfactual contrast to be possible at all, the factuality of real-world law must be established, as has already been emphasised several times. Only then can this law as 'fact' be contrasted with the law in the diegesis as 'fiction'. To work out the factuality of the *Kanun* as a corpus of customary law rules, it must be clarified how this customary law was able to develop, how it was received in social reality, and how this customary law is dealt with today.

---

[105] Karp (2015), p. 149. See also: Grosz (1995), pp. 29–34.

[106] According to Robert Elsie, the word *kanun* is derived from the Sumerian (*gi*), Akkadian (*qanu*), Hebrew (*qane*) and Greek (*kanna*) words for 'reed', until it became *kanun* in Turkish, meaning 'rule', 'norm', 'law', and was adopted by the Albanians. Cf. Elsie (ed.), *Der Kanun*, pp. XIII–XIV; see also Qerimi et al. (2022), pp. 289–299, here: p. 292.

5.3.3.1 The Factuality of the Kanun

As outlined in the theoretical part of the work, "the emergence of a customary legal principle presupposes a constant practice (*longa consuetudo*) based on the common conviction of the comrades involved (*consensus omnium*) to take account of a binding norm (*opinio iuris sive necessitatis*)."[107] In terms of legal sociology, the concept of customary law, according to Ernst Hirsch, is to be understood as the totality of customs in a social group to which normative character is attributed.[108] As Friedrich von Savigny explains, customary law was able to assert itself "as a kind of opposition of the subjects against the government."[109] Such an oppositional role to state legal systems can be attributed to the *Kanun*, whose rules were followed by the tribes of northern Albania for centuries in preference to state or ecclesiastical legislation and are still followed to this day in some cases.[110] Due to this supremacy, the *Kanun* survived not only as customary law but also as a form of cultural self-assertion,[111] which withstood the legal systems of all invaders of Albania, from ancient Rome to Byzantium, Serbia, Bulgaria, Turkey, Germany, Italy, and Yugoslavia.[112]

According to Islam Qerimi, the Albanian customary law (*Jus Albanicae ius non scriptum*) of the *Kanun* goes back to the customs and traditions of the Illyrians, the ancestors of the Albanians,[113] who colonised the western Balkan Peninsula around 4000 years ago.[114] According to Pupovci, the first Albanian customs date back to antiquity,[115] and Mary Durham surmises that the *Kanun* is the oldest European code, which could date back to the Bronze Age (1200 BC).[116] While the exact date of origin of the *Kanun* has not yet been clearly established, knowledge of the rules of the *Kanun* and its partial application can be traced back to modern Albania, even though the communist regime under Enver Hoxha tried in vain between 1944 and 1991 to ban the *Kanun* and eradicate its practice.[117] The resistance to new legislation is already expressed in the Albanian proverb "*bidàt t'ri n'katùnd t'vieter nuk qitet*", which translates as "one does not introduce new customs or laws into an old country."[118] According to the Italian Albanologist Ernesto Cozzi, this proverbial

[107] Sagan (2022), p. 202.

[108] Hirsch (1973), pp. 147–217, here: p. 172.

[109] Savigny (1840), p. 169.

[110] Elsie (2014b), pp. V–VI.

[111] Cf. Reinkowski (2005), pp. 121–142, here: p. 130.

[112] Qerimi et al. (2022), p. 290.

[113] Hasluck (1954), p. 10.
Thunmann (1976), pp. 169–366, here: p. 249.

[114] Cf. Qerimi (2014), pp. 7–9. The thesis of the Illyrian origin of the Albanian population is also supported by Ernesto Cozzi. Cf. on this: Cozzi (2021), p. 129.

[115] Qerimi et al. (2022), p. 294.

[116] Ebd., p. 293. See Durham (1991), p. 28.

[117] Voell (2003), pp. 85–101, here: p. 90.

[118] In the original: "*Questo principio esclude che vengano introdotte nuove leggi contrarie a quelle consuetudinarie esistenti*" (Cozzi, *Fra i Monti d'Albania*, p. 75).

principle rules out the possibility of introducing new laws that contradict the *Kanun*,[119] which explains the persistence of the *Kanun* in the remote mountains of northern Albania, despite all the reforms and occupying powers.

Stéphane Voell recalls the chaotic situation in Albania between 1991 and 1997, which can best be described with the Albanian proverb "*S'ka shtet, s'ka ligj* (There is no state. There is no law)."[120] This period saw massive emigration to Greece and Italy, numerous acts of violence against public institutions,[121] and the revival of the *Kanun* as a social practice not only in northern Albania but also on the outskirts of the capital Tirana. Péter Krastev questions this new strengthening of the *Kanun*: "Nobody understands why, nobody knows the precise rules or methods, nor if the situation seems to demand it they act according to the laws of blood feudalism."[122] In 1991, a party was even founded with the name "Revenge according to the Kanun", but it was declared unconstitutional.[123] What is certain is that to this day, no state power has succeeded in completely suppressing the *Kanun*.[124] According to Stephanie Schwandner-Sievers, the state has still not succeeded in penetrating the remote mountainous regions of northern Albania and enforcing state law.[125] Sandra Joireman points out that Hoxha's period of power and, above all, the codification of the *Kanun* by Shtjefën Gjeçovi have led to the fact that, although the *Kanun* can be found in written form in almost every household today, Albanians are paradoxically less familiar with its rules than they were at the time of oral tradition before communist rule.[126] Barbara Egeler confirms Joireman's observation when she states in unison that today's concrete adherence to the rules of the *Kanun* shows that Albanians still pass them on orally without, in most cases, having read the written text of the *Kanun* that is now available.[127] Sometimes inaccurate knowledge of the *Kanun* can lead to fatal mistakes in this context, such as the murder of women and children, which is actually forbidden according to the laws of the *Kanun*—"A woman does not incur blood" (§ XXVIII *Kanun*).[128]

Many Albanians therefore try to escape the blood revenge of their village by fleeing abroad,[129] others lock themselves and their families within their own four walls for fear of deadly retribution, as Dones marginally addresses in *Sworn Virgin* using the example of Hakia's family (SV 199).

---

119 Ebd.

120 Voell (2003), p. 86.

121 Ibid., pp. 87–88.

122 Krastev (2000), pp. 194–217, here: p. 200. See also: Reinkowski (2005), p. 138.

123 Cf. ibid., p. 138, footnote 66.

124 Dundes Renteln and Alan Dundes (1995), p. XV.

125 Schwandner-Sievers (1996), pp. 114–115.

126 Joireman (2014), pp. 235–248, here: p. 240.

127 Egeler (2010), pp. 96–98, here: p. 97.

128 In the following I refer to the English translation of the *Kanun* : Gjeçovi (1989), translation by Leonard Fox.

129 Bangerl (2019), p. 85.

Ejup Statovci defines Albanian customary law with the following words: "Customary law is more than a constitution, with which it is sometimes equated, it is more than any law. It is both a constitution, a code and a law, it is almost an entire legal and social system that also contains norms that have nothing to do with law and legal institutions."[130] Its customary legal norms were passed down orally from generation to generation,[131] "to regulate legal relations between people [...], the application of which is ensured by the local self-governing unit without state coercion in accordance with tradition."[132] In contrast to the legal corpora of other nations, the *Kanun* was never codified in writing until the beginning of the twentieth century, but was stored in the minds of the tribesmen and passed on orally to the next generation. The mysterious prince Lekë Dukagjini (1410–1481), who was revered for his brave resistance against the Turkish occupying power, summarised the most important rules of Albanian customary law in the *Kanun of Lekë Dukagjini*, which today represents the most important, if not the only[133] collection of Albanian *Kanuns*. At this point, Querimi also attempts to define what a *Kanun* is: "A Kanun is a legal and social complexity that is not in close relation with legal aspects, but as a basic source of ACL,[134] it is distinguished by a conglomerate of rules of constitutional, political, economic, religious, and family characters (Qerimi / Berisha, 2011)."[135] The development of different *Kanuns* is not surprising when one considers that, according to Ernesto Cozzi, there were at least twenty-eight tribes in Albania.[136] Given this heterogeneity, the Franciscan priest Shtjefën Gjeçovi spent 30 years at the beginning of the 20th century collecting and writing down the most important oral rules of the *Kanun*. His work was published posthumously in Scutari in 1933.

5.3.3.2 Counterfactual Contrasting

Gjeçovi's work, known today as the written *Kanun of Lekë Dukagjini*, is the standard work of the *Kanun* and consists of twelve books with 1,263 articles.[137] They deal with the church, the family, marriage, property, work, the transfer of property, the oral word (oath), honour, damage and compensation, criminal offences, and

---

[130] Statovci (1990), p. 517, cited in: Qerimi (2014), p. 11 (Since I unfortunately do not speak Albanian, I am forced to resort to the German reproduction of the quotations in Albanian).

[131] Qerimi et al. (2022), p. 291.

[132] Elezi (2003), p. 10, cited in: Qerimi (2014), p. 12.

[133] Egeler (2010), p. 96. "There was also the Kanun of the Albanian prince and national hero Skanderbeg, which is similar to the Kanun *Lekë Dukagjini*, the little-known Kanun of the mountains *Malsisë së Madhe* and the Kanun i Labërisë, which also has strong similarities with the Kanun *Lekë Dukagjini* (Egeler 2007, p. 14).

[134] ACL = Albanian Customary Law.

[135] Qerimi et al. (2022), p. 291.

[136] Cf. on this Cozzi (2021), pp. 115–127.

[137] Qerimi et al. (2022), p. 293. Cf. Gjeçovi (1993).

exceptional cases.[138] According to Karl Kaser, the most important pillars of the *Kanun* are honour and the word of honour, equality between men (without mentioning women, author's note) and the freedom to act according to the *Kanun* without being commanded by others.[139] Noel Malcolm summarises the basic structure of the *Kanun* in a similar way: "The foundation of it all is the principle of personal honour. Next comes the equality of persons. From these flows a third principle, the freedom of each person to act in accordance with his own honour, within the limits of the law, without being subject to another's command. And the fourth principle is the word of honour, the besë (def.: besa), which creates a situation of inviolable trust."[140] According to Giuseppe Valentini, personal honour and the word of honour (*besa*) occupy a special position in the *Kanun*,[141] because the loss of honour means social death. According to Stephanie Schwandner-Sievers, the term *besa* has to be defined more broadly in modern usage and can only be described in German in a rather rudimentary way as "peace pact, alliance, truce agreement, hospitable alliance, honour of the house, word of honour, oath, security guarantee, loyalty, fidelity and more."[142] According to the provisions of the *Kanun*, breaking the *besa* is the most serious offence against honour, such as betraying a friend or raping a woman.[143]

This pronounced concept of honour in the *Kanun* explains Hana's decision to take the vow of virginity to save her uncle's honour, which would have been violated by a possible refusal to marry. The practical reasons that as an unmarried woman, she ran the risk of being raped and that she would not have been able to manage the estate after her uncle's death are plausible, but take a back seat to the principle of family honour. In fact, according to the provisions of the *Kanun*, dishonouring her uncle would have meant social death for Hana: "A man who has been dishonoured is considered dead according to the Kanun" (§ 600 *Kanun*), insofar as the serious illness would have prevented Gjergj from upholding the family honour. This emerges from § 21, para. 1 of the *Kanun*, according to which the head of the family must safeguard the interests of the family members, which in Hana's case means that her uncle must ensure that she is married off: "'If I don't marry you off now while I'm still alive, you'll end up without a husband [...]. Maybe I've found the right person for you to marry. The day after tomorrow he'll be here.' [...] I want to see you settled. I've decided. I can't leave you alone'" (SV 131). If Hana had refused to marry without a vow of virginity, the honour of her uncle and the house would have been deeply wounded (§ 593–601). The possibility that Hana would have refused to marry is all the greater as the *Kanun* forbids an unmarried woman, even if she is an orphan, to choose her own future husband: "The young woman, even if her parents are not alive, does not have the right to concern herself about her

[138] See Gjeçovi (1989).

[139] Kaser (2008) (Studies on Southeast Europe, vol. 7), p. 29.

[140] Malcolm (1998), p. 18.

[141] Valentini (1969), pp. X–XI.

[142] Schwandner-Sievers (1996), p. 116.

[143] Ibid.

own marriage; the right is held by her brothers or other [male, author's note] relatives. The young woman does not have the right a) To choose her own husband; she must go to the man to whom she has been betrothed" (§ 31 *Kanun*). This is confirmed by Ernesto Cozzi: "If the girl is an orphan and has no relatives, the right to contract her marriage belongs to the pious person who has taken her in and given her paternal care."[144] In this sense, Uncle Gjergj, who took Hana in as an orphan and cared for her, is undoubtedly obliged to choose a husband for her.

The rules of the *Kanun* therefore leave Hana with only two options in her situation: Either she accepts marriage to the man her uncle has chosen for her, or she takes an oath of virginity, thereby saving the family honour and at the same time avoiding the obligation to marry: "Gjergj, *bre burrë*, now you have a son and the honor of the *kulla* will not die" (SV 146).

Ismail Kadare, an expert on the *Kanun*, aptly summarises Hana's metamorphosis into Mark in the light of the *Kanun* as follows:

> The story refers to an ancient if rare Albanian custom that has been preserved into the modern era, according to which, for various reasons – such as the absence of a man in a household or, as in Hana's case, the fear of rape – a 'conversion' of this kind was permitted and a woman could change her status from female to male. She would gain all a man's rights and freedoms, adopt male behavior and dress, take part in assemblies of elders, and go out to cafés to drink alcohol and smoke cigarettes, with the sole condition that she preserve her virginity. (SV 8)

According to the provisions of the *Kanun*, a girl can "swear perpetual virginity before twelve oath-keepers and then become a nun or servant of a priest, or she can dress as a man and live like a man, but without the right to vote in the assembly" (§ 1228 *Kanun*).[145] Section 1228 of the *Kanun* stipulates this equality between men and *Burrnesha*, with the exception of voting rights, with the following wording: "*The Virgins* (women who dress as men): They are not distinguished from other women, except that they are free to associate with men, although they have no right to a voice in the assembly." This provision makes it clear that it is not a question of gender reassignment ("They are not distinguished from other women" (!)) but of a social status based purely on external characteristics. There could be three motives for this sacrificial step: the desire to avoid an unwanted marriage (§ 31 *Kanun*), the preservation of family property despite the lack of male offspring (§ 88, § 92 *Kanun*),[146] or the care of parents in the absence of male offspring (*Amor filiale*).[147] The motivation of women to voluntarily renounce their female identity, family, and children in individual cases can be explained by the lawless position of women in the *Kanun*, which will be discussed in more detail below.

In this context, Laurence Hérault suggests that women seem to have no intrinsic value but are only there to bear male children in order to secure male offspring:

---

[144] Cozzi (2021), p. 164.

[145] Schmidt-Neke (2014), pp. XIII–XLIII, here: p. XXXIV.

[146] Durham (1928), p. 211. See also Kaser (1992), pp. 286–287.

[147] Martucci (2014), pp. 35–60, here: pp. 41–42. See also Young (2000), pp. 60–61. See further: Cozzi (2021), pp. 182–183.

"Women seem to have no value in themselves but only as providers of children, especially sons for the lineage."[148] This is confirmed by Robert Elsie: "Women enjoyed a very inferior status. The *Kanun* of Lekë Dukagjini explicitly stated: "'the woman is a tube in which the goods are transported' (alb. 'grueja âsht shakull për me bajtë')."[149] The *Kanun* literally reads: "A woman is a sack, made to endure" (XXIX *Kanun*). Mark Sadiku interprets this statement of the *Kanun* as meaning a sack to carry (bear) children, while the woman has no other rights that she can pass on or receive: "A woman has no other rights, only she is a purse to carry the child God has given her; she has no other rights, neither to give nor to take."[150] According to the laws of the *Kanun*, only the male line can and may continue (§ 90 *Kanun*) and this only through male descendants and inheritance: "The Kanun recognises the son as an heir, but not the daughter" (§ 88 *Kanun*). In this sense, the *Kanun* makes a clear distinction between the patriarchal paternal line ("Tree of blood", § 700 *Kanun*) with all rights and the rightless maternal line ("Tree of milk", § 701 *Kanun*). Even if there are no male descendants, succession through the daughters is out of the question: "If the male line of a house dies out, even though there may be a hundred daughters, none of them have the right to any share in the inheritance of their parents, nor do any of their sons or daughters" (§ 92 *Kanun*). The woman is therefore destined to join her future husband's family through marriage and is thus lost to her own family. For this reason, she is considered 'superfluous' for the household, i.e. worthless: "The Albanian woman does not inherit anything from her parents—neither possessions nor house; the Kanun considers a woman as a superfluity in the household" (XX *Kanun*). At this point, as Andrew Shryock emphasises, the pronounced imbalance between the rights of the man and the lack of rights of the woman clearly stands out.[151] Antonia Young describes the main features of this extremely patriarchal society in rural Albania:

> In anthropological terms, rural society in northern Albania is strictly patriarchal, patrilocal, exogamous and patrilineal. This means that the society is male dominated, normally men bring their wives from other villages into their own childhood home, and inheritance follows the male line, all 'social units, households, are based upon males who are recruited by birth, generation after generation.[152]

According to Berit Backer, Albanian tribal society is actually one of the most patriarchal societies in the world.[153] In this context, it may not be too surprising that every female birth was perceived as a disruptive factor for the smooth continuity of the male line and, as Paul Henri Stahl comments, mourned accordingly: "Even the

---

[148] Hérault (2009), pp. 273–284, here: p. 276.

[149] Cf. Elsie (2012) (internet-link in the bibliography). Elsie raises the question of how this sentence should be interpreted, namely in terms of the hard labour required of women, or in terms of childbearing.

[150] Sadiku (1943), pp. 271–279, here: p. 277.

[151] Cf. Shryock (1988), pp. 113–118.

[152] Young (2000), p. 13.

[153] Backer (1979), p. 314.

rafters wept."[154] Jana Arsovska confirms the disdain for women in Albanian society insofar as they are compared to half a man or half a dog,[155] and this is evident from the *Kanun*: "Blood of women is not equal to the blood of man" (§ XXVIII *Kanun).*

Both the woman and the man are married by the head of the household through an intermediary without the possibility of making their own choice (§ 30; § 31 *Kanun*). However, here too, there is a strong imbalance between the rights and duties of the man and those of the woman. On the one hand, the *Kanun* excludes women from all male rights and privileges and, on the other hand, releases them from male duties.[156] The *Kanun* then denies the woman any right to children and the home (§ 61 b *Kanun*), the only rights she is entitled to are "the right to ask her husband for sustenance, clothes and shoes" (§ 34 *Kanun*) and "1) To apportion everything produced in the house; 2) To give or lend flour, bread, salt, cheese or butter; 3) To order the women of the house to fetch water and wood, to bring bread to the workers, to wash, to dispose of the slops, to reap, to hoe, or to clean" (§ 22 *Kanun*). The wife's duties are thus limited to domestic tasks and the upbringing of the children, whereby she must always obtain her husband's consent and uphold his honour through unconditional obedience (§ 33 *Kanun*). While the woman's list of duties towards the man is disproportionately long, the opposite is true for the man: in addition to an infinitely long list of rights (§ 20; § 58; § 59 *Kanun*), he only has the duty to provide the woman with the necessary clothing and the necessities of daily life and to uphold her honour (§ 32 *Kanun*). On the other hand, he is free to rebuke, beat, and punish her (§ 58 *Kanun*). In the event of unfaithfulness, flight, or violation of hospitality,[157] he may even kill her without entering into a blood feud with her parents if her father has given him a rifle cartridge in return (§ XXXI *Kanun*), as Young explains in more detail: "Men's control of women is also outlined: 'the parents of his wife give him (the groom) a cartridge' as protection against 'two acts (for which) a woman may be shot in the back a) for adultery; b) for betrayal of hospitality' (to any guest). The preservation of this law continued to be demonstrated until quite recent times, the bridegroom's parents giving the groom a cartridge on the wedding day."[158] If the husband has not received a cartridge for his wife, a blood feud would be triggered if he were to murder her: "If a husband kills his wife, he incurs blood-feud with the woman's parents" (§ 963 *Kanun*). A woman may not even speak to guests without her husband's permission.[159] She can neither inherit nor bequeath (§ 88 ff. *Kanun*). Her only 'privilege' is that she is not subject to the right of feud and therefore may not be killed (§ 897 *Kanun*). The work that women must do includes fetching water, chopping wood, cooking food, transporting

---

[154] Stahl (1988), pp. 33–80, here: p. 41. For further information see Doja (1999), pp. 37–55.

[155] Cf. Arsovska (2006), pp. 161–184, here: p. 170. See also: Whitaker (1968), pp. 253–293, here: p. 267; Whitaker (1981), pp. 146–156, here: p. 151.

[156] Elsie (2014b), pp. IX–X.

[157] Arsovska (2006), p. 170.

[158] Young (2000), p. 20.

[159] Elsie (ed.) (2014a), pp. 50–51; see also: Elsie (2012).

fertiliser, irrigating fields (§ 22 *Kanun*), doing housework, serving the husband (§ 25 *Kanun*), bringing up children and maintaining the husband's clothes (§ 33 *Kanun*). Susan E. Pritchett Post summarises the essential provisions of the *Kanun* that relate to women, whereby their lack of rights becomes even more apparent:

1. the social order is strictly patriarchal.
2. marriage is not determined by the couple themselves but merely serves to extend the family and produce labour.
3. the man's family must pay a bride price.
4. the rights and duties of the spouses are clearly defined; the wife has a heavy workload, while the husband must above all protect her honour.
5. the woman has no inheritance rights.
6. the woman 'does not fall into the blood': since her blood does not have the same value as that of the man, the laws of blood revenge do not apply to her.
7. the woman is described as a tube through which the 'goods' 'slip'.
8. in the case of adultery or breach of hospitality, the husband has the right to kill the wife.[160]

These remarks on some details concerning the status of women in the Albanian *Kanun* are intended to provide the necessary background to better understand why women in some cases even voluntarily resort to the option of a vow of virginity while renouncing family and children. As Edith Durham emphasises, accepting the status of *Burrnesha* offers women the only way to escape marriage and thus the low status of women: "Marriage is arranged entirely by the head of the House. The children are betrothed in infancy or *in utero*. [...] The girl may—but it requires much courage on her part—refuse to marry the man. In that case she must swear before witnesses to remain [a] virgin all her life. Should she break this vow, endless bloodshed is caused."[161] In this context, Martucci weakens Durham's assertion that a possible breach of the vow of chastity would result in the death of the woman concerned by suggesting that it was primarily a question of not procreating offspring and not of abstaining from sexual intercourse.[162] Dvorsky confirms Martucci's thesis: "A virgin committed herself to abstaining from marriage, but not to chastity."[163] Other researchers seem to agree with this thesis,[164] or at least only a few seem to argue against it.[165] Carleton S. Coon, for example, very quickly revises his original thesis that breaking the oath was punished with burning by immediately countering: "If she breaks her oath, the elders will in theory, burn her alive. It is doubtful if this punishment has been exacted on any such person within the last few generations.

[160] Pritchett Post (1998), pp. 53–54.

[161] Durham (1985), p. 35.

[162] Martucci (2014), p. 50.

[163] Dvorsky (1909), p. 130.

[164] See also: Doja (1995), pp. 650–667, here: p. 652; Gopčević (1881), p. 460; Gopčević (1914), pp. 109–110.

[165] Cf. Durham (1985), p. 35.

[…] The second wore women's clothes. […] Since she spent the night with a junior member of my group of horse-drivers, I formed a poor opinion of the burning-alive theory."[166] Jan and Cora Gordon report on their attempt to find out whether breaking the oath would be punished with death, and receive an indirect negative answer from a sworn virgin on the grounds that it was not fear but a sense of honour that prevented them from doing so:

> Looking closer, we began to doubt the sex of this person . . .
> 'That girl . . . has vowed never to marry, so she dresses like a man and does man's work.'
> 'But if she breaks her vow,' we said, 'does her family pursue her to kill her?
> 'She does not ever break her vow . . . she would be ashamed to. And, anyway, no man would want her any more than he would want his sister . . .'
> Yet we repeated our questions, 'If? If? If?' we insisted.
> 'She would have to leave the clan then. . . she would be disgraced for ever.'
> 'But they would not kill her?' we asked.
> 'Oh, no. She can marry if she likes, but she would not want to. You understand . . . she has sworn she will not.'[167]

In contrast to these investigations, *Sworn Virgin* argues that breaking the vow of virginity would result in Hana's death (SV 68) and thus only leaving the country offers the possibility of cancelling the vow with impunity.

In *Sworn Virgin*, we find all three reasons that, as already discussed, can cause a woman to swear eternal virginity: She wants to nurse her terminally ill uncle Gjergj, who has no male offspring, without help. She does not want to dishonour him by refusing to marry. And finally, the estates that Uncle Gjergj leaves behind must be preserved and managed.

Hana's step can be explained by the situation of the woman in the *Kanun*, in that there are only two options open to her: an unwanted marriage and an existence without rights on the one hand and accepting the status of *Burrnesha* with the associated rights, but also sacrifices, on the other. If she had refused to marry, her fiancé would have been entitled to kill her: "If the girl does not submit and marry her fiancé, she should be handed over to him by force, 'together with a cartridge'; and if the girl tries to flee, her husband may kill her with the parent's cartridge, and the girl's blood is lost [remains unavenged], because it was with her cartridge that she was killed" (§ 43, al. 6 *Kanun*).

This opportunity for women to improve their social status in such a strictly patriarchal society can be interpreted as progressive on the one hand, but can also provoke outrage at the fact that women have to give up their identity and sexuality to enjoy rights. Ernesto Cozzi does not want to see the Albanian woman as the enslaved, oppressed woman she is often portrayed as. According to his observations, the honouring of women is not expressed in public, as 'gallantry' is alien to Albanian men, but they do respect them in the intimacy of the private sphere: "And they actually treat the weaker sex with love and respect […]."[168]

---

[166] Coon (1950), pp. 24–25.

[167] Gordon and Gordon (1927), pp. 238–239.

[168] Cozzi (2021), p. 175.

In addition to the few clues that the *Kanun* provides on the phenomenon of the *Burrnesha*, a historical-anthropological insertion should provide further information on this peculiar customary institution, which seems to contradict the general 'spirit' of the *Kanun.* According to Laurence Hérault, the phenomenon of the *Burrnesha,* also known as *Virgjëreshe*, *Virgjin*, *Vajzë* or *Betuar*,[169] has been documented by travellers in northern Albania, Kosovo, and Montenegro since the mid-19th century. Donato Martucci refers to the Albanologist Johann Georg von Hahn, who in his volume *Reise durch die Gebiete des Drin und Wadar* (1867) reports on four women who vowed eternal virginity and behaved like men. One of them made this vow because, like Hana, she did not want to marry.[170] According to Hérault, these women form a minority in one of the last tribal societies in Europe and dress and behave like men.[171] Antonia Young describes the phenomenon of sworn virgins as "women who have been chosen, been permitted and encouraged by their society or even parentally predestined, to become men."[172] They do what men do and women are not allowed to do: Many of them, though not all, wear men's clothing, a black gilet, short hair under a cap (*ksula*),[173] smoke tobacco, own guns, travel freely, alone or with other men, head the household, farm, marry off their sisters, etc.[174] Those who do not dress masculinely can be recognised as *Virgjëreshe* by their white headscarf *çalma*.[175] According to Ernesto Cozzi, who has many years of experience with various tribes in Albania, the *Burrnesha* are mainly distinguished by their short haircut and wear a turban (*shalli*) or a cap (*kaula*) and a kind of gilet (*gubére*), but otherwise, for many of them, they dress like women, even if they prefer to do men's work. Others do dress like men, but it must be clear, says Cozzi, that the *Burrnesha* remain women and are regarded as such, with the difference that they enjoy the respect of the tribal members.[176] Nevertheless, compared to men, they seem to have a hybrid status in some respects, as they have no voting rights in the council of family heads (§ 1228 *Kanun*), it is a disgrace for men to knowingly kill a virgin,[177] and they can neither bequeath nor inherit property. René Grémaud sees the virgin as a third genre, between man and woman: "In Balkan culture virgins were seen as a relatively unclassified category, clearly set apart from those who have become 'women' through matrimony and motherhood, and somehow akin to the

[169] See the testimony of one of the last living swear virgins 'Lali' (Diana Rakipi): Negri et al. (2019b) (internet-link in the bibliography).

See also the testimony of the sworn virgin Duni Grishaj: McLean (2022) (internet-link in the bibliography).

[170] Martucci (2014), p. 36. Cf. von Hahn (1867).

[171] Hérault (2009), p. 1.

[172] Young (2000), p. 69.

[173] Cf. Martucci (2014), pp. 46–47. Ernesto Cozzi does not speak of the *ksula*, but of the *listila*: Cozzi (1912), pp. 309–339; 617–626, here: p. 319.

[174] Hérault (2009), p. 7.

[175] Schultz (1907), pp. 1758–1763, here: p. 1760.

[176] Cf. Cozzi (2021), pp. 183–184.

[177] Grémaux (1993), pp. 541–281, here: p. 278.

male gender – which serves more or less as the marked prestige gender."[178] Hérault comments that the *Burrnesha* are not women in this sense, but almost men, to whom less of a resistive and more of an emancipatory quality can be attributed.[179] Martucci, on the other hand, insists that the *Burrnesha* fully remain women despite their masculine appearance, if only because they are not recognised as having all the rights of men:

> It is absolutely untrue that they were considered equal to men: virgins were and remained women. Some examples raise the question: all 'virgins' were allowed to attend all meetings with men, but could not speak or vote, a matter of exclusive importance. They could, if they were of age and orphans, administer the family estate as long as they remained 'virgins', but they had no right to sell property without the consent of the men of the brotherhood.[180]

Renouncing femininity and motherhood thus remain the only way for women, as Durham emphasises, to become bearers of rights almost equal to those of men[181] and, as Gilles de Rapper points out, to extend the patriarchal line by one generation. The solution remains a provisional one because virgin wives cannot pass on an inheritance.[182] In a lecture at the University of Leiden on 10 November 2012, Robert Elsie emphasised that the phenomenon of sworn virgins is "one of the most fascinating aspects of this culture", which was unique in Europe and still exists today.[183] Young notes that it is not always easy to obtain certainty about the number of *Burrnesha* still alive today, as they are not a conspicuous phenomenon in their community: "'Sworn virgins' are not a phenomenon, they are just a fact of life; the way they act is the way they organize their lives."[184]

In *Sworn Virgin*, the phenomenon of the sworn virgin is faithfully recreated according to the provisions of the *Kanun*. Hana takes on the appearance and lifestyle of a man to avoid an unwanted marriage, and the village accepts her easily and naturally as (almost) equal to the men. Uncle Gjergj accepts her oath by handing her the rifle. Only the oath in front of the twelve oath-keepers is not mentioned in the story. In connection with this requirement of the *Kanun*, Mary Durham points out that it was by no means easy to fulfil this condition: "If she could find twelve elders of her tribe group to act as co-jurors she could swear perpetual virginity. If she broke the vow the honour of the co-jurors was blackened, and a blood feud ensued. It was not easy for her to find twelve co-jurors."[185] Due to the difficulty of fulfilling the condition of twelve oath-helpers, according to Donato Martucci, many *Virgjëreshe* renounced this oath in practice,[186] as expressed in *Sworn Virgin*. It should also be

[178] Ibid., p. 281.

[179] Hérault (2009), p. 10. Cf. also: de Prosperis (2017).

[180] Martucci (2014), p. 47.

[181] Durham (1985), p. 63. See also the testimonies of oath virgins today in Favoino (2019).

[182] de Rapper (2000), pp. 457–466, here: p. 462.

[183] Elsie (2012).

[184] Young (2000), p. 65.

[185] Durham (1928), p. 194.

[186] Cf. Martucci (2014), p. 41.

noted that the *Kanun of the Lekë Dukagjuni* contains no specific information on this, and only one article (§ 1228 *Kanun*) explicitly refers to the figure of *Burrnesha*.

In the same vein, Antonia Young reports on one of her case studies, *Virgjëreshe* Pashke, who could have served Elvira Dones as a model for *Sworn Virgin*: Pashke is an orphan and was raised by her grandmother and uncle. After her grandmother's death, she lived alone with her uncle. When he fell seriously ill and she had to visit him twice a month in a hospital 80 km away, it became too dangerous for her to travel this long distance as a woman, which is why, as Young explains, she dressed like a man:

> A girl alone could not undertake such journeys. I did not have long to think through what I did. I took some of my uncle's clothes, my own in any case were only fit for rags. It was a time of such distress that I did not discuss it with anyone, just acted as I had to, and cannot see now that I could have done otherwise. I have done in my life whatever has been necessary, and this has been my fate.[187]

Like Hana, Pashke experienced her decision as situational and irrevocably willed by fate, which left her no alternative despite the personal suffering of giving up her female identity: "I am sorry for others who lead this kind of life. I had no other option, given my circumstances. I cannot go back on my decision."[188] Like Hana, Pashke cared for her uncle until his death and lived alone in the house afterwards.[189]

In addition to the case of Pashke, which deserves special attention because of its similarity to the fate of Hana in *Sworn Virgin*, other cases of *Burrnesha* still alive today are described: Isla Badenoch, in *The Burrnesha Archive*, gives the example of three men-women who indulge in cigarette and drink raki with men and wear men's clothes.[190] Barbara Mazzon cites the case of *Burrnesha* Ghero as an example of how the *Kanun* still prevails in Albanian reality and how girls today still see the vow of virginity as the only way out to achieve a better social position: "The norms of the ancient Kanun, as we have seen, are still in place and continue to weave the threads of invisible social bonds. There are still strongly male chauvinist contexts in which becoming a sworn virgin is the only way to rebel against subjugation."[191] From all the conversations with the *Burrnesha* who are still alive today, a strong will to ignore one's own sexuality and body as far as possible becomes clear, as is also expressed in *Sworn Virgin*: "One did what the honour of the Dodas demanded of one, and it was not proper to look at one's own naked body" (SV 178).

In the margins of the theme of the sworn virgins, on which Dones superficially focuses *Sworn Virgin*, the feudal law of the *Kanun* is addressed in passing with the mention of the now men less Frangaj family, whose men have been decimated by

---

[187] Young (2000), p. 78.

[188] Ibid., p. 91.

[189] Cf. Littlewood (2001), pp. 37–50, here; p. 46.

[190] Badenoch (2016).

[191] Mazzon (2018), pp. 35–36. See also interviews with virgins living today: Spankbecher (2021) (internet-link in the bibliography); Pelazza (2015) (internet-link in the bibliography); Favoino (2016) (internet-link in the bibliography); Mascioli (2017) (internet-link in the bibliography).

the blood feud (SV 29–30), on the one hand, and the fate of Hakia, who has to look after ten men who can only leave the *kulla* at the risk of death (SV 199), on the other. Dones presumably deliberately leaves the much better-known phenomenon of blood revenge according to the laws of the *Kanun* in the background, in favour of the hitherto less well-known figure of *Burrnesha*. Ismail Kadare, in particular, has already dealt extensively with Albanian feudal law in his well-known novel *Der Broken April* (1980)[192] and can be considered an expert on the subject.[193] Using the example of the Kryeqyqe and Berisha families, Kadare traces the course of the Albanian blood feud as it corresponds to the *Kanun*: the starting point of the feud between the two families, which has been going on for 70 years and has so far claimed the lives of 44 men, is the murder of a guest of the Berisha family, who was killed by a Kryeqyqe years ago. It should be noted that the *Kanun* equates the guest with God (§ 602 *Kanun*) and thus grants him an absolute special status (*besa*).[194] In this respect, the violation of hospitality means an unbearable loss of honour for the host, which must be avenged at all costs. Thus, according to the *Kanun*, "one could atone for the blood of a father, a brother – even one's child – but never for the blood of a guest."[195] Here Kadare refers to an old proverb, which Schwandner-Sievers relates almost literally to the high status of the guest/friend (alb. *mik*): "You can forgive the offence of the father, brother or cousin. But not that of the *mik*."[196] Against this background, Gjorg must avenge the murder of his brother and kill the murderer because of this long-standing family feud, which began with the violation of hospitality. To this end, he lies in wait for the murderer and calls him before he shoots. The killer turns the victim on his back and puts his rifle to his head.[197] The murder is then announced in the village and the victim's family is informed of the geographical location of the body.[198] A negotiating delegation can negotiate the small (24 h) and, if necessary, the great 'word of honour' (30 days) with the victim's family,[199] which protects Gjorg from revenge during this time. Soon, however, Gjorg will be among the other victims of the family feud, unless there is a blood reconciliation, which is usually most promising, according to Schwandner-Sievers, "when the incident that caused it happened a long time ago and no one alive has witnessed it."[200] Kadare puts it into Besian Vorpsi's mouth that the *Kanun* has so far resisted erasure by state law:

---

[192] Kadare (1990).
[193] See also: Young (2000), p. 44.
[194] Kadare (1990), p. 32.
[195] Ibid., p. 42.
[196] Schwandner-Sievers (1996), p. 116.
[197] Kadare (1990), p. 10.
[198] Ibid., pp. 11–12
[199] Ibid., pp. 13–16.
[200] Schwandner-Sievers (1996), p. 118.

> The *Rrafsh* ist the only region of Europe which [...] has rejected the laws, the legal institutions, the police, the courts, in short, all the structures of the state; which has rejected these things, you understand, because at one time it was subject to them, replacing them with other moral rules which are themselves just as adequate, so much as to constrain the administrations of the independent Albanian state, forcing them to recognize those rules, and thus to put the High Plateau, let's say nearly half of the Kingdom, quite beyond the control of the state.[201]

As already noted, Kadare's description of the blood feud in *Broken April* reflects the provisions of the *Kanun* very precisely: according to the *Kanun*, the stolen honour can only be restored through bloodshed (§§ 593–601 *Kanun*),[202] unless the bloodied families agree to a peaceful settlement of the feud (§§ 965–990 *Kanun*). Outside of the pacification procedure, a breach of honour can never be forgiven (§597 *Kanun*), because if the honour is not restored through the act of revenge, the person concerned is considered socially dead according to the *Kanun* (§ 600 *Kanun*). The *Kanun* counts the accusation of lying to the council of elders, breach of trust, desecration of the wife, weapons and bread, insulting the guest, housebreaking, breaking one's word, etc. (§ 601 *Kanun*) as violations of honour (alb. *Nderi*).[203] The law of blood revenge (*gjak, gjakmarrje*) refers, as has already been commented on with regard to *Sworn Virgin*, only to men, but not to women and sworn virgins (§§ 835–836 *Kanun*), which, as has also already been emphasised, is to be understood as an expression of the inferiority of women. Every blood feud carried out by killing entails a new blood feud against the murderer and his male relatives (§§ 843–873; §§ 898–900 *Kanun*).[204] In this way, the blood feud degenerates into an endless "ping-pong game"[205] between the feuding families, which drags on for generations and has led to a disproportionate decimation of the male population in many regions.[206] Adem Demaçi, winner of the Sakharov Prize in 1991 and known as the 'Mandela of the Balkans',[207] also took a critical look at this destructive phenomenon in his novel *The Serpents of Blood* (*Gjarpijt e Gjakut* 1958).[208] According to Kaser, it is an ancestor cult in which the soul of the murdered person only finds peace by killing the murderer.[209] In contrast, non-punishable killings such as suicide (§ 958–959 *Kanun*), the killing of a son by his parents, the killing of a wife by her husband (§ XXXI *Kanun*), or negligent killings (§ 932 *Kanun*) are not 'punishable' and therefore do not extend beyond the individual killing.[210] To escape the danger of

[201] Kadare (1990), pp. 72-73

[202] Schmidt-Neke (2014), pp. XXX–XXXI; Elsie (2014a), p. 134.

[203] See Qerimi (2014), p. 34.

[204] Schmidt-Neke (2014), p. XXXVI.

[205] Ibid., p. XXXVIII.

[206] Elsie (2014b), p. IX.

[207] Adem Demaçi (2005).

[208] European Parliament (2016), pp. 80–81. See also: Sozialistische Albanische Hefte (2009), pp. 29–30 (internet-link in the bibliography).

[209] Kaser (1992), pp. 275–279.

[210] Qerimi (2014), pp. 39–40.

being killed by the enemy family, the male members of the family concerned only have the alternative of hiding in their own house because as soon as they leave it, they can be murdered, as is alluded to in passing in *Sworn Virgin* (SV 199).[211]

To summarise, it should be emphasised that Elvira Done's novel *Sworn Virgin* presents a very faithful picture of Albanian customary law, except for the controversial assertion that the revocation of an oath of chastity always results in the death of the guilty party. The diegetic legal discourse also ignores the *Kanun*'s requirement for twelve oath-keepers, which, it seems, is also difficult to implement in real-world practice.

The narrative depiction of human behaviour in *Sworn Virgin* links law and literature in the closest possible way, even if the customary law provisions of the *Kanun* are not identified in the diegesis by legal paragraphs but only come to the fore through the contrasting of the fictional novel text with the real-world text of the *Kanun of Lekë Dukagjini*. The factuality of the *Kanun* as a collection of customary law rules is proven by the fact that it is a customary law that still exists today, which was passed down orally over generations and has been confirmed in writing since the beginning of the 20th century in the form of the *Kanun of Lekë Dukagjini*. The primarily oral character of the *Kanun* favours subjective hermeneutic imprecision, as is known from literature, just as the hermeneutics of the *Kanun* generally shows strong similarities with literary hermeneutics, in that it is interpreted over generations without any time limit, but without—in contrast to literature—having a textual reference until the beginning of the 20th century. Paradoxically, the emergence of written versions of the *Kanun*, such as the *Kanun of Lekë Dukagjini*, has done little to change this hermeneutical vagueness and lack of reference, as in many cases the customary law handed down orally is applied—sometimes incorrectly—without prior knowledge of the now written customary law. However, unlike in the literature, misinterpretations can have fatal consequences, as shown, for example, by the killing of women and children, which is forbidden in the *Kanun*. Due to the lack of a text for many generations, the hermeneutic rules and methods of interpretation of the hermeneutic circle that apply to legal texts were also difficult to apply to the *Kanun*. This leads to the paradoxical situation that literary hermeneutics is closer to the *Kanun* than legal hermeneutics.

As the example of the novel *Sworn Virgin* makes clear, literature fulfils the role of a textual substitute at the interface between the orally transmitted customary law of the *Kanun* and its lack of written form, whereby literary and legal hermeneutics are closely linked. It is now possible to use legal hermeneutics to interpret people's actions in *Sworn Virgin* in the light of the provisions of the *Kanun*. To do this, however, the customary law discourse in the diegesis must first be uncovered, as it does not appear to stand out from the literary text at first glance. Rather, it is the description of a special social status that Hana adopts to avoid an arranged marriage and to preserve the honour of her uncle's family. Her decision to swear eternal virginity and renounce marriage and children gives her (almost) all the rights of a man and

[211] Cf. Negri et al. (2019a) (internet-link in the bibliography).

thus leads to greater freedom for her in Albanian society. At first glance, it appears to be a gender issue that deals with female identity and the social position of women, as previous research has almost without exception shown. However, if one examines the diegesis in terms of its customary law discourse, with the real-world *Kanun* in hand, one realises that this is not ostensibly a gender issue, but rather a customary law issue that grants women the opportunity to assume a social position similar to that of men without changing or questioning their gender. Hana emphasises this explicitly in *Sworn Virgin*: " I'm not a transvestite, or a transsexual, and I'm not gay. I've never been any of these things. It's just that I swore to become a man, in a social sense, sixteen years ago. I had to do it because my circumstances forced me to" (SV 233). Hana's explanation corresponds to the meaning of § 1228 of the *Kanun*: "*The Virgins* (women who dress as men): They are not distinguished from other women, except that they are free to associate with men, although they have no right to a voice in the assembly." The customary law of the *Kanun* requires women to renounce marriage and children in return for improved social status but does not force them to act like men. It is up to them to decide whether they dress and behave like a man or whether they continue to dress like a woman. However, all *Burrnesha* wear short hair, a turban or a cap and mostly do men's work to match their new social status. They even seem to be allowed to have sexual intercourse, but on condition that they do not have children. In this sense, the law is purpose-bound and practically orientated: The purpose of the virgin oath is to feign the continuation of the male line in the absence of male offspring, to prolong the administration of the inheritance by one generation or to allow unmarried women to care for family members. The *Kanun* must therefore be understood and interpreted in terms of its practical effectiveness, which is precisely what the text of *Sworn Virgin* does by illustrating the purpose, application, and effect of the *Kanun* using a fictitious practical case. The individual case of 'Hana' is subsumed to a certain extent under the abstract norm of the *Kanun.* The text of *Sworn Virgin* functions here as a common hermeneutic reference for literature and law, in that *Sworn Virgin* provides an interpretative aid for this sparsely documented written special status of the *Burrnesha,* also known as *Virgjëreshe*, *Virgjin*, *Vajzë* or *Betuar*, which the oral *Kanun* lacks and which the written *Kanun of the Lekë Dukagjini* also does not provide in full, as the male-like status of the *Burrnesha* is only explicitly addressed in § 1228 of the *Kanun*, with the mention that the '*Virgins*' have no voting rights in the assembly. The scope of interpretation under customary law therefore remains so significant that it is meaningfully narrowed by the literary 'commentary' *Sworn Virgin.*

The counterfactual study of *Sworn Virgin* therefore proves the close interweaving of law and literature via the text as a hermeneutic reference, especially for the hitherto little-researched and little-known phenomenon of *Burrnesha.* This may not be so relevant in the case of feudal law, hospitality, honour, and all other areas of the *Kanun*, as these are only dealt with very marginally or not at all in *Sworn Virgin*, which is evidently due to the author's need to mainly focus on those aspects of the *Kanun* that are relevant to understanding the phenomenon of the sworn virgin. For example, the lawlessness of women is discussed in detail, the knowledge of which sheds a different light on the renunciation of marriage, family, and children. The better-known phenomenon of blood feud apparently seemed less relevant to the author, perhaps because it has already found its way into literature, as Ismail Kadare's well-known novel *Broken April* proves. Here, the exact course of the blood feud between the 'blood-feuding' families is described very precisely based on a 'case', whereby the relevant provisions of the *Kanun* are clearly and precisely reproduced.

Customary law and literature seem to fertilise each other in *Sworn Virgin*, as the diegetic text takes on the role of the lacking or inadequate writing of the orally transmitted law and conveys a concrete interpretative aid for the real-world *Kanun* via a 'fictional case'. In this sense, it can be argued that literature here assumes the role of translator between law and literature, acting as an area in which the interdiscourse unfolds a mediating function between law and literature.

5.4 *Unorthodox* (2012)[212] by Deborah Feldman

In her autobiographical novel *Unorthodox*, Deborah Feldman describes her childhood up until her marriage and the birth of her son in the Hasidic Satmar community in Williamsburg, New York. It was founded in 1946 by Rabbi Joel Teitelbaum, who had been rescued from the Bergen-Belsen concentration camp by the lawyer Rudolf Kasztner. Teitelbaum, who had led the Jewish community of Satu Mare on the border between Hungary and Romania, wanted to rebuild the European Jewish *shtetl* in New York with barely more than a dozen Holocaust survivors and increase its population. Today, the community has approximately 100,000 members who adhere to particularly strict rules in the belief that they can prevent a second Holocaust through deprivation and repentance.[213] The founding of the New York *shtetl* was influenced on the one hand by the feeling of guilt at having survived and on the other by the fear of God's 'punishment'. In this sense, the Holocaust is interpreted as God's punishment, which can only be countered in the future through unconditional religious obedience and the renunciation of assimilation efforts, such as those that took place in Europe. Life in the Satmar community, from birth to death, is strictly regulated down to the smallest detail, and anyone who does not submit unconditionally and uncritically becomes an undesirable foreign body that jeopardises the quest to appease God.[214]

---

[212] Feldman (2012). For citation purposes the sigle 'U' is used with the page number in the running text.

[213] Cf. Feldman and Ruzicska (2017) (internet-link in the bibliography).

[214] Cf. Deborah Feldman (2020) (internet-link in the bibliography).

5.4.1 Unorthodox*: Contents*

Deborah, called *mamaleh* by her grandmother (U 72; 121; 126; 156; 158), is the child of a failed marriage between a mentally ill, alcoholic and neglected father and a lesbian mother who has long since left the Satmar community (and her daughter) in New York's Williamsburg. As the offspring of ostracised parents, she becomes a problematic case of a different kind in the eyes of the community. She is brought up strictly according to Hasidic rules by her grandparents Zeidy and Fraida (Bubby), who are both Holocaust survivors (U 57). From an early age, Deborah tries to obtain books in secret to compensate for the emotional and intellectual emptiness that she must live with. Thanks to her secret reading, she excels in English lessons at the religious girls' school and becomes an English teacher at the same school at the age of 17. At 18, she is forced to marry Elie, a young man her grandparents have chosen for her. The psychological and religiously induced tension in her relationship with her own body leads to vaginismus in Deborah, which makes it impossible for her to bear a child immediately after the wedding. These intimate difficulties of the young married couple become a public affair because after all, childbearing and housekeeping are the main tasks of a woman. When she finally becomes pregnant with her son after numerous visits to the doctor and several therapies, she knows that she will do everything she can to offer her child a different life from the one she herself experienced. She managed to get accepted into the secular *Sara Lawrence College* outside the Satmar community to develop her writing skills. There she finds support from new friends who encourage her to leave Williamsburg for good with her son at the age of 23. Today, she lives as a freelance writer in Berlin. Her former husband Elie left the community 3 years after her and now also leads a normal life with a non-Jewish woman.[215] Feldman's story has been made into a film series that adheres relatively faithfully to her life in New York while interpreting her arrival and life in Berlin in a very different way.[216]

5.4.2 On the Explicit Legal Discourse in the Diegesis

In the ultra-orthodox Jewish community of Satmar in Williamsburg, New York, public and private life is regulated by religious rules, right down to the most intimate sphere. In this respect, the narrative of everyday life in *Unorthodox* appears to be congruent with religious law. One could almost claim that the diegesis is the 'law', insofar as it narrates the religious law, which is brought to life and visualised through explanatory commentary and first-person narration and embellished with Deborah Feldman's personal emotions and impressions. To a certain extent, the law

[215] Cf. Feldman and Ruzicska (2017).

[216] Unorthodox (Netflix). A series with Shira Haas, Amit Rahav, Jeff Wilbusch, directed by Maria Schrader, 2020 (https://www.netflix.com/at/title/81019069.

is created through the discourse in the diegesis by being formulated through words, whereby Feldman often refers to the terms 'law' and 'tradition' when she refers to important religious regulations. In this sense, diegetic discourse appears, following Foucault, and to paraphrase Rolf Parr, as "a practice of thinking, writing, speaking and also acting, which at the same time itself systematically produces the objects it deals with."[217] In the following, the objective is to filter out a selection of the Talmudic rules of life mentioned, as it would neither be possible nor reasonable to deal with all the details of the immensely complex, multi-layered, and all too extensive Talmudic law that can be extracted from the diegesis; this would unnecessarily go beyond the scope of the present work. Rather, the endeavour will be to test and explicate the methodological approach using a few illustrative examples, but not to put every single sentence in *Unorthodox* to the test, even if this would be quite conceivable in view of the density of rules in the narrative, insofar as the diegesis is the law here. Numerous Talmudic rules emerge from therefrom, which are tightened, not to say radicalised, by the Satmar rabbinate with specific regulations. They concern, roughly divided, general principles of Jewish 'being' (1.), prohibitions and commandments for women (2.) as well as religious festivals and traditions (3.) that determine the rhythm of the year.

(1.) The corpus of Talmudic rules is based on a contract with 'God', at the 'signing' of which "every Jewish soul was present when the Torah was handed down to the chosen people" (U 60). From this witnessing as the 'chosen ones' of God, the Jews have a special responsibility (*Midrash*): "There is no immunity for a Jewish soul" (U 60). Jews possess a "spark, a *tzelem Elokim*" (U 79), i.e. a small part of the divine light that makes them special. Non-Jews, on the other hand, have no soul. In addition to this 'contract with God', every head of a family in the Satmar community signed a contract with the Satmar rabbi, obliging the signatory himself, his family, and his descendants to obediently follow the Hasidic regulations within the Williamsburg community (*kehillah*) (U 60). In this context, the upbringing of children (*chinuch*) must be very strict and maintain great discipline: "It is the parent's spiritual responsibility that their children grow up to be God-fearing, law-abiding Jews" (U 18). Everyone is constantly watching others so that they can denounce spiritual or physical misdemeanours (U 18).

In everyday life, the young men study in learning collectives (*kollels*), where they are taught ancient religious texts (U 40), while the girls attend the Satmar School (U 21). None of these schools award a secular degree that would allow them to study in the outside world. The young men must grow a beard (U 64), spend every free minute studying the *Torah*, and are not allowed to talk to girls (U 64).

The food must be *kosher* and prepared *kosher*: The milk used must be tested by the rabbi (U 16). Meat and dairy dishes must be cooked and eaten separately (U 60). Cooking utensils that have come into contact with dairy products may not be used for other dishes. Conversation at the table is prohibited until the meal has begun (U 51).

217 Parr (2020), pp. 274–275.

It is forbidden to travel to Israel as long as the messiah has not come. Even relatives in Israel may not be visited, as this would mean the exclusion from the Satmar community (U 57). However, even in this case, the Jewish origin remains intact, because Jews remain Jews, no matter how hard they try to become a *goy* (U 96). "They may dress like one, speak like one, live like one, but Jewishness is something that can never be erased. Even Hitler knew that" (U 96).

(2.) The rules for women are even stricter than for men; gender segregation pervades everyday life. A girl is not allowed to be in a room with a man, even if other women are present. Only if there are several men present may she be alone with them, but she must leave the doors open and keep a physical distance: "No touching. No singing aloud, of course" (U 65). She may not place coins directly in the salesperson's hand but must place them on the counter (U 66). Female charms are to be concealed so as not to give men cause to 'sin'. In this sense, every part of the female body from the collarbone to the wrists and knees is to be covered *(ervah)* (U 36). If a man sees a part of the female body that must be covered, he sins (U 36). Hair as a female symbol must not be coloured (U 19) and must be hidden from view under a bonnet or wig. According to a later decree by the Satmar rabbi, all women must be completely shaven and wear a wig (U 24). Knitted clothing that lies directly on the skin is forbidden (U 32), which is why a blouse must be worn under every jumper. Skirts must cover the knee, trousers are unthinkable. Nothing may be red, since the colour 'red' is reminiscent of impure blood (U 61). Women are also not allowed to sing outside their own families and even then, only on special occasions (U 12), as singing could have a seductive effect.

The division of labour between husband and wife is clear: wives must provide their husbands with as many offspring as possible and take care of the household, while men devote themselves to studying the *Torah*.

Education that goes beyond the compulsory girls' school programme is strictly forbidden for women. Moreover, speaking English is not permitted, and the only colloquial language that is allowed is *Yiddish*: "An impure language, Zeidy says, acts like a poison to the soul" (U 26). Books, especially those in English, are forbidden (U 20; 26; 45; 80), and women are not even allowed to read the *Talmud* (U 26–28).

A married woman is considered unclean (*niddah*) for a fortnight a month "as soon as a one drop of blood exits her womb" (U 140) and may not be touched by her husband during this time: "He cannot see any part of her body. He cannot hear her sing" (U 140). He is not allowed to hand his wife "a plate of food" (U 140). After the end of menstruation, the woman must count seven clean days and check herself twice a day with a white cotton cloth for drops of blood. If no more blood can be detected with certainty, the newfound purity must be confirmed by a public ritual bath under the supervision of bathers (*mikvah*) (U 140–141; 156; 173).

(3.) *Shabbos* [Saturday, author's note] is a day off from work that is spent with the family (U 110). On this day, it is forbidden to use electricity or carry objects (U 110): "Every Jewish business must cease for the duration of the *Shabbos*, and the law requires that a Jew be the one to set things [switching on electricity, author's note] in motion again" (U 12).

Sukkot (U 13): For 8 days, meals are eaten in a specially built wooden hut made of leaves; no work is done during these days.

For the eight-day Passover (*Pesach*) festival (U 52), it is not permitted to buy nuts that have already been cracked, but they must be cracked at home by hand (U 47). During the *Pesach* celebrations, grated horseradish and bitter herbs reminiscent of the Exodus from Egypt are served in special "Passover jars" (U 48). For the *Passover seder* meal, the men put on long white linen coats, which are buttoned from top to bottom to symbolise angels and put "a belt at the waist" (U 50). Everyone gathers around the table, the children behind the adults, and rises for the *kiddush* with wine-filled silver goblets, the contents of which they must drink after the blessing (U 51). The last bite of *matzo* [unleavened bread, author's note] must be eaten before one o'clock in the morning. Before this, the *Haggadah* and a sermon (*drashah*) are read at the appropriate time (U 51).

Forty-nine days after *Pesach*, the community celebrates *Shavuos*, the day "that commemorates the day the Jewish people accepted the Torah at Mount Sinai" (U 53). During these 49 days, it is forbidden to listen to music, cut hair, or wear new clothes (U 53). During *Shavuos*, the house is decorated with flowers and ferns in memory of the barren Mount Sinai, which was adorned with flowers (U 59).

In May, the Satmar Hasidim gather from all over to attend the anti-Zionist march to express their desire for the destruction of Israel, because "faithful Jews wait for the messiah; they don't take up guns and swords and do the work themselves" (U 56).

On *Lag Ba'Omer*, the men dance around large bonfires that they light in all the streets, while the women are only allowed to watch from the windows (U 58).

On *Simchas Torah*, the women are allowed to catch a few glimpses of the rabbi and the men in the gallery at the top of the synagogue, separated from the men, through small holes in the partition wall (U 83). Downstairs in the synagogue, the *gabbaim*, the strong young yeshiva students, create "a human fence around the rabbi" (U 86). For the rest of the year, women are not allowed to go to the synagogue (*shul*), they are only allowed to pray at school or at home because their prayers do not count (U 87).

The marriage of marriageable girls (*kallah maidel*) is arranged by the family with the help of a matchmaker (U 119–137). The young woman is first introduced to the potential husband's parents, and if they agree, both husband and wife meet with their parents to set the festive day (*t'noyim*) on which the betrothal contract is signed (U 133–134) and the betrothed exchange gifts (U 135). On the engagement day, the mother-in-law presents her future daughter-in-law with a diamond ring and the *t'noyim* plate is broken as a symbol of devotion (U 135). Until the wedding, both brides and grooms are prepared for their marriage separately by marriage teachers (*kallah lessons*; *hashkafah courses*). Five days before the wedding, the bride must go to the *mikvah* to become pure, otherwise, she would not be able to go through with the wedding (U 140–141). On the wedding day, the bride and groom fast and pray from the morning until the wedding feast (U 163). For the actual wedding ceremony, the bride is seated on a white bridal chair entwined with silk flowers (U 164) and her face is covered with a white veil (*badeken ceremony*), as she is not allowed to see until the *chuppah ceremony* is over and the bride and groom are officially married (U 164–165). After the wedding blessing (*mesader kiddushin*), the husband slips the wedding ring over his wife's finger, glass is broken as a symbol of happiness, the white veil is lifted, and the newlyweds go to the neighbouring *yichud room*, where they eat a meal together for the first time alone (U 165). The feast then begins with dancing and music. When the feast is over, the couple goes back to the home and is expected to perform the sexual act that night, which neither of the partners knows about and which they have only heard about in the marriage course (U 168). Begetting and bearing children is the couple's most important task and is publicly observed. The wedding day is followed by seven festive days on which the bride is the best-dressed person (U 172). The prescribed frequency of sexual intercourse depends on the man's profession: every 6 months for a merchant, three times a week for a labourer and on Friday evenings for a Torah scholar (U 226). Only if there is an argument and the man does not apologise may the woman refuse sexual intercourse (U 227). After the birth of the child, male infants are circumcised (U 210), whereby the mother does not attend the ceremony so as not to suffer any emotional damage (U 210).

Four weeks after birth, the male infant undergoes the *pidyon haben* ceremony: Dressed in a pure white robe, he is placed on a golden tray and covered with the jewellery of the women present. "Six men grasp the tray [...] and hold it aloft" (U 212).

This perhaps somewhat 'dry' depiction of Talmudic discourse in the diegesis of the novel *Unorthodox,* shows how much the life of Hasidic Jews in the Satmar community is still constrained by prohibitions and commandments today, with women—as is so often the case—occupying a greatly underprivileged role. In the following chapter, this diegetic discourse will be contrasted with the actual laws of the *Torah* and the *Talmud*. In view of the immense wealth and complexity of the *Talmud* in particular, which overlays the *Torah*, it is necessary to make a very specific selection of those regulations that can and should be associated with the legal discourse in *Unorthodox*. It would neither be sensible nor possible to delve into the 9000 pages of the Babylonian *Talmud*.[218] As a result, it is inevitable that the following overview of the regulations of the *Torah* and *Talmud*—which intentionally concentrates on the most important topics dealt with by Feldman—cannot be considered an exhaustive discussion of this topic. It is important, on the one hand, to show which essential religious regulations Feldman refers to and, on the other hand, to explain the historical and social context of the Satmar community, which will be discussed in advance. The overall picture of the real Satmar Jews still living in Williamsburg, New York, today certainly contributes significantly to the understanding of the novel. This cannot be otherwise, because everyday life and religious rules are so closely interwoven in Judaism that one cannot be understood without the other.

---

[218] Stemberger (2019), p. 70.

5.4.3 History: The Ultra-Orthodox Jewish Satmar Community in Williamsburg, New York

In 1867, Hungarian Jews were granted civil rights and were asked to elect a representative for their ethnic group. No agreement could be reached between the assimilationist, traditional, and ultra-orthodox members of the faith and a split occurred between the Orthodox, Neologue, and *status quo* communities. Within the Orthodox community, there was a further split between the larger group of non-Hasidic moderate Orthodox Jews and the smaller group of ultra-Orthodox Jews,[219] who profess Hasidism.[220] While the latter group was of very minor importance in Hungary compared to the much larger group of more tolerant and more assimilated Jews, Jewish extremism was able to establish itself above all in Transylvania (Siebenbürgen), the part of Hungary that later became part of Romania. Its followers differed from the majority of their Jewish co-religionists, not only in their particularly strict religious outlook on life, but also in their resolutely anti-Zionist stance and rejection of the idea of the state of Israel.

Shulem Deen summarises the basic attitude of Hasidism very aptly in this context:

> The objective is self-imposed ghettoization. Distinct language and dress keep interactions with outsiders to a minimum and help maintain separation from the wider world. Restrictions on secular education and outside knowledge keep foreign ideas at bay. Bans on media and popular entertainment keep away any temptation. And so the Hasidim are spared the calamities of modernity.[221]

This self-imposed ghettoisation, which aimed to hermetically seal off the Jewish religious community from the modern outside world, was based on the strict retention of Yiddish as a colloquial language, the peculiarly distinctive clothing worn, and the almost complete ban on secular education to prevent the possibility of studying or working in the outside world. Raphael Schneller refers to this deliberate isolationism through language, dress, and lifestyle:

---

[219] The term *orthodox* denotes the deliberate more or less pronounced demarcation against Jewish assimilation in the society of the 'host country'. Cf. Jonathan Kaplan (2004), pp. 165–178, here: pp. 165–166. The more radical *Orthodoxy* is, the stronger the resistance to external influences on Jewish religious rules, customs, and traditions as well as to renewal, which leads to isolationist tendencies. The isolationism (*world-renouncer movement*) of the Satmar community in Williamsburg, New York, is a particularly extreme example of Jewish Orthodoxy, motivated by the endeavour to vehemently seal itself off from modernity encroaching from outside. Cf. Inbari (2016a), pp. 6–15.

[220] The *Hasidism* movement goes back to Israël Ben Eliezer (1700–1760), known as *Baal Shêm Tov*, who preached religious 'enthusiasm' and the possibility of experiencing enlightening union with God (*devokuss*) in everything one does. The term 'Hadis' means, roughly translated, 'the pious' (Pinsker (1975), pp. 230–246, here: p. 232). Ecstatic prayers and dances were supposed to help achieve this state. The Hasidim follow the 613 commandments of the *Torah* in the version of Joseph Caro (1488–1575). Based on Kabbalistic mysticism, the person of the *Rebbe* is intensely revered as a spiritual guide. Cf. Gutwirth (2004), pp. 53–93, here: pp. 14–30.

[221] Deen (2015), pp. 118–119.

> Its aim is total segregation from the wider society. […] Yiddish is the language of daily conversation and of instruction. The use of modern Hebrew is forbidden. The members dress in the same style as that of their ancestors in their land of origin and maintain other traditional patterns of personal and social behaviour. They adhere to the motto that 'Whatever is new is forbidden by the Torah' […].[222]

In this context, Lewis Glinert and Joseph Shilhav explain that the Yiddish language not only serves to differentiate them from the modern outside world but also from other Jewish groups: "Yiddish serves as a barrier, both symbolic and real, between Ultraorthodoxy and other Jews."[223] David Lehmann and Batia Siebzehner also highlight this systematic refusal to change: "Against the trend of secularisation, against the trend towards small families, against the trend towards a culture in which social status is determined overwhelmingly by economic means, against racial mixing, against the permissive society, against, against, against…This is a community, or better, a culture, in which the watchword appears to be 'any proposal for change say no'."[224]

As only a few of these Hasidic believers emigrated before the Second World War, merely a handful of them survived the Holocaust, including Rabbi Yoel Teitelbaum,[225] the only ultra-Orthodox leader of the Transylvanian (Transylvanian) Jewish community of *Satu-Mare*, which he had headed as rabbi since 1934.[226] He was rescued from the Bergen-Belsen concentration camp by the Zionist Rudolf Kasztner on the pretext that his survival was of particular interest to Israel.[227] Teitelbaum's first attempt to establish an ultra-Orthodox community in Jerusalem failed due to his hopeless over-indebtedness, which forced him to try his luck in the United States. Even there, he was not welcomed with open arms by the predominantly pro-Zionist Jews, until he managed to gather a small group of Holocaust survivors around him. In 1948, he and a dozen of these survivors founded the ultra-Orthodox Hasidic Satmar community in Williamsburg, New York, with the aim of preserving the original religious identity from the time before the Shoah.[228] As Glinert and Shilhav emphasise, this endeavour overlapped with the desire to recreate the Eastern European *shtetl* as a distinct and protected space elsewhere, "endeavouring to maintain the traditional *shtetl* 'small town' way of life within a dynamic, modern, urban Western environment so fundamentally dissimilar."[229] Teitelbaum's ideology is based on the condemnation of the Zionist movement—to which he owes his life (!)—as the cause of the Holocaust and thus on the radical rejection of the state of

[222] Schneller (1980), pp. 35–45, here: p. 36. See also Glinert and Shilhav (1991), pp. 59–86, here: p. 63.

[223] Ibid., p. 65.

[224] Lehmann and Siebzehner (2009), pp. 273–308, here: pp. 273–274.

[225] For further information on Yoel Teitelbaum, see: Inbari (2016b), pp. 131–172; Meisels (2011).

[226] Inbari (2016a), p. 139.

[227] Kaplan (2004), p. 165.

[228] Keren-Kratz (2023a), pp. 52–76, here: pp. 57–60.

[229] Glinert and Shilhav (1991), p. 63.

Israel and all other Jewish groups that recognise and support the Israeli state.[230] He recorded his anti-Zionist ultra-Orthodox ideas in his *work Va-yo'el Moshe*,[231] to which Menachem Keren-Kratz refers for explanatory purposes:

> The ideology expressed in *Va-yo'el Moshe* can be reduced to two fundamental principles. First, it claims that Zionism in general, and the State of Israel in particular, is the worst sin imaginable. This sin was so grave that God's only possible response to it was the Holocaust. Second, it claims that only a small group of Jews-namely, those who accept the ideas that Teitelbaum expressed in *Va-yo'el Moshe-are* 'true Jews', while all others who call themselves Jews are imposters who are either false or flawed.[232]

Teitelbaum endeavoured to clearly distinguish himself and his followers from other orthodox movements as a particularly fundamentalist religious community and to present the followers of his movement as the only 'true' Jews. In Teitelbaum's interpretation, the existence of the State of Israel is a grave sin that will bring punishment upon the Jews, who are destined to live in the diaspora due to persecution and pogroms until God redeems the Jewish people. This view rejects the idea of self-determination of the Jewish people as a state and at the same time denies the authority of secular law or democratic forms of government.[233] According to Teitelbaum, the only activities to which Jews should devote themselves are the study of the *Talmud Torah* and the leading of a pious religious life in accordance with religious law.[234] In this sense, 'true' Jews are not allowed to speak modern Hebrew, as this is the language of the State of Israel, which Teitelbaum holds responsible for the destruction of the Jewish faith. *Modern Hebrew must therefore not be spoken under any circumstances until the redemption by the messiah:* "The Land of Israel and the Holy Tongue [Hebrew], which are higher privileges, were taken from us at the time of the Destruction of the Temple because we were not worthy of them, and it will be restored at the Redemption which will be much higher and greater, as Redemption itself, which is the end goal of Creation, is the time when God will reign forever."[235]

Haim Lieberman therefore describes the Satmar community outright as haters of the Israeli state: "The State of Israel has many enemies in the world [. . .] Among its prominent haters are members of Neturei Karta of Jerusalem headed by the Satmar Rebbe and his Hasidim in Williamsburg [. . .] They are launching an inconceivable war against the great heavenly miracle and the earthly wonder, namely the Jewish state."[236] Teitelbaum's writings and ideology are still taught and commented on in the Satmar community today. Motti Inbari sees Teitelbaum's hatred of Israel as an

[230] Keren-Kratz (2023a), pp. 60-61.

[231] Teitelbaum (2023), Independently published 2023.

[232] Keren-Kratz (2023b), pp. 479–506, here: p. 479. See also: Keren-Kratz (2017), pp. 457–479, here: p. 471.

[233] Menachem Keren-Kratz (2023b), p. 494; Kaplan (2004), pp. 168–176.

[234] Menachem Keren-Kratz (2023b), p. 498.

[235] Glinert and Shilhav (1991), p. 73.

[236] Lieberman (1958), p. 1.

aversion to modernity, which could jeopardise power over an isolated group of people cut off from the outside world.[237]

Geographically, the Hasidic Satmar community is located in Williamsburg, one of the oldest neighbourhoods in Brooklyn, on the east side of Manhattan, in close proximity to other immigrant neighbourhoods, such as that of the Puerto Ricans, between the Bedford, Lee, Macy, and Division streets.[238] From 1948 onwards, the Hasidic Satmar community developed rapidly thanks to the commandment to produce as many children as possible to replace those lost in the Shoah. By the end of the 20th century, the initial dozen members had already grown to 40,000 Hasidim,[239] who pushed more moderate believers out of the neighbourhood and formed a closed, homogeneous ultra-orthodox community. By 2015, their number had risen to no less than 100,000 souls.[240]

As indicated, the Jews of Satmar deliberately set themselves apart from the 'other' Jewish and non-Jewish world through their peculiarly distinctive clothing: contrary to the general rule, the men button their black jackets from right to left. On *Shabbos* and holidays, the men wear high headgear made of fox tails, so-called *shtreimel*, as a special identifying mark of the Jews of Satmar.[241] Married women must shave their heads clean and cover them with a wig or headscarf.[242] However, given the fierce opposition to head shaving, Teitelbaum eventually had to withdraw this regulation.[243] The fact that even such pious and devoted women as Bubby in *Unorthodox* resist such violent suppression of femininity is shown by Zeidy's insistent tone when he implores his wife to shave her head for the sake of her reputation in the community (U 24). Women are not allowed to wear trousers, their skirts must reach below the knee and their legs must be covered with black stockings.[244] Men and women only wear long sleeves, even in summer, and the body must be almost completely covered.[245]

In *Unorthodox*, the details of the clothing of both men and women are described in detail, since clothing plays an essential role as a means of differentiation in Hasidic ideology. Feldman perceives the dress codes as a strongly marginalising factor vis-à-vis the outside world, especially from the moment she attends *Sarah Lawrence College* outside Williamsburg and compares herself to 'normally' dressed people: "I've started taking my wig off in college, even though my hair underneath is always a little matted. The wig makes me self-conscious, as do the skirts, but I don't own any normal clothing [...]" (U 230). As soon as she is able, she buys a pair

[237] Inbari (2016a), p. 2.

[238] Gutwirth (2004), p. 55. See also: Kranzler (1961), p. 15; Kranzler (1995a), pp. 287–288.

[239] Kranzler (1995b), p. 191; Rubin (1997), p. 11.

[240] Inbari (2016a), p. 155.

[241] Ibid., p. 159.

[242] Gutwirth (2004), p. 55; Inbari (2016a), pp. 159–160.

[243] Inbari (2016a), p. 160.

[244] Ibid.

[245] Ibid., pp. 158–159.

of jeans and seeks the approval of her fellow students (U 230). In *Unorthodox*, the religious clothing regulations are justified by the fact that they must conceal all female charms, which is why women must be covered from the collarbone to the wrists and knees (U 36). It remains to be seen whether the prohibition of the red colour as a reminder of impure blood (U 61) is justified, especially given that the *Torah*[246] does not prohibit the colour 'red' although it is associated with blood and sin (Genesis 25, 25). According to Konstantin Schuchardt, 'red' stands for blood and fire and is also "the colour of love and passion as well as the colour of anger and shame."[247] This may be a prohibition of the Satmar rabbinate, just as the regulation for girls not to wear knitted garments directly on their bodies (U 32) appears to be a specific Satmar regulation.

The members of the religious community attend schools especially set up for them – the *chaïder*, *yeshive gola* and the *kollel*[248] Talmud schools – without officially recognised qualifications.[249] In these schools, the Jewish rules of social and family life (*haloche*) are taught almost exclusively in Yiddish and ancient Hebrew.[250] The profane subjects are limited to the minimum required by American law (English lessons).[251] Girls receive significantly less religious education than boys, but slightly more English lessons.[252] Satmar women are denied access to public universities, as their internal degrees are not recognised in the outside world. University education is perceived as a danger to be avoided, as it could distract young people from religion.[253]

In *Unorthodox*, Feldman paints a picture, consistent with anthropological studies, of the restrictive, highly constrained educational system in the Satmar community, which is even more minimalist for women than for men, except for English lessons. The fear of a profane education is illustrated in the narrative by Zeidy's control and outbursts of anger: "'*Der tumeneh shprach*!' he thunders at me when he overhears me speaking to my cousins in English. An impure language, Zeidy says, acts like a poison to the soul. Reading an English book is even worse; it leaves my soul vulnerable, a welcome mat put out for the devil" (U 26).

Even though attempts are still being made to ban modern means of communication such as mobile phones, computers, the internet, email, etc., they have become an integral part of professional life in Williamsburg.[254] As early as the 1980s, several institutes opened offering IT training in compliance with strict orthodox rules. *Hatzoloh* (health) and *Shomrem* (security) are the organisations responsible for

[246] *The Torah: The Five Books of Moses*. Philadelphia : Jewish Publication Society of America 1999.

[247] Schuchardt (2016) (internet-link in the bibliography).

[248] Bomzer (1985).

[249] Gutwirth (2004), pp. 69–70.

[250] Inbari (2016a), pp. 157–158.

[251] Gutwirth (2004), pp. 69–71.

[252] Ibid., p. 72; Inbari (2016a), p. 156.

[253] Gutwirth (2004), p. 60.

[254] Ibid.

medical care and internal security.[255] The principle is always the same: everything must take place within the Satmar community to avoid contact with the outside world as far as possible.

Unorthodox therefore conveys a real picture of the history and everyday life of the Hasidic Satmar community that is very much in line with anthropological research. In a two-page introduction that precedes the novel, Feldman offers a cursory synthesis of the context to ease the reader's introduction and recalls the Hungarian-Romanian origins of the Jewish community of *Satu Mare*, the rescue of the rabbi of *Satu Mare* from the Holocaust by Rudolf Kasztner, Hasidism, the reproduction of the Eastern European *shtetl*, the distinction and isolationism as an assertion of otherness, and the programmed multiplication as 'revenge' for the Holocaust. She also hints at Teitelbaum's hostility towards the state of Israel without explicitly mentioning it (U *A Note from the Author*). This becomes clear several times in the story when she writes: "The rabbi has forbidden us from traveling to Israel. Until the messiah comes, the Promised Land is off-limits" (U 57).

During the biographical narrative, numerous other details shed light on the everyday reality of the Jews of Satmar, which is based on the religious regulations of Rabbi Joel Teitelbaum, the *Torah* and the *Talmud*, which will *be contrasted* with the religious-normative texts in the following.

Feldman's everyday reality can be seen, following Nelson Goodman, as "what is considered real or actual by the members of a society."[256] As it turns out, the detailed description of everyday life comes very close to this real everyday reality, as it seems to deviate only slightly from it. This reality is necessarily fictitious in the fictional novel *Unorthodox*, to use Wolfgang Iser's term, insofar as it is a literary work, i.e. a text that, as Ricœur emphasises, depicts the outside world.[257] As has already been emphasised several times, the study of *Unorthodox* is based on the endeavour to determine the degree of overlap or divergence between the life depicted by Feldman and the actual life of the Jews of Satmar with the help of scientific, historical, and sociological work. The depiction of the rules that govern this life is of great importance insofar as (orthodox) Jewish everyday life, as already emphasised, cannot be understood in isolation from religious rules. This especially applies to the ultra-Orthodoxy of the Satmar community, which does not follow American law—except for a few regulations, such as the minimum requirement to attend English lessons—but rather the sole religious rules of the *Torah* and the *Talmud*, which are overlaid and supplemented by their own, community-specific interpretations in a radicalising way. The way of life is thus normatively regulated by religion, secular law is replaced by the religious law of the *Torah* and the corresponding religious doctrine and interpretation by the *Talmud* and the commandments of the Satmar Rabbinate.

[255] Ibid., pp. 62–63.

[256] Zipfel (2001), p. 75.

[257] Ricœur (1991), pp. 17–18.

The *Talmud* summarises the stages of Jewish life in the sayings of the fathers in a few lines, whereby, as expected, no attention is paid to women:

> In the fifth year of life man is ready for the reading of the Torah, in the tenth for the reading of the Mishnah, in the thirteenth for the practice of the divine commandments, in the fifteenth for the explanation of the Mishnah, in the eighteenth for marriage, in the twentieth for the profession of life, in the thirtieth he attains to full strength, in the fortieth to full understanding, in the fiftieth to insightful counselling, in the sixtieth to set age, at seventy to old age, in the eightieth to old age, in the ninetieth to extinction, in the hundredth he is as if dead. (BT 22)[258]

The contrastive description of everyday reality as it comes to the fore in anthropological research on the one hand, and in *Unorthodox* on the other is at the same time the description of religious law, the normative character of which I will return to in a moment in the context of the explanations on the factuality *of Torah* and *Talmud*. However, and this should be expressly emphasised here, the following contrast of religious law must be limited to the most important aspects given the sprawling and often contradictory and extremely lengthy abundance of religious commentaries on the *Torah* down to the smallest, sometimes seemingly irrelevant details. This limitation to relevant examples is justifiable insofar as the aim of this work is to demonstrate a methodical approach to contrasting law in the diegesis and law in the actual legal texts, which can be accomplished effectively limiting to contrast a selection of relevant incidents in *Unorthodox* with correlating parts of Talmudic law.

5.4.4 Counterfactual Contrast: Torah/Talmud *vs Legal Discourse in the Diegesis*

Before moving on to the actual contrastive examination of the diegetic legal discourse with real-world legal texts, some preliminary remarks on the factuality of these texts are necessary.

5.4.4.1 Factuality of the Talmud-Torah

As is constantly emphasised, the factuality of these texts in the legal sense must be assured for a counterfactual diagnosis between diegetic (fiction) and real-world law (fact) to be possible.[259] Firstly, it should be pointed out here that the elaboration of the diegetic legal discourse in *Unorthodox* in the previous section was firstly carried out from a more anthropological and less legal perspective and, secondly, no distinction was made between the regulations that go back to Rabbi Teitelbaum, to the

[258] Fromer (2021), hereafter cited with the siglum "BT" and page number in the running text. See also: Geballe (2023), pp. 76–78, here: p. 77.

[259] See Sect. 3.4 on Counterfactuality.

Torah, or to the *Talmud*. Care was simply taken to separate the legal-anthropological discourse from the narrative in the sense of a special research perspective.[260]

In contrast, this chapter will discuss those diegetic legal discourses that correlate with the *Torah* and *Talmud* and can be contrasted with these texts. The fact that Teitelbaum's (pre-)writings are excluded from the study is due to their lack of factuality in the sense of Habermas' process of positive norm production,[261] even if they could possibly attain validity in the sense of Hans Kelsen insofar as they are actually followed by the members of the community.[262] As indicated,[263] the counterfactual investigation *strictu sensu* does not presuppose proof of practical compliance with the law, but rather factuality in the strict sense, which is to be regarded as having priority over the practical effect of legal norms. One could, of course, assume proximity to customary law in the spontaneous observance of the regulations by the Jewish members of the faith. However, this becomes invalid when one considers that the original '*usus*' emerges from society itself through *consensus omnium*, *opinio necessitatis* and *longa consuetuo* and cannot and must not be attributed to a specific law-producing person.[264]

The same question of factuality must now be posed *ipso facto* for the *Torah* and the *Talmud*. Can normative validity be claimed for these texts through the process of a canonised production of norms based on a basic law passed and accepted by a majority? François Ost explores this question, seeing the *Torah* as a consensual contract between God and the Jewish people. According to François Ost, the Book of *Exodus* in the Old Testament (synonymous with the *Torah*, author's note) can be read as the narrative of the first historical state treaty, long before Jean-Jacques Rousseau's *Contrat social*.[265] The exodus of the Jewish people from Egypt was an act of liberation from the yoke of slavery under the Egyptian pharaoh, while at the same time symbolised the assumption of responsibility with *Yahweh* (God) to negotiate the basic law of the Ten Commandments in dialogue: "And then the LORD said to Moses: Write down these commandments, for in accordance with these commandments I make a covenant with you and with Israel" (Exodus 34, 27).[266] This *sponsio*, in the sense of Gadamer's foreknowledge,[267] is interpreted by Ost in this context as an agreement that[268] obliged the Israelite people to negotiate with God through Mose's mediation in order to move from the unfree state of slavery to an institutionalised state of law. Naturally, this process towards responsible freedom

[260] Cf. Preisinger et al. (2014), p. 139.
[261] Cf. Habermas (1996), pp. 32–33.
[262] Cf. Kelsen (1965), p. 465.
[263] See the Sect. 3.4.2 on the facticity of law.
[264] Cf. Geis (2021), pp. 27–31.
[265] Cf. Draï (1988), p. 63.
[266] Ost (2004), pp. 59–60.
[267] Cf. Gadamer (1982), p. 267.
[268] Ost (2004), p. 67.

was not without difficulties, crises, and relapses, until finally the Ten Commandments were written down and signed as an institutionalising basic law.[269]

Raphaël Draï agrees with Ost's analysis of the 'contractual negotiation' between God (*Elohim, Yahweh*) and the Jewish people through the mediation of Mose: "In fact, even before these ten words were uttered, a real negotiation (*massa* or *matane*) took place between Israel and God, at God's initiative, concerning this covenant, its cause, its content and its goals."[270]

The *Torah* confirms this consensual agreement between God as the contractual 'initiator' and the Jewish people:

> The he [Moses, author's note] took the record of the covenant and read it aloud to the people. And they said, "All that the LORD has spoken we will faithfully do!" Moses took the blood and dashed it on the people and said, "This is the blood of the covenant that the LORD now makes with you concerning all these commands." (Exodus 24, 7–8)

This first treaty is disrupted by the idolatry of the Jewish people, who worship a golden calf in impatient anticipation of Mose's return from Mount Sinai: "As soon as Moses came near the camp and saw the calf and the dancing, he became enraged; and he hurled the tablets from his hand and shattered them at the foot of the mountain" (Exodus 32, 19). In a second attempt, the final sealing of the 'constituent' contract between God and the Jewish people finally succeeds: "The LORD said to Moses: "Carve two tablets of stone like the first, and I will inscribe upon the tablets the words that were on the first tablets, which you shattered" (Exodus 34, 1). "And the LORD said to Moses: Write down these commandments, for in accordance with these commandments I make a covenant with you and with Israel" (Exodus, 34, 27). The voluntary confirmation of this covenant by the Jewish people affirms the validity of the Divine commandments (Exodus 35).

Based on the metaphor of the contract, followed by the actual observance of God's commandments, the factuality of the *Torah* can be inferred. Naturally, this is not the adoption of a basic law by an earthly parliament, but rather a symbolic act that has been solidified and confirmed in the long history of the *Torah*, first through oral tradition and later through the written record of the *Torah* and the commentaries of the *Talmud* interpreting it.

In accordance with Ost and Draï's understanding of a contract, *Unorthodox* highlights a double contract in this context: a contract between every Jew and God, and a contract between every head of a family in the Satmar community and the Satmar rabbi (U 130). According to Feldman, the fact that the Jewish people witnessed the giving of the Ten Commandments by God to Mose is the inheritance of the "spark of *Zelem Elohim*" (U 172) as a trace of divine light and thus a special responsibility and status for every Jew. Non-Jews are excluded from this holy light and therefore have no soul. The ambiguity of the Talmudic texts, to paraphrase Roman Ingarden,[271]

---

[269] Cf. pp. 68–71.

[270] Draï (1999), pp. 19–60, here: p. 21.

[271] Ingarden (1968), p. 366.

results from the text-related interpretation[272] (it may be difficult to track down God's subjective intentions!) and mixes with fiction in ~~Un~~orthodox when Feldman writes in the *we-form*: "The *Midrash* says that every Jewish soul was present when the *Torah* was given to the Chosen People, and this means that *we* [author's emphasis], even if *we* do not remember it, were there and chose to accept the responsibility of being a Chosen One" (U 130).

The *negotiation* between God and the Jewish people initially gave rise to the oral tradition of the *Torah*, which Mose received from God on Mount Sinai (BT 9), and later to the written *Torah*, which in a narrower sense comprises the five books of Mose (*H'oumach*) and in a broader sense the books of the prophets (*Nebiim*) and the commentary writings *Ketoubim*.[273] The *Torah* contains 248 commandments and 365 prohibitions of a normative nature (*mitzvot*),[274] which can be traced back to the creation of the world and the Ten Commandments of God (*Michpat*). The oral tradition (*Mishnah*[275]) and its interpretation (*Gemara*[276]) as well as the written transcriptions and traditions of the *Torah* were expanded almost immeasurably by a wealth of interpretative commentaries known as the older Palestinian (also Jerusalemite) and the subsequent Babylonian *Talmud*.[277] As the Judaic scholar Günter Stemberger notes, the Babylonian *Talmud* alone comprises around 9000 (!) pages in the German translation by Lazarus Goldschmidt.[278] The Talmudic commentaries 'insert themselves', so to speak, between the *Torah* and the practical application of the norms and commandments and can be understood as a "collection of legal discourses, philosophical reflections and various explanatory stories and legends (Hebrew: *aggada*)." Judaism (BT 24)[279] insists on this Jewish religious law (*Halakha*), whose rigid 'core law' is enriched by the aforementioned numerous interpretative commentaries and discussions of the *Talmud* as well as the illustrative and explanatory stories it contains (*Midrash*[280]). These texts have been considered complete since the early 6th century. As the Central Council of Jews in Germany emphasises, the *Talmud* provides the key to the practical application of the commandments in everyday life (*Torat Chajim*),[281] it touches on all areas of life and, through interpretation, ensures that the norms of the *Torah* are adapted to practical life.[282] The Talmudic

[272] Cf. Schiesser (2007), pp. 20–33.

[273] Draï (1999), p. 19.

[274] Ibid., p. 35.

[275] The *Mishnah* is the "most important transcript of the oral tradition" of the *Torah*. Cf. Zentralrat der Juden in Deutschland (2023), p. 201.

[276] The *Gemara* is the "transcript of the rabbinical discussions of the Mishnah". Cf. Zentralrat der Juden in Deutschland (2023), p. 200.

[277] See Draï (1999), pp. 67–73. Cf. Stemberger (2019), pp. 41 and 51.

[278] Cf. Stemberger (2019), p. 70. See also: Goldschmidt (2002).

[279] See also: Berger (2019), p. 152.

[280] *Midrash* refers to the explanatory narratives in the *Talmud* to clarify gaps in the text of the *Torah* and passages that are difficult to understand (Zentralrat der Juden in Deutschland 2023, p. 200).

[281] Ibid., pp. 14–15.

[282] Cf. Stemberger (2019), pp. 55–67.

writings can be understood as a guide to subsuming real-life situations into the rules of the *Torah*, i.e. as a link between the abstract norm and the actual situation.[283] To this end, rabbinic hermeneuticians used a series of rules of interpretation such as analogy, inference from the lesser to the greater and vice versa, inference from the particular to the general and vice versa, and contextual interpretation.[284]

This is where the interdisciplinary connection between law and literature via the text as a link and interdiscursive medium comes into its own: the *Torah* as a whole text, and not just individual paragraphs of the law, must be interpreted to be applied to practical situations, i.e. to everyday Jewish life. This situation is similar to a literary work that would be interpreted as a coherent text in its entirety, every sentence, every paragraph, every chapter. Here, the literary text meets the literary-normative text, as does the discourse of the Talmudic text on every detail of the *Torah* in long treatises. It should be noted that these are indeed literary *and* normative texts, as the legal interpretations are supplemented by numerous non-normative narratives, the so-called *haggadic* texts (*Haggadah*), which include tales of all kinds, fables, parables, wisdom, prayers, lamentations for the dead, etc.[285] It is therefore not surprising that literary and legal hermeneutics are especially close here.[286] They differ essentially only in their objectives: the Talmudic commentaries aim at the practical applicability of the rules in everyday life, which a reading of the *Torah* limited to reception aesthetics and literary interpretation could not achieve.[287] Even the legal hermeneutic circularity[288] is recognised by the *Torah* in that, as already mentioned, it lays down its own guidelines for interpretation. The analogical approach is familiar both to the literature[289] and to the law.[290] The conclusion from the lesser to the greater or vice versa, from the particular to the general or vice versa, corresponds to the legal principle of avoiding conflict between norms through conflict rules[291] and the hierarchical principle of the legal system.[292] Contextual interpretation can be found in literary intertextuality and interdiscourse,[293] in the overall legal context (systematic interpretation[294]), and in Gadamer's hermeneutic circle.[295] Both disciplines are also familiar with grammatical-textual interpretation, which searches

283 Cf. Möllers (2023), pp. 126–131.
284 Cf. Stemberger (2019), pp. 55–62.
285 See ibid., pp. 158–267.
286 Cf. Bleich (1989), pp. 3197–3203.
287 Cf. Jauß (1981), p. 475.
288 Cf. Zippelius (2006), p. 58.
289 Cf. Ost (2014), pp. 120–121; Albrecht (2015), pp. 285–292.
290 Cf. Möllers (2023), pp. 253–258.
291 Cf. ibid., pp. 153–164.
292 See Zippelius' concept of 'circularity': Zippelius (2006), p. 58.
293 Cf. Müller-Seidel (1986), pp. 46–60; Ternès (2016), pp. 35–37.
294 Cf. Möllers (2023), p. 153.
295 Cf. Gadamer (1982), p. 267.

for the generally known semantic meaning of the words forming the text.[296] It is undisputed that the commentaries of the Talmudic hermeneuticians have a normative-constitutive effect that the literary hermeneutician lacks because it is only through their interpretation that the legal text of the *Torah* becomes practically applicable. However, interpretations are also refuted and invalidated by new discussions; they intersect, overlap, and contradict each other. The discussion about how the prohibition of carrying (an object) on *Shabbat* is to be understood and interpreted (BT 141–165) alone testifies to the relative indeterminacy of the normative force of individual interpretations. As in literature, Talmudic interpretation takes place in a time-unbound chain of successive interpretations over many years. Perhaps the *Torah* and *Talmud* could be described as literary law books, which demonstrate interdisciplinarity and interdiscursivity particularly well. Interdiscursivity as the interlocking of different epistemes in the text[297] is well illustrated here by the close interweaving of everyday religious practice, which is the subject of both sociological and theological studies, with jurisprudence.

To illustrate these epistemic interdependencies, reference should be made to Joel Berger's remark that the texts of the *Torah* and the *Talmud* not only regulate everyday Jewish life in all its facets but also fulfil a distinguishing function, because Judaism is "more of a view of life, a way of life, [which] differs from other religions in the fulfilment of the Jewish commandments", whereby behind this distinction is the "endeavour of a minority to assert its distinctiveness in a different environment."[298] Faith and piety are visible in Judaism and must be expressed through external signs because purely spiritual faith is neither perceptible nor demonstrable. What counts is the visible observance of religious rules, not internalised faith.[299]

5.4.4.2 Counterfactual Contrast

This striving for outward visibility as a religious affiliation—without regard to feelings or spiritual states—is repeatedly emphasised in *Unorthodox* Zeidy's only concern is that his family follows the rules, as the following dialogue makes clear: "'But Fraida,' Zeidy entreated, 'the rebbe said! It's a new rule. All men are telling their wives to do it. You want me to be the only man whose wife doesn't shave her hair? […] You want the rebbe should know that I couldn't get my wife to follow the rules?'" (U 24). It is not the mental balance and happiness of the children that are considered successful child-rearing, but the success of raising them to be "God-fearing, law-abiding Jews" (U 18). Hence, it is not the spiritual and psychological well-being that counts, but the external appearance, the judgement of third parties, which takes place in the community through constant mutual observation: "Instead,

296 Larenz (1991), p. 320

297 Parr (2015), pp. 289–302.

298 Berger (2019), p. 15.

299 Ibid., p. 17.

we watch each other closely, ever ready to point out someone's spiritual or physical failing." (U 18). To paraphrase Wolfgang Iser, Feldman portrays this real basic attitude of the Jewish community in the diegesis, which she then fleshes out in the literature.[300] In narrative fiction, the fact that Judaism is primarily about the outward proof of religious obedience is explained and illustrated with many details from Feldman's personal experience, whereby the almost identical proximity to the real world is unmistakable. The counterfactual variation approaches zero here, without losing its justification as a method.[301] Rather, through its methodical approach, it fulfils an additional function of gaining knowledge,[302] which unfolds from a multitude of individual events that furnish the diegesis of *Unorthodox* and which, if they are to be reduced to a common denominator, serve the purpose of differentiation and demarcation from the *other* world.

The clothing regulations are a particularly visible sign of the people's distinction as a distinct minority: Animal fibres must not be mixed with plant fibres in the fabric of clothing, the long temple curls (*pejes*)—"You shall not round off the side-growth on your head, or destroy the side-growth of your beard" (Leviticus 19, 27)—protrude from the black caps or hats, *tallit* and *zizit* are worn visibly (BT 323).[303] The *tefillin*[304] must be put on for the morning prayer (BT 84). The *zizit* on the prayer shawl should remind the believers that they have committed themselves to obey the Lord's commandments: "Every time you see the tassels, they should remind you of my commandments. They should remind you to live according to my instructions and not let your thoughts and lustful eyes lead you to disobedience. Then you will be a holy people, a people who belong entirely to their God."[305]

The close interweaving of religion and secular existence corresponds to the central role that the *Talmud* assigns to continuous learning through the study of the *Torah* and its Talmudic interpretation as a means of rising above the materiality of life. As Daniel Krochmalnik explains, learning is seen as the highest duty, one that outweighs all other duties.[306] The students and scholars of the Talmud, who "grasp easily and forget rarely" (BT 14), without ever being boastful of their knowledge, deserve the highest recognition. The incessant occupation with the holy scriptures in a collective context (synagogue and Torah school *yeshiva*), charity, and observance of the commandments guide the pious Jewish life: "You shall eat bread with salt, drink even water measured out, you shall sleep on the ground, you shall lead a life of privation and in all this you shall devote yourself restlessly to it [...]. Much

[300] Cf. Iser (1983), pp. 121–125.

[301] Cf. Nünning (1995), p. 46.

[302] Cf. White (1991), pp. 101–122.

[303] *Tallit* is the prayer shawl, *zizit* are the threads hanging from the corners of the prayer shawl.

[304] *Tefillin* are "prayer straps worn by men during morning prayers on weekdays" (Zentralrat der Juden in Deutschland (2023), p. 202).

[305] 4. Mose 15, 39, cit. *Gute Nachricht Bibel. Altes und Neues Testament*, Stuttgart: Deutsche Bibelgesellschaft 2018 (internet-link in the bibliography).

See also: Berger (2019), pp. 89–93.

[306] Krochmalnik (2017), pp. 155–161, here: p. 155.

Torah, much life [...]. Higher than the study of doctrine is the good deed. Knowledge is without foundation if it is not based on action [...] (But higher than action is the fear of God)" (BT 16). Every sin has unforeseeable consequences; one's own will must take a back seat to the will of God (BT 17), because "the bliss of one hour in the hereafter is worth more than all the joys of this life" (BT 18). Earthly life is understood as a preliminary stage of a higher fulfilment, which makes the self-castigating and self-punishing attitude of the believers shown in *Unorthodox*, albeit criticised, easier to understand.

The continuous study of the holy scriptures as a male life practice (women are excluded from this) is not derived from the *Torah* but was interpreted into the *Torah* by the rabbinical commentaries. Just how far-fetched these interpretations can be is shown by the interpretation of the sentence "And on the table you shall set the bread of display, to be before Me always" (Exodus 25, 30). As Daniel Krochmalnik explains, this sentence is about the weekly changing of the bread "without any intermittence (mMen 11,7)." The old loaves are taken away from one side, while at the same time, the fresh loaves are pushed into their place from the other side.[307] From this commandment of uninterrupted physical nourishment, the Talmudists derive the commandment of uninterrupted *Torah* study in a very far-fetched analogy, although it is not formulated anywhere in the *Torah*.[308] Nor is there an explicit prohibition on women studying in the *Torah*. Krochmalnik concludes from this that profane learning and teaching materials should be permitted alongside *Torah* study, as there is no reference to the exclusivity of *Torah* study to the exclusion of all others, whereby "Torah study is not properly understood if one fears competition from the study of philosophy and wants to prohibit it with legal measures."[309] If one now assumes that the study of philosophy is perfectly compatible with the study of the *Torah*, the analogy "from an investigated, well-known case to a less well-known, unclear situation"[310] also seems to confer plausibility to an extension to secular studies in general. In plain language, this would mean that it is equally as conceivable to allow men or women to study English, or any other secular subjects. It can be here deduced that the ban on the study of secular subjects and the prohibition of the *Torah* for women, which is denounced in *Unorthodox*, contradicts the commandments of the *Torah* and seems to go back to the will of the Satmar rabbi. Feldman's resistance to this ban on learning and reading runs like a golden thread through the novel *Unorthodox*, and forces her into fearful concealment: "There's something new under my mattress this week, and soon [...] I will shut the door to my room and retrieve it, the wonderful leather-bound volume with its heady new-book smell. It's a section of the Talmud, with the forbidden English translation [...]" (U 26). The secret reading is highly risky if it is discovered, because books "are only for men" (U 26), which is why Zeidy's house search for leavened food

[307] Krochmalnik (1996), pp. 73–83, here: p. 78.

[308] Cf. Eco (2004), p. 391: Eco, too, evokes the concept of continuous prayer and study.

[309] Krochmalnik (1996), p. 80.

[310] Knorr-Cetina (2016), p. 107.

before Pesach (Exodus 12, 15) harbours the danger that the hidden books will be discovered: "I hide my books under the bed [...], and once a year, when Zeidy inspects the house for Passover, poking through our things, we hover anxiously, terrified of being found out" (U 26).

The male monopoly on religious learning is reflected in the *Talmud* in the fear expressed that too much 'chatting' with women could distract men from studying the *Torah*: "Spare your words for a woman, be it a stranger or your own. Whoever chats a lot with her brings evil upon himself, is distracted from the Torah and ends up in hell" (BT 21). The analogous argument implies the reverse conclusion that women should also not 'gossip' too much with men to devote themselves to *Torah* study, assuming that the *Torah*, mentioned previously, seems not to specifically prohibit women from learning.

Alongside the debate about teaching and learning, a latent sense of guilt is a second narrative thread running through the story of *Unorthodox* Even the writings of the *Talmud* reveal how deeply the Jewish faith is anchored in a culture of guilt, self-punishment, and self-mortification. Enduring suffering and restrictions, praying regularly in the community of the synagogue (BT 122), and living a God-fearing and kind life serve to redeem sins (BT 113–114).

This feeling of guilt, which goes hand in hand with voluntary self-mortification, is scrutinised in *Unorthodox*: "It is guilt that drives my grandparents to inflict continuous suffering upon themselves, bear laborious burdens, never once accepting the possibility of easement?" (U 42). Feldman uses the example of her grandparents Zeidy and Bubby to illustrate the suffering imposed by the *Talmud* to redeem sin. The diegetic fiction here fulfils a strong explanatory function about the foundations of orthodox religious obedience, which forbids questioning the why of the suffering or the rules. Thus, she surmises that for Zeidy, pain is a form of self-purification when he says his prayer to God in tears on Friday night (U 42–43), because, as the *Talmud* says, "the most precious things are acquired through suffering: the Torah, the return of the Jews to Palestine and the reward in the hereafter" (BT 71). To emphasise this feeling of guilt in its elusive form, Bubby and Zeidy ask themselves why they were allowed to survive the Holocaust. Zeidy muses: "So many times I wondered why I was allowed to live [...]. But with time, it became clear to me that all of my children and grandchildren had to be born, and it is my responsibility to make sure they grow up to be good Jews, *ehrliche Yidden*, to give meaning to my survival" (U 43). Zeidy goes on to explain that suffering is to be endured as a just punishment: "To treat a problem is to evade the suffering that God felt you deserved" (U 100). Theodor Adorno, one of these survivors, coupled the feeling of guilt with the question of "whether after Auschwitz you can go on living – especially whether one who escaped by accident, one who by rights should have been killed, may go on living."[311] George Steiner argues that it is precisely this unspeakably inhumane experience of the Shoah that forms the lowest common denominator of Jewish

[311] Adorno (1983), p. 363.

identity, despite all the conflicts and differences of opinion that exist between the numerous groups of religious and non-religious orientations of varying degrees:

> The Shoah, the memory of Auschwitz, the recurring fear that somewhere and somehow the massacres could begin anew, form the central cohesion of Jewish identity today. Therein lies the one and only bond that unites the Orthodox Jew and the atheist, the practising and completely secularised Jew, the Israeli people and the diaspora, the Zionist and the anti-Zionist, the extremely conservative Jew [...] and the Jewish Trotskyist or communist.[312]

Feldman uses the example of her grandfather's pious and abstemious lifestyle, which is characterised by prayer, the study of sacred texts, and efforts to ensure strict observance of religious rules by all family members, to illustrate the intensive prayer and religious study required to free oneself from the burden of debt until the end of one's life: "Zeidy wakes up at four in the morning to go to study the Torah at the synagogue across the street" (U 39). He makes sure that his granddaughter behaves according to the rules: "He only wants to hear that I'm conducting myself properly so no one will say he has a disobedient granddaughter" (U 13). Zeidy believes, as Bubby explains, that "if we go to extreme lengths to make God proud of us, he'll never hurt us again, like he did in the war" (U 25). In this awareness of atonement and in the conviction that God will one day appear as Saviour in this way, prayers are said every morning and evening (BT 90).

One of the most important events that interrupts the prayer and study routine of Satmar Jews is marriage, which serves to ensure procreation, as the *Torah* states: "Be fertile and increase, and fill the earth" (Genesis 9, 1). To this end, it must be ensured that everyone marries, which is why marriage and procreation take place according to institutionalised rites and commandments.[313] Marriage does not serve the personal happiness of the bride and groom, but solely the rational purpose of optimised procreation and must take place between the ages of 20 and 24.[314] From this point of view, contraception is generally prohibited unless there are valid medical reasons.[315] The choice of the marriage partner is made by the family with the help of professional matchmakers according to criteria of social standing, which is particularly high among good *yeshiva* (*Torah*) students. Time is crucial in this context, as there are usually many brothers and sisters on the waiting list.[316]

Unorthodox describes numerous details about the marriage process, from the matchmaking, the betrothal ceremony, the marriage lessons, the purity regulations before the wedding day, the wedding ceremony itself, and the obligatory coitus on the wedding night. Of particular importance is the ceremony of the *chuppah*, which is mentioned in *Unorthodox* (U 164–165) and symbolises the bride's entry into the domain of her future husband. From this point onwards, the marriage is legally

---

[312] Steiner (1987), pp. 194–212, here: pp. 200–201.

[313] Lehmann and Siebzehner (2009), pp. 280–281.

[314] Geballe (2023), p. 77.

[315] Deen (2015), pp. 194 ff. See also: Lehmann and Siebzehner (2009), p. 285.

[316] Lehmann and Siebzehner (2009), pp. 291–294.

binding according to Talmudic law.[317] Feldman's fiction here illustrates the Satmar regulations and customs that are not found in the *Torah* and links them to the feelings and emotions of the biographer, who tells of her own wedding. The normative content of these rituals remains undefined here and is more comparable to social practices that become customary law (*opinio necessitatis*) over time (*longa consuetudo*) through general agreement (*consensus omnium*).[318]

Normative misogyny emerges much more clearly from the *Torah* when the woman is required to desire the man and at the same time be subject to him: "And to the woman He said, 'I will make most severe Your pangs in childbearing; In pain shall you bear children. Yet your urge shall be for your husband, And he shall rule over you'" (Genesis 3, 16). The woman is primarily obliged to bear children, to fulfil her husband's sexual desires (to have as many children as possible), and to submit completely to her husband throughout her life (sic!). The devaluation of women according to the *Torah* is strongly reminiscent of the no less contemptuous treatment of women according to the *Kanun* unless they assume the status of *Burrnesha*. In fact, misogyny is taken literally and practised by the Satmar community: A woman is a birthing machine who spends her daily life uneducated between domestic and religious duties, caring for her numerous children, up to eighteen in number.

In *Unorthodox*, Feldman fights against this misogyny with small and large gestures of rebellion at home and school, until she finally decides to leave the Satmar community and her husband forever with her son, without the possibility of returning—even if, according to Talmudic law, it is not possible to discard the 'Jewishness' inherited from the mother. Even a Jew who commits a serious sin remains a Jew: "From there it may be inferred that even when the Jewish people have sinned, they are still called 'Israel'."[319] In *Unorthodox*, Bubby explains this principle as follows: "A Jew can never be a *goy*,[320] she says, even if they try their hardest to become one. They may dress like one, speak like one, live like one, but Jewishness is something that can never be erased. Even Hitler knew that" (U 96). The explanatory function of literature for less meaningful norms is very clearly practised here.

A long chapter of the *Torah* is dedicated to female impurity during the menstrual period (*niddah*) and the 7 days after:[321]

> When a woman has a discharge of blood for many days at a time other than her monthly period or has a discharge that continues beyond her period, she will be unclean as long as she has the discharge, just as in the days of her period. Any bed she lies on while her discharge continues will be unclean, as is her bed during her monthly period, and anything she sits on will be unclean, as during her period. Anyone who touches them will be unclean;

[317] Homolka (2009), p. 77.

[318] Cf. Geis (2021), pp. 28–31.

[319] *Babylonischer Talmud*, 44a, 2: https://halakhah.com/sanhedrin/sanhedrin_44.html.

According to the Palestinian (Jerusalem) *Talmud*, all Jews belong to Israel, except those who, in synthetic terms, slander the *Torah*, i.e. the Jewish faith (Guggenheimer 2010, p. 5; 328).

[320] Non-Jew.

[321] Cf. also: Ehrlich and Stemberger (2006), pp. 602–618.

> they must wash their clothes and bathe with water, and they will be unclean till evening. When she is cleansed from her discharge, she must count off seven days, and after that she will be ceremonially clean. On the eighth day she must take two doves or two young pigeons and bring them to the priest at the entrance to the tent of meeting. The priest is to sacrifice one for a sin offering and the other for a burnt offering. In this way he will make atonement for her before the LORD for the uncleanness of her discharge. (Leviticus 15, 25–30)

The Jews of Satmar observe these impurity and purity laws to the letter, except for the sacrifice of the turtledove on the eighth day. Today, the cleansing bath (*mikvah*) takes its place. Non-compliance with many of the *Torah*'s rules is severely punished, as is the case here: "'If a man has sexual relations with a woman during her monthly period, he has exposed the source of her flow, and she has also uncovered it. Both of them are to be cut off from their people." (Leviticus 20, 18). Note the *Torah*'s particular hostility towards the body, which speaks of 'shame' in connection with the female vagina and describes natural bodily functions such as menstruation as 'unclean', so unclean that the husband may neither touch his menstruating wife nor come into contact with things that have been touched by his wife. The menstruating woman is completely demonised and treated like a leper, and it is evident from this view that sexual intercourse is forbidden during these 2 weeks. This disqualification of female menstruation and the segregation of women as impure beings seems to stand in inexplicable contradiction to the woman's main function as a birthing machine, which could not function at all without the menstrual cycle.

This tabooing and devaluation of the female body is forcefully addressed in *Unorthodox*. For women, the first sexual intercourse on their wedding night is usually their first encounter with the male sex and their own body. They discover that they have a vagina that they have never used before, as both premarital sex and masturbation are taboo and strictly forbidden. As a result of this body-hostile upbringing, Feldman suffers from vaginismus, which makes sexual intercourse almost impossible. Seeking medical help enlightens her: "I read that the condition is most common in women who grow up in repressive religious environments. I begin to understand that years of hiding from my body have taught it to hide from me" (U 184). To make matters worse, she becomes infected with shingles during the monthly *mikvah* ritual, as the water in the plunge pool is not disinfected and remains the same for many women. The visit to the doctor confirms this: "The doctor [...] tells me I have orbital shingles, which he claims, looking at Eli's religious garb, I probably caught in the ritual bath" (U 174).

The *Talmud* does not stop at the most intimate sphere of man, for procreation is, as already mentioned, a supreme commandment (Genesis 9, 1). Thus it determines very precisely, depending on the man's activity and neglecting the woman's activity, how often man and woman should have intercourse: "If the man has a lot of free time, twice a week if he is a labourer, once a week if he is a donkey driver, once a month if he is a camel driver, once every six months if he goes to sea." Scholars, on the other hand—and this is where the importance of *Torah* and *Talmud* study comes into play—must have sexual intercourse once a week on the evening of *Shabbos*, the only study-free day. In *Unorthodox*, these regulations are reproduced very faithfully (U 226–227). If the woman refuses to have intercourse for more than 12 months, this is grounds for divorce.[322]

If a child is born male, it must be circumcised on the eighth day after birth: "Every male among you shall be circumcised. You are to undergo circumcision, and it will be the sign of the covenant between me and you." (Genesis 17, 10–11; 36). Circumcision is to be understood as a ritual to confirm the covenant with God, from which the woman seems to be excluded. If it is the first-born son, he must be ransomed (*Pidyon haben*) on the 31st day of life by a descendant of the Cohen[323] in exchange for 100 g of silver (Exodus 13, 15).[324] In *Unorthodox*, the newborn is presented to the rabbi on a tray covered with the jewellery of the women present (U 212). The fact that, as mentioned in *Unorthodox*, the woman does not attend the circumcision ceremony for psychological reasons is probably a specific feature of the Satmar rabbinate.

In addition to the obligation to bear as many offspring as possible, women have numerous other domestic duties, which Homolka lists with reference to the *Talmud*: "grinding flour, baking bread, washing clothes, cooking food, making the bed and working the wool"[325] and, as Berger lists, observing the *kosher* dietary rules.[326] According to *the Torah*, meat must be bled: "But you must not eat meat that has its lifeblood still in it" (Genesis 9, 4). Only the meat of hoofed animals that have claws, chew the cud, and are quadrupedal may be eaten, which results in the prohibition of pork, rabbit, and game meat. Only aquatic animals with scales and fins are *kosher*. Seafood of all kinds, however, is forbidden (Leviticus 11, 10–12). Animals moving on the soil are banned as well: "'Every creature that moves along the ground is to be regarded as unclean; it is not to be eaten. You are not to eat any creature that moves along the ground, whether it moves on its belly or walks on all fours or on many feet; it is unclean" (Leviticus 11, 41–42). *Meat and dairy products must never touch each other. The same applies to kitchen utensils, cutlery and crockery, which are to be used separately for meat and dairy products.*

The woman is responsible for organising the preparations for holidays and feasts, which determine the rhythm of the year. *Shabbos* is the weekly day of rest that begins with the onset of darkness on Friday evening and ends on Saturday when the first three stars[327] (provided they are not covered by clouds!) light up. For the

---

[322] Homolka (2009), p. 102.

[323] The surname Cohen, which still exists today, testifies to the fact that the descendants of the Jewish priests, the *Kohanim*, still exist. The *Kohanim* were the staff of the temple and are still subject to special rules today: They may not marry divorced women, may not enter cemeteries, and should avoid contact with the dead. A first-born son can only be redeemed by a Cohen (unless the father is a Cohen himself). Cf. Evers (2022) (internet-link in the bibliography).

[324] Michael Rosenkranz (2013b) (internet-link in the bibliography).

[325] Homolka (2009), p. 100.

[326] Berger (2019), p. 99.

[327] Ibid., p. 197.

duration of *Shabbos*, nothing that is not necessary may be worn,[328] no fire may be lit (today this means any kind of energy, author's note), no money may be taken in hand and, of course, no work may be done (BT 140–141).[329] The *Torah* punishes those who do not comply with the prohibition of work on *Shabbos* with death: "For six days, work is to be done, but the seventh day shall be your holy day, a day of sabbath rest to the LORD. Whoever does any work on it is to be put to death. **3** Do not light a fire in any of your dwellings on the Sabbath day" (Exodus 35, 2–3). The strictness of the *Torah* certainly has a deterrent effect on deep believers, but the threat of death, if Shabbos is not observed, seems disproportionately exaggerated from the today's perspective.

In *Unorthodox*, further *Shabbos* prohibitions and commandments are explained. Not only is it forbidden to use electricity, but it must also be switched on again by a Jew at the end of *Shabbos*, which is one of Feldman's father's side jobs: "The non-Jewish employees are already working when he arrives […], and when my father walks through the wide utility building and flips the switches […]" (U 7–8). Feldman's cousins are not allowed to visit anyone with their babies on *Shabbos* because they must be carried (U 101). The Talmudic discussions about the prohibition of carrying and when and how it can be circumvented are explained in *Unorthodox* through the debate on the *eiruv*: "Halacha, or Jewish law, forbids carrying on one's person in public domain, but with an *eiruv*, a symbolic fence surrounding public property, the area is considered private, and carrying children, house keys, and other necessary items becomes legal" (U 101).

One of the most important annual festivals out of several celebrations during the course of the year—*Pesah*, *Shavuos*, *Rosh Hashanah*, *Yom Kippur*, *Sukkot* (Leviticus 23, 1–44)—is *Pesah*, which commemorates the liberation of the Jews from Egyptian slavery. In remembrance of the life of poverty on the one hand, and the hasty departure on the other, which left no time for the bread dough to rise, it is the highest commandment to remove all food containing leavening agents from the house on the day before *Pesah* and to eat only unleavened bread for the following 8 days (BT 166–167; Exodus 12, 15; U 53).[330] The consumption of bitter herbs also symbolises the remembrance of this difficult time.[331] At this juncture, the commentators in the *Talmud* engage in lengthy discussions about the exact time of the beginning and end of Pesah (BT 166–193).

In *Unorthodox*, reference is made to the commandment to chop nuts with one's own hands, as it is forbidden to buy nuts that have already been chopped. This regulation seems unusual and can probably be traced back to the Satmar rabbinate (U 47).

[328] On this point, the commentators engage in page-long debates in the *Talmud* as to what is to be understood by this (BT 141-165). Even a handkerchief seems to be dispensable and should not be worn (BT 141). What does this mean in the case of a severe cold? [Author's question].

[329] See also: Berger (2019), p. 100.

[330] See ibid., pp. 204–205.

[331] Ibid., pp. 215–216.

The *Lag Ba'Omer* festival of joy takes place between *Pesah* and *Shavuos*,[332] where bonfires are lit, and people dance and sing around them. Here too, the discriminatory supporting role of women is emphasised in *Unorthodox*, as they are not allowed to join in the dancing, but only to watch the male revelry from the window (U 58). *Lag Ba'Omer* is followed by *Shavuos*, the festival of the first fruits and at the same time the 'giving of the *Torah*', on which the handing over of the *Torah* from God to Mose is celebrated.[333] On this occasion, all houses are decorated with branches and flowers (U 59).

Rosh Hashanah and *Yom Kippur* also play an important role. *Yom Kippur* is a strict fast day on which the focus is on mutual reconciliation and the forgiveness of sins committed:[334] "The tenth day of this seventh month is the Day of Atonement. Hold a sacred assembly and deny yourselves, [...]. Do not do any work on that day, because it is the Day of Atonement, when atonement is made for you before the LORD your God" (Leviticus 23, 27–28). *Rosh Hashanah*, on the other hand, is a day of remembrance that is celebrated with the blowing of the shofar horn (Leviticus 23, 24) and also marks the first day of the new year according to the Jewish calendar.[335] All horns of animal origin, with the exception of cattle, are permitted.[336] *Shavuos* is a holy day of rest (Leviticus 23, 21), *Sukkot* is a seven-day festival celebrated in a hut built according to precise specifications[337] (Leviticus 23, 40–43).[338] Meals must be eaten in this hut for 7 days.[339] *Sukkot* ends on the eighth day with the ceremony of *Simchas Torah* when the *Torah* scrolls are taken from their shrine and ceremoniously carried around. However, this is a rabbinical addition that is not mentioned in the *Torah* or the *Talmud*.[340]

Feldman comments that the timing of *Simchas Torah* offered women the only opportunity to go to synagogue (U 87). *Rosh Hashanah* and *Yom Kippur* are only briefly mentioned in *Unorthodox* as school holidays (U 88). We learn that *Yom Kippur* is a day of repentance when Bubby Feldman, reacting to the attack on the New York Twin Towers (9 September 2001) on 13 September 2001, begs Feldman to repent on the day of *Yom Kippur* (U 106). This diegetic link between the horrors of the worst terrorist attack of all time and *Yom Kippur* emphasises the role of the Day of Atonement and Reconciliation—it is certainly not a festival of joy.

The anti-Zionist parade mentioned in *Unorthodox* also finds no normative equivalent in the Jewish legal texts (U 56).

[332] Guggenheimer (2014), p. 126.

[333] Michael Rosenkranz (2013c) (internet-link in the bibliography).

[334] Berger (2019), p. 199.

[335] Guggenheimer (2014), p. 351.

[336] Ibid., p. 436.

[337] Ibid., p. 211.

[338] Zentralrat der Juden in Deutschland (2023), p. 14.

[339] Guggenheimer (2014), p. 262.

[340] Rosenkranz (2013a) (internet-link in the bibliography).

In summary, the members of the ultra-Orthodox Jewish religious community Satmar in Williamsburg (New York) deliberately seal themselves off as hermetically as possible from the outside world to follow their strict religious traditions and rules in a kind of artificially created *shtetl* modelled on the European *shtetl Satu Mare* in present-day Romania. In a limited space, within sight of the secular world, the maintenance of otherness is supported by observing the commandments of the *Torah* and their interpretation in the *Talmud* and other rabbinical texts. The fact that these religious rules are lived and practised daily makes it impossible to draw a line between Talmudic law and everyday life, and this close interdependence means that all members of the community know Talmudic law *nolens volens*, at least as far as their personal lives are concerned. Talmudic law is a daily lived law, which is why literature that tells of life according to the rules of the *Talmud Torah*, as in the case of the novel *Unorthodox*, also tells of law. It is thus unsurprising that in *Unorthodox* the degree of divergence between diegetic law and Talmudic real-world law is negligible. This is even more a reason for the literature to play a strongly illuminating and commenting role here since the diegetic fiction also explains and illustrates Talmudic law very well for laypeople of the Jewish faith. *Unorthodox* does indeed appear here as a legal commentary. The commandments and prohibitions with which Feldman is confronted in her everyday life, the basic attitudes of her community such as isolationism, anti-Zionism, feelings of guilt, being a girl and a woman, learning—or rather, the prohibition of learning –, the holidays, the stages of her life on the path from child to married woman and finally leaving the community, are at the same time part of Talmudic law, which she reproduces realistically and simultaneously enlivens and sensitises through the technique of first-person narration.

Because the literary discourse in *Unorthodox* is largely congruent with the Talmudic legal discourse, the boundaries between literature and law are almost completely blurred. As indicated, they differ from each other essentially in their purpose, since the religious norms are intended to regulate practical life in concrete terms, while literature remains in its commentary function. Apart from this point of differentiation, literature and law can be seen here as fused in disciplinary terms: The limit of the representability of normativity is overcome by literature insofar as normativity 'flows' from the narrative: the description of everyday life with its commandments and prohibitions is at the same time the description of law, insofar as law and the practice of life are one in the Orthodox Jewish Satmar community. The literature here explains and comments on Talmudic law in its factual form (*Torah*, *Talmud*) as well as in its hybrid form at the interface between customary law (Rabbinic regulations) and applicable factual law. In *Unorthodox*, human actions are described that are simultaneously an expression of normativity, whereby literary fiction and legal factuality merge into one another. The literary text here does not anticipate possible legal states but describes their actual state and rubs up against the limits of the depiction of this normative actual state. The language used is that of Talmudic law, whereby literary and legal terminology are not mutually exclusive in a disruptive way.

This blurring of disciplinary boundaries is already evident in the *Talmud* itself, as already indicated, in that the text of the *Torah* is interpreted according to the rules of literary and legal hermeneutics. The text of the *Talmud* combines literature and law, insofar as the legal commentaries are supplemented and illustrated by numerous literary, non-legal insertions. The textual-grammatical interpretation of the *Torah* text sometimes follows certain rules of interpretation, which the *Torah itself* explicates in the sense of Zippelius' circularity. It can also be postulated that Gadamer's hermeneutic circle comes into its own where the long series of successive interpretations of individual commandments of the *Torah* presupposes knowledge of the preceding interpretative proposals on the one hand and requires Talmudic prior knowledge on the other.

In the continuity of the remarks on the *Talmud* as a normative-literary text, the fusion of hermeneutical rules can also be asserted for the interpretation of *Unorthodox*, insofar as the diegesis and law coincide.

Unorthodox then offers an interesting example of the fusion of law and literature, which does not lead to a relevant counterfactual variation due to the practical lack of differentiation of the diegetic legal discourse from the Talmudic discourse, but which benefits greatly from this for an interdisciplinary acquisition of knowledge.

5.5 *Repenti* (2017) by Claude Chossat[341]

In *Repenti*, Claude Chossat reports on his career as a convicted felon who buys his release by cooperating with the justice system but does not benefit from the judicial and legal protection afforded to judicial informants. This is even more dangerous for him as he is one of the first to dare to break the *omerta*, the unwritten law of silence that surrounds Corsican criminality. As a now publicly known informant who reveals names and facts, he is threatened with *vendetta* or revenge. In plain language, this means the daily threat of murder.

Chossat comes from a middle-class Corsican family, his mother is a civil servant, and his father works for the state electricity company EDF. Although he was considered a quiet boy, he became a delinquent during his secondary school years (robbery with weapons and assault) and served a seven-year prison sentence (2000–2007) in Borgo prison near Bastia. During this time, he met Francis Mariani, one of the co-founders of the Corsican gang *Brise de Mer*, and witnessed Mariani's preparations to escape from prison. After his own release, Chossat contacted Mariani and became his chauffeur, bodyguard, and 'man for everything' to support Mariani in the hunt for Richard Casanova and his brother-in-law Jean-Luc Germani.

[341] Chossat (2017). For citation purposes, the siglum 'R' is used with the page number in the running text. There is no translation in English available, all the translations are mine.

5.5.1 The Corsican Gang Brise de Mer

Chossat's *Repenti* report can be read against the backdrop of the Corsican criminal organisation *Brise de Mer*, whose origins date back to the 1970s. It begins in a simple café called *Brise de Mer*[342] in the old harbour of Bastia. A group of 20 to 30 young people from all social classes met regularly in the back room of the café to get to know each other better and made plans to gain political and economic power over parts of Corsica. To do this, the 'competition' needed to be eliminated in advance, especially the then-powerful *Corte* clan under Louis Memmi, who had amassed a considerable fortune in slot machines through violence and blackmail. Through this, they were greatly respected, and equally as feared. The cold-blooded murder of Memmi on 10 September 1981[343] marked the birth of the *Brise de Mer*, followed by more than 20 murders of recalcitrant members of the *Corte* clan and disagreeable witnesses until the north of Corsica fell into the hands of the *Brise de Mer*.[344] In judicial proceedings involving members of the clan, judges, witnesses, and jurors are blackmailed to obtain an acquittal. The first evidence of this is the trial before the jury court in Dijon, France, against three members of the *Brise de Mer*—Robert Moracchini, Pierre-Marie Santucci, and Georges Seatelli—who were involved in the murder of Daniel Ziglioli, a member of the 'Memmi' clan and owner of the flourishing discotheque *Le Castel*. Despite clear evidence and the testimony of a police officer, the three accused were acquitted in May 1985.[345] Twelve men with no hierarchical relationship led the *Brise de Mer*,[346] including Francis Mariani and Richard Casanova, and governed unimaginable financial wealth through investments in and outside Corsica, in public construction, nightclubs, casinos, gambling dens and slot machines, restaurants and cafés, luxury tourism, etc. They lent money to companies in return for interest and extorted payments from companies and businesses. In 1999, the assets of the *Brise de Mer* were roughly estimated at one billion francs (approx. 153 million euros), five hundred bank accounts, and countless properties. The tax evasion was just as colossal.[347] This financial power gave the representatives of the *Brise de Mer* access to the 'powerful' in politics and business,[348] as illustrated by the fact that otherwise, Casanova would not have been able to escape from prison for 16 years without

[342] The café still exists today under the name *Le Méditerranée*.

[343] Lazard and Galland (2020), pp. 26–28.

[344] Ibid., p. 30.

[345] Ibid., pp. 29–34.

[346] These twelve men include Richard Casanova, Francis Mariani, Maurice Costa, Paul-Louis Guazzelli, Angelo Guazzelli, Francis Guazzelli, Robert Moracchini, Francis Santucci, Pierre-Marie Santucci, Georges Seatelli, Alexandre Chevrières, and Dominique Rutily.

[347] Lazard and Galland (2020), pp. 52–53.

[348] Cf. Franck Guérin, Documentary film "Omerta, le gang de la Brise de mer" in 4 parts, Patrick Spica Productions, 2023, here part 1: "Usu Corsu: à la manière corse" (internet-link in the bibliography).

having to hide himself. The political 'patrons' of the *Brise de Mer* included Bernard Squarcini, former director of the French secret service,[349] Charles Pasqua, former French Minister of the Interior,[350] the French Minister of Justice, Éric Dupont-Moretti, former lawyer and defender of the *Brise de Mer* until recently, and Paul Giacobbi, former regional president of Corsica.[351] In financial terms, the *Brise de Mer* had a 'patron saint' in Michel Tomi, a Corsican by birth who has built up an empire of casinos and gambling dens in Africa.[352]

Richard Casanova, one of the most important strategic heads of the *Brise de Mer*, came from a wealthy family in the centre of Bastia and got a good education. He initially became a criminal for the ideal of Corsican independence: at the age of 20, he joined the FLNC (*Front de Libération Nationale Corse*)[353] and committed numerous bank robberies to finance the activities of his organisation. In 1980, he was caught red-handed and sentenced to prison. Betrayed and abandoned by his FLNC comrades-in-arms, Casanova turned to the *Brise de Mer* after his release a year later and became one of its leading members. He successfully planned their criminal activities. One of these operations, whose preparation and strategy can clearly be traced back to him, will go down in history as one of the biggest bank robberies: On 25 March 1990, the *Brise de Mer*, with the help of the bank's internal accomplices, succeeded in opening and emptying the safes at the headquarters of the Swiss bank UBS in Geneva without leaving any traces of a break-in. The loot amounted to 220 kg of banknotes worth around 54 million euros.[354] All the money taken was divided equally among the twelve leading members of the *Brise de Mer*, including those who did not take part in the crime.

While Casanova and other members of the *Brise de Mer* skilfully 'white-washed' the money they had amassed through investments, Francis Mariani spent a lot of time in prison and, after his respective releases, squandered the money by investing in car rallies, his youthful passion. Unlike Casanova, he came from a poor peasant family, left school at the age of 14 and became a father at 16. He was characterised, above all, by his fearlessness and willingness to use violence.

The decline of the *Brise de Mer* is heralded by internal rivalries that developed between Richard Casanova and Francis Mariani in particular. While most of the leading members of the *Brise de Mer* were content with the wealth they have amassed so far, a rivalry broke out between Mariani and Casanova for the free territories of Corsica, which were no longer controlled by the *Armata Corsa* and the *Colonna* clan. Mariani was convinced that Casanova, with the help of his brother-in-law Jean-Luc Germani and his friend Michel Tomi, was building up his own

[349] Lazard and Galland (2020), p. 56.

[350] Ibid., p. 82.

[351] Ibid., pp. 58–60.

[352] Ibid., pp. 82–83.

[353] The FLNC was founded in 1976.

[354] Lazard and Galland (2020), pp. 46–47.

group against the interests of the *Brise de Mer* to secure these now free territories for himself.[355]

It should be noted that the zones of influence in the north of the island of Corsica were previously divided between the *Brise de Mer* and the *Armata Corsa* and were respected by both sides until the assassination of Dominique Savelli, a member of the *Brise de Mer*. This act of violence, motivated by an attempt to seize some of the *Brise de Mer*'s thriving businesses, triggered a state of war between the two factions. The *Brise de Mer*'s response followed shortly thereafter: they murdered the leader of the *Armata Corsa*, François Santoni,[356] and seven other members, decimating *the Armata Corsa* to the point of insignificance. Parallel to the hostilities between the *Brise de Mer* and the *Armata Corsa*, the murder of Robert Feliciaggi, a member of the *Colonna* clan, on 10 March 2006 triggered a new series of murders, to which Jean Colonna himself also fell victim on 1 November 2006.

Another reason for the development of the enmity between Mariani and Casanova is Mariani's jealousy of the seemingly invulnerable Casanova, who, thanks to powerful accomplices in politics and business who reached as far as Africa, managed to remain at large for 16 years despite court convictions, while he, Mariani, was repeatedly sent to prison.[357] Mariani also followed Casanova's financial enrichment in Africa under the patronage of Michel Tomi with growing envy.

When Mariani was the victim of a botched attack on 22 November 2007 in which he was injured in the arm, he was convinced that Casanova and Germani were behind it and did everything in his power to murder them. To this end, he hired Claude Chossat to help him carry out the plan. Mariani did indeed murder Casanova on 23 April 2008,[358] albeit without Chossat's direct involvement.

At this point in the internal dissolution of the *Brise de Mer*,[359] Claude Chossat joins Mariani, and this is where his report in *Repenti* (2017) starts.[360]

---

[355] Ibid., pp. 87–91.
Follorou (2022), pp. 15–16.

[356] Lazard and Galland (2020), p. 125.

[357] Cf. Guérin, Documentary film, part 2: "Le temps des Braquos", part 3 : "Le Casse du siècle", part 4 : "Ainsi finit la Brise" (internet-link in the bibliography).

[358] Cf. ibid., part 4 : "Ainsi finit la Brise".

[359] After Casanova's death, a series of murders decimated the *Brise de Mer*: Francis Mariani († 12.1.2009), Pierre-Marie Santucci († 10.2.2009), Francis Guazzelli († 15.11.2009), and Maurice Costa († 7.8.2012). Cf. Follorou (2022), p. 223.

[360] If the *Brise de Mer* has been hollowed out and decimated from within, this does not mean the end of Corsican gangsterism. According to Frédéric Ploquin, a new *Balagne* gang is already forming in northern Corsica around the Federicci family, which has already gained experience in Marseille. Cf. Ploquin (2010), pp. 91–102, here: p. 98. Corsica thus continues to perpetuate gangsterism (Ploquin 2010, p. 91).

5.5.2 Repenti *by Claude Chossat*

Claude Chossat is a 'repenti', i.e. a confessed criminal who co-operates with the police. His decision to tell the justice system the truth about his 2 years as Francis Mariani's confidant, chauffeur, and bodyguard is fuelled by the danger to his own life and limb. Chossat's complicity in Mariani's murder of Casanova within the *Brise de Mer* has landed him in the mills of Corsican *vendetta*, or revenge. It is certain that Casanova's brother-in-law, Jean-Luc Germani, will avenge Casanova's death (R 23). Mariani himself can also become dangerous in his bloodlust.

5.5.2.1 Previous History

To escape endogenous revenge, Chossat fled with his family to Switzerland, where he was arrested in September 2009 and extradited to the French justice system. At this point, he offered himself to the judiciary as a collaborator in the hope of obtaining a reduced sentence and benefiting from a borrowed identity and suitable protective measures in accordance with section 132-78 of the French Criminal Code.[361] Although Chossat was released from prison after 3 years (R 213), he was denied this special protection for judicial collaborators. He is thus a self-proclaimed 'repenti' without legal status: "Confessed criminal in fact but not in law" (R 10). He is the first Corsican 'repenti' who dares to break the *omerta* and sign his testimony transcripts. Judge Guillaume Cotelle confirms that this is an isolated case: "The singularity of Mr Chossat's case was that an actor from the Corsican milieu accepted to speak, giving details and names, which was very significant in the insular context."[362] Claude Choquet, a former judge, echoes this sentiment and confirms the historical

---

[361] In France, the law 'Perben' II of 9 March 2004 (Loi n° 2004-204 du 9 mars 2004), amended on 6 December 2013, provides for special protection and reintegration measures, such as a borrowed identity and appropriate security measures, which are determined on a case-by-case basis (Art. 706-63-1 French Criminal Code), in addition to the possibility of exemption from or reduction of punishment for collaborators in justice (Art. 132-78 French Criminal Code). Section 132-78 of the French Criminal Code stipulates that defendants who intended to commit a criminal offence can be exempted from punishment if their information helps to prevent this offence and identify accomplices. If the offence has already been committed, the informants can benefit from a reduced sentence if they provide information that helps to put an end to the offence or prevent harm: "In the cases provided for by law, persons who have attempted to commit a crime or an offence shall be exempt from punishment if, after having informed the administrative or judicial authority, they have helped to prevent the commission of the offence and, where appropriate, to identify the other perpetrators or accomplices. In the cases provided for by law, the term of imprisonment of persons who have committed a crime, or an offence shall be reduced if, after having informed the administrative or judicial authority, they have made it possible to stop the crime or offence, to prevent it from causing damage or to identify the other perpetrators or accomplices." See also: Mihman (2005), pp. 6–11; Viennot and Desprez (2017), pp. 115–135.

[362] Mucchielli (2019b), pp. 1–2, here: p. 1.

uniqueness of Chossat's revelations, which have enabled the judiciary to gain a deeper insight into the criminal context in Corsica:

> When Mr Chossat decided to speak, I realised that this was an extraordinary, almost historic event, because he was the first to speak. He enabled us to make great strides in this area where we were in the dark. We were aware of the settling of scores, but we only had the surface and not what was going on underneath, because of the code of silence that prevails in Corsica.[363]

According to Chossat, several illegal financial transactions could be punished thanks to his information (*Cercle de jeux parisien*, *Bateaux Promenade en Mer*, money laundering, etc.; see R 108–112)[364] and yet, after his release from custody in 2012, he must ensure his own safety.[365]

Chossat puts his life on the line every day because according to the rules of the *vendetta*, the breach of confidentiality must not go unavenged. He is even more at risk because his testimony transcripts have inexplicably left the confidentiality of the court files and have been leaked to the press: "You speak in confidence to the law and find yourself on the front page of *Le Monde*? I was promised that my confessions would be protected by the greatest secrecy, and now I find myself in the closet as never before, thrown in the face of all those who would dismiss me!" (R 205–206). The judiciary has broken its word to keep the case strictly confidential, and Chossat's breach of *omerta* is now becoming public. It is an unwritten law in Corsica that nobody knows anything or passes on information. For the members of the *Brise de Mer*, confidentiality is part of an unconditional principle of solidarity that guarantees the continued existence of the criminal organisation. For the population, it is a survival strategy, because anyone who talks dies an unnatural death. The Italian judicial collaborator Tommaso Buscetta formulates the *omerta* very aptly: "I know nothing, I have seen nothing. But if even this nothingness arouses suspicion, then I know less than nothing, I have seen less than nothing."[366] Claire Sterling points out that anyone who breaks this duty of confidentiality is a traitor: "Anyone who helps the police uncover a crime, collaborates with law enforcement officers or seeks justice in court is an infame—a traitor and renegade",[367] who falls victim to the *vendetta* through their dishonour. Chossat knows this only too well when he himself states: "The moral of the story is that in Corsica, it is an unwritten law that if you speak out and sign your name, you are condemned to death" (R 260).

Chossat knows that this restless life will never end, for the arms of the *vendetta* reach far and for a long time: "All I know is that as long as I live, I will continue to live the life of a hunted man, but in the open air" (R 255). As he does not know whether he will die a natural death, he has written *Repenti* with the help of a journalist, on the one hand to ease his conscience and on the other to write down in his own

---

[363] Ibid.

[364] Cf. Pelletier (2019) (internet-link in the bibliography).

[365] Cf. Le Parisien (2019) (internet-link in the bibliography).

[366] Galluzzo (1985), p. 21.

[367] Sterling (1990), p. 31.

words the truth that he wants to leave behind as a testament: "This truth, I want to tell it, it's my testament" (R 11). This truth is intended to prevent other young people in Corsica from slipping into crime and to warn them of the unreliability of the justice system, which has not honoured its promise of state protection under the pretext that Chossat is involved in the Casanova murder case.[368]

5.5.2.2 Repenti: Contents

Claude Chossat was not born into crime; his parents led a normal middle-class life (R 38). During his childhood and youth, he was looked after by his grandparents during the day until his parents returned home from Ajaccio to the village of Cuttoli-Corticchiato (R 37) in the evening. He was a good pupil, and his childhood was normal (R 37–43). He attended a vocational school and worked for 2 years in an electronics company (R 45–46) until he encountered the milieu of small-time hustlers, therewith engaging in his first criminal activities. A burglary in the home of an elderly couple in 2000, in which Chossat's role is initially limited to waiting in the driver's seat of the car parked in the street for his comrades to drive off, becomes his undoing when he is called in by them to help break into the couple's safe. The victims' daughter manages to alert the police, who catch Chossat in the act, but not his accomplices, who were already on the run (R 49–51). These unfortunate circumstances lead to 7 years in the Borgo prison on the outskirts of Bastia (R 55–56), where three members of the inner circle of the *Brise de Mer* (R 57–61) are also imprisoned at the same time: Pierre-Marie Santucci, Maurice Costa, and Francis Mariani.[369]

While the three criminals soon leave the prison through the big door thanks to a false fax,[370] Chossat serves his sentence in full. After his release from prison, his attempt to set up a construction company fails due to debts of 50,000 euros, forcing him to give up his business and putting him in a precarious situation. As a result, he turns to Mariani for help, who agrees to pay off the debt, but not without taking the opportunity to hire Chossat as his personal chauffeur, bodyguard, and man for everything (R 98). He now had him firmly in his grip, from which it is difficult to escape. Chossat was supposed to help him track down Richard Casanova and Jean-Luc Germani: "A week ago, someone tried to kill me. You're going to help me find them." (R 78). He instructs his new assistant to get him 25,000 euros worth of weapons.[371] Mariani kills Casanova on 23 April 2008 and not Jean-Luc Germani, as

[368] Cf. France 3 Corse ViaStella (2017) (internet-link in the bibliography).
Cf. Cohen (2017) (internet-link in the bibliography).
Regarding the judicial collaborator, see: Abdessalem (2019) (Internet-link in the bibliography).

[369] Lazard and Galland (2020), p. 67.

[370] Ibid., pp. 68–69.

[371] Ibid., p. 95.

originally planned.[372] The grinder of *vendetta* is now set in motion, as Germani will avenge the death of his brother-in-law and thus initiate the downfall of the *Brise de Mer*.[373] He will thereby not only turn Mariani but also Claude Chossat into an eternal victim (R 10): "The Fire of Vengeance" (R80).

Repenti is an account of the unwritten laws of Corsican *vendetta* and of the impossible lives of those who must fear them. In the following section, the passages in *Repenti* that refer to this customary law of revenge (*vendetta*) are analysed to create an overall picture, which is subsequently contrasted counterfactually with the real-world practice of *vendetta* in the section hereafter.

5.5.3 *Explicit Discourse on the* Vendetta *in the Diegesis*

In *Repenti*, Claude Chossat refers to the unwritten laws of *vendetta* (R 260), and thereby to the culture of murder and revenge in which the slightest conflict is settled with a gun: "This culture of death and revenge, where everything is settled with a gun, where we see innocent people murdered, people dying because they did someone a favour or for no reason at all" (R 261).

The mechanism of this *vendetta* is illustrated in *Repenti* by the feud between Mariani and Casanova and by the numerous murders in response to dishonour, an insult, a refused service, a murder or even for trivial reasons in general. The danger of the *vendetta* is omnipresent, it lies like a leaden layer over the whole of Corsica and parts of southern France.

Mariani killed Richard Casanova, one of the leading members of the *Brise de Mer*'s inner circle (R 99)—"I have killed Richard Casanova" (R 18)—and not, as originally planned, Casanova's brother-in-law Jean-Luc Germani. This act represents a serious breach of the absolute and unspoken duty of solidarity among the members of the *Brise de Mer* (R 18), which until then had been its strength. It marks the beginning of their disintegration and now makes Mariani and Chossat predictable victims of the inevitable circle of death that characterises the *vendetta*:

> How do you explain to them [Chossat is referring to his daughters and his wife, author's remark] that in Corsica, the land of the Mafia, resentment kills? How can I explain to them all my stories with Francis Mariani, his fight to the death with Richard Casanova, which led to the implosion of *La Brise de Mer*, the madness in which I found myself, the violence of the prison, the greed of the Corsican Mafia, this circular culture of death and revenge, in which not only criminals but also innocent people fall to the ground? (R 32)

There can be no doubt that Jean-Luc Germani will avenge Casanova's death when he lifts his brother-in-law's coffin onto his shoulder as a sign of his intention to take revenge: "With a dry eye, Jean-Luc Germani walks over to his brother-in-law's

[372] Ibid., p. 99.

[373] Ibid., p. 102.

coffin and lifts it onto his shoulder. A sign that he has lost his honour. A sign that the tragedy has only just begun" (R 23).[374]

When it comes to getting rid of inconvenient people or avenging the murder of a member of their own clan—"'*Ci vole à caccià lu*' [He must be removed]!" (R 113) –, then the murder in question is decided in cold blood in the closest circle of the *Brise de Mer*: "When it comes to deciding on an assassination, they're all there [...]" (R 114). Every murder is followed by another murder: "One dead leads to another [...]" (R 132), blood must be repaid with blood: "Blood will be avenged in blood" (R 182).

Francis Mariani is the most bloodthirsty of them all; after the murder of Casanova, he boasts a total of 54 murders: "I'm up to 54. So, one more or one less...'" (R 155). Here, Chossat realises the danger. In the months that follow, Mariani murders Daniel Vittini and Jean-Claude Tasso (R 167) to pave the way for his son Jacques Mariani by eliminating as many of the troublemakers as possible (R 155). Daniel Vittini, a long-time friend of Mariani, dies due to envy because his son Alexandre was sentenced to a shorter prison term than Mariani's son Jacques (R 164).[375] In January 2009, the relentless *vendetta* also overtakes Francis Mariani: he falls victim to an explosion in his own hangar (R 179).[376] The threat of the *vendetta* now hovers all the more clearly over the surviving members of the *Brise de Mer* as long as Jean-Luc Germani is at large: "And the survivors of La Brise can already make the sign of the cross – they know it. With the summit decapitated, Jean-Luc Germani on the loose and obsessed with revenge, the most legendary gang of recent years is making its last stand" (R 179). The heads of the *Brise de Mer* do indeed fall one by one: Pierre Marie Santucci on 10 February 2009 (R 184),[377] Francis Guazzelli on 15 November 2009,[378] Christian Leoni on 28 October 2011, and Maurice Costa on 7 August 2012 (R 257). Angelo Guazzelli and Jean-Luc Germani are sentenced to prison terms (R 157–258).

In 2010, Claude Chossat was under investigation in six criminal cases: embezzlement of company assets, car theft, and murder of Tasso and Casanova, which is why he remained in custody for almost 3 years until 2012 (R 208–213).

It is very difficult for him to return to freedom as he does not benefit from the specific protection for judicial collaborators and is not given a new identity that could help him cover his tracks to escape the *vendetta*. Chossat must constantly erase his tracks, install surveillance cameras, and change his place of residence, because ever since the French newspaper *Le Monde* publicised his 'betrayal', he has been threatened with the consequences of the *vendetta*, la *mala morte*, the violent death (R 233). The judiciary has denied him the status of judicial collaborator on the flimsy grounds that, on the one hand, it cannot be proven that his statements would

[374] Ibid., p. 129.

[375] Ibid., p. 106.

[376] Ibid., pp. 107–111.

[377] Ibid., pp. 111–112.

[378] Ibid., p. 112.

have prevented crimes and, on the other, the Perben II dispositive was not yet in force at the time of his statements in 2009. In fact, it took 10 years for this to finally become legally binding (2004–2014), but without the inconsistencies and practical weaknesses that still exist having been rectified.[379]

In 2019, Chossat was again sentenced to 8 years in prison for criminal complicity in the murder of Richard Casanova.[380] Public prosecutor Pierre Cortès even demanded 15 years, as he doubted the sincerity and effectiveness of Chossat's collaboration with the judiciary.[381] In 2021, Chossat was again sentenced to 7 years in prison for involvement in a criminal organisation (arms procurement) in the context of the murder of Jean-Claude Tasso. This last prison sentence will be offset by the 8 years in the 'Casanova' case. Both murders, that of Casanova and that of Tasso, were probably committed by Francis Mariani alone, while Chossat merely acted as an accomplice.[382]

In the following section, as already mentioned above, the diegetic discourse in *Repenti* with reference to the customary law of Corsican *vendetta* is contrasted with the real law custom of *vendetta*. The prerequisite for this, as has already been asserted several times, and thus also here, is the demonstrable factuality of this custom, which is now discussed in detail.

5.5.4 *Counterfactual Contrast:* Vendetta *vs Customary Law in the Diegesis*

In contrast to the oral tradition of the Albanian customary law of the *Kanun*, which, as explained in Sect. 5.3, which was last recorded in writing at the beginning of the twentieth century, the rules of the Corsican *vendetta* have not yet been codified into writing. While the lack of written evidence makes it difficult to establish the factuality of this *custom*, it does not make it impossible, as it only requires going back further into the historical past to find the roots and models for the modern application of the rules of *vendetta*. Historicity can shed light on the process of tacit agreement on the normative character of the rules of *vendetta*[383] and the stringency or consequences of their non-observance.[384] As shown below, the feuding behaviour of modern Corsican banditry remains strongly indebted to its historical heritage.

---

[379] Cf. Janouel (2024), pp. 1–2, here: p. 1.

[380] Salvi (2019) (internet-link in the bibliography).

[381] Mucchielli (2019a, 2019c).

[382] Bouschon (2021) (internet-link in the bibliography). Cf. Foreix (2019) (internet-link in the bibliography).

[383] Cf. Puchta (1828), pp. 139 ff. (cf. Sect. 3.4.2 on the factuality of the law).

[384] Cf. Hahn (2019), p. 190 (cf. Sect. 3.4.2 on the factuality of the law).

5.5.4.1 Factuality of the *Vendetta*

The Corsican *vendetta* probably dates back to the thirteenth century, when Corsica fell under the rule of the Italian city-state of Genoa in 1284.[385] To understand the mechanism of the *vendetta*, which, as Chossat shows in *Repenti*, is still very much alive, the evolution of the island's structural organisation throughout history must be taken into account. Unlike on the mainland, where in the Middle Ages religious power was in the hands of the Church and civil power in the hands of the feudal lords, in Corsica, as Antoine Casanova summarises, the feudal lords had to share their power with the judges, recruited from the people, as third actors:

> The seigniorial and ecclesiastical powers coexisted with the popular magistrates, who represented the parishes and groups of parishes, administered justice, waged war, met in general assemblies that had the power to send embassies to Pisa or to the Pope and to appeal to the powers of the 'mal governo' of the counts and lords. The secular lords, the ecclesiastical lords, the magistrates and the institutions of the rural communities and groups of parishes thus had equal and coexistent political and legal capacities and personalities.[386]

These people's judges represented the community of a *piève* or associations of several *pièves*, sat in judgement, waged wars, or sent delegations to the Pope to denounce the mismanagement (*mal governo*) of the feudal lords. The appearance of these representatives of the people, who were recognised by the inhabitants of a *piève*, led to the subsequent coexistence of state and non-state power structures, which basically continues to this day and is based on the geographical division of Corsica into *pièves*, as once established by the Church.[387] The aim of this territorial organisation was to locate the religious communities in the geographical vicinity of a church as their centre of life.[388] As Antoine Casanova notes, it was not uncommon for these representatives of the people to later become feudal lords by usurpation of power.[389] They then ruled over the inhabitants of a *piève* or a clan[390] and received a voluntary tribute from the peasants, the so-called *accato*,[391] which, according to Francis Pomponi, was imposed arbitrarily and collected by force over time. In this sense, it can be seen as the forerunner of the mafia racket: "The transition from *accatto* to racket came about as clan chiefs established themselves as a parallel power within the state apparatus, diverting public demands for their personal

[385] In a treaty signed in Versailles on 15 May 1768, Genoa sold the island to France, with whom it has remained to this day, without ever completely abandoning its aspirations for independence.

[386] Casanova (1981), pp. 81–130, here: p. 95.

[387] Broc (2014), p. 33.

[388] Pergola (1979), pp. 89–111, here: p. 91.

[389] Casanova (2005), pp. 239–265, here: p. 252.

[390] The Corsican clan structure corresponds to a hierarchisation within the social groups, which could be made up of the following member categories: *amici* (friends), *sequaci* (followers), *aderenti* (members), and *parenti* (family in the narrow and broad sense). Cf. Pomponi (1978), pp. 7–30, here: p. 8; Marchi van Cauwelaert (2011), pp. 437–438.

[391] Casanova (2005), p. 252.

gain."[392] Gangs (*partitu*) formed around these self-appointed feudal lords,[393] usually grouped around an influential mayor and became politically active, as Georges Ravis-Giordani notes: "Each partitu is an aggregate of smaller family, lineage or 'clan' groups (a group of supporters grouped around an influential mayor at the level of a canton or even one or two communes). The family and relatives of the *capi partitu* are always present and active in political life."[394] Clans in the broader sense and family intermingled in the *partitu* and functioned parallel to state institutions. Stephen Wilson speculates that the small number of surnames in Corsica is an indication of the clan system in Corsica, which goes far beyond the biological family: "Various families which had no blood ties decided to give up their individual names and to take collectively either the name of one of them, or an entirely new name. The small number of Corsican surnames, to which we have alluded, would support this speculation."[395] Often the common place of residence connects the members of the clan (*ceppu*): "This [...] usually derived more directly from residence in the same locality."[396] This clan structure, which extended from the biological family (*parenti stretti),* through the extended family (*parentelli*) and the unrelated clan members to the political associations,[397] also corresponds to the geographical structure of the so-called *pièves*, which has remained the template for the administrative units (municipalities and municipal associations) to this day.[398] Figure 5.1 from 1730 illustrates Corsica's close-knit geographical structure. Family, 'allies' and politics thus intertwined at the local level of the *pièves* and formed the basis for the system of *vendetta*, as François-Guillaume Robiquet explains: "The system of *vendetta* makes each family to an independent power [...]. The families then group together in party interests, and the powerful men of each party protect all their members."[399] Jacques Busquet confirms that a clan could extend to an entire *piève*: "Villages and entire counties were involved [...]."[400]

Jacques Follorou points to the continuing legacy of this clan structure and the strong local ties of Corsicans to their villages as the basis for banditry, which the state has still not been able to get under control: "Corsican banditry cannot be understood without knowledge of its context, its history and its territory'. [...] 'With its roots in a clan-based culture and a strong attachment to the land and to family heritage, it has a long tradition, both on the island and on the mainland, of settling scores [...] and has long been ignored by the authorities in favour of terrorism'."[401]

[392] Pomponi (1978), p. 12.

[393] Ibid., p. 8.

[394] Ravis-Giordani (2005), pp. 317–337, here: p. 325.

[395] Wilson (1988), p. 180.

[396] Ibid.

[397] Raggio (1990), pp. 937–954, here: p. 948.

[398] Trochet (2022), al. 31–32. (internet-link in the bibliography).

[399] Robiquet (1835), p. 396.

[400] Busquet (2022), pp. 193–223, here: p. 220.

[401] Follorou (2022), p. 15.

Fig. 5.1 Francis Pomponi, *Pieve et paesi – Communautés rurales corses*, Paris: CNRS Éditions 1978, p. 321

To this day, according to Follorou, the Corsican mafia functions according to the rules of the clan, led by feared and respected bosses who enrich themselves with threats, violence and rackets and, thanks to the generalised *omerta*, evade the reach of justice. They operate for all to see, suppressing the state and suffocating the population: "The Corsican mafia have become quasi-public figures. They weigh heavily on society."[402] In this extra-judicial system of power, the rules of *vendetta*

[402] Ibid., p. 240.

are the ideal instrument for maintaining the power of one's own clan and control over the population.

5.5.4.2 Counterfactual Contrasting

In *Repenti*, Chossat aptly summarises this leaden pressure of the clan, the *Brise de Mer*: "La Brise de mer, the heart of the Corsican mafia, was just that. Racketeering, dirty murders, an empire of terror built on crime money and the attraction of power" (R 8). Crime is divided between geographically bound clans and their leaders (R 123), the Clan *Corte* (Memmi) (R 71), the *Brise de Mer*, the *Armata Corsa* (R 92), the Clan *Federici* (R 59; R 94), the Clan *Petit Bar* (Ange-Marie Michelosi) (R 130), and the *French Connection* (Colonna), which at times respect each other and at other times are at war with each other. The murder of a member of an opposing clan can destroy the precarious balance, as the murder of Robert Feliciaggi, followed by that of Jean Jérôme Colonna, shows. These two murders inevitably trigger the 'mechanism' of *vendetta* and threaten to decimate the *Brise de Mer* clan (R 123). The bond with the village of childhood, the family, and the villagers remains even for those Corsican women and men who have left the island. In this context, Chossat cites the prominent example of Bernard Squarcini, the former head of the French secret service, who regularly visits his family in the village of Cuttoli-Corticchiato and whose brother oversees Corsica's penal institutions (R 43), which may give Corsican criminals certain advantages.

Within the clan, the rule of absolute cohesion is the highest commandment in life as well as in and after death: "Not to mention the fact that the group was based on a few intangible rules, the most important of which was absolute solidarity between its members. They owed each other assistance in life and after life" (R 65). Internally, the *vendetta* fulfils the function of cementing the clan members, while externally, it performs the function of intimidation, of gaining power, or as a means of asserting oneself against enemy clans. The clan is like a family whose members stick closely together. If one of these members dies, other family members or friends take over their role to maintain the group (R 71). This group solidarity (R 114) also manifests itself in the fact that the murder of a clan member must be avenged as one. This is made clear by the example of the murder of Dominique Rutily, one of the 12 leading members of the *Brise de Mer*: as Chossat describes, in this situation all the other clan members travel together to Sarthène in southern Corsica as a sign of cohesion to avenge Rutily's death, because cohesion is the indispensable prerequisite for the clan's continued existence: "It was urgent to avenge his [death, author's comment] firstly in symbolic terms, as the safety and omnipotence of the Breeze were at stake" (R 65). At the height of its power, the *Brise de Mer* can rely on the services of the population, the police, the judiciary, and politics, i.e. on a wide-meshed network that hears nothing and sees nothing, and which covers its criminal activities like a protective cloak (R 117–119). Bernard Squarcini also holds his hand over them and makes compromising information about members of the *Brise de Mer* disappear (R

119). Clan thinking and *vendetta* are two sides of the same coin, they are part of the Corsican identity and the historical legacy that continues to this day.

The Corsican *vendetta* is originally, like the right of feud in the *Kanun*, an act of reasoned revenge to make up for a loss of honour. It is based on the idea of bloody reparation for violations of family honour that the state system does not effectively sanction; it is a system within a system.[403] Moreover, it is an integral part of a social model and characterises its identity, whereby it is not the degree of violence, but the intensity of the violation of honour that determines the degree of retribution.[404] As Caroline Parsi shows, this principle is also taken into account in Corsican case law and can lead to acquittal in many cases despite murder.[405] The *vendetta* comprises a corpus of unwritten rules that are passed on orally from generation to generation[406] and are perceived as normative, i.e. binding, due to long traditional practice. Here, I recall Jellinek's description of the normativity of customary law norms, which in turn determines their factual existence: "The continuing practice generates the notion of the normative nature of this practice, and the norm itself thus appears as an authoritative commandment of the community, i.e. as a legal norm."[407] These customary law 'norms' are applied, as Stephen Wilson emphasises, when honour (*onore*) is violated, which in extreme cases can only be restored through blood:[408] "Blood vengeance was subject to 'law', if indeed it did not constitute a system of law"[409] Paoli Pompei emphasises the normative nature of these rules, which govern the exercise of *vendetta* in a binding manner: "Revenge, as practised in Corsica, has its own set of rules that cannot be ignored."[410] Busquet points out that the corpus of customary law norms of the *vendetta* has a violence-regulating function.[411] Abbé Antoine Bartoli compares the regularity of the *vendetta* with the duel: "Like an ordinary duel, the vendetta is subject to fixed, determined laws."[412] Albert Surier emphasises the tacit agreement on the mandatory, regulated course of the *vendetta*, which nobody would contravene.[413] In 1835, François-Guillaume Robiquet was the only person to observe a decline in the rules of *vendetta*: "Today, vengeance no longer seems to be subject to any rules, or at least, if there are still any, observing them has become the exception."[414] Parsi argues against Robiquet, stating that a murder committed according to the rules of *vendetta* is considered a noble and nec-

---

[403] Busquet (1994), pp. 194–195.

[404] Parsi (2013), pp. 247–261, here: p. 253.

[405] Ibid., pp. 253–257.

[406] Ibid., p. 252.

[407] Jellinek (1921), p. 339.

[408] Wilson (1988), p. 91.

[409] Ibid., p. 197.

[410] Pompei (1821), p. 209.

[411] Busquet (1920) (section II A). See also Tihanyi (1998), pp. 72–73.

[412] Bartoli (1898), pp. 255–256.

[413] Surier (1934), pp. 46–47.

[414] Robiquet (1835), p. 394 (footnote 1).

essary act and is therefore not punishable under state law in the eyes of most Corsicans.[415] In this sense, customary law takes precedence over state law.

This compelling character of revenge, which makes the violence legible and resembles a perpetual duel according to certain rules, in which the murdered and those to be murdered take turns, is confirmed by Chossat: "One death leads to another" (R 132), and "Blood will be avenged in blood" (R 182). A murder calls for murder because an unavenged murder is a rejection of solidarity with one's own clan (R 65). The duel is fought between clans or individuals in the interests of the clan. If one member is killed, the whole clan must avenge this murder to symbolically demonstrate unity (R 65). In territorial power struggles, entire clans face each other and whoever kills more and faster gains territory. The *Brise de Mer* practises this as indicated when it succeeds in decimating the Clan Memmi to such an extent that it can take over their territory (R 71). In the eyes of those involved, but also in the eyes of the Corsican population, this action is not strange, as the laws of the *vendetta* and not those of the French penal code regulate conflicts, power struggles, violations of honour or solidarity, or demonstrations of solidarity (R 44–45). The *Brise de Mer* does not shy away from the 'correct' application of the laws of *vendetta*, which help it to consolidate its power, but it is panicky about acts of revenge that do not follow the rules of *vendetta* but personal motives, as is the case between Mariani and Casanova. In fact, the disregard for the unwritten rules of the *vendetta*, as it turns out, heralds the downfall of the *Brise de Mer* (R 18; R 156; R 174; R 179).

The rules in this context are the result of a long historical development which, as already mentioned, dates back to the thirteenth century. This historical genesis gives rise to four main triggers for taking revenge: dishonouring a woman by touching or kissing her (*attacar*),[416] breaking a promise, murdering a close relative, and convicting a close relative in court on the basis of false testimony.[417] In addition to these four main offences, various insults such as verbal abuse, spitting on an opponent's weapon, damage to property, the killing of pets, etc.[418] can also trigger revenge and, according to Wilson, bind relatives up to the third, fourth, and in some cases even the fifth and sixth degree of separation.[419] Jacques Busquet, however, contradicts this, as the historical archives of the *civile governatore* demonstrably show that the *vendetta* did not extend beyond the third degree of kinship.[420] On the other hand, there is widespread agreement that the main obligor is always the closest male relative in good physical condition (son, father, brother, cousin, nephew, brother-in-law, etc.).[421] In some cases, the bond of solidarity of the *vendetta* can also extend to

---

415 Parsi (2013), p. 247.

416 Busquet (1994), pp. 112–118. *Attacar* refers to the act of touching when it forces a woman to marry the perpetrator of this act in order to save her honour.

417 Wilson (1988), p. 197.

418 Cf. ibid., pp. 92–127.

419 Ibid., p. 189.

420 Busquet (1994), p. 105.

421 Wilson (1988), pp. 190–193. See also: Busquet (1920), pp. 341–342; Carrington (1971), p. 82; Feydel (1799), pp. 68–69; Rossi (1900), p. 115 ; Culioli et al. (2022), pp. 206–207.

neighbours or even, as Jean-François-Ignace Réalier-Dumas comments, to an entire village.[422] Only women, children,[423] old men, and friars, but not the village priests, who are sometimes clan heads themselves,[424] are exempt from the obligation to take revenge.[425] The *vendetta* must be carried out within 25 years of the offence. The family, i.e. the *parenti* of the murderer, had to pay a monetary tribute to the family of the murdered person (which has become obsolete today). Anyone who, contrary to the code of honour, declares his intention to evade the duties and risks of the *vendetta* is accused of disgrace (*rimbeccu*).[426] He is ostracised by society and accused of evading revenge.[427] As Abbé Bartoli explains, in this case, the loss of honour is tantamount to social death, because those who lose their honour must remain silent, they are publicly ostracised and lose influence and prestige: "In Corsica, anyone who has not avenged a father, a brother, a murdered relative or a deceived daughter can no longer appear in public. [...] As one sees it, he is a dead man, without any consideration; he has no more credit, no more prestige; he exerts no influence on his companions."[428]

After Francis Mariani is lucky enough to escape an attack in which he was injured in the arm, he is obsessed with the desire for revenge and this is the reason for employing Claude Chossat: "A week ago, someone tried to kill me. You're going to help me find the people who did this" (R 78). The fervour of revenge—"the fire of vengeance" (R 80)—now guides his actions, he cannot do otherwise, and it could not be otherwise (R 85). Francis Mariani immediately realises that it is a matter of honour for Jean-Luc Germani, Richard Casanova's closest male relative, to avenge his murder when he soberly states immediately after the crime: "I may already be dead" (R 20). Mariani's suspicion becomes a certainty when Germani symbolically lifts Casanova's coffin onto his shoulder at the funeral, thereby confirming his intention to restore his honour, that of his family, and that of the deceased through revenge: "Jean-Luc Germani walks up to his brother-in-law's coffin and lifts it onto his shoulder. A sign that he will avenge the deceased" (R 23). Now it is certain that Francis Mariani (R 179) and Pierre-Marie Santucci (R 184) are hit by the revenge. However, a violation of honour can also be avenged on one of the offender's relatives instead of directly on the offender, as Chossat describes using the example of an incident in Borgo prison: A fellow inmate, Alexandre Rogliano, humiliates Pierre-Marie Santucci during a football match in the prison yard. A short time later, his unsuspecting brother, Pascal Rogliano, is found dead (R 61–63). As Chossat emphasises, the *Brise de Mer* never grants amnesty (R 132). As a judicial informant and traitor, he himself is in constant danger of falling victim to the *vendetta* (R200), indeed, he is

[422] Réalier-Dumas (1819), p. 19.
[423] Busquet (1994), p. 107.
[424] Ibid., pp. 107–108.
[425] Parsi (2013), p. 253.
[426] Ibid., p. 252.
[427] Busquet (1994), pp. 108–109.
[428] Bartoli (1898), p. 254.

already dead: "I have chosen to throw a stone into the pond of omerta. And I'm already dead" (R 206; R 216). The unwritten law of *vendetta* condemns Chossat to death, since he signed his recorded statements about Corsica's mafia system.

As soon as a family decides to take revenge, it announces this explicitly or implicitly after the funeral, possibly with an oath,[429] because the feud between the clans must not be a 'surprise war'.[430] When placed within this intricate system of custom law, the symbolism of lifting Casanova's coffin onto Germani's shoulder explicitly announces the start of the feud to those present (R 23). Violette Lazard and Marion Galland confirm this form of revenge announcement: "On the island, only close friends and family carry the coffin of the deceased, and in the codes of organised crime, the pallbearers are also the ones who take revenge."[431]

In anticipation of the *vendetta*, the family withdraws into a kind of *retreat*, where alcohol consumption and food intake are restricted, the men grow hair and beards, and the murder victim's bloodstained shirt is hung up in the parlour to remind them of their duty to take revenge.[432] Advocate General Félix Bertrand reports a scene of a *vendetta* between two men that leads to a new revenge, as the woman of the house announces: "I will drive a stake through the wall to hang up the bloody clothes of our two dead men, showing them to the children who are left to me, and I will address the *rimbecco* to them until we are avenged."[433] For fear of a counter-attack, Bertrand says, the families become like those buried alive, they lock themselves in their fortified houses without taking part in social life: "So, to escape these perils, how many men consented to groan, for whole years, in the anguish of a painful captivity! How many remained stubbornly locked up in their homes as if in a tomb! In some villages, almost entire generations passed without taking any part in social life."[434] Jean-Baptiste Marcaggi also reported on this in a text from 1929: "The houses of families with a vendetta remained closed at all times. The windows were barricaded with large oak beams, leaving only narrow slanting slits which served as battlements."[435] Bertrand refers in particular to the high death toll that the *vendetta* claimed in Corsica, for example, in just 30 years, between 1685 and 1715: 28,715 victims were mourned in this period alone.[436] He counted around one hundred and fifty murders in connection with the *vendetta* every year since he took office in 1858.[437]

---

429 Parsi (2013), p. 252.

430 Wilson (1988), p. 197. See also: Robiquet (1835), p. 394 (footnote 1): "In Corsica in the past, war did not begin until it had officially been declared"; Pompei (1821), pp. 209–210. Busquet explains that this is the so-called declaration of *guardarsi*, which can be compared to 'Look after yourself' (cf. Busquet 2022, p. 204).

431 Lazard and Galland (2020), p. 129.

432 Wilson (1988), p. 198.
Marcaggi (2022), pp. 9–131, here: p. 52; Busquet (1994), pp. 100–103.

433 Bertrand (1870), p. 19.

434 Ibid., *La Vendetta*, p. 22.

435 Marcaggi (2022), p. 51.

436 Bertrand (1870), p. 38 and footnote 1.

437 Ibid.

While *Repenti* does not mention the symbolism of the reduced food intake, the men's hair and beard growth and the display of the bloody shirt, which do not seem to have survived to this day, the escape from social life, the *retreat* to escape the death of revenge, applies to Chossat. Since his statements became public knowledge, he has become the target of the *vendetta* and lives away from society, locked up in his home, which is equipped with alarm devices and video cameras and which he constantly and restlessly monitors. He rarely leaves the house and when he does, it is only under the highest security precautions, which severely interferes with his normal family life and professional activities (R 25–33).

Mariani also transforms his house into a fortress with a sophisticated system of surveillance cameras after the failed attempt on his life. He even has an underground tunnel dug to serve as his escape route (R 86–87). Today's *retreat* may differ from that of the nineteenth century in terms of technical means, but the principle remains the same. Those who fear being exposed to an act of revenge try to protect themselves and delay the time of what is probably an unnatural death.

Robert Colonna d'Istria, a well-known Corsican personality, quotes Pierre Bonardi (1887–1964), a connoisseur of the Corsican mentality, to illustrate the spirit of the *vendetta*:

> Say to the Corsican: "I am lost, I am tired, and I am hungry. His bed and table are yours. You want to pay? You are doing him a disservice! But if you ask him: 'For what price will you sell me this chair or this tree?', he will answer: 'A million'. His sense of value is not the same as yours. Tell him: 'I need your field to dance in', he will reply: 'Take my field' and smile as he sees his crop plundered. Claim a legitimate easement to cross his garden, he will take up his gun… If word gets out that you are ill? The whole village will go and reap your wheat or finish your grape harvest. But if you have caused your neighbour's vegetable patch to lose five minutes of watering, vengeance may come with its bloody procession.[438]

In some cases, the *vendetta* can be settled by a mediator (*paceru*). His arbitration award is generally recognised as legally valid and recorded in writing in a book of 'peace' (*pace*). The subsequent mutual promise of friendship (*amicizia*) and alliance (*parentella*) then seals the end of the feud. In *Repenti*, however, no reference is made to this possibility.

As the *vendetta* and the fear of its practice paralysed many villages in Corsica, in 1755 Pascal Paoli made an unsuccessful attempt to eradicate the *vendetta* through repression—at that time through the law of *Giustizia Paolina:*[439] with this in mind, two mediators (*paceri*) and a judge were assigned to each village, and the death penalty was introduced for murderers.[440] However, the consequences of these measures were not as hoped for; on the contrary, they led to a revival of resistance to state institutions.[441]

---

[438] Colonna d'Istria (2018), p. 237.

[439] Simon Timotei (2021) (internet-link in the bibliography).

[440] Busquet (1994), pp. 291–292.

[441] Lenclud (2012), pp. 239–240. Pascal Paoli made an unsuccessful attempt to turn Corsica into a nation and, to this end, drafted the world's first democratic constitution in 1755, thirty years before the American constitution. See also: Eisenmenger (2010), pp. 430–446.

According to Bertrand, *vendetta* and banditry are closely linked, because once you are involved in a feud, you become a bandit, constantly changing your location, exchanging your home for the wilderness of the *maquis* and intimidating the population with your fearlessness. Even if banditry no longer exists in this form today, modern Corsican gangsterism, as shown in *Repenti* using the example of the *Brise de Mer*, continues to wield power through unscrupulous scaremongering, blackmail, murder and racketeering, and dominates politics and the economy alongside the state. Bertrand already observed in the nineteenth century that these *héros du makis* dominated public life, influenced elections, set sales prices, extorted financial contributions from wealthy citizens, etc. Their power allowed them to do everything, and the population obeyed, supported, and entertained them. The authority of these *héros du makis* surpassed that of the state, as Bertrand notes: "Their authority also knew no bounds. It often thwarted administrative orders, court rulings and even the provisions of the law."[442] The fact that laws, court rulings and other regulations mean little is also clear in *Repenti*: in Borgo prison, the "Club Med" (R 55) of prisons, Mariani, Santucci and Costa set the rules, not the prison administration: "They, the men of La Brise, are the ones who keep order, their own order" (R 59) and, incidentally, they leave prison early thanks to a forged fax, "a false legal document sent to the management of Borgo" (R 73), which a bribed bailiff has had authenticated (R 74). The bribery or intimidation of aldermen, judges, and witnesses (R 142–143) systematically steered the outcome of trials against members of the *Brise de Mer* in their favour. Richard Casanova's sixteen-year escape from punishment and prison proves the superiority of the *héros du makis* over state legislation, which is even made possible by high-ranking accomplices in the state hierarchy itself: The French Ministry of the Interior issues Casanova a false passport in the name of Éric Rossi and Bernard Squarcini removes Casanova's name from the wanted list for organised crime (R 119). In 2006, Casanova was arrested in agreement with the police for the sake of form. Contrary to the opinion of the public prosecutor's office, however, he was released just a few months later, on 22 November 2006, on bail of 150,000 euros, which a cousin and a casino operator posted for him (R 124). Lazard and Galland report on such practices of witness intimidation and jury tampering in connection with the first major trial against the *Brise de Mer* in the murder case of Daniel Ziglioli before the Dijon jury court, which, contrary to expectations and despite overwhelming evidence of the murder, ended with the acquittal of the three defendants:[443] This is clear proof of the *Brise de Mer*'s supremacy over state law.

The counterfactual contrast between the fictional and the factual custom that determines the still unwritten rules of the Corsican *vendetta* results in a systemic fusion of law and literature, as it is literature alone that puts the still unwritten rules on paper. In these circumstances Luhmann's idea of differentiated systems[444] does not work, because law and literature form the same system here. The custom of the

[442] Bertrand (1870), pp. 41–42.

[443] Lazard and Galland (2020), pp. 30–34.

[444] Cf. Sect. 3.2.2 on the Interdiscourse, footnote 120.

modern *vendetta* as customary law comes into its own here through its first written form, if one assumes that Claude Chossat was the first to put some of its current rules on record. Seen in this light, *Repenti* fulfils less the task of interdiscursively connecting different epistemes but rather constitutes the rules of the Corsican vendetta for the first time via literary discourse. In this sense, it is precisely this diegetic discourse, to paraphrase Rainer Diaz-Bone, that creates the custom of the *vendetta*.[445] There is no need for 'translation' through literature of the legal vocabulary, insofar as the literary discourse fulfils the task of describing the regularities of the Corsican *vendetta*. This does not require a legal vocabulary, such as that of the criminal trials in *Repenti*, which are merely a peripheral phenomenon of *vendetta*, but not *vendetta* itself.

The lack of a written codification of the *vendetta* since the thirteenth century prevents any attempt to interpret its provisions according to the rules of legal hermeneutics. Instead, literary hermeneutics must be used here, in that *Repenti* can be read and interpreted in conjunction with historical and contemporary texts that deal with this phenomenon from different perspectives. The recourse to intertextuality plays an important role here, as not only literary but also historical and anthropological writings must be consulted to understand the *vendetta*. The interpretation of the feudal law in *Repenti* thus obeys the rules of literary hermeneutics to the latter.

It can therefore be argued that literature constitutes (customary) law in the first place so that law and literature coincide at this point (the *vendetta*). The interdisciplinary connection between law and literature could not be stronger, insofar as the text is the only hermeneutic reference and is naturally subject to the vagueness that results from the unbound nature of literary interpretation across historical periods.

To summarise, it should be noted that *Repenti's* depiction of the customary law of *vendetta* in force in today's Corsica is very realistic and truthful. This is demonstrated by the comparison between the statements in the diegeses and the scientific, historical, anthropological and journalistic contributions consulted. The factuality, i.e. the binding nature and enforceability of the norms on which the *vendetta* is based, emerges from these studies, which trace its origin and development back to the thirteenth century. The legal factuality as a prerequisite for the counterfactual contrast should therefore once again be fulfilled.

Chossat's *Repenti* makes an interesting contribution to clarifying the interpretation and application of the rules of *vendetta* in contemporary Corsica, the details of which have largely remained obscure in practice due to the unspoken principle of *omerta*. As the first contemporary judicial informant, Chossat therefore provides valuable information on whether and how the rules of *vendetta* are applied today in Corsica (and in the south of France), where the legacy of the historical, topological, and anthropological evolution of the island is unmistakable. It is precisely this heritage that explains the clan system and the laws of revenge as two sides of the same coin that cannot be considered separately. While the clan forms the basis for action, the *vendetta* fulfils the function of maintaining group cohesion on the one hand and serves to acquire and

[445] Cf. Sect. 3.2.1 on the discourse, footnote 88.

maintain power on the other. The 'correct' application of its rules in the interests of the collective ensures the continued existence of the clan and its power influence; the individual, 'incorrect' application of its rules leads to its downfall.

This awareness is conveyed in *Repenti* using the example of the *Brise de Mer*, the violent expansion of their sphere of power through the decimation of opposing clans and their disintegration as a result of the endogenous rivalry between Casanova and Mariani, as well as Chossat's collaboration with the judiciary. The unity and absolute solidarity among the twelve leading members of the *Brise de Mer* is guaranteed as long as the internal unity and solidarity are not disturbed by individual, internal desires for revenge and the *vendetta* serves as proof of solidarity to ward off external attacks on members of the *Brise de Mer*. Vengeance as an instrument in the hands of the clan as a closed group promotes its expansion of power through the elimination of opposing clans and 'disruptive' individuals. It fends off threats to their continued existence, such as those posed by Chossat's denunciation and Mariani's solo endeavours. Moreover, it defends its honour and cohesion against attacks on its members, whereby this is not only a question of unity, but also of honour. The *Brise de Mer* does not hesitate to seize new territories and sources of financial income. The stronger its position, the more successfully it can win over politicians, officials, witnesses, judges, and the population to its side and operate under the protection of the *omerta*. This requires the consolidation of its position of power, which it achieves through terror, violence, threats, and intimidation: the *vendetta* is the ideal instrument for this, it is the fuel for establishing and maintaining a system in the state that is above state legality.

In contrast, the *Brise de Mer* greatly fears the *vendetta* in the hands of the individual when it seeks to satisfy individual needs regardless of clan interests. As the examples of Mariani and Chossat show, revenge as an instrument of selfish ends triggers a devastating process of collective destruction, which is responsible for the decline of the *Brise de Mer*. However, it does not mean the end of the Corsican clan system as such, which continues to be cyclically renewed, changed, and destroyed by the coming and going of new gangs and new desires for power, which profit from the law of *omerta* and complicity right up to the highest spheres of the state. As an invisible phenomenon in the shadow of state legal institutions, the *vendetta* serves this purpose well.

5.6 *A Slap in the Face* (2016) by Abbas Khider[446]

Abbas Khider was born in Baghdad in 1973. After 3 years in prison in Iraq for anti-regime activities, he went through the painful experience of being an illegal refugee in Egypt, Tunisia, Italy, Turkey and Greece,[447] until he found asylum in Germany.

---

[446] Khider (2018) (in German: *Ohrfeige* published by Hanser in Munich in 2016). For citation purposes, the sigle 'ASF' is used with the page number in the running text.

[447] El-Kaddouri (2017), pp. 39–51, here: pp. 39–40.

Julia Encke welcomes *A Slap in the Face* as the first "novel about a home for asylum seekers"[448] while Lorenz B.M. Moosmüller identifies the "struggle in the face of the harassment and obstacles of the German asylum system" as the central theme of the novel. Khider conveys "the dishonest, repressive asylum system from the perspective of an asylum seeker", the "everyday racism in German society, as well as the dishonest machinations of some asylum seekers [...]."[449]

Khider opposes "the administrative system that has turned us into strange, bored creatures. On the one side are the locals as these creatures, on the other are asylum seekers who only live in fear: First for their residence permit, then before it is revoked. And in between is the 'system'."[450] The Germans are portrayed in the novel as bored and mostly heartless figures who distance themselves from the refugees. According to Khider, this is partly due to the language barrier and partly to the dullness and exhaustion of the professional groups who constantly must deal with the refugees: "Caretakers, Caritas employees, police officers. And these people, who are constantly with the asylum seekers, are exhausted over time."[451] Who gets a residence permit at the end of a long bureaucratic, often aporetic and standardised procedure is not predictable, but a matter of luck: "There is bad luck and good luck, nothing more. The majority are unlucky, most are deported at some point. They always live in fear that their residence permit will not be extended or will be revoked. That they will lose their job and that they will be treated badly by the immigration authorities. [...] And almost everyone has these fears. Only those who eventually manage to obtain German citizenship no longer have them."[452]

According to Thomas Hummitzsch, Khider shows "in symbolic miniatures the abysses of the European asylum directives and the consequences of their hasty implementation [...]", while at the same time making it clear "that it is usually the imposed hopelessness that leads migrants into crime."[453] Those who want to integrate into the host country are prevented from doing so by "the regime that formally calls itself European immigration and asylum policy."[454] Hummitzsch sees a further difficulty in the globalised indifference of the system, which is bowing to populist and racist tendencies in Europe.[455]

In this context, *A Slap in the Face* thematises the asylum-seeking refugee using the fictional Iraqi refugee Karim Mensy, who gets caught up in the machinery of German asylum law, whose rigidity, inconsistencies, and legal uncertainty cause him to oscillate between the hope of asylum and despair over deportation without the possibility of returning to Iraq. Attempts at integration while waiting for the

---

448 Encke (2016) (internet-link in the bibliography).

449 Moosmüller (2017), p. 1.

450 Heinrich (2016) (internet-link in the bibliography).

451 Ibid.

452 Ibid. Cf. also Vertlib (2016) (internet-link in the bibliography).

453 Hummitzsch (2016) (internet-link in the bibliography).

454 Ibid.

455 Hummitzsch (2015) (internet-link in the bibliography).

official asylum decision are doomed to failure from the outset due to language barriers. All that remains is the paralysing, inactive wait for a fateful decision. The often-stubborn interpretation of the law by the official apparatus without regard for the individual human fate leads to aporias and incomprehensible decisions.[456] Instead of promoting the integration of refugees, it is, as Khider shows, on the contrary, made more difficult, if not prevented. One example of this, according to Roland Freisitzer, is the bureaucratic hurdles involved in being allowed to attend German courses at all.[457] And that's not all: "How," asks Khider in *A Slap in the Face*, "does not being able to live in my homeland or abroad affect me?"[458]

5.6.1 A Slap in the Face*: Contents*

Karim Mensy, Iraqi asylum seeker no. 3873 (ASF 4), ties Mrs Schulz, an official at the immigration office in Niederhofen an der Donau, to her office chair to force her to finally listen to him (ASF 1–11). She is one of the officials "who decide how I may or should live" (ASF 3), she is the one who destroys hopes "with the weight of your oversized stamp" (ASF 3). Mensy describes to Mrs Schulz how he was only able to flee Iraq with the assistance of the expensive services of obscure smugglers, how he ended up in Germany by chance, although he wanted to go to France, and was put in an asylum centre there. It was only through the equally obscure services of intermediaries in Munich's 'Enlil' that he was able to find undeclared work and was helped with the convoluted administrative procedures and formalities involved in obtaining a residence permit as an asylum seeker in return for payment:

> The smugglers offer everything an Iraqi in Munich – and probably in the whole of Bavaria – urgently needs: black market job announcements, details about applying for asylum, work and residence permits, information about specialist immigration lawyers, people who arrange marriages of convenience, matchmakers between girls from back home and Iraqis living in Germany, and a money transfer office (ASF 14–15).

Mensy fled Iraq because he suffered from gynaecomastia and was at risk of being persecuted as a homosexual in his home country (ASF 80–83). As an official reason to improve his chances of obtaining asylum, he claims to have insulted Saddam Hussein and his wife (ASF 101–102). After several stays and long waits in various asylum centres (Munich, Zirndorf, Bayreuth, Niederhofen an der Donau), he is recognised as a person entitled to asylum and receives a residence permit limited to 2 years and a blue passport for persons entitled to asylum and homeless people (ASF 150). Mensy's hopes of obtaining a permanent residence permit after these 2 years are dashed, however, when his asylum application is revoked after the fall of Saddam Hussein (ASF 23) on the grounds that Iraq no longer poses a threat to him. Now he

---

[456] Cf. Granzin (2019) (internet-link in the bibliography).

[457] Freisitzer (2016) (internet-link in the bibliography).

[458] Zühlsdorff (2016) (internet-link in the bibliography).

has no choice but to leave Germany and try to apply for asylum again in another country.

In the following, attention is focused on the *explicit legal discourse in the narrative* as it appears to the reader without knowledge of real-world German asylum law. Based on this legal discourse in the narrative, the evident legally relevant information is worked out and brought together to form a preliminary overall legal picture as it emerges from the text. In the second step, the asylum law currently in force in Germany is explained and contrasted with the overall legal picture.

5.6.2 On the Explicit Legal Discourse in the Diegesis

The examination of the legal discourse in *A Slap in the Face* brings to mind Jürgen Fohrmann's and Harro Müller's comparison of the discourse to an unknown game: "It looks as if the rules of an unknown game can be discovered by observing the course of the game."[459] In fact, Karim Mensy has been discovering the rules of the German asylum system in the course of his experiences since he set foot on German soil. His smugglers have told him that as soon as he encounters police officers, he should make his wish for asylum known in English (ASF 35). According to the provisions of the Common European Asylum System (CEAS), which will be discussed in more detail later, an asylum application is any form of expression indicating that the person concerned is seeking international protection.[460]

The legal discourse is gradually unfolded, supplemented, and completed in *A Slap in the Face*, following the stages of German asylum law. The latter is described very precisely in the work using the specific official vocabulary, as will be shown below. Apart from a few exceptions, such as the three-month period for leaving the country if the asylum permit is withdrawn (Art. 38 of the German Asylum Act AsylG), which will also be discussed later, there are only very minor deviations from the German asylum legislation, with which the author Abbas Khider is obviously very familiar. In *A Slap in the Face*, there is, to paraphrase Johannes Angermüller, an interplay of "'language', 'practice' and 'context',"[461] in the sense that the official language of the German asylum administration, the practical (fictitious) case of Mensy, and the wider context of the German asylum system are brought together. Khider explains and comments on the German asylum system by linking specialised legal vocabulary with the experiences of Mensy and other asylum seekers who share the same fate. In *A Slap in the Face*, the legal discourse dominates the actions and deeds of the fictional characters, whose equally fictional dialogues have the function of both illustrating and evaluating the real German asylum system. Real and diegetic legal discourse are thus very closely linked and are

[459] Fohrmann and Müller (1988), p. 16.

[460] European Asylum Support Office (2020), p. 26.

[461] Angermüller (2014), p. 25.

staged through fictional-imaginary elements, especially when it comes to uncovering inconsistencies and contradictions in the system. A vivid example of such structural inconsistencies is the difficulty for asylum seekers to obtain funded language lessons as quickly as possible to facilitate integration: this requires a full year of work in Germany (ASF 154–155), but at the same time asylum seekers are not allowed to work during the long wait for a decision on their asylum application. This sets off an aporetic cycle, as all efforts to use the long waiting times for training or qualification are cancelled out without prior language acquisition:

> To get into that college I had to sit a different exam, and to be allowed to sit that exam I needed a language certificate – the general intermediate certificate from the Goethe-Institute, which involved courses for language levels A1 to B2 [...]. Preparing for the entrance exam would therefore take at least twelve months and cost a fortune. Otherwise, I would have to work twelve months in order for the job centre to fund my language course. I could therefore have begun to study, at the earliest, three years after my Iraqi high-school diploma had been recognized. (ASF 154–155)

As is shown here, Khider's legal discourse in *A Slap in the Face* is not just limited to depicting the asylum system in the story, but as an expert on the system, he emphasises its weak points, whereby description, illustration, and criticism of the system are closely interwoven. In connection with the diegetic legal discourse, Khider, to paraphrase George Mead, uses the asylum seeker Mensy and his interactions with other asylum seekers to create a system of meaning "generated by a group of individuals participating in a social process of experience and behaviour."[462] This involves the way in which asylum seekers communicate about the asylum system, advise each other, and exchange information, as the following example shows when Rafid, a flatmate in the asylum centre, explains to Mensy:

> You'll never get a residence permit if they find out you are here because you deserted. You'll get a temporary stay of deportation. That status does allow you to live outside the hostel, but you'll be tied to Bayreuth and you will not be allowed to travel, study or work. If you do not want a residence permit, then be truthful. (ASF 62)

Similarly, another asylum seeker, Zacharias, explains to Mensy what arguments he can use to improve his chances of being granted asylum:

> You have six options if you want to convince the judge. Either you have done something against the regime and they are hunting you, or you are a Christian, a communist, a member of a Shiite party, a homosexual or belong to a minority. There are no other options for an Iraqi'. (ASF 95)

Khider's good knowledge of the German asylum system is reflected in the story; the fiction serves not only to explain the asylum system but also to scrutinise it.

With this in mind, Karim Mensy asks Mrs Schulz from the Foreigners' Registration Office why no one is concerned about his difficulties with his residence permit, the Foreigners' Registration Office, the Federal Criminal Agency, the Federal Intelligence Service, the Office for the Protection of the Constitution (ASF 11) and the Federal Office for Migration and Refugees (ASF 54) and how he is

[462] Keller (2013), p. 40.

supposed to know "how does not being able to live in my homeland or abroad affect me?" (ASF 11).

After Mensy must get out of the lorry transporting him somewhere in Germany, even though he wants to travel to his uncle in France, he hurries to the nearest train station and is asked by the police there to identify himself. As he has no passport, the handcuffs click (ASF 41), and he is taken to the Dachau police station (ASF 38). After his personal details have been recorded, he must strip stark naked in an adjoining room and is examined down to his most intimate parts (ASF 36–37). Signatures, photographs, and fingerprints follow (ASF 37). His five-hundred-dollar note is withheld as a fine for illegal presence on German soil (ASF 43; 50). He is locked in a prison cell (ASF 38–39) and a few days later, he is first taken to an asylum centre in Munich and then to Zirndorf, as Munich is overcrowded (ASF 43). His belongings are returned to him and his handcuffs are removed, but he is only allowed to apply for asylum in Germany, i.e. in the country where he was apprehended (ASF 43–44). He is given a ticket to travel from Zirndorf to another asylum centre in Bayreuth (ASF 50). There he " had to go to the administrative office for questioning" (ASF 61), where he was given a so-called 'identity card. [...] This was a document confirming that I had a three-month residence permit. It was a green, oblong document bearing my photo and personal details" (ASF 61). He also must appear at an appointment on 21 February 2001 at 8:30 a.m. (ASF 99) at the Federal Office for Migration and Refugees for "a hearing for an asylum application" (ASF 99) to check if he qualifies "for asylum, if you are a refugee as defined by the Geneva Refugee Convention or if there are other obstacles to deportation" (ASF 61). The aim is to convince the judge that, on the one hand it is impossible to return home and, on the other, that Germany is the first country of asylum (ASF 64). A fellow resident of the Bayreuth asylum centre, Rafid, summarises the legal situation for Mensy, as already mentioned, by listing the valid grounds for asylum (ASF 95). The hearing lasts 80 min and Mensy must answer 40 questions on four categories—person, reasons for asylum, travel route, other—with the help of an interpreter (ASF 100–105). While waiting for the court's decision, he is not allowed to accept any work apart from an 'integration job' with an hourly wage of one mark (ASF 145).

After several months, Mensy's application is granted, and he receives a blue passport for homeless people and asylum seekers (ASF 150) and a residence permit limited to 2 years (ASF 150). One month after receiving the decision, Mensy must leave the asylum centre and look for a flat and a job (ASF 151). As a temporary solution, he applies to the social welfare office and receives a room in a homeless shelter and three hundred and eighty marks a month (ASF 153–154). However, to be able to study in Germany, he needs to "attend a college for a year and sit the equivalent German exams" (ASF 154), as his Iraqi school leaving certificate is not recognised equivalent to the German *Abitur*. To do this, however, he needs proof of language level B2 in German and, to receive funding for a German course from the German labour office, he must have worked for at least 1 year (ASF 154–155). After the attack on the New York Twin Towers on 11 September 2001, however, his job search is made even more difficult (ASF 158–160) and Mensy is summoned twice, for no particular reason, to an interview with the criminal investigation department, where he has to answer numerous questions, including whether he has contacts with Al-Qaeda or any of the other 44 terrorist organisations (ASF 161–163).

After the fall of Saddam Hussein, Mensy even had his asylum application revoked and was told to return to his home country immediately (ASF 23). With the help of a lawyer, he obtains a two-month extension to gain time (ASF 25–26). At the end of this period, his blue asylum seeker passport is taken away and he receives a toleration document that restricts his freedom of movement to a radius of 30 km around his place of residence—"'mandatory residence'" (ASF 54)—and is also only an intermediate stage before deportation: "Your residence permit will soon be over. Your asylum seeker passport will then also be taken away from you. After that, the best you'll get is a tolerated stay permit, and you won't be allowed to travel more than thirty kilometres from Niederhofen. All this is only done so that you can be deported later" (ASF 24). In this situation, he ultimately has no choice but to try to apply for asylum in another country, contract an expensive fictitious marriage, or marry a local woman (ASF 26).

This depiction of the legal discourse on asylum and immigration in *A Slap in the Face* is now contrasted in the following chapter with the real-life German asylum law, whereby attention is selectively focused on the issues that Abbas Khider particularly addresses in his novel.

5.6.3 *Counterfactual Contrast: German Asylum Legislation vs Legal Discourse in Diegesis*

As with the previous counterfactual analyses, the factuality of the law must also be established here in order to enable the counterfactual contrast between real and fictional asylum law.[463] It has already been mentioned several times that law, unlike literature, must fulfil the task of regulating concrete facts, i.e. it must be valid and effective in order to have a practical effect, although for our purpose, I remember, it is its validity that is decisive.

This requirement gives rise to the imperative of legal facticity, which, as Habermas emphasises, is artificially created by the positive setting of norms in conjunction with the enforceability of these norms.[464]

5.6.3.1 Factuality of German Asylum Law

It is worth recalling Habermas' concept of the 'artificially produced facticity' of law: "For an empirical approach, the validity of positive law is in the first instance characterized tautologically, in that the law is considered to be whatever acquires

[463] See Sect. 3.4 on Counterfactuality.

[464] Cf. Habermas (1996), p. 50.

the force of law on the basis of legally valid procedures [...]."[465] If one applies Habermas' criteria of positive-artificial legal production to German asylum law, legal facticity, in this sense, is based on three hierarchically organised levels, namely the international level (Geneva Refugee Convention [GRC] and associated protocols), the European level (CEAS), and the national level (German Asylum Act). In this context, it should be recalled one last time that norms are only effective if, to paraphrase Georg Jellinek, they emanate from external authority and their binding nature is guaranteed by external powers.[466] With this in mind, it must first be clarified how international and European norms can develop their effect under German law. This is done through the ratification procedure in accordance with section 59, al. 1 of the German Basic Law (GG): "Treaties that affect the legislative powers of the Bundestag or relate to subjects of federal legislation require the approval of the Federal Government and the Bundestag as well as the federal states in accordance with section 77 GG." According to this fundamental provision, the ratification of international treaties requires the consent of the *Bundestag*, the approval of the *Bundesrat*, and the signature of the *Federal President*. Only after the ratification procedure has been completed, the ratification act has been published, and the ratified treaty has been deposited do international treaty norms take effect in German law.[467] This is how the 1954 Geneva Convention on Refugees, which is of particular interest here, was ratified by Germany. As far as the Common European Asylum Law (CEAS) and the associated European directives and regulations are concerned, these are directly binding for all contracting states of the European Union from their publication in the EU Official Journal and must be transposed into national law within a certain period (usually 2 years). For Germany, the legally binding nature of the European standards in national law results from the series of binding EU directives of the CEAS.[468] To paraphrase Hans Kelsen, the factual-normative 'being'[469] of European asylum law can be derived from this, which stands hierarchically above national law. In contrast, the factual-normative 'being' of German asylum law results from the German legislative process and the promulgation of the law on 2 September 2008 (BGBl. I p. 1789), last amended by the Returns Improvement Act of 21 February 2024 (BGBl. I No. 54).

5.6.3.2 Counterfactual Contrast

According to these international, European and national provisions, German asylum law is based on three pillars, which are arranged hierarchically as follows: 1. international agreements, 2. the German Basic Law, and 3. the German Asylum Act.

---

[465] Ibid., p. 29.

[466] Jellinek (1921), p. 333.

[467] JuraForum (2024) (internet-ink in the bibliography).

[468] Directive 2013/32/EU, Directive 2013/33/EU, Regulation (EU) N. 604/2013, Regulation (EU) N. 2024/1347.

[469] Cf. Jellinek (1921), pp. 333–337.

According to the wording of section. 1, A al. 2 of the "Convention Relating to the Status of Refugees" (Geneva Refugee Convention, GRC) of 28 July 1951, refugee status is granted to any person who.

> owing to a well-founded fear of being persecuted [my underlining] for reasons of race, religion, nationality, membership of a particular social group or political opinion, is outside the country of his nationality and is unable or, owing to such fear, is unwilling to avail himself of the protection of that country; or who, being stateless, is outside the country of his habitual residence as a result of such events and is unable or, owing to such fear, is unwilling to return to it.[470]

The *well-founded fear* of persecution implies a subjective and objective assessment of refugee status. The subjective element requires the assessment of the asylum application to take the personal situation of the asylum seeker into account:

> Personal reasons, the applicant's family background, his membership of a particular racial, religious, national, social or political group, his own assessment of his situation, his personal experiences – in other words, anything that might indicate that the decisive motive for his application is fear. However, the fear must be justified. But even exaggerated fear can be justified if, judging by the circumstances of the case, such a state of mind can be regarded as justified.[471]

Subjectively justified reasons for the fear of persecution can also include future fears due to the legal handling, experiences of others or individual characteristics, the experience of life-impairing discrimination or a strong feeling of insecurity:[472]

> These fears do not necessarily have to be based on the applicant's own personal experiences. From what happened to his friends and relatives and other members of his race or social group, for example, it can be concluded that his fear that he too will sooner or later become a victim of persecution is well-founded. The laws of his home country and, above all, the way in which they are applied are of importance here. The individual's situation must be assessed according to the circumstances that apply only to him. The possibility of being persecuted is probably greater for a known person than for an unknown person. All these factors, i.e. a person's character, background, influence, wealth or character, may justify the conclusion that his fear of persecution is well-founded.[473]

The objective element requires the assessment of the actual political and legal situation in the country of origin as a credibility factor for the justification of the fear of personal persecution: "Knowledge of the conditions in the applicant's home country can, in any case, be an important factor in assessing the applicant's credibility."[474]

In *A Slap in the Face*, Mensy can claim both subjective and objective reasons for fear: The subjective reasons certainly include his suffering from gynaecomastia, which, due to the false assumption of homosexuality, exposes him to persecution not only by the Iraqi state but also by Iraqi society: "endowed with both a magnificent penis and an ample bosom. […] Back then in Baghdad I was also afraid that

[470] UNHCR Austria (2003), p. 11.

[471] Ibid., p. 13.

[472] Cf. ibid., pp. 15–16.

[473] Ibid., p. 13.

[474] Ibid.

local lads would rape me if they ever discovered that I was half woman" (ASF 80). The objective reasons for Mensy's fear stem from Saddam Hussein's dictatorship and political persecution. The fact of having already been a victim of persecution can be seen as an additional plausibility of the fear of persecution.[475] The GRC defines persecution as a "threat to life or freedom [...] on account of [...] race, religion, nationality", undesirable political beliefs, or membership of a social group.[476]

Persecution may be based cumulatively on several of the grounds listed in section 1 A, al. 2 of the Refugee Convention (race, religion, nationality, membership of a social group, political opinion) or on just one of these grounds. Furthermore, an application for asylum can only be made if the applicants are outside their country of origin at the time of application:

> A general requirement for obtaining refugee status is that the applicant in possession of a nationality must be outside the country of that nationality. There are no exceptions to this rule. International protection cannot be granted if a person is under the territorial sovereignty of their home country.[477]

According to section 16a of the German Basic Law (GG), politically persecuted persons are entitled to asylum in Germany if they can prove that they are being politically persecuted in their country of origin or can expect inhuman or degrading punishment or treatment there. If these conditions are not (or are no longer) met, the asylum seeker may be refused asylum, or the decision of asylum may be withdrawn. The legislator can also determine those countries of origin whose nationals are not granted asylum due to the favourable or protective legal situation.

Mensy faces such humiliating treatment in addition to persecution and punishment in Iraq, where he must hide his gynaecomastia under difficult circumstances: "I still couldn't bring myself to tell her my problem. [...] Swimming baths became a total no-go zone for me. [...] I'm still plagued by a constant fear of men beating, humiliating or raping me, and of being mocked or considered disgusting by women" (ASF 81–83). Mensy is particularly afraid of the upcoming military service, where there is a risk of being humiliated and sexually abused as '*al-Arif*' because of his breasts (ASF 83).

If, on the one hand, the contracting states of the GRC are obliged to grant asylum protection if the necessary conditions are met, they also have the option of withdrawing this protection from the asylum seeker as soon as it is no longer justified due to new factors.In certain cases, the granting of asylum can be revoked in accordance with section 1 C of the Refugee Convention if the circumstances due to which the protection of the country of origin was guaranteed no longer apply.[478] However, the situation of refugees who can invoke "compelling reasons based on past persecution" (Art. 1C (6), 2) and who cannot reasonably be expected to return despite

[475] Ibid., p. 14.

[476] Ibid., p. 15.

[477] Ibid., pp. 23–24.

[478] Ibid., pp. 30–31.

changed circumstances in their country of origin always precludes the withdrawal of asylum protection. With this clause, the GRC refers to the.

> situation of a person who has suffered very severe persecution in the past and whose refugee status is not necessarily terminated, even if fundamental changes have taken place in their country of origin. […] It is often argued that a person who has suffered particularly severe persecution – or whose family has suffered particularly severe persecution – cannot be expected to return to the country in question. Even if there has been a change of regime in the country in question, this does not always mean a complete change in the attitude of the population, nor does it mean, in view of past experiences, that the mental state of the refugee has completely changed.[479]

In *A Slap in the Face*, Mensy's right to asylum is revoked on the grounds that Saddam Hussein has been overthrown by the US army, and he can now safely return to his home country (ASF 23). However, the fall of Hussein in no way means the end of the dangers, because even if Iraq is no longer formally a dictatorship, the country is still in chaos, as Mensy explains in *A Slap in the Face*: "Bombs are exploding every day. Armies from around the globe and loyalists to Saddam are shooting each other to bits. […] Iraq isn't a state anymore; it's the scene of a battle between the major powers and a bunch of fanatics" (ASF 24). In *A Slap in the Face*, the German authorities' revocation of the right to asylum is based solely on the fall of Hussein, without taking the real conditions in Iraq into account, which continue to pose a threat to Mensy. It is especially important to emphasise that the basic attitude of Iraqi society towards alleged homosexuality—even if it is only apparent in Mensy's case—does not change overnight because of political upheaval, and thus, Mensy still must fear punishment and humiliation and cannot return to his country. In this context, it must therefore be pointed out that the German authorities failed to comply with section 1C (6), 2 GRC, according to which they should have taken Mensy's special situation into account. Above all, it should have been considered that the attitude of the Iraqi population towards homosexuality as a cultural factor does not change merely because of political upheaval. In addition, other factors determining Mensy's individual situation should have been considered, such as his financial inability to escape the risk of persecution as a homosexual through surgery and the ongoing life-threatening situation in Iraq due to the violent and chaotic state of war. While the Geneva Convention (GRC) and its Protocol from 31 January 1967[480] set out the criteria for determining the definition of a refugee under international law, the form and details of the asylum procedure are left to the respective contracting states. In this context, the Office of the United Nations High Commissioner for Refugees (UNHCR[481]) emphasises the need for a humane, understanding and competent handling of the asylum procedure:

---

479 Ibid., p. 37.

480 Convention relating to the Status of Refugees ("Geneva Refugee Convention"), United Nations, Treaty Series, vol. 189, 28 July 1951; amended by the Protocol relating to the Status of Refugees, United Nations, Treaty Series, vol. 606, 31 January 1967.

481 UNHCR = United Nations High Commissioner for Refugees.

> It should never be forgotten that someone seeking to be recognised as a refugee is in a particularly vulnerable position. Not only are they in a foreign environment, [but] they may also have to contend with considerable technical and psychological difficulties when they have to present their case to the authorities of a foreign country – very often in a foreign language. Their application should therefore be processed by qualified officials who have the necessary knowledge and experience as well as an understanding of the difficulties and needs of the applicant.[482]

The appeal to understanding the individual situation of the asylum seeker stands out here in particular. This also includes the prohibition of expulsion or refoulement of the refugees if this would threaten their life or freedom on the grounds of section. 1, A al. 2 GRC.

In *A Slap in the Face*, Khider highlights the lack of humanity and individualisation in the processing of asylum applications. Asylum seekers are not treated as people, but as numbers, as Mensy bitterly states: "For you I was asylum seeker 3873 or something. Worth no more than the numbers I had to take, then sit and wait" (ASF 4). The individual situation of the asylum seeker must take a back seat to the administrative rigidity that destroys any hope of human understanding: "It was a pointless wait, which I only put up with because I hoped I'd be understood and given a chance" (ASF 4).

The binding nature of the Geneva Convention on Refugees for the Member States of the European Union is clearly emphasised in Article 78 of the Treaty on the Functioning of the European Union (TFEU):[483] "In accordance with Article 78(1) TFEU, the common policy on asylum, subsidiary protection and temporary protection must be in conformity with the Geneva Convention relating to the Status of Refugees and the Protocol of 31 January 1967 and 'other relevant treaties'."[484] This is also emphasised in recital 3 of the EU[485] Reception Directive of 26 June 2013: "The European Council agreed […] to work towards a Common European Asylum System (CEAS) based on the full and inclusive application of the Geneva Convention […], […] in order to respect the principle of non-refoulement (Art. 33 GRC)"[486] and the prohibition of punishment for illegal entry (Art. 31 GRC) is taken into account in the run-up to formal recognition of asylum.[487]

In *A Slap in the Face*, however, this prohibition of punishment is not considered in any way, as the German police officers detain Mensy when they check him at the railway station and retain his $500 note as punishment for illegal entry (ASF 43; 50). He could have avoided this penalty if he had reported to the police immediately

[482] UNHCR Österreich, *Handbuch*, p. 55.

[483] Treaty on the Functioning of the European Union (TFEU). Official Journal of the European Union, C 326/49, 26.10.2012.

[484] European Asylum Support Office (2020), p. 22.

[485] EU: European Union.

[486] Directive 2013/33/EU of the European Parliament and of the Council laying down standards for the reception of applicants for international protection, 26.06.2013. This directive is binding for all EU states, except for Denmark.

[487] European Asylum Support Office (2020), p. 22.

after entering German territory (ASF 43), but he had no opportunity to do so, as he had been forced to get out of the lorry transporting him on German soil at an unknown location without prior notice. This shows a certain inconsistency in the German asylum system, as it is impossible in practice for refugees to apply for asylum without already being in the country of destination, even if only to go from the place of arrival to the nearest police station, as in Mensy's case. Asylum seekers not only face penalties for illegal immigration but above all deportation from the country of destination. The CEAS is committed to the principle of non-refoulement, which prohibits the Member States of the EU from returning refugees "to a country where they face persecution." Its scope of application also extends to asylum seekers "as long as no final decision has been taken on their application."[488]

As indicated, the revocation of asylum recognition puts Mensy in an impossible situation: he is not allowed to stay in Germany but must continue to expect persecution in Iraq and has no certainty of being granted asylum in another country. From this point of view, the confiscation of the German asylum passport is in practice tantamount to an unlawful return, which does not do justice to Mensy's individual subjective and objective situation. In *A Slap in the Face*, Mensy's aporetic situation is summarised in the question of "how does not being able to live in my homeland or abroad affect me?" (ASF 11).

Another supranational source of law that is binding for the EU Member States is the European Convention on Human Rights (ECHR). Its legally binding nature for Germany, as for the other contracting states, is set out in section 6, al. 3 of the Treaty on European Union (TEU): "Fundamental rights, as guaranteed by the European Convention for the Protection of Human Rights and Fundamental Freedoms and as they result from the constitutional traditions common to the Member States, shall constitute general principles of the law of the Union."[489] Further obligations arise for Germany from the Charter of Fundamental Rights of the European Union (EU Charter), particularly concerning the provisions on human dignity (Art. 1 EU Charter), the prohibition of torture and inhuman punishment (Art. 4 EU Charter), the right to liberty and security (Art. 6 EU Charter), and the right to non-discrimination (EU Charter 21).[490]

The CEAS was created with the aim of establishing a minimum standard of reception conditions for asylum seekers for all EU Member States, which—in accordance with the provisions of the ECHR and the EU Charter for a Decent Life—should ensure comparable conditions throughout the EU. The practical and legal implementation of the CEAS is based on three EU directives and two EU regulations[491] to standardise the asylum procedure in the EU by establishing

[488] European Union Agency for Fundamental Rights (2016), p. 1.

[489] Rudolf Streinz (ed.), EUV/AEUV. *Vertrag über die Europäische Union und Vertrag über die Arbeitsweise der Europäischen Union*, Munich: C.H. Beck 2012 (2nd ed.), Art. 6.

[490] Charter of Fundamental Rights of the European Union, 26.10.2012 (C 326/391).

[491] Directive 2013/33/ ('EU Reception Directive'), Directive 2011/95/EU ('EU Qualification Directive'), Directive 2013/32/EU ('EU Asylum Procedures Directive'), EU Regulation No. 604/2013 ('Dublin III Regulation') and EU Regulation 603/2013 ('Eurodac II Regulation').

common minimum standards (Qualification Directive, Reception Directive), harmonising the conditions for granting and withdrawing refugee status (Asylum Procedures Directive), determining the state responsible for the asylum procedure (Dublin III Regulation), and setting up an electronic archive for comparing fingerprints (Eurodac Regulation). These minimum standards for asylum seekers are measured against an adequate standard of living that guarantees a livelihood and the protection of physical and mental health (Art. 17, al. 2 Directive 2013/33/EU).[492]

According to section 13, al. 2 of the Dublin III Regulation (V-V), an asylum application must be submitted in the Member State "responsible for the irregular border crossing of a third-country national into the EU."[493] This is intended to avoid conflicts of responsibility between Member States and multiple applications in several Member States. As Daniele Saracino explains, the aim is to prevent "secondary movements [...] by asylum seekers travelling from one Member State, where they should have lodged their application, to another."[494] In accordance with this provision, Mensy must and may only apply for asylum in Germany (ASF 43–44), as this is the first time he has illegally set foot on European soil, even if he would have preferred to travel to France to see his uncle. To effectively prevent multiple applications, the D-III Regulation is linked to the Eurodac II Regulation (E-II Regulation), which establishes a common database in which Member States are obliged to store the personal data and fingerprints of all migrants over the age of 14.[495] With this in mind, Mensy's fingerprints are taken at the police station in Dachau as soon as he sets foot on German soil (ASF 37).

Contrary to this principle of responsibility for the initial application, section 17 D-III-V allows another Member State to examine the asylum application, even if it is not originally responsible, provided it is informed by the Member State previously responsible. In this sense, Mensy, who is ultimately on German soil against his will, would be entitled to apply for asylum in France based on family ties in accordance with section 17 (2) D-III-V.

The European minimum standard of the CEAS comes into operation as soon as the person seeking protection applies for asylum, whereby "any act by which the wish to obtain international protection is expressed in any way to any authority"[496] is considered an asylum application. Mensy expresses this immediately when he is checked by the police at Dachau station: "I am from Iraq. Seeking asylum. Asylum, please" (ASF 35).

---

[492] According to attempts of a more precise interpretation, an 'adequate standard of living' includes access to necessary food, clothing, housing (centres, private houses, flats, hotels, etc.; section 18 Directive 2013/33/EU), to medical examinations and social services, and receipt of vouchers or cash benefits (section 2, letter g Directive 2013/33/EU).

[493] Saracino (2019), p. 102.

[494] Ibid., p. 103.

[495] Ibid., pp. 103–104.

[496] European Asylum Support Office (2020), p. 26.

As long as the applicants have not received a legally binding decision on their application, they will benefit from international protection.[497] Within 15 days, the applicants must be informed of the benefits and obligations and of the persons and organisations providing advice in a language they understand (Art. 5 Directive 2013/33/EU).

Following this labarinthine process, Mensy is assigned to an asylum centre in Bayreuth and receives a so-called "identity card" in the administration office, which "confirms a three-month residence permit" (ASF 61) as well as a note with the date on which he is to appear for an official hearing to determine the validity of his asylum application (ASF 61; ASF 99). He does not receive any further information.

In the period between the submission of the application and the final decision on the asylum application, the applicant must be granted freedom of movement within the territory of the host Member State (Art. 7, al. 1 Directive 2013/33/EU), irrespective of any residence requirement.

Section 15 of the Directive 2013/33/EU also stipulates that applicants should be granted access to the labour market and vocational training after 9 months of residence at the latest, even if they are still awaiting a decision on their asylum application (Art. 16 Directive 2013/33/EU). Contrary to this, Mensy in *A Slap in the Face* is not granted access to regular work even after a nine-month waiting period but is only entitled to an 'integration job' with an hourly wage of one "deutschmark" (ASF 145).

When examining asylum applications, the individual situation of the applicant must be considered, in accordance with international legal sources, considering the actual situation in the country of origin (Art. 10 Directive 2013/32/EU). A personal interview with the applicant must precede the decision by the competent authority (Art. 14 Directive 2013/32/EU). In *A Slap in the Face*, Mensy is interviewed for 80 min at the Federal Office for Migration and Refugees with the help of an interpreter and must answer 40 questions (ASF 99–100).

In the event of refusal or revocation of the grant of asylum, the Member State concerned must ensure that the applicants do not face a risk to life and liberty in their country of origin on grounds of race, religion, nationality, membership of a particular social group, or political opinion (Art. 38 Directive 2013/32/EU), whereby the competent authority must rely on information from EASO, UNHCR, the Council of Europe, and other relevant international organisations to assess the situation in the country of origin (Art. 37 Directive 2013/32/EU). In other words, a pragmatic and realistic assessment of the 'safe' country of origin is sought. As already noted, in *A Slap in the Face* this assessment is done very superficially in the case of Iraq, as it is limited solely to the fact of Saddam Hussein's overthrow.

Section 16a of the German Basic Law (GG) expressly recognises the right to asylum for politically persecuted persons in concordance with international agreements and conventions, whereby a list of 'safe' countries can be drawn up on a legal basis. German asylum law essentially follows international and European

[497] Ibid., pp. 29–31.

guidelines in this respect, albeit with certain deviations and restrictions, especially since 1993. As Klaus Behnam Shad emphasises, the unrestricted German right of asylum following the original section 16 al. 2 GG of 1949 has developed into a restrictive right of asylum with the current section 16a GG since 1993. The reason for this was the massive increase in the number of refugees in the 1990s, which led to outbreaks of violence, as shown by the attacks on asylum centres in Mölln and Rostock-Lichtenhagen.[498] These past experiences characterise the spirit of current German asylum legislation, which now tends towards a more restrictive stance, in that recognition of refugee status can be refused or revoked even if the asylum seekers are not in danger in at least part of their country of origin[499] (Art. 3e AsylG). The right to asylum is therefore essentially limited to persons who must fear for life and limb everywhere in their country of origin. In line with this criterion, the list of safe countries of origin was expanded to include the Balkan states, Ghana, and Senegal (Art. 29a AsylG). Behnam Shad criticises this approach for being abstract criteria that do not necessarily correspond to reality, as people from these countries could still be politically persecuted in individual cases. Such categorical and standardised generalisations are indeed problematic and are clearly addressed in *A Slap in the Face*, where the overthrow of Saddam Hussein justifies the expulsion of Mensy from Germany which is even more incomprehensible since Iraq is still not on the list of safe countries.

In line with these tightening trends, since the adoption of the German asylum acceleration package on 23 October 2015, rejected asylum applications can lead to more effective and faster deportation of the applicant without a deadline being specified.[500]Asylum applications are decided on by the Federal Office for Migration and Refugees (Art. 5 AsylG) or a branch office of the same that is assigned to the foreigner's reception centre (Art. 14 AsylG). The officials at these branch offices process the applications, conduct the hearings, and issue the decisions, usually through the same person.[501] It is precisely this personal union that Ms Schulz embodies in *A Slap in the Face*, as Mensy ironically states: "That must be because you are in charge of everything that makes our lives easier or tougher: residence permits, identity cards, work, deportation decisions, pocket money – eighty euros, later reduced to the forty – and doctor's certificates" (ASF 136).

In many municipalities, the entire spectrum of immigration law (issuing and extending residence permits, tolerated stay permits, expulsions, deportations, employment permits, and integration courses) is handled by the municipal immigration authorities (ABHen).[502] The police officer, who recognises the foreigner as an

[498] Lüthke and Müller (2014), pp. 125–133, here: pp. 126–128.

[499] The German Asylum Act was last amended on 21 February 2024 (BGBl. No. 54).

[500] Wissenschaftliche Dienste des Deutschen Bundestags, "Änderungen des Asyl- und Aufenthaltsgesetzes seit Januar 2015 mit den Schwerpunkten Asylpaket I und II.", *Deutscher Bundestag*, WD – 3000 - 018/16, 21.1.2016, pp. 7–8 (internet-link in the bibliography). Cf. Asylverfahrensbeschleunigungsgesetz, 20.10.2015, BGBl. I 2015, 1722.

[501] Lahusen et al. (2022), pp. 174–247, here: p. 174.

[502] Bogumil et al. (2023), pp. 37–175, here: p. 108.

asylum seeker, must officially take them in and forward them to the responsible reception centre (asylum centre) (Art. 19 AsylG). This also happens to Mensy, who, after being arrested by the police in Dachau, is taken to the asylum centre in Munich, which is unable to take him in due to overcrowding (ASF 54–55).

Except for special cases, the asylum seekers must be heard in person before a decision is made on their application (Art. 24 AsylG), whereby the period up to the decision on the asylum application may not exceed 18 months (Art. 24 AsylG). During this time, asylum seekers are exempt from the requirement of a residence permit (Art. 55 AsylG) but are obliged to live in the asylum centre assigned to them (Art. 47 AsylG) and are restricted in their freedom of movement to the district of the responsible immigration authority (Art. 56 AsylG). In *A Slap in the Face*, Mensy is interviewed by the Federal Office for Migration and Refugees (ASF 105) and waits in the asylum centre in Bayreuth for the asylum decision.

During the first 6 months of waiting for the asylum decision, no gainful employment may be carried out (Art. 61 AsylG), unless with the express permission of the Federal Employment Agency or in state or municipal institutions serving the public interest for a fee of 80 cents per hour (Art. 5 AsylbLG). In deviation from German asylum legislation, Mensy may work a maximum of 80 h per month at an hourly wage of one mark (ASF 145).

According to the Asylum Seekers' Benefits Act (AsylbLG), asylum seekers receive food, accommodation, heating, clothing, healthcare, and household consumer goods to cover their needs (Art. 3 AsylbLG). Mensy in *A Slap in the Face* receives the most necessary clothing (ASF 57), food (ASF 49), and pocket money (ASF 50). In addition, there is a monthly allowance of 204 euros for single adults (Art. 3a AsylbLG) to cover personal needs if the asylum seeker does not live in an asylum centre.

If the asylum application is rejected, the deadline for leaving the country is 30 days, which is extended by a further 30 days in the event of an appeal. If asylum that has already been granted is revoked, the deadline for voluntary departure is 3 months (Art. 38 AsylA). With the help of a lawyer, Mensy manages to extend his deadline to 2 months before leaving the country (ASF 33), but not to 3 months, as stipulated in Art. 38 AsylG for persons who have already been granted asylum once. At the end of this two-month period, Mensy must hand in his blue asylum passport (ASF 25).

The granting of asylum can be revoked if the circumstances that justified the asylum application cease to exist significantly and permanently so that the foreigner's fear of persecution can no longer be considered well-founded (Art. 73 AsylG). In *A Slap in the Face*, as already mentioned several times, Mensy's grant of asylum is revoked on the grounds that since the removal of Saddam Hussein's dictatorship, the situation in Iraq is no longer dangerous for him and there is no compelling reason for him to remain in Germany (ASF 23).

The German immigration authority's decision to revoke Mensy's asylum authorisation could be based on an incorrect interpretation of international and national asylum law if one considers its wording: According to the GRC, an asylum seeker cannot be expected to return to his or her home country despite changed circumstances if it can be assumed that the basic attitude of the population has not changed despite a change of regime and the asylum seeker's psychological state of fear due to past experiences remains.[503] As indicated, the GRC refers to subjective and objective reasons for fear.[504]

When the Federal Office for Migration and Refugees in *A Slap in the Face* solely focuses on the fact that with the fall of Saddam Hussein, all Mensy's fears and anxieties have been dispelled and he can safely return to his home country, it ignores the fact that on the one hand, the hostile attitude of the population towards the suspicion of homosexuality and, on the other hand, the ongoing state of war in Iraq renders a return to Iraq by no means safe for Mensy.

The CEAS is based on the full and comprehensive application of the GRC, which means that the principle of non-refoulement (Art. 33 GRC) must be upheld by the national legislation of the European Member States. In this sense, according to section 38 of Directive 2013/32/EU, each Member State must ensure that the asylum seekers do not face a threat to life and liberty in their country of origin due to race, religion, nationality, membership of a particular social group, or political opinion. As emphasised earlier, section 3e of the German Asylum Act restricts this principle in that an asylum seeker can already be deported if there is no longer any danger in at least part of their country of origin.

Despite domestic tightening, German asylum legislation remains committed to the spirit of the GRC and the CEAS, and thus it can be argued that the immigration authorities in Mensy's case did not carefully consider his previous experiences or the subjective (gynaecomastia, risk of being arrested as a homosexual; ASF 80–83; 85) and objective (state of war) elements. If one follows Fikentscher's *case-norm theory*, the immigration office has by no means 'ascended and descended' in the sense of Gadamer's hermeneutic circle between norm and fact until it is certain that norm and fact correspond.[505] For a standard-compliant interpretation and application, it would have had to examine Mensy's personal reasons, his family background, his membership in a particular social group, his own assessment of the situation and his personal experiences, as required by the GRC.[506] The omission of this hermeneutic endeavour neglects the meaning and purpose of the prohibition of return as a core element of the CEAS,[507] which aims to ensure that asylum seekers are not exposed to physically or psychologically justified fear.

To summarise, it should be noted that the legal discourse in *A Slap in the Face* is almost congruent with German asylum law. Abbas Khider's knowledge of the German asylum system is evidently fuelled by his own experience as a former asylum seeker when he traces Mensy's path as an asylum seeker accidentally and involuntarily abandoned on German soil in the light of international, European, and

---

503 UNHCR Österreich. *Handbuch*, p. 37.

504 Ibid., p. 13.

505 See Fikentscher (1977), pp. 201–202.

506 UNHCR Österreich. *Handbuch*, p. 13.

507 Möllers (2023), p. 182.

German asylum legislation. In doing so, he makes use of the relevant legal vocabulary, whereby the legal episteme in *A Slap in the Face* is clearly discursively constituted: The text conveys and explains the German asylum system using the case of 'Mensy' and in this way develops a legal-literary 'case history' for the purpose of illustrating the real law.

Khider's main aim is to use this 'case' to highlight the gaps and inconsistencies in the German system, which make the integration of asylum seekers considerably more difficult, and to highlight the disregard for the core principle of non-refoulement on which the CEAS is based. Khider's text also emphasises the hermeneutical fuzziness in the interpretation of the GRC and the CEAS in German law, where the German authorities rely solely on the fact that Saddam Hussein was overthrown to withdraw Mensy's right to asylum. Such a simplistic interpretation of the law bears witnesses to the dangers of human subjectivity on the one hand and to Germany's endeavour to interpret international and European asylum law very restrictively on the other. The hermeneutic vagueness of the literature is combined here with possible vagueness in the subjective interpretation of the law, which, however, has no practical consequences in the literature, while in law it can sometimes have fatal consequences for the person concerned.

As the Mensy case in *A Slap in the Face* shows, the hasty transposition of European asylum directives into national law can lead to inconsistencies in the practical application of the law if the requirement of a teleological and humane interpretation of the law is not considered. In this sense, the application of German asylum law in *A Slap in the Face* appears on the one hand to be misappropriated, as it prevents rather than promotes the integration of asylum seekers, and on the other hand, the individual situation is not adequately subsumed under the abstract norm. Gadamer's hermeneutic circle as a meaningful aid to interpretation does not appear to have any practical application here if asylum seekers are denied the opportunity to learn German, work, or study during the long waiting time for an asylum decision which often exceeds 1 year.

The demand for a humane and individualised interpretation of the criteria that decide on a possible revocation of the granting of asylum is also not met in the Mensy case if the international texts and the UNHCR guidelines are interpreted incorrectly in grammatical and teleological terms. Grammatically, the semantics of the word 'fear' in relation to the individual case is neglected: instead of solely relying on the fact that Iraq is no longer ruled by Saddam Hussein, the German authorities should have considered the meaning of individual fear in Mensy's specific situation, i.e. the fact that the fall of Hussein by no means ended the war in Iraq, and especially the fact that Mensy would still be persecuted in his home country because of his gynaecomastia. In this sense, the hasty interpretation of the refoulement criteria, which is due to the rigidity of the authorities, does not do justice to the subjective or objective significance of the fear of persecution in his home country.

In *A Slap in the Face*, Germany's endeavours to simplify and speed up the deportation of asylum seekers as much as possible (Art. 3e AsylG; asylum acceleration package) become clear, and this is at the expense of the humane assessment of individual human destinies. Literary fiction creates the fictional fate of Mensy to emphasise the real asylum law and its weaknesses more clearly. Contrastive analysis between diegetic and factual law reveals only very slight deviations here, as Khider constitutes the legal discourse in *A Slap in the Face* very faithfully and thus clearly highlights the discursive and hermeneutic points of intersection between literature and law. Literature that deals with positive law, as in *A Slap in the Face*, does not have a law-constituting effect, but it does have a critical and illustrative function here, which could provide 'food for thought' and perhaps also trigger reflections on possible changes and improvements to German asylum law. Raising awareness of the weaknesses, shortcomings, and incoherence of the current legal system is an important first step, and *A Slap in the Face* certainly makes an effective contribution to this.

References

Abdessalem, Safouane. 2019. Mafia corse: comment la France collabore avec les repentis, In *Café Babel,* 15.11.2019, https://cafebabel.com/en/article/how-french-authorities-collaborate-with-reformed-criminals-5dce9cd1f723b36c2228eead.

Abela, Frédéric. 2022. Affaire Merah: dix ans après les attentats de Toulouse et Montauban, retour sur l'effroyable parcours du tueur au scooter, *LA DEPECHE* 10.3.2022, https://www.ladepeche.fr/2022/03/09/recit-affaire-merah-dix-ans-apres-les-attentats-de-toulouse-et-montauban-retour-sur-leffroyable-parcours-du-tueur-au-scooter-10158549.php.

Adorno, Theodor. 1983. *Negative Dialectics*. New York: Continuum.

Agamben, Giorgio. 1998. *Homo sacer. Sovereign Power and Bare Life*. Stanford: Stanford University Press.

Agresti, Jean-Philippe. 2023. Préface. In *Quand la littérature moderne (ré)invente le droit. Œuvres choisies du XXe siècle à aujourd'hui*, ed. Gil Charbonnier and Franck Petit. Paris: LexisNexis.

Albrecht, Andrea (2015): "Analogieschlüsse und metaphorische Extensionen", in: Andrea Albrecht, Lutz Danneberg, Olav Krämer, Carlos Spoerhase (eds.), *Theorien, Methoden und Praktiken des Interpretierens*, Berlin/Munich/Boston: De Gruyter, 271–299.

Alix, Julie. 2017. La qualification terroriste après l'arrêt du 10 janvier 2017 (affaire dite 'de Tarnac'), *Actualité Juridique Pénale*: 79.

Anastasi, Markeliana, and Renata Martini. 2023. Elvira Dones' Novels. The Language of the Literature, The New Literary Phenomenon. *Specialusis Ugdymas / Special education* 44 (1): 428–439.

Angermüller, Johannes. 2014. Einleitung. In *Diskursforschung. Ein interdisziplinäres Handbuch. Theorien, Methodologien, Kontroversen*, ed. Johannes Angermüller, Martin Nonhoff, Eva Herschinger, et al., vol. 1, 16–36. Bielefeld: transcript.

Arsovska, Jana. 2006. Understanding a 'Culture of Violence and Crime': the Kanun of Lek Dukagjini and the Rise of the Albanian Sexual-Slavery Rackets. *European Journal of Crime and Criminal Justice* 14 (2): 161–184.

Backer, Berit. 1979. *Behind the Stone Walls: Changing Household Organization among the Albanians of Yugoslavia*. Oslo: University of Oslo.

Badenoch, Isla. 2016. *The Burrnesha Archive*. Copenhagen: The Royal Danish Academy of Fine Arts.

Bangerl, Sarah. 2019. *Der Kanun. Das albanische Gewohnheitsrecht und seine Rolle bis ins beginnende 21. Jahrhundert*. Graz: Diploma Thesis Karl-Franzens-Universität Graz.

Bartoli, Antoine F. 1898. *Histoire de la Corse*. Vol. 1. Paris: Orphélins-Apprentis.

Berger, Joel. 2019. *Gesetz – Ritus – Brauch*. In *Einblicke in jüdische Lebenswelten*. Heidelberg: Winter.
Bertrand, Félix. 1870. *La Vendetta, le banditisme et leur suppression. Tableau de mœurs corses*. Paris: Hurteau.
Bleich, Susanne. 1989. Die literarische und die juristische Hermeneutik – Ein Vergleich. *NWJ* 1989 (50): 3197–3203.
Boccou, Jean-Christoph. 2021. *La vierge jurée*. Paris: Nouveaux Auteurs.
Bogumil, Jörg, Jonas Hafner, and André Kastilan. 2023. Lokales Integrationsmanagement in Deutschland – Eine Bestandaufnahme. In *Lokales Integrations- management in Deutschland, Schweden und Frankreich*, ed. Jörg Bogumil, Sabine Kuhlmann, Jonas Hafner, et al., 37–175. Baden-Baden: Nomos.
Bomzer, Herbert W. 1985. *The Kolel in America*. New York: Shengold.
Bond, Emma, and Daniele Comberiati. 2013. Narrare il colonialismo e il postcolonialismo italiani. La 'questione' albanese. In *Il con- fine liquido. Rapporti letterari e interculturali fra Italia e Albania*, ed. Emma Bond and Daniele Comberiati, 2–27. Nardò: Besa.
Bouschon, Axelle. 2021. Claude Chossat condamné à 7 ans de prison pour association de malfaiteurs, *Franceinfo* 11.5.2021, https://france3-regions.francetvinfo.fr/corse/claude-chossat-le-repenti-autoproclame-condamne-a-7-ans-de-prison-2087662.html.
Broc, Damien. 2014. *Dynamiques politiques, économiques et sociales dans la corse médiévale: le diocèse de Nebbio (XIème siècle – c. 1540)*, Doctoral thesis, Corte: Université Pascal-Paoli.
Busquet, Jacques. 1920. *Le droit de la vendetta et les paci corses*. Paris: Pedone.
Busquet, Jacques. 1994. *Le droit de la vendetta et les paci corses*. Aubervilliers: Éditions du CTHS.
Busquet, Jacques. 2022. Le Droit de la vendetta du XVe au XVIIIe siècle. In *La Corse et la Vendetta. Anthologie-Le tragique*, ed. Gabriel X. Culioli et al., 193–223. Paris: Éditions Vannina.
Cabrillac, Rémy. 2022. La decision. *La Semaine Juridique (édition générale)* (3): 141.
Cahn, Olivier. 2017. Sauriez-vous reconnaître un 'terroriste'? *Grief* 1 (4): 127–138.
Carrington, Dorothy. 1971. *Granite Island. A Portrait of Corsica*. London: Longman.
Casanova, Antoine. 1981. Pensée paysanne, histoire sociale et récit des chroniqueurs (le cas du Corse Giovanni Della Grossa). In *Les genres et l'histoire, XVIIIe-XIXe siècles (II), Annales littéraires de l'université de Besançon*, 81–130. Paris: Les Belles Lettres.
Casanova, Antoine. 2005. Évolution historique des sociétés et voies de la Corse. In *La chaîne et la trame. Ethnologie et histoire de la Corse*, ed. Antoine Casanova, Georges Ravis-Giordani, and Ange Rovere, 239–265. Ajaccio: Albiana.
Charbonnier, Gil, and Franck Petit. 2023. *Quand la littérature moderne (ré) invente le droit. Œuvres choisies du XXe siècle à aujourd'hui*. Paris: LexisNexis.
Chetrit, Jonathan. 2022. *Toulouse 12 mars 2012. L'attentat de l'école Ozar Hatorah par ceux qui l'ont vécue*. Paris: Albin Michel.
Chossat, Claude. 2017. *Repenti*. Paris: Fayard.
Cohen, Patrick. 2017. Un repenti de la mafia corse raconte. *C à Vous* 19 (9): 2017. https://youtu.be/GgPefmKVrzs?si=C_LLtsdDP7meDLuw.
Colcombet, François. 1991. Rapport n° 2244, tome 1, Exposé général. Examen des articlesAN 1991, 93.
Colonna d'Istria, Robert. 2018. *Une famille corse: 1200 ans de solitude*. Paris: Plon.
Conseil Supérieur de la Magistrature. 2019. *Recueil des obligations déontologiques des magistrats*. Paris: Direction de l'information légale et administrative. http://www.conseil-superieur-magistrature.fr/sites/default/files/atoms/files/csm_recueilobligationsdeontologiques.pdf.
Coon, Carleton S. 1950. *The Mountains of Giants. A Racial and Cultural Study of the North Albanian Mountain Ghegs*. Cambridge/Massachusetts: Peabody Museum Press.
Cordignano, Fulvio. 1933. *L'Albania attraverso l'opera e gli scritti di un grande missionario italiano il P. Domenico Pasi S. I. (1847–1914)*. Vol. 1. Rome: Istituto per l'Europa Orientale.
Cozzi, Ernesto D. 1912. La donna albanese con speciale riguardo al diritto consuetudinario delle Montagne di Scutari. *Anthropos* 1912 (VII): 309–335. 617–626.

Cozzi, Ernesto D. (2021): *Fra i Monti d'Albania. Cenni su gli usi e i costumi delle Montagne Albanesi*, ed. by Peter Bartl / Bardhyl Demiraj, Wiesbaden: Harrassowitz.
Culioli, Gabriel X., et al., eds. 2022. *La Corse et la Vendetta. Anthologie – Le tragique*. Paris: Éditions Vannina.
de Prosperis, Eva. 2017. *Io sono una burnesha. Viaggio nell'Albania delle vergini giurate*. Catania: Villaggio Maori Edizioni.
de Rapper, Gilles. 2000. Entre masculin et féminin. La vierge jurée, l'héritière et le gendre de la maison. *L'Homme* 2000 (154–155): 457–466.
Deen, Shulem. 2015. *All Who Go Do Not Return: A Memoir*. Minneapolis: Graywolf Press.
Demaçi, Adem. 2005. *Die Schlangen des Blutes*. Frankfurt am Main: Weimarer Schillerpresse.
Doja, Albert. 1995. Le sexe de la naissance: masculin/féminin dans la société traditionnelle. *Ethnologie française* 25 (4): 650–667.
Doja, Albert. 1999. Morphologie traditionnelle de la société albanaise. *Social Anthropology* 7 (1): 37–55.
Dones, Elvira. 2014. *Sworn Virgin*. London/New York: And Other Stories.
Draï, Raphaël. 1988. *La Traversée du désert. L'invention de la responsabilité*. Paris: Fayard.
Draï, Raphaël. 1999. La Thora écrite. In *Raphaël Draï, La Thora. La Législation de Dieu*, 19–60. Paris: Michalon.
Dundes Renteln, Alison, and Alan Dundes, eds. 1995. *Folk Law. Essays in the Theory and Practice of Lex Non Scripta*. Wisconsin: University of Wisconsin.
Dupuis, Frederick. 2021. Un avocat peut-il déjeuner avec un magistrat?. *La lettre juridique* n° 875, 2.9.2021, online: https://www.lexbase.fr/revues-juridiques/72004194-focus-un-avocat-peut-il-dejeuner-avec-un-magistrat-a0
Durham, Mary E. 1928. *Some Tribal Origins, Laws and Customs of the Balkans*. London: Unwin Brothers.
Durham, Mary E. 1985. *High Albania*. London: Virago Press.
Durham, Mary E. 1991. *Brenga e Ballkanit*. Tirana: Argeta LMG.
Dvorsky, Victor. 1909. *Černohorskoturecká hranice od ústí Bojany k Taře*. Prague: Nákl. České akademie císaře Frantisška Josefa pro vědy, slovesnost a umění.
Eco, Umberto. 2004. *The Name of the Rose*. London: Vintage.
Egeler, Barbara. 2007. *Der Kanun – Gewohnheitsrecht als rechtliche Grundlage für Unrecht? Die Ausdehnung auf Tätigkeiten illegaler Natur und der damit verbundene Einfluss auf Delikte ethnischer Albaner in der Schweiz, degree thesis Hochschule*. Luzern: Kompetenzzentrum Wirt- schaftskriminalistik.
Egeler, Barbara. 2010. Albanisches Gewohnheitsrecht und Häusliche Gewalt. *Neue Kriminalpolitik* 22 (3): 96–98.
Ehrlich, Ernst L., and Günter Stemberger, eds. 2006. *The Jerusalem Talmud*. Vol. XXXIV. Berlin/New York: De Gruyter.
Eisenmenger, Daniel. 2010. Die vergessene Verfassung von Korsika 1755. Der gescheiterte Versuch einer modernen Nationsbildung. *Geschichte in Wissenschaft und Unterricht* 61 (7/8): 430–446.
Elezi, Ismet. 2003. *Njohuri për të drejtën zakonore mbarëshqiptare*, Pristina.
El-Kaddouri, Warda. 2017. 'Gott rette mich aus der Leere!' Verlust, Religiosität und Radikalisierung in den Fluchtnarrativen von Abbas Khider und Sherko Fatah. In *Niemandsbuchten und Schutzbefohlene. Flucht-Räume und Flüchtlingsfiguren in der deutschsprachigen Gegenwartsliteratur*, ed. Thomas Hardtke, Johannes Kleine, and Charlton Payne, 39–51. Göttingen: Vandenhoeck & Ruprecht.
Elsie, Robert. 2012. "Kanun of Lekë Dukagjini", Albanian Symposium University of Leiden, 10.11.2012 (video), https://www.youtube.com/watch?v=U9H-hEbskKcA&ab_channel=ALBFACT
Elsie, Robert, ed. 2014a. *Der Kanun. Das albanische Gewohnheitsrecht nach dem sogenannten Kanun des Lekë Dukagjini*. Berlin: Osteuropa Zentrum.

Elsie, Robert. 2014b. Vorwort. In *Der Kanun. Das albanische Gewohnheitsrecht nach dem sogenannten Kanun des Lekë Dukagjini*, ed. Robert Elsie, V–XI. Berlin: Osteuropa Zentrum.

Encke, Julia. 2016. Vom Warten wird man immer blöder. In *Frankfurter Allgemeine,* 30.1.2016, https://www.faz.net/aktuell/feuilleton/buecher/fluechtlingsroman-vom-warten-wird-man-immer-bloeder-14030679.html

European Asylum Support Office. 2020. *Reception of applicants for international protection. Reception Conditions Directive (2013/33/EU). EASO training series for members of courts and tribunals.* Luxembourg: Publications Office of the European Union.

European Parliament. 2016. *Sakharov Prize for Freedom of Thought*, 80–81. Luxembourg: Publications Office of the European Union.

European Union Agency for Fundamental Rights. 2016. *Guidelines on reducing the risk of refoulement in the context of external border management in or in co-operation with third countries.* Vienna: Publications Office.

Evers,Raphael.2022.DieHerkunft,derStatusunddieRollederKohanimimdrittenTempel,In*Orthodoxe Rabbinerkonferenz – Das Rabbinat Deutschlands,* https://www.ordonline.de/religion-aktuelles/dwar-thora/die-herkunft-der-status-und-die-rolle-der-kohanim-im-dritten-tempel

Favoino, Paola. 2016. Burrneshe, le vergini giurate d'Albania, In *telecastrovillari* 2.2.2016, https://www.youtube.com/watch?v=h_GhA4Ix6tY&ab_channel=telecastrovillari

Favoino, Paola. 2019. *A JE BURRNESH.* Rome: Leporello books.

Feldman, Deborah. 2012. *Unorthodox.* New York: Simon & Schuster.

Feldman, Deborah. 2020. Viele Aussteiger nehmen sich das Leben (Interview mit Olivia Röllin), in: *SRF Kultur Sternstunden* 19.5.2020, https://youtu.be/mBLk6FUszXA?si=yGS8AULA5UcBq7Br

Feldman, Deborah, and Christian Ruzicska. 2017. Unorthodox, In *Körberstiftung,* 5.12.2017, https://youtu.be/eGFtBF0FxuM?si=8B3N7Zie_BpkP-6p

Feltrinelli Editore. 2007. Elvira Dones presenta 'Vergine giurata', 10.10.2007, https://youtu.be/-aMaI911A-M

Feydel, Gabriel. 1799. *Mœurs et Coutumes des Corses.* Paris: Garnery.

Fikentscher, Wolfgang. 1977. *Methoden des Rechts in vergleichender Darstellung.* Vol. IV. Tübingen: J.C.B. Mohr.

Fohrmann, Jürgen, and Harro Müller. 1988. Einleitung: Diskurstheorien und Literaturwissenschaft. In *Diskurstheorien und Literaturwissenschaft,* ed. Jürgen Fohrmann and Harro Müller, 9–21. Frankfurt am Main: Suhrkamp.

Follorou, Jacques. 2022. *Mafia corse. Une île sous influence.* Paris: Robert Laffont.

Foreix, Yann. 2019. Procès de Claude Chossat: le 'repenti' de la Brise de Mer condamné à 8 ans de prison, *Le Parisien*, 9.11.2019, https://www.leparisien.fr/faits-divers/proces-de-claude-chossat-le-repenti-de- la-brise-de-mer-condamne-a-8-ans-de-prison-08-11-2019-8189676.php

Foucault, Michel. 1972. *The Archeology of Knowledge.* New York: Pantheon Books.

France 3 Corse ViaStella. 2017. Claude Chossat le repenti corse livre les secrets du banditisme. In *Youtube*, 22.9.2017, https://youtu.be/vgRk0OnhTk8?-si=KV7wNIiLzZMoYe4i.

Freisitzer, Roland. 2016. Abbas Khider: 'Ohrfeige', In *sandammeer.at – Literaturzeitschrift im Internet, March 2016,* https://www.sandammeer.at/rez16/khider-ohrfeige.htm.

Frei-Tomic, Gallus. 2018. Elvira Dones 'Hana', ink press, In *Literaturblatt*.ch, 20.3.2018, https://literaturblatt.ch/elvira-dones-hana-ink-press.

Fromer, Jacob, ed. 2021. *Der Babylonische Talmud.* München: Anaconda.

Gadamer, Hans-Georg. 1982. *Truth and Method.* New York: Crossroad.

Galluzzo, Lucio. 1985. *Das gebrochene Schweigen. Tommaso Buscetta: Mafia-Capo und Verräter.* Vienna/Munich, J&V.

Gas, Valérie. 2002. Attentats de 1995: le procès tant attendu, In *Rfi,* 30.9.2002, http://www1.rfi.fr/actufr/articles/033/article_17194.asp.

Geballe, David. 2023. Der richtige Zeitpunkt: In welchem Alter man eine Familie gründen sollte. In *Die Lehren des Talmud*, ed. Zentralrat der Juden in Deutschland, 76–78. Gütersloh: Gütersloher Verlag.

Geis, Max-Emmanuel. 2021. Gewohnheitsrecht. In *Handbuch Rechtsphilosophie*, ed. Eric Hilgendorf and Jan C. Joerden, 27–31. Berlin/Heidelberg: J. B. Metzler.

Gherlone, Laura. 2019. Women's Writing Between the Border and the Non-Place: The Emerging Female Discourses in Migrant Literature / A escrita feminina a fronteira e o não lugar: discursos femininos em ascensão na Literatura Italiana de Migração. *Revista do Estudios do Discurso* 14 (2): 7–24.

Gjeçovi, Shtjefën. 1989. *Kanuni i Lekë Dukagjinit / The Code of Lekë Dukagjini*. New York: Gjonlekaj Publishing Company. translation by Leonard Fox.

Gjeçovi, Shtjefën. 1993. *Kanuni i Leke Dukagjinit: me parathenie të at Gjergj Fishtës*. Tirana: Albinform.

Glinert, Lewis, and Joseph Shilhav. 1991. Holy Land, Holy Language: A Study of an Ultraorthodox Jewish Ideology. *Language in Society* 20 (1): 59–86.

Goldschmidt, Lazarus. 2002. *Der Babylonische Talmud*. Frankfurt am Main: Jüdischer Verlag.

Goldsmith, Rosie. 2019. The Riveting Interviews: Rosie Goldsmith talks to Elvira Dones. In *The Riveting Interviews* 14.8.2019, https://youtu.be/JRIC9brKRm4?si=SBNypTvgjYSMEWIb.

Gopčević, Spiridion. 1881. *Oberalbanien und seine Liga. Ethnographisch-politisch-historisch geschildert*. Leipzig: Duncker & Humblot.

Gopčević, Spiridion. 1914. *Das Fürstentum Albanien, seine Vergangenheit, ethnographischen Verhältnisse, politische Lage und Aussichten für die Zukunft*. Berlin: H. Paetel.

Gordon, Jan, and Cora J. Gordon. 1927. *Two Vagabonds in Albania*. New York/London: Dodd, Mead and Company/John Lane.

Granzin, Katharina. 2019. Der Mensch im Durchgangsland, In *Frankfurter Rundschau,* 11.1.2019, https://www.fr.de/kultur/literatur/mensch-durchgangsland-11130928.html.

Grémaux, René. 1993. Woman Becomes Man in the Balkans. In *Third Sex, Third Gender. Beyond Sexual Dimorphism in Culture and History*, ed. Gilbert Herdt, 241–281. New York: Zone Books.

Grosz, Elisabeth. 1995. *Space, Time, and Perversion*. New York: Routledge.

Gubert, Romain. 2023. Attentat à Arras: qui était Dominique Bernard, le professeur de français tué?, In *Le Point*, 16.10.2023, https://www.lepoint.fr/societe/attaque-a-arras-qui-est-l-enseignant-qui-a-ete-tue-13-10-2023-2539224_23.php#11.

Guggenheimer, Heinrich W., ed. 2010. *The Jerusalem Talmud*. Vol. 51. Berlin/Boston: De Gruyter.

Guggenheimer, Heinrich W., ed. 2014. *The Jerusalem Talmud*. Vol. 80. Berlin/Boston: De Gruyter.

Gutwirth, Jacques. 2004. Williamsburg, bastion Satmar. In *La Renaissance du hassidisme*, ed. Jacques Gutwirth, 53–93. Paris: Odile Jacob.

Habermas, Jürgen. 1996. *Between Facts and Norms. Contributions to a Discourse Theory of Law and Democracy*. Cambridge/Massachusetts: MIT Press.

Hahn, Judith. 2019. Wirksamkeit des Rechts. In *Grundlegung der Kirchenrechtssoziologie. Zur Realität des Rechts in der römisch-katholischen Kirche*, ed. Judith Hahn, 189–233. Wiesbaden: Springer.

Hasluck, Margaret. 1954. *The Unwritten Law in Albania*. Cambridge: Cambridge University Press.

Hegemann, Sophie. 2023. *Kulturen des Ausnahmezustandes. Antiterrorpolitik in Frankreich, Belgien und Deutschland von 2015–2017*. Wiesbaden: Springer.

Heinrich, Kaspar. 2016. Abbas Khider. Wir sollten nicht plötzlich alles infrage stellen, In *Planet Interview,* 11.5.2016, https://www.planet-interview.de/interviews/abbas-khider/48826.

Hérault, Laurence. 2009. Les 'vierges jurées': une masculinité singulière et ses observateurs. *Sextant* 2009 (27): 273–284.

Hirsch, Ernst. 1973. Rechtssoziologie. In *Die Lehre von der Gesellschaft*, ed. Gottfried Eisermann, 147–217. Stuttgart: Enke.

Homolka, Walter. 2009. *Das Jüdische Eherecht*. Berlin: De Gruyter.

Hummitzsch, Thomas. 2015. Schluss mit der 'Globalisierung der Gleichgültigkeit', In *Intellectures,* 12.10.2015, https://www.intellectures.de/2015/10/12/schluss-mit-der-globalisierung-der-gleichgueltigkeit. Access 10 May 2024.

Hummitzsch, Thomas. 2016. Inside Refugee oder: Abbas Khider und sein Roman zur Stunde, In *Intellectures,* 2.2.2016, https://www.intellectures.de/2016/02/02/inside-refugee-oder-abbas-khider-und-sein-roman-zur-stunde.

INA. 2021. 1996: l'attentat du RER B à la gare du Port Royal, In *L'INA éclaire l'actu,* 2.12.2021, https://www.ina.fr/ina-eclaire-actu/1996-l-attentat-du-rer-b-a-la-gare-de-port-royal.
Inbari, Motti. 2016a. *Jewish Radical Ultra-Orthodoxy Confronts Modernity, Zionism and Women's Equality*. Cambridge: Cambridge University Press.
Inbari, Motti. 2016b. The Life and Work of Rabbi Yoel Teitelbaum, Founder of the Satmar Hasidic Court in New York. In *Jewish Radical Ultra-Orthodoxy Confronts Modernity, Zionism and Women's Equality*, ed. Motti Inbari, 131–172. Cambridge: Cambridge University Press.
Ingarden, Roman. 1968. *Vom Erkennen des literarischen Kunstwerks*. Tübingen: Niemeyer.
Iser, Wolfgang. 1983. Akte des Fingierens. Oder: Was ist das Fiktive im fiktionalen Text? In *Funktionen des Fiktiven*, ed. Dieter Henrich and Wolfgang Iser, 121–151. Munich: W. Fink.
Janouel, Pierre. 2024. Les repentis: un dispositif à reformer, In *Dalloz Actualité,* 28.2.2024, pp. 1-2.
Jauß, Hans R. 1981. Zur Abgrenzung und Bestimmung einer literarischen Hermeneutik. In *Text und Applikation: Theologie, Jurisprudenz und Li- teraturwissenschaft im hermeneutischen Gespräch*, ed. Hans R. Jauß, Manfred Fuhrmann, and Wolfhart Pannenberg, 459–481. Munich: W. Fink.
Jellinek, Georg. 1921. Staat und Recht. In *Allgemeine Staatslehre*, ed. Georg Jellinek, 332–379. Berlin/Heidelberg: Springer.
Joireman, Sandra F. 2014. Aiming for Certainty: the Kanun. *Blood Feuds and the Ascertainment of Customary Law, The Journal of Legal Pluralism and Unofficial Law* 46 (2): 235–248.
JuraForum. 2024. Ratifikation: Definition und Bedeutung im Völker- und Vertragsrecht, *Lexikon* 5.6.2024, https://www.juraforum.de/lexikon/ratifikation-ratifizierung.
Kadare, Ismail. 1990. *Broken April*. New York: New Amsterdam Books.
Kalo, Valbona, and Mirela Shella. 2024. Anthropological and Literary Reading of Sworn Virgins: A Study on the Influence of Tradition in Society and Literature. *Journal of Educational and Social Research* 14 (5): 276–290.
Kaplan, Zvi Jonathan. 2004. Rabbi Joel Teitelbaum, Zionism, and Hungarian Ultra-Orthodoxy. *Modern Judaism* 24 (2): 165–178.
Karabash, René. 2022. *Vierge jurée*. Paris: Tropismes.
Karp, Karol. 2015. Cultura e viaggio. *Vergine giurata di Elvira Dones, Echo des études romanes* XI (2): 147–157.
Kaser, Karl. 1992. *Hirten, Kämpfer, Stammeshelden*. Vienna: Böhlau.
Kaser, Karl. 2008. *Patriarchy after Patriarchy. Gender Relations in Turkey and in the Balkans, 1500–2000*. Vienna/Münster: LIT.
Keller, Reiner. 2013. Das Wissen der Wörter und Diskurse. Über Sprache und Wissen in der Wissenssoziologischen Diskursanalyse. In *Diskurs – Sprache – Wissen. Inter- disziplinäre Beiträge zum Verhältnis von Sprache und Wissen in der Diskursforschung*, ed. Willy Viehöver, Reiner Keller, and Werner Schneider, 21–49. Wiesbaden: Springer.
Kelsen, Hans. 1965. Was ist juristischer Positivismus? *JuristenZeitung* 20 (15): 465–469.
Keren-Kratz, Menachem. 2017. Rabbi Yoel Teitelbaum – the Satmar Rebbe – and the Rise of Anti-Zionism in American Orthodoxy. *Contemporary Jewry* 37 (3): 457–479.
Keren-Kratz, Menachem. 2023a. Satmar and Neturei Karta: Jews against Zionism, *Modern Judaism. A Journal of Jewish Ideas and Experience* 43 (1): 52–76.
Keren-Kratz, Menachem. 2023b. *Va-yo'el Moshe*: The Most Anti-Zionist and Anti-Israeli Jewish Text in Modern Times. *The Jewish Quarterly Review* 113 (3): 479–506.
Khider, Abbas. 2018. *A Slap in the Face*. Calcutta: Seagull Books.
Kienzle, Florian. 2020. *Ein Nehmen und Geben. Die Geschlechter in der albanischen Literatur*. Wiesbaden: Harrassowitz.
Klein, Christian. 2013. Erzählung. In *Literatur und Wissen. Ein interdisziplinäres Handbuch*, ed. Roland Borgards and al., 17–21. Stuttgart/Weimar: J. B. Metzler.
Klein, Christian, and Matías Martínez. 2009. *Wirklichkeitserzählungen. Felder, Formen und Funktionen nicht-literarischen Erzählens*. In *Wirklichkeitserzählungen. Felder, Formen und Funktionen nicht-literarischen Erzählens*, ed. Christian Klein and Matías Martínez, 1–13. Stuttgart/Weimar: J. B. Metzler.

Knorr-Cetina, Karin. 2016. *Die Fabrikation von Erkenntnis. Zur Anthropologie der Wissenschaft*. Berlin: Suhrkamp.
Kołakowski, Leszek. 1967. *Kultura i fetysze*. Warschau: Państwowe Wydawnictwo Naukowe.
Kranzler, George. 1961. *Williamsburg. A Jewish Community in Transition*. New York: Feldheim.
Kranzler, George. 1995a. *Hasidic Williamsburg. A Contemporary American Hasidic Community*. New Jersey/London: North Vale.
Kranzler, George. 1995b. The Economic Revitalization of the Hasidic Community of Williamsburg. In *Ethnographic Studies of Hasidic Jews in America*, ed. Janet S. Belcove-Shalin. Albany: State University of New York Press.
Krastev, Péter. 2000. The Price of Amnesia. Interpretations of Vendetta in Albania. In *Albania and the Albanian Identities*, ed. Antonia Zhleyazkova, 194–217. Sofia: IMIR.
Krochmalnik, Daniel. 1996. 'Du sollst darüber nachsinnen Tag und Nacht'. Glauben und Lernen in der jüdischen Tradition. *Zeitschrift für theologische Urteilsbildung* 11 (1): 73–83.
Krochmalnik, Daniel. 2017. Religion des Lernens. *Zeitschrift für christlich-jüdische Begegnung im Kontext* 2017 (3): 155–161.
Lahusen, Christian, Karin Schittenhelm, and Stephanie Schneider. 2022. Lokale Behördenpraxis und die Europäisierung des *street levels*. Modi, Promotoren und Anpassungen in den deutschen und schwedischen Asylbehörden. In *Europäische Asylpolitik und lokales Verwaltungshandeln. Zur Behördenpraxis in Deutschland und Schweden*, ed. Christian Lahusen, Karin Schittenhelm, and Stephanie Schneider, 174–247. Bielefeld: transcript.
Larenz, Karl. 1991. *Methodenlehre der Rechtswissenschaft*. Berlin/Heidelberg: Springer.
Lazard, Violette, and Marion Galland. 2020. *Vendetta. Les héritiers de la Brise de Mer*. Paris: Plon.
Le Parisien. 2019. [Podcast] Claude Chossat, le repenti 3/5, In *Youtube*, 7.8.2019, https://youtu.be/ziIH_tALZ5M.
Lehmann, David, and Batia Siebzehner. 2009. Power, Boundaries, and Institutions: Marriage in Ultra-Orthodox Judaism. *Archives européennes de sociologie* L (2): 273–308.
Lenclud, Gérard. 2012. *En Corse. Une société en mosaïque*. Paris: Éditions de la Maison des sciences de l'homme.
Lieberman, Haim. 1958. *Der Rebbe und der Satan*. New York: Marstin Press.
Link, Jürgen. 1983. *Elementare Literatur und generative Diskursanalyse*. München: W. Fink.
Littlewood, Roland. 2001. Three Into Two: The Third Sex in Northern Albania. *Anthropology & Medicine* 9 (1): 37–50.
Lüthke, Albrecht, and Ingo Müller. 2014. Ausländerfeindliche Gewalt – das Beispiel Rostock-Lichtenhagen. In *Strafjustiz für Nicht-Juristen. Ein Ratgeber für Schöffen, Pädagogen, Sozialarbeiter und andere Interessierte*, ed. Albrecht Lüthke and Ingo Müller, 125–133. Wiesbaden: Springer.
Malabat, Valérie. 2022. *Droit pénal spécial*. Paris: Dalloz.
Malcolm, Noel. 1998. *Kosovo: A Short History*. New York: New York University Press.
Marcaggi, Jean-Baptiste. 2022. Fleuve de sang. In *La Corse et la Vendetta. Anthologie – Le tragique*, ed. Gabriel X. Culioli et al., 9–131. Paris: Éditions Vannina.
Marchi van Cauwelaert, Vannina. 2011. *La Corse génoise. Saint-Georges, vainqueur des 'tyrans' (milieu XVe – début XVIe siècle)*. Paris: Classiques Garnier.
Martínez, Matías, and Michael Scheffel. 2019. *Einführung in die Erzähltheorie*. Munich: C. H. Beck.
Martucci, Donato. 2014. Donne che diventano uomini? Le vergini giurate nella cultura tradizionale Albanese. *Anuac* III (2): 35–60.
Mas, Marion. 2023. L'interprétation en question dans *La vengeance m'appartient* de Marie NDiaye et *La Décision* de Karine Tuil. *Revue critique de fixxion française contemporaine* 2023 (26): 1–10.
Mascioli, Paola. 01/09/2017. Burrneshe, le vergini giurate d'Albania - i centenari di Sardegna, *Timonieri*, https://www.youtube.com/watch?v=rC602fAyWyc&ab_channel=TIMONIERI.
Mayaud, Yves. 2020a. *Prévention du terrorisme*. Paris: Dalloz.

Mayaud, Yves. 2020b. *Terrorisme – Infractions, poursuites pénales et indemnisation*. Paris: Dalloz.

Mazzon, Barbara. 2018. *Le Vergini Giurate: donne libere di costringersi e costrette a liberarsi in Albania*. Milan/Udine: Mimesis.

McLean, Tui. 2022. The last of Albania's 'sworn virgins', BBC 10.12.2022, https://bbc.com/news/world-europe-63904744.

Meisels, Dovid. 2011. *The Rebbe – The Extraordinary Life & Worldview of Rabbeinu Yoel Teitelbaum, the Satmar Rebbe*. Lakewood/NJ: Israel Bookshop Publications.

Mihman, Alexis. 2005. Exemption et réduction de peine pour les repentis: apports de la loi du 9 mars 2004, dite loi 'Perben'. *Droit pénal.*, Étude Nr. 1, § 26–11.

Möllers, Thomas M. J. 2023. *Juristische Methodenlehre*. Munich: C. H. Beck.

Moosmüller, Lorenz B. M. 2017. *Ich triumphiere mit den Mitteln der Literatur. Abbas Khiders Subversion und ironische Distanznahme als Erzählverfahren und Positionierungsstrategien im Kontext der sogenannten Migrationsliteratur*, Master's thesis, University of Vienna.

Mucchielli, Julien. 2019a. Procès du 'repenti' corse Claude Chossat: 'Ses déclarations sont extraordinaires, il s'auto-incrimine'. In *Dalloz Actualité,* 29.10.2019.

Mucchielli, Julien. 2019b. Procès du 'repenti‹ corse Claude Chossat: 'C'était le premier à parler', In *Dalloz Actualité,* 5.11.2019.

Mucchielli, Julien. 2019c. Procès du 'repenti' corse Claude Chossat: 'Je vous invite à ne pas adhérer au discours victimaire de Claude Chossat'. In: *Dalloz Actualité,* 8.11.2019.

Müller-Seidel, Walter. 1986. *Die Deportation des Menschen. Kafkas Erzählung 'In der Strafkolonie' im europäischen Kontext*. Stuttgart: J. B. Metzler.

Negri, Marco, Marianna Di Piazza, and Roberto Di Matteo. 2019a. Solo il sangue lava il sangue, il codice d'onore Albanese, In *Insideover* 1.2.2019, https://it.insideover.com/reportage/donne/albania-sospesa/68033-2.html

Negri, Marco, Marianna Di Piazza, and Roberto Di Matteo. 2019b. 'Diresti mai che sono donna?' Lali, l'ultima vergine giurata, In *Insideover* 2.2.2019, https://it.insideover.com/reportage/societa/albania-sospesa/68038-2.html

Nünning, Ansgar. 1995. *Von historischer Fiktion zu historiographischer Metafiktion, vol 1: Theorie, Typologie und Poetik des historischen Romans*. Trier: Wissenschaftlicher Verlag Trier.

Ost, François. 2004. *Raconter la loi. Aux sources de l'imaginaire juridique*. Paris: Odile Jacob.

Ost, François. 2014. Penser par cas: la littérature comme laboratoire expérimental de la démarche juridique. *Revue interdisciplinaire d'études juridiques* 2014 (2): 99–131.

Parr, Rolf. 2015. Autorität und Geltung zwischen Spezial- und Interdiskursen. In *Erzählung und Geltung. Wissenschaft zwischen Autorschaft und Autorität*, ed. Safia Azzouni, Stefan Böschen, and Carsten Reinhardt, 289–302. Weilerswist: Velbrück Wissenschaft.

Parr, Rolf. 2020. Diskurs. In *Foucault Handbuch. Leben – Werk – Wirkung*, ed. Clemens Kammler, Rolf Parr, and Ulrich J. Schneider, 274–277. Berlin: J. B. Metzler.

Parsi, Caroline. 2013. Le crime d'honneur en Corse (deuxième moitié du XIXe siècle). *Hypothèses* 16 (1): 247–261.

Pelazza, Luigi. 2015. Vergini Giurate fino alla morte, In: *Le Iene,* 7.5.2015, https://www.iene.mediaset.it/video/pelazza-vergini-giurate-fino-alla-morte_68840.shtml.

Pellegrini, Franca. 2013. Traslazioni narrative: strategie di mediazione in *Vergine giurata* di Elvira Dones e *Rosso come una sposa* di Anilda Ibrahimi. In *Il confine liquido. Rapporti letterari e interculturali fra Italia e Albania*, ed. Emma Bond and Daniele Comberiati, 149–166. Nardò: Besa Muci.

Pelletier, Eric. 2019. Claude Chossat, le repenti de la mafia corse à visage découvert, In *Le Parisien,* 27.10.2019, https://youtu.be/OVGTC4T-BiOY?si=YjPjmtb3Jvyj2RlC.

Pergola, Philippe. 1979. Une pieve rurale corse: Santa Mariona di taleini. Problèmes d'archéologie et de topographie médiévales insulaires. *Mélanges de l'école française de Rome* 91 (1): 89–111.

Pinsker, Sanford. 1975. The Idea of Community. *Social Research* 42 (2): 230–246.

Ploquin, Frédéric. 2010. Parrains et caïds. L'inépuisable vivier français. *Pouvoirs* 132 (1): 91–102.

Pompei, Paoli. 1821. *État actuel de la Corse. Caractère et mœurs de ses habitants*. Paris: Kieffer/Moreau.

Pomponi, Francis. 1978. À la recherche d'un invariant historique: la structure clanique dans la société corse. In *Piève et paesi. Communautés rurales corses*, ed. Max Caisson, Antoine Casanova, François-Josep Cast, et al., 7–30. Paris: CNRS Éditions.

Poncela, Pierrette. 2016. Les naufragés du droit penal. *Archives de politique criminelle* 1 (38): 7–26.

Pozo Sánchez, Begoña. 2022. Vergine giurata: la novela de Elvira Dones donde confluyen género y migración. In *Nuevos itinerarios e investigaciones en la literatura y cultura italiana*, ed. Daniele Cerrato, 151–159. Madrid: Dyckinson.

Preisinger, Alexander, Pascale Delormas, and Jan Standke. 2014. Diskursforschung in der Literaturwissenschaft. In *Diskursforschung. Ein interdisziplinäres Handbuch, vol. 1: Theorien, Methodologien, Kontroversen*, ed. Johannes Angermüller, Martin Nonhoff, Eva Herschinger, et al., 130–139. Bielefeld: transcript.

Pritchett Post, Susan E. 1998. *Women in Modern Albania: Firsthand Accounts of Culture and Conditions from Over 200 Interviews*. London: McFarland.

Puchta, Georg F. 1828. *Das Gewohnheitsrecht, part 1*. Erlangen: Palm'sche Verlagsbuchhandlung.

Qerimi, Islam. 2014. *Gewohnheitsrecht in Albanien: Rolle und Herkunft des Kanun bei den Albanern*. Hamburg: Bachelor + Master Publishing.

Qerimi, Islam, Ahmet Maloku, and Elda Maloku. 2022. Customary Law and Regulation: Authenticity and Influence. *Journal of Governance & Regulation* 11 (4): 289–299.

Raggio, Osvaldo. 1990. Etnografia e storia politica. La faida e il caso della Corsica. *Quaderni storici (nuova serie)* 25 (75/3): 937–954.

Ravis-Giordani, Georges. 2005. L'alta pulitica et la bassa pulitica: valeurs et comportements politiques dans les communautés villageoises corses (XIXe-XXe siècles). In *La chaîne et la trame. Ethnologie et Histoire de la Corse*, ed. Georges Ravis-Giordani, Antoine Casanova, and Ange Rovere, 317–337. Ajaccio: Albiana.

Réalier-Dumas, Jean-François-Ignace. 1819. *Mémoire sur la Corse*. Paris: Planchet.

Reinkowski, Maurus. 2005. Gewohnheitsrecht im multinationalen Staat: Die Osmanen und der albanische Kanun. In *Rechtspluralismus in der Islamischen Welt: Gewohnheitsrecht zwischen Staat und Gesellschaft*, ed. Michael Kemper and Maurus Reinkowski, 121–142. Berlin/New York: De Gruyter.

Ricœur, Paul. 1991. *From Text to Action. Essays in Hermeneutics II*. Evanston: Northwestern University Press.

Robiquet, François-Guillaume. 1835. *Recherches historiques et statistiques sur la Corse*. Paris/Rennes: Chez Duchesne.

Rolle, Chelsea. 2024. Décider ne va pas sans responsabilité. *Le Regard Libre* 2024 (3): 42–43.

Romano-Martín, Yolanda. 2011. Vergine giurata de Elvira Dones: el tercer sexo en Albania. *Revista internacional de culturas y literaturas* 2011 (11): 199–212.

Romeo, Caterina. 2019. Attraversamenti di confini e pratiche di scrittura nella narrativa di Elvira Dones. *OBLIO* IX (36): 79–86.

Romeo, Caterina. 2023. *Interrupted Narratives and Intersectional Representations in Italian Postcolonial Literature*. Cham: Palgrave Macmillan.

Romeo, Caterina, and Áine O'Healy. 2022. Narrating the Transnational Trajectories and Transgender Performances of the Sworn Virgin. *The Italianist* 42 (2): 1–21.

Rosenkranz, Michael. 2013a. Schemini Atzereth – Fest des achten Tages und der Torah-Freude, *Talmud.de*, 29.11.2013, https://www.talmud.de/tlmd/schemini-atzereth-fest-des-achten-tages-und-der-torah-freude.

Rosenkranz, Michael. 2013b. Pidyon ha Bechor – Die Auslösung des Erstgeborenen, *Talmud.de*, 5.12.2013, https://www.talmud.de/tlmd/pidyon-ha-bechor-die-ausloesung-des-erstgeborenen/.

Rosenkranz, Michael. 2013c. Schawuot – Fest der Torahgebung", *Talmud. de*, 29.11.2013, https://www.talmud.de/tlmd/schawuot-fest-der-torahgebung.

Rossi, Giovanni. 1900. *Corses d'après l'histoire, la légende et la poésie*. Paris: Hachette.

Rubin, Israel. 1997. *Satmar. Two Generations of an Urban Island*. New York: Peter Lang.

Sadiku, Mark. 1943. Il Kanun di Lekë Dukagjini secondo la versione di Mark Sadiku, primo della Djelmnija di Shala, ripresa sotto dettatura il 20 febraio 1940 da P. Bern. Palaj O. F. M. In *Studime e Tekste (Serie giuridica 1)*, 271–279. Rome: Instituti i Studimevet Shqiptare.

Sagan, Adam. 2022. *Rückwirkende Rechtsprechungsänderung. Eine methodologische und dogmatische Studie zur zeitlichen Dimension höchstrichterlicher Rechtsprechungsänderungen im Privatrecht.* Baden-Baden: Nomos.

Salvi, Ellen. 2019. Le 'repenti' corse retourne en prison, *Mediapart* 9.11.2019, https://www.mediapart.fr/journal/france/091119/le-repenti-corse-retourne-en-prison.

Saracino, Daniele. 2019. *Solidarität in der Asylpolitik der Europäischen Union.* Wiesbaden: Springer.

Schiesser, Giaco. 2007. Autorschaft nach dem Tod des Autors. Barthes und Foucault revisited. In *Autorschaft in den Künsten: Konzepte – Praktiken – Medien. Zürcher Jahrbuch der Künste*, ed. Corina Caduff and Tan Wälchli, 20–33. Zürich: Museum für Gestaltung.

Schmidt-Neke, Michael. 2014. Der Kanun der albanischen Berge: Hintergrund der nordalbanischen Lebensweise. In *Der Kanun. Das albanische Gewohnheitsrecht nach dem sogenannten Kanun des Lekë Dukagjini*, ed. Robert Elsie, XIII–XLIII. Berlin: Osteuropa Zentrum.

Schneller, Raphael. 1980. Continuity and Change in Ultraorthodox Edu- cation. *Jewish Journal of Sociology* 1980 (22): 35–45.

Schuchardt, Konstantin. 2016. "Rot", In *Jüdische Allgemeine,* 10.5.2016, https://www.juedische-allgemeine.de/glossar/rot/#:~:text=Rot%20ist%20die%20Farbe%20der,%C2%BBDam%C2%AB%20(Blut).

Schultz, E. 1907. Albanisches Mannweibertum. *Die Woche. Moderne Illustrierte Zeitschrift* 9 (40): 1758–1763.

Schwandner-Sievers, Stephanie. 1996. Zur Logik der Blutrache in Nordalbanien: Ehre, Symbolik und Gewaltlegitimation. *Sociologus* 46 (2): 109–129.

Ségur, Philippe. 2017. Droit et littérature. Éléments pour la recherche. Éléments pour la recherche. *Revue Droit & Littérature* 2017 (1): 109–123.

Shryock, Andrew. 1988. Autonomy, Entanglement, and the Feud: Prestige Structures and Gender Values in Highland Albania. *Anthropological Quarterly* 61 (3): 113–118.

Simon, Stéphane, and Alexis Kebbas. 2023. *Les derniers jours de Samuel Paty*. Paris: Plon.

Sozialistische Albanische Hefte. 2009. Buchvorstellung: Die Schlangen des Blutes. Roman von Adem Demaçi. *Sozialistische Albanische Hefte* 2009 (3): 29–30. http://www.kpd-ml.org/doc/partei/soz_albanische_hefte_3.pdf.

Spankbecher, Flugutel. 2021. Frei um jeden Preis – Albaniens Schwurjungfrauen Doku, In *Arte,* 31.12.2021, https://www.youtube.com/watch?v=T7ffCgSZuO4&ab_channel=FlugutelSpankbecher.

Stahl, Paul H. 1988. La regione tribale Albanese. *Incontri Meridionali* 1988 (3): 33–80.

Statovci, Ejup. 1990. Një monument madhor i kültures së lashtë shqiptare. *Përparimi – Revistë shkencore* 1990(5).

Steiner, George. 1987. Das lange Leben der Metaphorik. Ein Versuch über die 'Shoah'. *Akzente. Zeitschrift für Literatur* 34 (3): 194–212.

Stemberger, Günter. 2019. *Der Talmud. Einführung, Texte, Erläuterungen.* München: C. H. Beck.

Sterling, Claire. 1990. *Die Mafia. Der Griff nach der Macht.* Berne/Munich/Vienna: Scherz.

Surier, Albert. 1934. *Notre Corse. Études et souvenirs*. Paris: Étienne Chiron.

Tardy-Joubert, Sophie. 2020. Karine Tuil, du droit à la littérature ou la réflexion sur la condition humaine. *Droit & Littérature* 2020 (4): 27–29.

Teitelbaum, Yoel. 2023. *Sefer va-yo'el Moshe: Le-va'erdine ha-shalosh shevu'ot* / ישמח משה - חלק א': ביאור נדיר ונפלא על התורה, על פי החסידות והקבלה לספר בראשית ושמות (1960), Independently published.

Ternès, Anabel. 2016. *Intertextualität. Der Text als Collage*. Wiesbaden: Springer.

Thomas, Jean-Luc, and Christian Taveira. 2022. Attentats de Toulouse et Montauban: Jonathan Chetrit, témoin de la tuerié de l'école Ozar Hatorah, raconte l'horreur 'par ceux qui l'ont vécu', In *CNEWS,* 19.3.2022, https://www.cnews.fr/france/2022-03-19/attentats-de-toulouse-et-montauban-jonathan-chetrit-temoin-de-la-tuerie-de-lecole.

Thunmann, Johann E. 1976. "Untersuchungen über die Geschichte der östlichen europäischen Völker", part 1. In *Über die Geschichte und Sprache der Albaner und der Wlachen*, ed. Johann Thunmann and Harald Haarmann, 169–366. Buske: Hamburg.
Tihanyi, Catherine. 1998. *Violence on the Rebound: A Semiotics of Justice, Feud, Colonialism and Self in and around the Corsican Chronicles*, Doctoral thesis, Simon Fraser University.
Timotei, Jacques Simon. 2021. Coutumes et croyances corses: La Vendetta (A vendetta), In *Corsica Mea*, 9.7.2021, https://www.corsicamea.fr/coutumes/vendetta.htm.
Trévidic, Marc. 2011. *Au cœur de l'antiterrorisme*. Paris: JC Lattès.
Trochet, Jean-René. 2022. *L'Europe avant l'État*. Rennes: Presses Universitaires de Rennes. https://doi.org/10.4000/books.pur.165002.
Tuil, Karine. 2022. *La décision*. Paris: Gallimard.
Tuil, Karine. 2023. La littérature, force de changement social, Inaugural address at Sciences Po de Paris, 14.9.2023, https://www.sciencespo.fr/fr/actualites/automne-2023-karine-tuil-titulaire-de-la-chaire-d-ecrivain-de-sciences-po/.
UNHCR Austria (2003[1979]), *Handbook on Procedures and Criteria for Determining Refugee Status under the 1951 Convention and the 1967 Protocol relating to the Status of Refugees*, Geneva, September 1979, new edition December 2003.
Valentini, Giuseppe, ed. 1969. *Le leggi delle montagne albanesi nelle relazioni della missione volante 1880–1932*. Florence: Olschki.
Vertlib, Vladimir. 2016. Sag ja nicht die Wahrheit! *Die Presse* 5 (8): 2016. https://www.diepresse.com/5064168/sag-ja-nicht-die-wahrheit.
Viennot, Camille, and François Desprez. 2017. L'appréhension ambiguë de la trahison par la procédure pénale. *Droit et Cultures* 74 (2): 115–135.
Voell, Stéphane. 2003. The Kanun in the City. Albanian Customary Law As a Habitus and Its Persistence in the Suburb of Tirana, Bathore. *Anthropos* 98 (1): 85–101.
von Hahn, Johann G. 1867. *Reise durch die Gebiete des Drin und Wadar*. Denkschriften der kaiserlichen Akademie der Wissenschaften, XV, Vienna: Carl Gerolds Sohn.
Wagner, Wolfgang. 2023. *BESA – eine albanische Rettung*. Wien: Buchschmiede.
Whitaker, Ian. 1968. Tribal Structure and National Politics in Albania, 1910–1950. In *History and Social Anthropology*, ed. Ioan M. Lewis, 253–293. London: Tavistock Publications.
Whitaker, Ian. 1981. 'A Sack for Carrying Things': The Traditional Role of Women in Northern Albanian Society'. *Anthropological Quarterly* 54 (3): 146–156.
White, Hayden. 1991. Der historische Text als literarisches Kunstwerk. In *Auch Klio dichtet oder die Fiktion des Faktischen. Studien zur Tropologie des historischen Diskurses*, ed. Hayden White, 101–122. Stuttgart: Klett-Cotta.
Wild, Gerhard. 2017. Kindler Kompakt. *Französische Literatur der Gegenwart*. In *Französische Literatur der Gegenwart*, 9–27. Stuttgart: J. B. Metzler.
Wilson, Stephen. 1988. *Feuding, Conflict and Banditry in Nineteenth-Century Corsica*. Cambridge et al: Cambridge University Press.
Xhaho, Armela. 2013. Sworn Virgins, Male and Female Berdaches: A Comparative Approach to the So Called 'Third Gender' People. *Gender Questions* 1 (1): 112–125.
Young, Antonia. 2000. *Women Who Become Men: Albanian Sworn Virgins*. Oxford/New York: Berg.
Zentralrat der Juden in Deutschland, ed. 2023. *Die Lehren des Talmud*. Gütersloh: Gütersloher Verlag.
Zipfel, Frank. 2001. *Fiktion, Fiktivität, Fiktionalität: Analysen zur Fiktion in der Literatur und zum Fiktionsbegriff in der Literaturwissenschaft*. Berlin: Schmidt.
Zippelius, Reinhold. 2006. *Juristische Methodenlehre*. Munich: C. H. Beck.
Zühlsdorff, Henning. 2016. Heinrich-Heine-Gastdozent 2016: Abbas Khider, Universität Leuphana, 18.8.2023, https://www.leuphana.de/portale/heinrich-heine-gastdozentur/abbas-khider.html.

Chapter 6
Concluding Remarks and Outlook

As indicated, the aim of this study was to further strengthen the more established, older American research approaches in the interdisciplinary field of law and literature—which are now also hesitantly beginning to gain a foothold in Europe—and to continue them on European soil. This seems to be an even more important task given that the first attempt to formalise law and literature research within the framework of the Münster Collaborative Research Centre SFB 1385 "Law and Literature" came to an end in June 2024. Further institutionalised and broader-based research initiatives that go beyond the individual initiatives that have been established have not (yet) taken place, at least in the European countries to which this study is dedicated. The emphasis here is on the 'yet', because I would like to campaign for the further development and coordinated expansion of this highly interesting interdisciplinary branch of research. There is no reason to believe that literary scholars cannot develop legal sensitivity, just as lawyers can be equipped with literary skills because both are united by the text as the central object of investigation, which each discipline accesses (or can access) in its own way. This mode of access can certainly be changed, and it does not require an insurmountable effort to deal with the rules of interpretation, linguistic peculiarities, discursive regularities and language patterns of the other discipline that are specific to law or literature. This is precisely the aim of my work, namely, to show that interdisciplinary work is possible, even desirable, and to provide guidance on how this can be achieved. Pointing out the theoretical points of intersection between jurisprudence and literary studies on the one hand, and demonstrating the practical, methodical application of this theoretical knowledge using examples from contemporary literature on the other, are in the service of this endeavour to pave the way for further interdisciplinary work.

In my research practice, I have encountered literary scholars who originally had no intention of studying law and yet who today lead interdisciplinary law and literature research in their country. The same can be said for lawyers. For example, one of my research colleagues in literary studies told me that she is currently working

A. Juster, *Law, Literature and Legal Counterfactuals*, Law and Visual Jurisprudence 16, https://doi.org/10.1007/978-3-032-03792-3_6

on literature and maritime law and has immersed herself in reading the relevant textbooks on a self-taught basis.

Christine Baron, the leading scholar in law and literature in France today, is a good example to confirm my assumptions: She studied literature and philosophy and yet today she is *the* country's interdisciplinary reference when it comes to law and literature. She never tires of showing how much law and literature intersect, overlap and are mutually dependent by referring to current issues that move society, such as women's rights.[1]

Law can be found wherever society exists, and human actions and interactions need to be channelled. Literature absorbs society into itself and, *ipso facto,* can hardly represent it as a lawless space. As Dieter Grimm and Christoph König point out, law and literature are in a chiastic relationship with one another, insofar as literature can use the narrative of individual cases to highlight legal contexts, questions, and shortcomings and draw general conclusions from them, while law proceeds in the opposite direction from the abstract norm under which the concrete individual case is subsumed: "While legal norms aim at a generality to be interpreted concerning concrete cases, literary works owe themselves to an individualisation of general presuppositions produced within the text [...]."[2] Erich Maria Remarque refers to such a pedagogical effect of literature, which breaks down the indeterminate generality to a level that the reader can grasp concretely, in connection with collective memory, when he states that a message can only be conveyed vividly through the text if an individual case is extrapolated and presented from the indeterminate generality:

> The difficult thing is that we can't rely on our imagination. When I say: five million died, this number says nothing. Five million deaths do not equal one death [...]. But if I say five died, then this difficulty could be minimised. And if I tell you that one died – a person I created for you to know and understand [...], then perhaps I have told you something you should know about the Nazis.[3]

This consideration can be applied analogously to the relationship between law and literature: abstract legal norms receive their vivid concretisation through the literary depiction of individual fates. Literature and law therefore support and assist each other via the medium of the text: the pedagogical, explanatory, illustrative, demonstrative, foreshadowing, and anticipatory function of the literary text supports and illuminates the understanding of the normative legal text, the literary text provides points of reference for the application of the law in individual cases, it criticises grievances of incorrect or lacking application of the law, and it anticipates legal developments or wishes for them.

This connection is clear in all the works analysed in this study: Karine Tuil's *La décision* for example, explains French terrorism legislation with its strengths, deficits, problems, and challenges based on the individual case of Alma Revel as a judge

[1] An example of this is Baron's contribution to the '*#MeToo*' debate: Baron (2023), pp. 1–10.
[2] Grimm and König (2020), p. 13.
[3] van Gelder (1948), p. 256. Cf. on this: Juster (2022), pp. 95–115.

and as a person and places it in the context of France, which is constantly threatened by terrorist attacks. The legal norms of criminal law and criminal procedure lose their abstractness through the fictitious subsumption of the offence of 'returnee from an IS training camp' under French law, of which Abdeljalil Kacem and his wife Sonia Dos Santos were guilty as concrete-fictitious examples.

In *Sworn Virgin* by Elvira Dones, the literary text gives the customary law of the *Kanun*—which, until the beginning of the twentieth century, was only passed down orally—a concrete form in the figure of Hana Doda, who takes the oath of eternal virginity according to the rules of the *Kanun*. The hitherto little-known customary law institution of *Burrnesha*, i.e. the possibility for women to become (almost) socially equal to men, is presented here in detail through the medium of the literary text, in a way that could not emerge from a mere reading of the *Kanun* of Lekë Dukagjini, which has survived in writing today. In addition to numerous provisions that define the lawlessness of women, the status of the *Burrnesha* recognised by customary law is only found in the written *Kanun* very laconically and not very informatively in a paragraph under the section 'Exceptions': "*The Virgins* (women who dress as men): They are not distinguished from other women, except that they are free to associate with men, although they have no right to a voice in the assembly" (§ 1228 *Kanun*). *Sworn Virgin* illustrates the complementary role of literature in the process of finding and clarifying the law particularly explicitly using the example of the individual case of 'Hana' and at the same time offers an interpretation proposal for the less meaningful § 1228 of the *Kanun*. The connection between law and literature proves to be particularly close in this context, as the literature also takes on the task of interpreting the law. Closely linked in this way, law and literature form a unity in need of interpretation via the medium of the text. Incidentally, this seems to apply generally to customary law (*usus*) when it is constituted, supplemented and/or interpreted by literature. This close relationship can also be observed in Claude Chossat's *Repenti* when the author deals with the unwritten laws of the Corsican *vendetta*. Chossat's text acts as a discourse on the customary rules of the *vendetta*, which, unlike the *Kanun*, were never set down in writing, which is why their rules are only made visible through literature. Once again, it is the individual fate, namely that of the author, that is used as an illustration to convey a systemic overall picture of the mechanisms of *vendetta* in Corsica. The real-life case of 'Claude Chossat' is used to concretise and explain the rules of *vendetta*, which otherwise form a system in the underground of the public state system that is difficult for outsiders to understand and grasp. In this context, the constitutive and explanatory function of literature is particularly effective. It illuminates for the reader the hopelessness of those who, for whatever reason, are drawn into this system of customary law. Moreover, it opens new perspectives on the motives and behaviour of Chossat and those who get caught up in the dynamics of this particular mechanism and its own laws. It also points to the relativity of value systems, which can change depending on the cultural context. The pedagogical function of literature, emphasised by Richard Weisberg, Marta Nussbaum, and C.R.B. Dunlop, also comes to the fore in *Repenti*, insofar as Chossat's account of his experiences is intended to help curb the bloody violence in Corsica and prevent the deaths of many more victims through education (R 261). Customary law discourse and literary text form a unity here, which undergoes an initial interpretation through Chossat's writing endeavours, which the recipients take up and in turn reinterpret based on their previous knowledge and the knowledge acquired through reading. From this, it is evident that Gadamer's hermeneutic circle is always peeking out from a corner.

A very strong correlation between the legal and literary texts can also be seen in Deborah Feldman's *Unorthodox*, in that her text seems to complement the endless series of previous interpretations of the *Talmud*. With her autobiographical narrative, the author provides her personal interpretation of the *Talmud Torah*, which at the same time acts as a critical commentary. In *Unorthodox*, her criticism is primarily directed against the seemingly aporetic and absurd interpretation of the law by the Satmar rabbinate. Feldman's own interpretation of the law clashes with that of her community, whereby the resulting knot of conflict not only fails to unravel but hardens to such an extent that Feldman feels compelled to break out of her living environment for good. In this sense, *Unorthodox* refers to the relevant-critical potential of literature, which reveals the inconsistencies, contradictions, and incompatibilities of Talmudic law in the interpretation of the Satmar rabbinate with keen observation. *Unorthodox* is an interpretative narrative about the interpretation of the Talmud-Torah *text*, the diegesis 'is' Talmudic law, whereby literary and legal discourse and literary and legal interpretation enter a close interrelationship.

In Abbas Khider's *A Slap in the Face*, German asylum law and its literary representation confront each other in a clearly chiastic manner, to refer to Dieter Grimm and Christoph König: Using the fictitious individual fate of asylum seeker Karim Mensy, Khider takes stock of the shortcomings, gaps, inadequacies, and contradictions of German asylum law on the one hand, and denounces its impractical, inadequate, and individually inappropriate application due to the sometimes aporetic and nonsensical rigidity of the administrative apparatus and its functionaries on the other. The literary statements show, on the one hand, the failure to achieve the goal of enabling the practical integration of asylum seekers and, on the other hand, the ill-considered, unrealistic and less-than-humane interpretation of asylum law by those who must apply it. The incoherence of the insurmountable hurdles that prevent asylum seekers from learning German alone shows the nonsensical discrepancy between the abstract norm and its practical effectiveness. Khider's text criticises not so much the substantive asylum law as the inappropriate subsumption of each individual case under the abstract norm, or rather: the failure of legal effectiveness in the attempt to avoid the strenuous process of subsuming the individual case under the abstract norm by rigidly standardising individuals and circumstances, although these are completely unsuitable for standardisation. In this sense, *A Slap in the Face*, like *Unorthodox*, can be read as a critique of the interpretation of the law, which calls less for a change in the law than for a more pragmatic and humane interpretation and application of (asylum) law. In addition, Khider's text fulfils an explanatory and illustrative function vis-à-vis positive law by using the individual case of Mensy to 'retell' in detail the stages of the German asylum procedure with its pitfalls and difficulties for asylum seekers.

In addition to the examples discussed in the present study, the thesis that interdisciplinary work between law and literary studies is both plausible and made possible by the commonality of the *text* in need of interpretation as a site of interdiscourse could be, I believe, substantiated by a long series of works. Numerous examples, to which reference was made in Chap. 2, can prove this.

Cedric Essi cites an interesting, because very topical, example of the close interdisciplinary link between law and literature, with reference to the constant interaction between the two disciplines in *Critical Race Theory* (CRT), which is to be understood as "an already established transdisciplinary *lingua franca*" that links the humanities and law as a result of American *law schools*.[4] In this context, according to Essi, the American legal scholar Patricia J. Williams in particular demonstrates the "interdependence of legal oppression and African-American literature" in her work[5] and thus makes a decisive contribution to the American *law and literature* movement.[6] In Germany, Emilia Roig is currently examining the various forms of discrimination such as racism, sexism and classism and, in her recently published book *Why We Matter: Das Ende der Unterdrückung* (2021),[7] addresses the normative pressure of discriminatory thought patterns in society.

In her recently published volume *L'irai chercher Kafka. Une enquête littéraire* (2024), Lea Veinstein links Kafka's literary work with the series of civil lawsuits that were filed in Germany and Israel between 2008 and 2016 to clarify the ownership of Kafka's estate (his original manuscripts). Most recently, the Israeli Supreme Court ruled that Kafka's estate should fall to the State of Israel and be administered by the National Library of Israel and made accessible to the public.[8] Veinstein's literary text deals here with procedural law, which determines the fate of Kafka's original writings, which in turn have a close relationship with the law, considering that Kafka, who was himself a lawyer, constantly deals with the law in his works. The interdisciplinary interweaving of law and literature certainly reaches a climax here.

All these examples show, as Doron Rabinovici notes, that "law in literature is more than just a commentary on the legal text. Rather, it discusses what one's own being encompasses and how the actions of the individual are to be evaluated. [...] It does not pronounce judgement, but it drives the investigation within us further. [...] It is not a judge, but a witness."[9] Rabinovici brings the relationship between law and literature to another vector when he ascribes to literature the function of testimony

---

[4] Essi (2024), here: pp. 198–212.

[5] Ibid., p. 200. See also: Williams (1987), pp. 401–434; Williams (1993); Williams (1998); Williams (2021a, b) (internet-link in the bibliography); Williams (2024).

[6] Cf. Essi (2024), p. 204. Essi points out that Williams was honoured with the *James Boyd White Award* by the *Association for the Study of Law, Culture, and the Humanities* (ASLCH) for her significant contributions.

[7] Roig (2021).

[8] Veinstein (2024), pp. 251–259.

See in detail on the trial of Kafka's estate: Balint (2018).

[9] Rabinovici (2013), here: pp. 54–55.

on the one hand and that of an incentive for further investigation on the other. While the law develops its normative power through its enforceability, with the claim to effectively regulate specific circumstances, literature lacks this compelling enforceability. However, it can facilitate and promote the enforcement of the law or hinder and impede it. If normative rules are perceived by society as appropriate, necessary, or sensible in relation to certain specific circumstances, they are in most cases already followed without coercion. Rules that are perceived as inconsistent, contradictory, inappropriate, or unfair, on the other hand, meet with resistance that must be broken by coercion. Grimm and König confirm this analysis of the relationship between law as a normative medium and literature as a non-normative medium:

> A literary author can indeed claim to make valid statements which, because of their validity, should have a behaviour-determining effect. [...] Nor can the author give the claim any validity in the legal sense. It is up to the reader to decide whether to attribute authoritativeness to the text. Legal norms, on the other hand, are inherently authoritative. The addressee cannot evade them. However, they can violate them and must then expect sanctions.[10]

Literature draws its potential from illustration and explanation, it can point out, convince, or criticise and, through this illustrative-commentary function via the fiction of concrete facts, has a serious potential for influence that can have a positive or negative effect on the current or future body of law and the application of the law. However, even if the literature fulfils an important function of critical commentary, it can by no means be attributed a normative validity. At this point, reference should be made to Eva-Maria Konrad's erroneous thesis that literature can be ascribed a normative claim as soon as it presents a coherent contradictory argumentation on legal issues and the narrative figures are methodologically coherent:

> This is where we can hook into the analysis of *Das Gewicht der Worte (The Weight of Words)* and establish that the novel can in any case be understood as normative insofar as it not only evaluates the language of law in general, but in particular a specific object, namely the legal situation with regard to a self-determined death and the corresponding assisted suicide, as inhumane. Furthermore, one could even discuss the prescriptive nature of the text, as the changes to the law that are called for are repeated and explicitly formulated as normative sentences. The novel therefore not only presents norms descriptively but also evaluates and demands the corresponding changes prescriptively.[11]

Konrad's remarks provide an interesting example of the terminological and semantic differences that are partly responsible for the difficulties in understanding between the academic disciplines. Against this background in particular, my work aims not only to highlight interdisciplinary points of contact and dividing lines, but also to fulfil a pedagogical task for future interdisciplinary work between law and literary studies by 'demonstrating' and 'sensitising'. In this specific case, it becomes clear that Konrad equates the legal concept of 'normativity' with the grammatical request sentence, also known as the imperative sentence, with which the speaker "wants the person addressed to do something specific."[12] When Konrad brings liter-

---

[10] Grimm and König (2020), pp. 8–9.

[11] Konrad (2024), here: p. 273.

[12] Hoberg and Hoberg (2016), p. 350.

ary normativity into play, she is referring to the critical voice of the author Pascal Mercier who, in his novel *Das Gewicht der Worte* (2020),[13] questions the current legal situation regarding euthanasia and expresses the obvious wish that it should change. However, the literary expression of criticism and wishes for change can in no way claim to be enforced by force—in Konrad's example, this would mean enforcing Mercier's wish for a change in the legal situation on euthanasia with police force if necessary—as is inherent in legal norms. In other words, the literary 'normativity' mentioned by Konrad is by no means to be equated with the normativity of legal provisions that are issued by a legitimised authority and enforced by force in the event of non-compliance.[14] As Matthias Mahlmann confirms, the critical and observational function of literature as a catalyst for ethical and legal reflection should not be confused with a normative claim in the legal sense:

> A place where law can reassure itself of its own civilisational foundations, a place of self-renewal through critical reflection, [...] is literature. Through criticism of individual and political ways of life and the emergence of better alternative worlds, it can be a source of material legal ethics that is able to provide standards [sic] for the normative architecture of human societies, which is created by law in the present with assertive power across cultural and political boundaries.[15]

Literature observes, it depicts the world in which we live in a variety of ways, it imitates actions and presents them in its own way. With this understanding of literature as a mimetic medium, Aristotle already refers to man's pleasure in imitation as the basis of the arts, because man is "the most 'mimetic' living being [...]: *τό τε γὰρ μιμεῖσθαι σύμφυτον τοῖς νθρώποις ... μιμητικώτατόν ἐστι (sc. τῶν ζῴων).*"[16] According to Martin Hose, the term 'mimesis' describes a "practice that can be described and defined quite precisely: an object (an object, a behaviour, an action) is consciously/intentionally reproduced by a 'practitioner' in such a way that there is a relationship between the object and the product that can be grasped with the term similarity."[17] Aristotle formulates this human practice as follows:

> It seems that the art of poetry has produced two specific causes that are inherent in human nature. For imitation is innate in human beings from an early age [...] because they are the species most fixated on imitation and make their first **learning progress through imitation** [my emphasis]. And (innate to) all is the pleasure of imitation. A clear sign of this is what happens in practice (i.e. the experience of art). For **we see images** of **what we regard as immediate events with sorrow, images that are made with specific precision** [my emphasis] [...].[18]

Aristotle's concept of mimesis makes an interesting contribution to understanding the relationship between law and literature. It has already been emphasised several

[13] Mercier (2020).

[14] Cf. Jellinek (1921), p. 337.

[15] Mahlmann (2013), here: p. 17.

[16] Hose (2023), p. 30.

[17] Ibid.

[18] Ibid., pp. 107–108.

times that both law and literature are related to society: Law is the regulator of social relations *par excellence* and therefore cannot be conceived without society, while social coexistence necessarily encounters law. Similarly, literature cannot be thought of in isolation from human society, and here Aristotle's concept of mimesis provides a valuable aid to understanding: Human beings, including authors, writers and poets, cannot escape the need for imitation, because if they could, they would be able to think the world beyond themselves in spheres that are unthinkable in principle. In this sense, man's mimetic behaviour explains the unavoidable link between literature and society, between literature and human ontology, both of which are inconceivable without law. As Thomas Metscher makes clear

> Art [is] thus necessarily related to people who take a stand in the world and relate to the world [...]. Art is worldly and opens the world [...]. This means that the world always finds its way into art in a perspectival refraction [...], which implies world judgements and world interpretations, i.e. acts of affirmation and negation of the designed world [...]. Understood in this way, all art has normative implications, often borders on explicit (conceptually formulated) systems of norms, and is even able, **at least in literature, to reflect the underlying systems of norms conceptually** [my emphasis] [...].[19]

Literature thus refers to human actions from which it attempts to draw conclusions and lessons, which it observes, describes, evaluates, and criticises, just as the law is brought to life by these actions, which it can promote, command, or suppress. Literature imitates to *learn*, and the law regulates and *standardises* to enable human coexistence. Literature is pedagogical and anticipatory, with a particularly keen eye for grievances (Aristotle's sorrow). Law, on the other hand, is inherently standardising and binding.

Theodor Adorno goes beyond the Aristotelian instinct of imitation by ascribing an anticipatory power to human thought as "part of the mimetic faculty", which, as Ernst Bloch adds, endows people with a "utopian rationality."[20] Reiner Wild takes up this idea when he speaks of the anticipatory function of literature, which he sees *as*

> *thinking ahead and anticipating possibilities of human behaviour and forms of consciousness as a counter-image to the existing; in this it necessarily has the character of an appeal.* The proximity to the critical function is unmistakable; both the critical and the anticipatory function have their common basis in the utopian quality of literature.[21]

Reiner Wild explains the anticipatory character of literature with the gift of closely observing the existing and anticipatory expansion of the space of the possible beyond the boundaries of the here and now. Literature can anticipate the occurrence of desirable changes (utopias) or negative shortcomings such as crises, challenges, or deterioration of the current situation (dystopias).[22]

---

[19] Metscher (2004), p. 28.

[20] Ibid., p. 10.

[21] Wild (1982), p. 130.

[22] Ibid., pp. 135–136.

Kafka expresses this anticipatory, seismographic quality of literature in one of his conversations with Gustav Janouch when, in response to the question of whether he could say anything about his future literary plans, he compares writing to a seismograph: "Can one foretell how one's heart will beat tomorrow? No, it is not possible. Yet the pen is only a seismographic pencil for the heart. It will register earthquakes, but not foretell them."[23] Referring to Janouch's conversations with Kafka, Boris Blahak surmises that in his novel fragment *The Missing Person*,[24] Kafka not only records earthquakes that are about to occur but also seems to process the "perception of political earthquakes that are about to occur or are occurring."[25] As indicated, Hans Müller-Dietz uses the concept of the seismograph to describe the anticipatory, prescient power of literature in comparison to the temporally 'lagging' developments of law: "This 'cultural lag', the cultural delay of law [...] is contrasted with the more seismographic character of literature, which picks up on processes of social change earlier and more quickly, if not even assuming a pioneering function."[26] Anett Lüttecken confirms the seismographic character of literature in her studies on Heinrich von Kleist when she states that literature functions like a seismograph whose 'vibrations' anticipate and register the "change in views, values and modes of representation."[27] Thomas Klinkert demonstrates this using the example of Marcel Proust and Louis-Ferdinand Céline, who already announced future changes as a result of the First World War in their writings: "This can be seen in literary texts by contemporaries who, in a sense, function as seismographs of such changes."[28] The existing order is destroyed in the writing process and replaced by the fiction of a future new order.[29] Günther Höfer sees Ödön von Horvath's *Der ewige Spießer* (1930, 1st part *Herr Kobler wird Paneuropäer*) as the seismograph of "the prevailing European consciousness."[30] Ashraf Noor also attributes seismographic characteristics to Thomas Mann's novel *Doctor Faustus* (1947), which, like a "seismograph", registers the smallest "changes in the image of truth."[31] As Patrick Eser and Jan-Henrik Witthaus emphasise, recent contemporary literature also demonstrates "the potential of literature as a seismograph of crisis scenarios"[32] with

---

[23] Janouch (1953), p. 38.

[24] Kafka's unfinished novel *Amerika: The Missing Person* (orig. *Der Verschollene*) was written between 1911 and 1914, at a time of upheaval, in the shadow of the imminent outbreak of the First World War on 28 July 1914 and the imminent decline of the Austro-Hungarian monarchy, which was sealed on 12 November 1918 with the proclamation of the democratic Republic of German-Austria.

[25] Blahak (2012), here: p. 248.

[26] Müller-Dietz (1990), p. 21. Cf. also: Schwarz (2009), pp. 213–238.

[27] Lütteken (2004), here: p. 190.

[28] Klinkert (2024), here: p. 80.

[29] Ibid., p. 85.

[30] Höfler (2023), here: p. 469.

[31] Noor (2024), here: p. XIII.

[32] Eser and Witthaus (2023), here: p. 7. Examples of such 'seismographic' literature can be found on the subject of the 'pandemic' in Oster and Witthaus (2021). On the topic of the financial crisis, see Hahn and Liebermann (2021). On the topic of capitalism see Gonnermann et al. (2021).

reference to the current social debates surrounding the COVID-19 pandemic, the financial crisis, and the capitalist worldview. The abundance of references to the anticipatory character of literature in a wide variety of genres and epochs, the list of which could be continued, thus seems to demonstrate a relatively broad consensus that literature is a strongly observational medium that not only detects social trends and developments in the present but also attempts to anticipate them, whereby this characteristic is by no means limited to legal relationships but encompasses all topics that affect human life.

If we now return to the exemplary works on which our counterfactual-interdisciplinary experiment is based as 'test material', this seismographic quality can also be recognised here without great difficulty: In Karine Tuil's *La décision*, the author uses the figure of Alma Revel to highlight the material, organisational, and psychological burdens of the anti-terror judge and—at the same time—to highlight the weaknesses of the system. In material terms, the high workload due to the chronic shortage of personnel is striking, as the number of cases entrusted to the Paris anti-terrorism department is increasing rapidly without additional judges with appropriate experience in anti-terrorism operations being (or being able to be) recruited at the same pace. The constant pressure of work, coupled with the heavy psychological strain of being confronted with scenes of horror and violence as well as the depression and/or helpless aggression of victims and their families, makes working conditions more difficult and takes its toll on both the mental and physical health of judges. Added to this is the agonising question of making the right decision in each individual case, which is made even more difficult by the fact that the French terrorism law now allows returnees from known terrorist areas to be remanded in custody or kept in custody even before a specific crime has been committed. By fictionalising the social microcosm of the 'anti-terrorism department in the Parisian *Palais de Justice*, Tuil anticipates the question of how to deal with the increasing volume of terrorism-related criminal cases in relation to the limited number of available judges to handle each individual case responsibly and carefully. The main challenge is providing the necessary resources to fulfil the requirement to avoid 'wrong' decisions and miscarriages of justice as far as possible. In addition, *La décision* anticipates the search for the right way to deal with the questionable principle of presumption of guilt based on the intention to commit a crime instead of the usual principle of presumption of innocence. At this point, the literature triggers a forward-looking debate about the 'right' equilibrium between reliable evidence and the need to prevent terrorist attacks. On a human level, Tuil's text points to the psychologically problematic isolationism of the investigating judge, who bears the responsibility of making the 'right' decision about detention or freedom almost alone, if one disregards the work in binomials.

Regarding Elvira Dones' novel *Sworn Virgin*, the critical-anticipatory quality of literature can be seen in the current debate on the relationship between men and women in contemporary society, which Dones enlivens with forward-looking questions using the example of the fictional character Hana. Given the almost total oppression of women by men in Albanian society, insofar as they follow the rules of the *Kanun*, the possibility of almost equal social status with men through the oath of virginity seems strange and therefore raises a series of questions that point to current and future debates about the relationship between men and women in society. How do almost complete oppression on the one hand and almost complete equality with men on the other rhyme in the same society? Should this be seen as a progress for women or rather as a step backwards, considering that the status of *Burrnesha* is linked to the renunciation of marriage and children? These questions are in the realm of diegesis and are even more relevant as the rules of the *Kanun* are still applied and followed in parts of northern Albania and Albanian women still take the vow of virginity voluntarily or under duress. Why is it the woman and not the man who has to make the sacrifice of renouncing family and children if she wants to improve her social status and the rights associated with it? Why is male status always presented as a desirable reference parameter? Dones' fictional narrative serves as a starting point for further reflections on the relationship between men and women, which continues to be determined by persistent stereotypes and preformed, inherited standards. With *Sworn Virgin*, Dones projects the possibility of decoupling biological gender from outward appearances such as clothing, preferences, behaviour, and activities. She asks about the possibility of performing undifferentiated male or female activities or behaviours without giving up the innate female or male identity. These considerations give rise to the forward-looking question of whether the cultural patterns of femininity and masculinity that have been imprinted over generations can give way to gender neutrality, detached from biological sex, to achieve true gender equality.

Deborah Feldman's *Unorthodox* is also about women's lack of rights, only here it is not caused by customary law but by the religious rules of the *Talmud Torah* and, even more, by the conservative orthodox interpretation of the latter. The male-dominated community of orthodox Jews of the Satmar community in New York provides an example of extreme 'isolationism' from modern society: it denies itself education and progress and prevents the slightest contact with the outside world. This is where Feldman's criticism comes in, which not only denounces the deliberate discrimination against women but also emphasises the denial of progress as a principle of maintaining power and control and anticipates the expected gradual softening of this rigid corset. Digital technologies are also penetrating through closed doors, opening a window to the outside world for more and more young members of the community, until some of them, like herself, take the plunge into the unknown. At the time that *Unorthodox* was published, only a small number succeeded in doing so, but this number is now growing steadily thanks to the supportive actions of former members who assist the 'deserters' to take their first steps into freedom. Ignorance is the building block on which arbitrary power is based. As soon as information, new horizons, experiences, and knowledge come into play, the power structure is dangerously perforated—as Feldman demonstrates with her own example—until it is finally questioned, criticised, and rejected because of this critical questioning. *Unorthodox* anticipates the expected gradual decline of the Satmar community's influence. At the same time, it raises the question of the extent to which people are shaped by their childhood experiences and family memories, which often go back several generations. Feldman questions how this can be dealt with and how far one's own ability to detach oneself from family and historical preconditions can reach: In her case, she is caught up in the 'boomerang' of her family history, which seems to mean that present and past always remain closely interwoven in the human psyche.

Claude Chossat's *Repenti* sheds light on the workings of the laws of the Corsican *vendetta*, knowledge of which explains why it is impossible for those who fall into the mills of this *vendetta* to free themselves from its clutches. Anyone who gets caught up in its wheels, willingly or unwillingly, must 'run with it' at the risk of their lives. In his book, Chossat criticises the unreliability and arbitrariness of the judiciary, which, contrary to the agreements, refused him protection for judicial collaborators. If Chossat had foreseen this turn of events, he would not have co-operated with the judiciary, as the status of a judicial collaborator is tantamount to a death sentence if he does not enjoy legal and police protection. Chossat's clarification of the workings of the Corsican *Brise de Mer* and other mafia organisations in Corsica and the south of France also points to the high hurdles that, it would seem, are preventing any hope of eradicating the Corsican *vendetta* and its breeding ground in the future. The betrayal of Chossat by the judiciary that has now been publicised and the ineffective legal instrument for protecting collaborators in the judiciary also suggest that only a few new informants will be recruited from the ranks of the Corsican mafia in the future. In this sense, *Repenti* anticipates the continuation of the violent *status quo* for the island of Corsica.

In conclusion, it should be noted that Abbas Khider's novel *A Slap in the Face* is primarily a blatant criticism of the misguided humane and situation-appropriate interpretation of asylum law. It is not asylum law that is being questioned in principle, but rather its misguided interpretation by unmotivated functionaries, the consequences of which are exacerbated by official rigidities, and which result in the individual circumstances of the asylum seeker not being pragmatically and purposefully subsumed under the abstract norm. The result is a contradictory asylum policy plagued by inconsistency and incoherence, which on the one hand prevents asylum seekers from integrating into German society as quickly as possible, contrary to the practical purpose of asylum legislation, and on the other hand imposes deportations that do not take into account the individual situation of the asylum seekers in the real context of their country of origin. With this finding, Khider's *A Slap in the Face* anticipates the pre-programmed failure of the asylum system in this form.

From these concluding remarks on Khider's *A Slap in the Face*, we shall finally move on to a concluding word on the attempt, thus concluded for the time being, to develop an interdisciplinary working method for the research field of law and literature.

6.1 Conclusion

The aim of the present work, which was hopefully achieved, was to develop an interdisciplinary method for the research field of law and literature. To this end, it was first necessary to work out the separating elements between literature and law to then better align the two fields of knowledge. The common intersection resulting from the process of these investigations is remarkable and seems to offer a good basis for further interdisciplinary research endeavours in this field. The interdisciplinary work is supported, by the common double reference of written *text* and human society by common techniques of text access, i.e. interpretation and discourse that are shared between the two disciplines. However, the normative quality of law, in the sense of authoritative enforceability, which literature lacks and which is explained by the different functions of law and literature in society, remains an essential dividing point.

Testing the interdisciplinary research method based on exemplary contemporary literature has shown the indissoluble link between both disciplines and human society: While literature depicts, explains, illustrates, comments on, or criticises society in all its facets, the law aims at the pragmatically effective disciplining and regulation of interpersonal relationships so that society can function at all.

This division of tasks and simultaneous interweaving of law and literature could be established in different ways in the literary texts analysed: When it comes to the examination of positive law in literature, as demonstrated by Tuil's *La décision* and Khider's *A Slap in the Face*, the relationship between law and literature is complementary: Literature comments on and explains existing legal relationships, points out their weaknesses, and refers to possible future demands for change or improvement. Deborah Feldman's autobiographical work *Unorthodox*, stands for a hybrid case of the depiction of positive law that needs interpretation, in which law and literature intervene in the process of text interpretation in a mutually complementary manner. If, as in Sworn Virgin, the aim is to explain incompletely documented customary law, the overall diegetic context results in a gap-filling interpretation that meaningfully complements and perfects the law as the object of investigation. If the literature attempts to convey unwritten customary law completely, as is the case in Chossat's *Repenti*, the diegesis plays a constitutive role in that it makes previously unknown customary law visible in the first place, albeit without any normative claim, which is always reserved for the law.

From this condensation of insights gained from the present work, a positive finding seems to emerge in favour of the suitability of legal counterfactuals as a method. It is hoped that this can contribute to further interdisciplinary research between law and literature and perhaps even to the gradual development of an institutionally coordinated field of research in Europe. This would be in the interests of both literary studies and legal studies: For the former, it would make the social benefits more demonstrable in a 'cost-benefit' orientated society such as ours; for the latter, it would support better access, knowledge and understanding for non-legally trained readers—vital to better understand the world we live in.

References

Balint, Benjamin. 2018. *Kafka's Last Trial: The case of Literary Legacy*. New York: WW Norton & Co.

Baron, Christine. 2023. Tribunaux réels, tribunaux imaginaires. *Revue critique de fixxion française contemporaine (online)* 26:1–10.

Blahak, Boris. 2012. Reflexe einer mitteleuropäischen Endzeitstimmung in Franz Kafkas Romanfragment *Der Verschollene*. In *Kafka und Prag. Literatur-, kultur-, sozial- und sprachhistorische Kontexte*, ed. Peter Becher, Steffen Höhne, and Marek Nekula, 231–252. Cologne/Weimar/Vienna: Böhlau.

Eser, Patrick, and Jan-Henrik Witthaus. 2023. Soziale Ungleichheiten und 'Realismus' als Paradigma – literatur- und kulturwissenschaftliche Vorüberlegungen. In *Renaissancen des Realismus? Romanistische Beiträge zur Repräsentation sozialer Ungleichheit in Literatur und Film*, ed. Patrick Eser and Jan-Henrik Witthaus, 1–18. Berlin/Boston: De Gruyter.

Essi, Cedric. 2024. Der Fall Prof. Patricia J. Williams. Critical Race Theory als Hermeneutik zwischen Recht und Literatur. In *Rechtsnorm und ästhetische Reflexion. Studien zum Verhältnis zwischen den Hermeneutiken des Rechts und der Literatur*, ed. Gideon Stiening, 197–216. Berlin: J. B. Metzler.

Gonnermann, Annika, Sina Schuhmaier, and Lisa Schwander, eds. 2021. *Literarische Perspektiven auf den Kapitalismus. Fallbeispiele aus dem 21. Jahrhundert*. Vol. 84. Tübingen: Narr Francke Attempto.

Grimm, Dieter, and Christoph König. 2020. Lektüre und Geltung – Einleitung. In *Lektüre und Geltung. Zur Verstehenspraxis in der Rechtswissenschaft und in der Literaturwissenschaft*, ed. Dieter Grimm and Christoph König, 7–23. Göttingen: Wallstein.

Hahn, Kurt, and Marita Liebermann, eds. 2021. *Finanznarrative als Krisennarrative: literarische und filmische Modellierungen 'kapitaler' Erschütterungen in der Romania*. Berlin/Vienna: Peter Lang.

Hoberg, Ursula, and Rudolf Hoberg, eds. 2016. *Der kleine Duden. Deutsche Grammatik*. Berlin: Dudenverlag.

Höfler, Günther. 2023. 2.4.3.3. Paneuropabewegung. In *Ödon-von-Horvath-Handbuch*, ed. Nicole Streitler-Kastberger and Martin Vejvar, 469–471. Berlin/Boston: De Gruyter.

Hose, Martin. 2023. *Aristoteles, Poetik. Einleitung, Text, Übersetzung und Kommentar mit einem Anhang: Texte zur aristotelischen Literaturtheorie*. Vol. 1. Berlin/Boston: De Gruyter.

Janouch, Gustav. 1953. *Conversations with Kafka. Notes and Reminicences*. New York: Frederick A. Praeger.

Jellinek, Georg. 1921. Staat und Recht. In *Allgemeine Staatslehre*, ed. Georg Jellinek, 332–379. Berlin/Heidelberg: Springer.

Juster, Alexandra. 2022. Vergessen, um zu überleben – sich erinnern, um fortzuleben. In *Peter Weiss Jahrbuch (2022/31): Facetten des Exils*, ed. Arnd Beise and Michael Hofmann, 95–115. Bielefeld: Aisthesis.

Klinkert, Thomas. 2024. Der Zusammenhang von Krieg, Stadt und Erinnerung bei Proust und Céline. In *Stadt – Krieg – Literatur: Stadt und Urbanität unter den Bedingungen des Krieges 1914–1945*, ed. Henning Hufnagel, Thomas Klinkert, and Olaf Müller, 79–98. Berlin/Boston: De Gruyter.

Konrad, Eva-Maria. 2024. Recht durch Literatur? Das Misslingen des normativen Anspruchs in Pascal Merciers *Das Gewicht der Worte*. In *Rechtsnorm und ästhetische Reflexion. Studien zum Verhältnis zwischen den Hermeneutiken des Rechts und der Literatur*, ed. Gideon Stiening, 269–299. Berlin: J. B. Metzler.

Lütteken, Anett. 2004. Die zwei Renaissancen des Heinrich von Kleist. In *Heinrich von Kleist – Eine Dichterrenaissance*, ed. Anett Lütteken, 151–310. Berlin/Boston: Max Niemeyer.

Mahlmann, Matthias. 2013. Die wechselseitige Humanisierung von Recht und Literatur. In *"Fechtschulen und phantastische Gärten": Recht und Literatur*, ed. Andreas Kilcher, Matthias Mahlmann, and Daniel Müller Nielaba, 16–19. Zürich: vdf Hochschulverlag.

Mercier, Pascal. 2020. *Das Gewicht der Worte*. München: Hanser.
Metscher, Thomas. 2004. *Mimesis*. Vol. 10. Bielefeld: transcript.
Müller-Dietz, Heinz. 1990. *Grenzüberschreitungen. Beiträge zur Beziehung zwischen Literatur und Recht*. Baden-Baden: Nomos.
Noor, Ashraf. 2024. Translator's Introduction. In *Displacements. Selected Essays on German-Jewish Literature and Modernity.*, transl. by Ashraf Noor, ed. Stéphane Mosès, XI–LVI. Berlin/Boston: De Gruyter.
Oster, Angela, and Jan-Henrik Witthaus, eds. 2021. *Pandemie und Literatur*. Vienna/Berlin: Mandelbaum.
Rabinovici, Doron. 2013. Sprache und Schuld. In *"Fechtschulen und phantastische Gärten": Recht und Literatur*, ed. Andreas B. Kilcher, Matthias Mahlmann, and Daniel Müller Nielaba, 37–55. Zürich: vdf Hochschulverlag.
Roig, Emilia. 2021. *Why We Matter. Das Ende der Unterdrückung*. Berlin: Aufbau.
Schwarz, Claudia. 2009. Sentenced to 'Storification'. A Trial on Legal Narratives. In *Legal Narratives. European Perspectives on U.S. Law in Cultural Contact*, ed. Gudrun M. Grabher and Anna Gamper, 213–238. Vienna/New York: Springer.
van Gelder, Robert. 1948. *Prominente plaudern*. Vienna: Humboldt Verlag.
Veinstein, Lea. 2024. *J'irai chercher Kafka. Une enquête littéraire*. Paris: Flammarion.
Wild, Reiner. 1982. *Literatur im Prozeß der Zivilisation. Entwurf einer theoretischen Grundlegung der Literaturwissenschaft*. Stuttgart: J. B. Metzler.
Williams, Patricia J. 1987. Alchemical Notes: Reconstructing Ideals from Deconstructed Rights. *Harvard Civil Rights – Civil Liberties Law Review* 22 (2): 401–434.
Williams, Patricia J. 1993. *The Alchemy of Race and Rights*. London: Virgo Press.
Williams, Patricia J. 1998. *Seeing a Color-Blind Future: The Paradox of Race*. New York: Macmillan.
Williams, Patricia J. 2021a. *Giving a Damn. Racism, Romance, and Gone with the Wind*. London: TLS Books.
Williams, Patricia J. 2021b. "How Not to Talk about Race", In *The Nation*, 18.10.2021, https://www.thenation.com/article/society/talk-about-race.
Williams, Patricia J. 2024. *The Miracle of the Black Leg: Notes on Race, Human Bodies, and the Spirit of Law*. New York: The New Press.

Legal References

German Jurisprudence

BVerfG 17.5.1960 – 2 BvL 11/59 ua, BVerfGE 11, 126 (130) – Nachkonstitutioneller Bestätigungswille.
BVerfG 9.5.1978 – 2 BvR 952/75, BVerfGE 48, 246 (257) – Ehrenamtliche Richter.
BVerfG, Beschluss 5.4.1990 – 2 BvR 413/88 – Besorgnis der Befangenheit eines Bundesverfassungsrichters.

French Jurisprudence

Cass. soc., 18 novembre 1998, n° 94-43.840.
Cass. Crim. 10 janvier 2017, n° 16-84596, Dr. Pénal 2017, comm. 35, note P. Conte. (aff. dite »de Tarnac«).
Conseil Constitutionnel décision n° 2016-611 QPC du 10 février 2017.
Conseil Constitutionnel décision n° 2017-682 QPC du 15 décembre 2017.
Conseil Constitutionnel décision n° 2020-845 QPC du 19 juin 2020.

Legal Texts

Asylverfahrensbeschleunigungsgesetz vom 20.10.2015, BGBl. I 2015, 1722.
Charter of Fundamental Rights of the European Union, 26/10/2012, C 326/391.
Convention relating to the Status of Refugees ("Geneva Refugee Convention"), United Nations, Treaty Series, vol. 189, 28 July 1951; amended by the Protocol

A. Juster, *Law, Literature and Legal Counterfactuals*, Law and Visual Jurisprudence 16, https://doi.org/10.1007/978-3-032-03792-3

relating to the Status of Refugees, United Nations, Treaty Series, vol. 606, 31 January 1967.

Deutsches Asylgesetz vom 2. September 2008 (BGBl. S. 1798) in der Fassung vom 21. Februar 2024 (BGBl. I Nr. 54).

Deutsches Asylbewerberleistungsgesetz (AsylbLG) in der Fassung vom 7. August 1997 (BGBl. I S. 2023), zuletzt geändert durch das Rückführungsverbesserungsgesetz vom 21. Februar 2024 (BGBl. I Nr. 54).

DIRECTIVE 2011/95/EU OF THE EUROPEAN PARLIAMENT AND OF THE COUNCIL of 13 December 2011 on standards for the qualification of third-country nationals or stateless persons as beneficiaries of international protection, for a uniform status for refugees or for persons eligible for subsidiary protection, and for the content of the protection granted (L 337/9), "Directive of Qualification".

DIRECTIVE 2013/32/EU OF THE EUROPEAN PARLIAMENT AND OF THE COUNCIL of 26 June 2013 on common procedures for granting and withdrawing international protection (L 180/60), "Directive of Asylum-proceeding".

DIRECTIVE 2013/33/EU OF THE EUROPEAN PARLIAMENT AND OF THE COUNCIL of 26 June 2013 laying down standards for the reception of applicants for international protection (L 180/96), "Directive of admission".

Streinz, Rudolf (ed.) (2012): EUV/AEUV. *Vertrag über die Europäische Union und Vertrag über die Arbeitsweise der Europäischen Union*, München: C.H. Beck.

Treaty on the Functioning of the European Union (TFEU). Official Journal of the European Union, C 326/49, 26.10.2012.

REGULATION (EU) No 604/2013 OF THE EUROPEAN PARLIAMENT AND OF THE COUNCIL of 26 June 2013 establishing the criteria and mechanisms for determining the Member State responsible for examining an application for international protection lodged in one of the Member States by a third-country national or a stateless person (L 180/31), "Dublin-III-Regulation".

REGULATION (EU) No 603/2013 OF THE EUROPEAN PARLIAMENT AND OF THE COUNCIL of 26 June 2013 on the establishment of 'Eurodac' for the comparison of fingerprints for the effective application of Regulation (EU) No 604/2013 establishing the criteria and mechanisms for determining the Member State responsible for examining an application for international protection lodged in one of the Member States by a third-country national or a stateless person and on requests for the comparison with Eurodac data by Member States' law enforcement authorities and Europol for law enforcement purposes, and amending Regulation (EU) No 1077/2011 establishing a European Agency for the operational management of large-scale IT systems in the area of freedom, security and justice (L 180/1), "Eurodac-II-regulation".

REGULATION (EU) 2024/1347 OF THE EUROPEAN PARLIAMENT AND OF THE COUNCIL of 14 May 2024 on standards for the qualification of third-country nationals or stateless persons as beneficiaries of international protection, for a uniform status for refugees or for persons eligible for subsidiary protection and for the content of the protection granted, amending Council Directive 2003/109/EC and repealing Directive 2011/95/EU of the European Parliament and of the Council (L series).

Index

A. Juster, *Law, Literature and Legal Counterfactuals*, Law and Visual Jurisprudence 16, https://doi.org/10.1007/978-3-032-03792-3

MIX
Papier aus verantwortungsvollen Quellen
Paper from responsible sources
FSC® C105338

If you have any concerns about our products,
you can contact us on
ProductSafety@springernature.com

In case Publisher is established outside the EU,
the EU authorized representative is:
Springer Nature Customer Service Center GmbH
Europaplatz 3, 69115 Heidelberg, Germany

Printed by Libri Plureos GmbH
in Hamburg, Germany